Andrea Pizarro Pedraza

Linguistic Taboo Revisited

Novel Insights from Cognitive Perspectives

DE GRUYTER
MOUTON

ISBN 978-3-11-068515-2
e-ISBN (PDF) 978-3-11-058275-8
e-ISBN (EPUB) 978-3-11-058051-8
ISSN 1861-4132

Library of Congress Control Number: 2018934500

Bibliographic information published by the Deutsche Nationalbibliothek
The Deutsche Nationalbibliothek lists this publication in the Deutsche Nationalbibliografie;
detailed bibliographic data are available on the Internet at http://dnb.dnb.de.

© 2019 Walter de Gruyter GmbH, Berlin/Boston
This volume is text- and page-identical with the hardback published in 2018.
Typesetting: fidus Publikations-Service GmbH, Nördlingen
Printing and binding: CPI books GmbH, Leck

www.degruyter.com

Andrea Pizarro Pedraza
Linguistic Taboo Revisited

Cognitive Linguistics Research

Editors
Dirk Geeraerts
Dagmar Divjak
John R. Taylor

Honorary editors
René Dirven
Ronald W. Langacker

Volume 61

Keith Allan
Foreword

Taboo refers to a proscription of behaviour for a specifiable community of one or more persons at a specifiable time in specifiable contexts (Allan & Burridge 2006: 11). When words are tabooed, what is in fact tabooed is the use of those words in certain contexts; in other words, the taboo applies to instances of language behaviour. As originally recognized in the Pacific islands when first visited by Europeans, taboos prohibited certain people, either permanently or temporarily, from certain actions, from contact with certain things and certain other people. A tabooed person was ostracized. The term *taboo* came to be used of similar customs elsewhere in the world, especially where taboos arose from respect for and fear of metaphysical powers; it was later extended to political and social affairs, and generalized to the interdiction of the use or practice of anything, especially an expression or topic considered offensive and therefore to be avoided or prohibited by social custom. Where something physical or metaphysical is said to be tabooed, what is in fact tabooed is its interaction with a specifiable group of persons. In principle any kind of behaviour can be tabooed. For behaviour to be proscribed it must be perceived as in some way harmful to an individual or the community; but the degree of harm can fall anywhere on a scale from a breach of etiquette to real fatality.

There are people who would like to erase obscene terms like *cunt* and slurs like *idiot* and *nigger* from the English language; less passionate people recognize after a few moments reflection that this is a wish impossible to grant. Such words are as much a part of English as all the other words in the language (see Allan 2015, 2016, 2018 for discussion). However, there is evidence that 'swear words' occupy a different brain location from other vocabulary; part of the evidence is that people said never to have uttered taboo language earlier in their lifetime sometimes, when senile dementia has set in, lose the ability to speak normally but do readily recall and utter taboo words (cf. Comings & Comings 1985, Jay 2000, Finkelstein Forthcoming). Certain tabooed behaviours are prohibited by law; all tabooed behaviours are deprecated and lead to social if not legal sanction.

To engage in tabooed behaviour will cause offence to others and consequently it is dysphemistic. The use of tabooed words to insult someone is dysphemistic. The use of swear words has a number of motivations, one of them is the auto-cathartic 'letting off steam' e.g. with expletives such as *Fuck!* or *Shit!* (this actually works, see Stephens, Atkins & Kingston 2009). A standard way of trying to avoid giving offense is to substitute a euphemistic locution for such dysphemisms, e.g. *Fiddle-di-dee!* and *Sugar!* which might be called euphemistic dysphemisms –

though just plain euphemism seems acceptable. In many circumstances it is dysphemistic to refer to faecal matter as *shit*; a standard euphemism for it is *poo*. Or, to call a spade a spade, the orthophemism is *faecal matter* or *faeces*. Although the particular context of use affects such judgements, dysphemism is typically impolite because it is offensive; orthophemism ('straight-talking') is polite and so is euphemism ('sweettalking'). Typically, euphemism is more figurative and colloquial, orthophemism more literal and more formal. Sometimes euphemisms are flamboyant verbiage, e.g. when a traffic bottleneck is described as a 'localised capacity deficiency'. Where such jargon causes offence, these are dysphemistic euphemisms.

There can be sound reasons for mandating specific parts of our lives out of bounds: for instance, rules against incest are eminently rational from an evolutionary point of view; communities remain healthier if human waste is kept at a distance; many food prejudices have a rational origin; and avoidance-speech styles help prevent conflict in relationships that are potentially volatile. To an outsider, many prohibitions are perplexing and seem silly; but they are among the common values that link the people of a community together. What one group values another scorns; so, shared taboos are a sign of social cohesion.

This book, *Linguistic taboo revisited: novel insights from cognitive perspectives*, derives from papers delivered at workshops organized by Andrea Pizarro Pedraza which took place in two conferences: the 13th International Cognitive Linguistics Conference held in July 2015 at Northumbria University, England and the 10th AELCO International Conference held in October 2016 at the University of Alcalá, Spain. The cultures represented in this volume include American, Australian, and British English, Dutch, Egyptian Arabic, Kikuyu, Persian, Polish, and Spanish and its net spreads to include the violations of taboos by people with Obsessive Compulsive Disorder and Tourette's syndrome (which causes coprolalia and copropraxia). The principle aim of *Linguistic taboos revisited* is to approach taboo language from perspectives inspired by cognitive linguistics. There is therefore much discussion of metaphor, metonymy and other figurative language as means of managing taboo topics. This is a very enlightening volume by a panoply of international scholars. You will enjoy a good read.

References

Allan, Keith. 2015. When is a slur not a slur? The use of *nigger* in 'Pulp Fiction'. *Language Sciences* 52: 187–199.
Allan, Keith. 2016. The reporting of slurs. In *Indirect Reports and Pragmatics*, ed. by Alessandro Capone, Ferenc Kiefer & Franco Lo Piparo. Cham: Springer. Pp. 211–232.
Allan, Keith. 2018. Getting a grip on context as a determinant of meaning. In *Further Advances in Pragmatics and Philosophy. Part 1. From Theory to Practice*, ed. by Alessandro Capone, Marco Carapezza & Franco Lo Piparo. Cham: Springer. Pp. 177–201. doi: 10.1007/978-3-319-72173-6_9.
Allan, Keith & Kate Burridge. 2006. *Forbidden Words: Taboo and the Censoring of Language*. Cambridge: Cambridge University Press.
Comings, David E. & Brenda G. Comings. 1985. Tourette Syndrome: Clinical and psychological aspects of 250 cases. *American Journal of Human Genetics* 37: 435–450.
Finkelstein, Shlomit R. Forthcoming. Swearing and the brain. Chapter 7 in *Oxford Handbook of Taboo Words and Language*, ed. by Keith Allan. Oxford: Oxford University Press.
Jay, Timothy. 2000. *Why We Curse: A Neuro-Psycho-Social Theory of Speech*. Philadelphia: John Benjamins.
Stephens, Richard, John Atkins & Andrew Kingston. 2009. Swearing as a response to pain. *NeuroReport* 20 (12): 1056–1060.

Table of contents

Keith Allan
Foreword — V

Andrea Pizarro Pedraza
Introduction — 1

Miguel Casas Gómez
1 **Lexicon, discourse and cognition: terminological delimitations in the conceptualizations of linguistic taboo** — 13

Part I: Construal

Eliecer Crespo-Fernández
2 **The axiological and communicative potential of homosexual-related metaphors** — 35

Ivana Moritz
3 **Metonymy-based euphemisms in war-related speeches by George W. Bush and Barack Obama** — 55

Pedro J. Chamizo-Domínguez
4 **Ambiguity and vagueness as cognitive tools for euphemistic and politically correct speech** — 79

Part II: Cultural Conceptualization

Réka Benczes, Kate Burridge, Keith Allan, Farzad Sharifian
5 **Old age revolution in Australian English: Rethinking a taboo concept** — 99

Magdalena Zawrotna
6 **Taboo subjects as insult intensifiers in Egyptian Arabic** — 117

Mohsen Bakhtiar
7 **Emotion concepts in context: Figurative conceptualizations of *hayâ* 'self-restraint' in Persian** — 141

Moses Gatambuki Gathigia, Daniel Ochieng Orwenjo
and Ruth Wangeci Ndung'u
8 A Cognitive Linguistics approach to menstruation as a taboo in Gĩkũyũ —— 161

Anna Kuzio
9 The socio-cognitive aspects of taboo in two cultures: A case study on Polish and British English —— 179

Barbara De Cock and Ferran Suñer
10 The influence of conceptual differences on processing taboo metaphors in the foreign language —— 201

Part III: Cognitive Sociolinguistics

Tom Ruette
11 Why do the Dutch swear with diseases? —— 225

Andrea Pizarro Pedraza
12 Calling things by their name: Exploring the social meanings in the preference for sexual (in)direct construals —— 245

Ana M. Cestero Mancera
13 The perception of the expression of taboos: a sociolinguistic study —— 269

Part IV: Interdisciplinary Approaches

Habibollah Ghassemzadeh
14 Scrupulosity, sexual ruminations and cleaning in Obsessive – Compulsive Disorder —— 293

Shlomit Ritz Finkelstein
15 Swearing as emotion acts —— 311

Index —— 329

List of contributing Authors

Ana M. Cestero Mancera
Departamento de Filología, Comunicación y Documentación
Universidad de Alcalá
anam.cestero@uah.es

Andrea Pizarro Pedraza
Faculty of Philosophy, Arts and Letters
Institut Langage et Communication (ILC)
Université catholique de Louvain
Belgium
andrea.pizarro@uclouvain.be

Anna Kuzio
University of Zielona Góra
Poland
a.kuzio@in.uz.zgora.pl

Barbara De Cock
Faculty of Philosophy, Arts and Letters
Institut Langage et Communication (ILC)
Université catholique de Louvain
Belgium
barbara.decock@uclouvain.be

Daniel Ochieng Orwenjo
Department of Languages and Communication Studies
Technical University of Kenya, Nairobi
Kenya
orwenjo@ gmail. com

Eliecer Crespo-Fernández
Departamento de Filología Moderna
Universidad de Castilla-La Mancha
Eliecer.Crespo@uclm.es

Farzad Sharifian
School of Languages, Literatures, Cultures and Linguistics
Monash University
Australia
farzad.sharifian@monash.edu

Habibollah Ghassemzadeh
Roozbeh Hospital
Department of Psychiatry
Tehran University of Medical Sciences
Iran
hghassemzadeh@tums.ac.ir, hghassemzadeh@gmail.com

Ferran Suñer
Faculty of Philosophy, Arts and Letters
Institut Langage et Communication (ILC)
Université catholique de Louvain
Belgium
ferran.sunermunoz@uclouvain.be

Ivana Moritz
Faculty of Education
University of Osijek
Croatia
imoritz@foozos.hr

Kate Burridge
School of Languages, Literatures, Cultures and Linguistics
Monash University
Australia
kate.burridge@monash.edu

Keith Allan
School of Languages, Literatures, Cultures and Linguistics
Monash University
Australia
keith.allan@monash.edu

Magdalena Zawrotna
Faculty of Philology
Jagiellonian University in Kraków
Poland

Miguel Casas Gómez
Department of Philology
Universidad de Cádiz
Spain

Mohsen Bakhtiar
Department of English and American Studies
Eötvös Lorand University, Budapest
Hungary
mbakhtiar61@gmail.com

Moses Gatambuki Gathigia
Department of Languages
Karatina University
Kenya
gatambukimoses@gmail.com; mgathigia@karu.ac.ke

Pedro J. Chamizo-Domínguez
Departamento de Filosofía
Facultad de Filosofía y Letras
Universidad de Málaga
Spain
pjchamizo@uma.es

Réka Benczes
Institute of Behavioural Sciences and Communication Theory
Corvinus University of Budapest
Hungary
reka.benczes@uni-corvinus.hu

Ruth Wangeci Ndung'u
Department of Communication, Languages and Linguistics
Pan Africa Christian University, Nairobi
Kenya
wrndungu@gmail.com

Shlomit Ritz Finkelstein, PhD
Department of Psychology
Emory University, Atlanta
USA
finkelstein@emory.edu

Tom Ruette
Quantitative Lexicology and Variational Linguistics
University of Leuven
Belgium
tom.ruette@kuleuven.be

Andrea Pizarro Pedraza
Introduction

Linguistic taboo revisited is a collection of papers adopting cognitive frameworks to reconsider taboo-related phenomena, such as taboo concepts and words, euphemism, dysphemism, insults or political correctness. It emerges from the growing interest of taboo researchers in the cognitive facets of this complex phenomenon, and more precisely, in how those facets interplay with, and are grounded on, social and cultural dynamics in particular settings.

The study of linguistic taboo is the study of forbidden or dispreferred meanings and words (Allan and Burridge 1991: 12) that refer to problematic areas of reality such as sexuality, ethnicity, religion, economic status, aging, death, illness, or bodily functions, among others, and the expression of these concepts through euphemism (mitigated expression), orthophemism (neutral expression) or dysphemism (offensive expression), along an "x-phemistic continuum", as defined by Allan and Burridge (2006). Other non-referential phenomena such as swearing and insulting, that build on these or any sensitive aspects as well (Jay 2000), are also part of linguistic taboo. The inventory of taboo topics is variable and can be expanded circumstantially: the ones mentioned above are well-known taboos in many societies, but others could enter the list, if they become problematic for a society or even just in a particular situation. What is (un)mentionable for a speaker in a given moment is the result of an assessment of the communicative situation: who are the interlocutors, what is the relationship between them, what are they talking about, where are they, or how do they want to be perceived, are questions that determine what becomes a taboo (Allan and Burridge 2006: 11).

This complex linguistic phenomenon is part of the broader group of behavioural interdictions or restrictions, a distinction that was already made by Frazer (1875). Originally, *taboo* was imported from the Tongan languages to refer to ritual prohibitions from those cultures (Allan and Burridge 1991: 12). The first taboo studies were thus carried out in Ethnography and Anthropology. They described systems of prohibitions and their similarities in a variety of cultures (Frazer 1932; Radcliffe-Brown 1952; Thomas 1911). In those works, it was already observed that taboo systems also included forbidden words and sounds, which might even affect languages as a whole, as is the case of many Austronesian languages (Allan and Burridge 1991: 35–36). In a taboo system, certain behaviours are prohibited and if the prohibition is violated, the individual will be punished by the group or by supernatural powers (Frazer 1875). In that case, a number of purification rituals need be put in place to escape the taboo condition. Later, the works of Freud (1991 [1913]) were key for the expansion of the concept of *taboo* to behaviours within Western societies, since his studies observed similarities in the rituals of exotic cultures and those of his neurotic patients. In time, the realm of application of taboo grew considerably. Nowadays, the term can be applied to any socially imposed prohibitions or restrictions, with social or even legal consequences, and studies about taboo are present in a variety of disciplines, including Psychiatry, Psychology, Sociology or Cultural Studies. Still, the linguistic facet of the phenomenon is obviously very prominent.

Within Linguistics, in the last decades, linguistic taboo has finally received increasing attention, but as with any emerging subject, the contributions are scattered and rather uncoordinated. Research on linguistic taboo is often revisiting the definition of the phenomenon and refreshing the state of the art, a fact that can sometimes lead to confusion about what is linguistic taboo exactly, what is its position within linguistic theory, and what methods are there to study it. The next section briefly summarizes some of these aspects.

1 Taboo in linguistic theory

For a long time, linguistic taboo has been relegated to a peripheral position within Linguistics. This is not surprising if we consider two crucial facts: the extralinguistic difficulty motivated by the social stigmatization of the phenomenon, and the linguistic difficulty based on its inherent complexity.

First, until the 20th century was well advanced, linguists were still defending the seriousness of the subject and denouncing the stigmatization of the taboo topics even within scientific research (Alonso 1964). As Andersson and Trudgill (1992) argue, judging taboo words (among other linguistic phenomena) as *bad language* is a matter of ideology, therefore it is crucial to "keep science and opinions apart" (p. 189) in order to investigate what lies behind bad language use. Although the situation has improved for researchers, it is fair to say that working with taboos still implies facing more practical problems than other phenomena, especially in data collection regarding topics such as sexuality, illness or death. Why would a linguist deal with such uncomfortable topics? Many of us have faced this kind of (not always innocent) question. Yet in the very question lies the answer: studying linguistic taboo means understanding the systems of beliefs, the regimes of language, truth and knowledge (Irvine 2011) regarding the immorality or inappropriateness of what cannot be said, and why these topics (or particular words) produce strong reactions in some speakers. It also means understanding the linguistic resources for veiling or disguising the forbidden, or on the contrary, for enhancing it with the purpose of using its powerful affective meanings for a variety of purposes. The very fact that languages allow for the existence of forbidden meanings and words, and their alternatives, can shed light on aspects such as how (social) meanings are acquired, categorized, perceived and dealt with in discourse.

Second, a theoretical and practical difficulty comes from the fact that linguistic taboo affects various levels of discourse and has therefore been quite problematic to define and analyse. There is variation in situating the scope of the phenomenon, which has been defined as semantic, pragmatic, sociolinguistic, and more recently, also cognitive. Semantic studies have focused on the phenomenon of taboo at the level of Lexical Semantics: the linguistic means to create alternative expressions and the description of particular semantic fields or concepts (Kany 1960; Galli de Paratesi 1964; Senabre 1971; Montero Cartelle 1981; Casas Gómez 1986; Chamizo Domínguez and Sánchez Benedito 2000; etc.), or on a more lexicographic vein, specialized dictionaries focusing on taboo semantic fields (for instance, about sexuality, Rodríguez González 2011; Rodríguez González 2008; Cela 1989; Coll 1991; Richter 1993; etc.) or types of x-phemistic expressions (Lechado García 2000; Martín 1974; Ayto 1993; Green 2006; etc.). Pragmatic studies analyse the functions of taboo words or expressions in particular communicative situations or genres (Crespo-Fernández 2007; Jay and Janschewitz 2008; etc.). In this respect, the study of euphemism and mitigation strategies has caught considerable attention, as well as dysphemism and offense, sometimes related with impoliteness (Pizarro Pedraza and De Cock 2018; Crespo-Fernández 2018). On the other hand, sociolinguistic approaches research the social patterns in the use of particular x-phemistic expressions, by focusing particularly on the social meanings of euphemism or dysphemism, for instance (De Klerk 1992; López Morales 2005; Stenström 2006; Christie 2013; Cestero Mancera 2015; Pizarro Pedraza 2015; among others).

In fact, linguistic taboo participates in all of the mentioned linguistic dimensions in different ways; however, the perspective taken in this book is that taboo is primarily a semantic phenomenon, in line with the Cognitive Semantic tenet that "language is all about meaning" (Geeraerts 2006: 3). In this sense, the taboo prohibition falls on concepts or, more abstractly, on meanings, rather than only on words. The semantic nature of taboo doesn't go against the existence of taboo words: it is obvious that certain lexical items are tabooed, such as slurs or insults. However, the stigmatization that falls on those words is due to the fact that they refer to a tabooed concept. Formally, words like *fuck* or *cunt* do not have anything offensive *per se*; it is because the concepts they refer to are problematic, and because the link with the taboo meanings is transparent, that they are taboo. The stigmatization of taboo concepts does not have linguistic causes, since it is extralinguistically determined: as already mentioned, "bad language" depends on the ideologies of each particular social group (Andersson and Trudgill 1992). Consequently, linguistic taboo is also a sociolinguistic phenomenon, which varies across and within societies, assigning different degrees of prohibition to taboo concepts.

Besides its semantic nature and its sociolinguistic variation, the expression of linguistic taboo is also crucially determined by situation-dependent pragmatic factors that determine what is offensive and what is not, often in terms of face protection and threat (Allan and Burridge 2006: 34). Thus, it is not surprising that perspectives on linguistic taboo have been varied and have focused on different facets of the phenomena, depending on the interest of the research.

As might be deduced from the previous paragraphs, linguistic taboo shows some overlap with other linguistic phenomena such as (im)politeness, linguistic aggression, hedging, as well as with particular perspectives focusing on language and sexuality, ethnicity, and various situations such as censorship, political correctness, or illegal behaviours, such as slander. Although not all the works dealing with those problems use the concept of "linguistic taboo", they are often related to it. Moreover, the study of linguistic taboo can hardly avoid touching on non-linguistic aspects, which makes it also highly interdisciplinary. This added complexity is also its biggest appeal: linguistic taboo is of interest to many disciplines within the Humanities and the (Social) Sciences. The cognitive aspects of the phenomenon are a crucial part of the web that links the disciplines interested in cognition with those that focus on social reality. It is precisely on that connection that this book wants to dig in.

2 A cognitive perspective on linguistic taboo

Linguistic taboo triggers interesting questions related with the processes of acquisition, processing and production of problematic concepts. Often the focus has been put on what makes them different from the rest of the concepts. Apparently, speakers learn quite early to use some taboo phenomena like cursing (at 1 or 2 years of age, or as soon as they learn to speak) in moments loaded with strong negative emotions like anger or frustration (Jay 2000). Moreover, they also learn about their inappropriateness in episodes of negative conditioning, through punishments, that can be recalled long after childhood (Jay, King and Duncan 2006). This negative conditioning seems to be connected with the emotional content that these words are loaded with: in experiments measuring skin response, it has been proven that the body reacts strongly to these words (MacWhinney, Keenan, and Reinke 1982, in Allan and Burridge, 2006: 42). The fact that taboo words are special has been further underlined by the evidence that they survive in patients with dementia and aphasia who have lost linguistic fluency (Jay 2009: 155). Words are learnt with this sort of transversal categories of "allowed" or "forbidden" (Jay 2009: 158), and at the same time, speakers learn alternative, adequate expressions, and the situations in which they can appear, namely in what types of contexts, physical and social environments and with what kind of interlocutors (Jay and Janschewitz 2008).

Since the categorization of concepts as taboo happens in a particular society (at the beginning, the family), the range of taboo concepts and their degree of tabooization is socially dependent, as are the learned adequate equivalents. Same as for other concepts, similar construals of taboo concepts within a society might show patterns in the shared conceptualization of those concepts by particular groups (Kristiansen and Dirven 2008). In this line, the relation between taboo and conceptual metaphor has caught some attention: on the one hand, in what respects the relation between the speakers' conceptualization of taboos and their use and understanding of metaphorical expressions (Pfaff, Gibbs and Johnson 1997), and on the other hand, in what respects the conceptual associations between taboo target concepts and non-taboo sources and their sociocultural motivations (Chamizo Domínguez 2004; Crespo-Fernández 2015). Nonetheless, linguistic taboo is also construed in discourse through other phenomena such as conceptual metonymy (Gradečak-Erdeljić and Milić 2011) or vagueness (Grondelaers and Geeraerts 1998), although they have not received as much consideration yet.

Due to this growing interest in the relation between taboo and Cognitive Linguistics in general, and with the intention of motivating research and debate, in 2015 I organized a session within ICLC 13 (Northumbria, July 2015) with the name "Cognitive perspectives on Linguistic Taboo". The small session, which included five papers (versions of which are included in this volume), focused on different aspects of linguistic taboo. The discussions initiated then were responsible for the project of the present volume: there was not enough research, but there was enough interest. After that session, I launched an open call for papers, for which I received more proposals than this book could handle. After a difficult selection based on double-blind reviews, the project of the book was outlined and pre-approved, and the project started. In the meantime, I organized a second session in AELCO (Alcalá de Henares, October 2016) in Spanish and focusing on conceptual metaphor, which was also successful and rich in discussion. It became even clearer that the growth of the interest in taboo from Cognitive Linguistic perspectives was steady. The present volume does not aim to cover all possible questions about taboo and Cognitive Linguistics; rather it intends to propose a broad range of studies that will hopefully motivate discussion and further research.

3 Overview of the volume

The purpose of this book is to bring to the readers a collection of papers about different taboo phenomena written from a cognitive perspective, in the broad sense. As the taboo phenomenon itself, the book is purposefully heterogeneous. Since a main goal of this volume was to provide a view on the cultural variation of taboos, a variety of languages and cultures are represented (English, Spanish, Polish, Dutch, Persian, Gikūyū and Egyptian Arabic) as well as taboo topics (sexuality, illness, ageing, war, shame, race, religion...). The contributors work within cognitive linguistic frameworks such as conceptual metaphor and metonymy, cultural conceptualization or cognitive sociolinguistics, but also at the interface of Pragmatics, Discourse Analysis, Applied Linguistics, and at the interdisciplinary borders with Psychiatry. The methods used in the studies are also varied, ranging from corpus analysis, interviews or surveys to experiments.

Since the complexity of the phenomenon has often led to conceptual and practical confusion, in **Chapter 1** Miguel Casas Gómez provides a review of the state of the art and a theoretical discussion on linguistic taboo, in order to clarify the object(s) of study, the commonly used concepts and their evolution, and the linguistic phenomena they refer to.

In order to illustrate the mentioned complexity, the theory is supported by 14 case studies providing novel insights into a very broad range of taboo-motivated phenomena (euphemism, dysphemism, swearing, political correctness, coprolalia, etc.), divided in four parts.

Part I focuses on *Construal* and particularly on three productive phenomena for the study of linguistic taboo: metaphor, metonymy and vagueness. In **Chapter 2**, Eliecer Crespo-Fernández analyses English metaphors about homosexuality in the COCA corpus. The metaphorical expressions are classified in four conceptual metaphors based on the domains of CONTAINER, ANIMAL, CRUISING and WOMAN. He classifies the particular examples according to their axiological value and analyses their different communicative functions, which are highly dependent on the context. Interpretation is enriched with historical information about the expressions and explanations of cultural discourses about homosexuality and the values related to it. In **Chapter 3,** Ivana Moritz studies euphemisms based on metonymy in war related-speeches by George W. Bush and Barak Obama. Metonymical expressions are more frequent than metaphorical euphemistic expressions, which shows some interesting evidence on the euphemistic potential of metonymy versus metaphor. The author provides an analysis of the concepts that are most often conveyed through metonymy and explains the role of this mechanism in political discourse. In **Chapter 4**, Pedro Chamizo Domínguez argues that political correctness is based on euphemism, which in turn relies on vagueness and ambiguity to reach its effects. Through the qualitative analyses of a variety of examples in different languages, the author shows the tension that exists between the need for prohibiting and the political incorrectness of forbidding derived from May 68. He exemplifies how vagueness and ambiguity work for political correctness at the lexical semantic level (synonymy) and at the speech act level (indirect speech acts).

Part II focuses on the relation between taboos and *Cultural Conceptualization*. It includes six case studies that present taboo phenomena through the meanings they have in their particular societies. In **Chapter 5**, Réka Benczes, Kate Burridge, Keith Allan and Farzad Sharifian analyse the taboo of AGEING in Australian English, through the names and expressions referring to "old age" in Australian newspapers from 1987 to 2014. Their findings show the crucial social changes related to extended longevity that are reflected in a reconceptualization of the concept of AGEING through new conceptual categories, conceptual metaphors and cultural schemas. In **Chapter 6**, Magdalena Zawrotna studies the use of the taboo categories FAMILY, SEX and RELIGION as insult intensifiers in Egyptian Arabic. Based on evidence from different sources (field research, online sources and questionnaires), the author illustrates how taboo words have undergone a process of grammaticalization, through which they have lost their original meanings but retained their emotional load for the new function of intensification, in which the offensiveness of the original domain gives rise to a graded intensification, where RELIGION is the most intense. In **Chapter 7**, Mohsen Bakhtiar analyses the concept of HAYÂ 'self-restraint' in Persian. It is a regulatory force that prevents (linguistic) taboo behaviours. In a corpus of newspapers, the author studies 150 examples of collocates and metaphorical expressions to provide an interpretation of the cultural conceptualization of the concept and its relation to other key concepts, as well as a comparison to the concept of SHAME in English. **Chapter 8** deals with the concept of MENSTRUATION in the African language Gĩkũyũ. Through interviews, Moses Gatambuki Gathigia, Daniel Ochieng Orwenjo and Ruth Wangeci Ndung'u collect metaphorical expressions referring to the target concept. In their analysis, they identify several conceptual metaphors with positive and negative implications, and they interpret the current cultural and embodied meanings within the studied speech community, but also in line with its traditions. In **Chapter 9**, Anna Kuzio proposes a contrastive analysis of taboos among Polish and British English speakers. Through a number of questionnaires, the author contrasts the general perception about taboo language, and more specifically, the contexts of use, the kind of interlocutor and the communicative intentions that allow for the use of taboo. The study finds significant differences among Polish and British English speakers that can be linked to cultural variations related to politeness and social norms in both cultures. The last chapter of this part, **Chapter 10**, contributes with a study on the factors that influence the processing of taboo metaphors in a foreign language. Their authors, Barbara De Cock and Ferran Suñer, report on the results of their experiment on the processing of sexual metaphors in Spanish by Belgian students who are native speakers of French. Their results show the significant impact of an experience in a country where the L2 is spoken, rather than other factors included in the analysis, such as conceptual similarity, presence of context or the students' L2 level.

Part III brings together three quantitative studies with a *Cognitive Sociolinguistics* perspective on the variation of taboo concepts. In **Chapter 11**, Tom Ruette investigates disease-based swearing in Dutch in Belgium and the Netherlands on a corpus of Twitter data, in order to prove the hypothesis that the stronger taboo on diseases present in Calvinism will motivate a preference for swearing with diseases in the Netherlands, rather than with other domains. Through the application of Global Spatial Autocorrelation to his data, he provides evidence of geographical patterns that partially prove his hypothesis, but also point in other explanatory directions related to swearing preferences in rural versus urban areas. **Chapter 12** focuses on the variation of sexual concepts (body parts and physiology) on a corpus of interviews in Spanish collected by the author, Andrea Pizarro Pedraza. Through logistic regression, the author studies the preference for a direct sexual expression according to a number of linguistic and social factors. Her results show that the use of direct expressions is related to formality, whereas the preference for indirect expressions can indicate informality, affect or euphemism. In **Chapter 13,** Ana María Cestero Mancera reports on a sociolinguistic study of the perceived expression of taboos in Madrilenian Spanish. Through a questionnaire, the author explored how speakers perceive their own use of taboo expressions from the fields of DEATH, RELIGION, SEXUALITY and SCATOLOGY. The different provided contexts are an important source of variation, as well as the variables sex, age and level of education, but not the district the speakers come from. When comparing these results with data from interviews, the author finds that reported use is different from actual use.

Finally, the volume ends with two chapters from *Interdisciplinary Approaches*, which constitute **Part IV**. In **Chapter 14**, Habibollah Ghassemzadeh presents psychiatric, cultural and linguistic aspects of Obsessive Compulsive Disorder that are related to taboos, such as religious scrupulosity and sexual ruminations and their linguistic expressions. Through evidence from different experiments and studies, the author explains that for OCD patients, the violation of a taboo very often triggers washing rituals and cleansing vocabulary as a physical response to the threat of moral cleanness, although these rituals and concepts are present in a lesser degree throughout society. Finally, in **Chapter 15**, Shlomit Ritz Finkelstein analyses the phenomenon of involuntary swearing (coprolalia and copropaxia) in patients with Tourette disorder. Based on interview data with patients, the author shows that swearing in TS, while being automatic, is not random, but rather fine-tuned to situational specificities, such as particular social or cultural prohibitions. In that sense, as long as the hearer reacts automatically to it, involuntary swearing constitutes an effective speech act, and particularly, an emotion act. However, a non-automatic response by the hearer can lessen the offense done by the involuntary swearing.

In sum, the fifteen chapters collected in *Linguistic taboo revisited* intend to promote theoretical discussion and further research on the complex phenomenon of linguistic taboo. As the editor, I am conscious that the field of taboo is far too complex and varied to be fully covered by these chapters, nonetheless their heterogeneity is intended to provide the reader with a variety of questions and topics that connect linguistic taboo with aspects of Cognitive Linguistics and linguistic theory in general. Hopefully, the problems posed by taboo phenomena, both theoretical and methodological, will spark the interest of other researchers to replicate, discuss or follow up on any of these studies. Then, the main intention of this volume to give taboo a more central position in linguistic research will have been fulfilled.

References

Allan, Keith & Kate Burridge. 2006. *Forbidden words*. New York: Cambridge University Press.
Alonso, Dámaso. 1964. Para evitar la diversificación de nuestra lengua. *Presente y futuro de la lengua española. Actas de la Asamblea de Filología del I Congreso de Instituciones Hispánicas*. Madrid: Cultura Hispánica.
Allan, Keith & Kate Burridge. 1991. *Euphemism and Dysphemism. Language Used as Shield and Weapon*. New York, Oxford: Oxford University Press.
Allan, Keith & Kate Burridge. 2006. *Forbidden Words*. New York: Cambridge University Press.
Andersson, Lars-Gunnar & Peter Trudgill. 1992. *Bad Language*. London: Penguin Books.
Ayto, John. 1993. *A Dictionary of Euphemism*. London: Bloomsbury.
Casas Gómez, Miguel. 1986. *La interdicción lingüística. Mecanismos del eufemismo y disfemismo*. Cádiz: Servicio de publicaciones de la Universidad de Cádiz.
Cela, Camilo José. 1989. *Diccionario secreto*. Madrid: Alianza.
Cestero Mancera, Ana María. 2015. La Expresión Del Tabú: Estudio Sociolingüístico. *Boletín de Filología* 50 (1). 71–105.
Chamizo Domínguez, Pedro J. 2004. La función social y cognitiva del eufemismo y del disfemismo. *Panace@* V (15).
Chamizo Domínguez, Pedro J. & Francisco Sánchez Benedito. 2000. *Lo que nunca se aprendió en clase. Eufemismos y disfemismos en el lenguaje erótico inglés*. Granada: Comares.
Christie, Christine. 2013. The Relevance of Taboo Language: An Analysis of the Indexical Values of Swearwords. *Journal of Pragmatics* 58. 152–169.

Coll, José Luis. 1991. *El Eroticoll. Diccionario erótico*. Madrid: Tema de hoy.
Crespo-Fernández, Eliecer. 2007. *El eufemismo y el disfemismo. Procesos de manipulación del tabú en el lenguaje literario inglés*. Alicante: Publicaciones Universidad de Alicante.
Crespo-Fernández, Eliecer. 2015. *Sex in Language. Euphemistic and Dysphemistic Metaphors in Internet Forums*. London: Bloomsbury.
Crespo-Fernández, Eliecer (ed.). 2018. *Taboo in Discourse: Studies on Attenuation and Offence in Communication*. Bern: Peter Lang.
De Klerk, Vivian. 1992. How Taboo Are Taboo Words for Girls? *Language in Society* 21. 277–289.
Frazer, James George. 1875. Taboo. In *Encyclopaedia Britannica*, 9th ed.
Frazer, James George. 1932. *The Golden Bough: A Study of Magic and Religion*. 3rd. ed. London: MacMillan and Co. Limited.
Freud, Sigmund. 1991. Totem Und Tabu. In *Gesammelte Werke*. Vol. IX. London: Imago Publishing Co.
Galli de Paratesi, Nora. 1964. Semantica dell' eufemismo. L'eufemismmo e la repressione verbale con esempi tratti dall' italiano contemporaneo. *Pubblicazioni della Facoltà di Lettere e Filosofia* XV (1). Torino: G. Giappichelli Editore.
Geeraerts, Dirk (ed.). 2006. *Cognitive Linguistics: Basic Readings*. Berlin/New York: Mouton de Gruyter.
Gradečak-Erdeljić, Tanja & Goran Milić. 2011. Metonymy at the Crossroads: A Case of Euphemisms and Dysphemisms. In Benczes, Réka, Antonio Barcelona & Francisco José Ruiz de Mendoza Ibáñez (eds.), *Defining Metonymy in Cognitive Linguistics. Towards a Consensus View*. Amsterdam/Philadelphia: John Benjamins Publishing Company.
Green, Jonathon. 2006. Slang Dictionaries, English. In *Encyclopedia of Language & Linguistics*, 403–406.
Grondelaers, Stefan & Dirk Geeraerts. 1998. Vagueness as a Euphemistic Strategy. In Athanasiadou, Angeliki & Elżbieta Tabakowska (eds.), *Speaking of Emotions: Conceptualisation and Expression*, 357–374. Berlin/New York: Mouton de Gruyter.
Irvine, Judith T. 2011. Leaky Registers and Eight-Hundred-Pound Gorillas. *Anthropological Quarterly* 84 (1). 15–39.
Jay, Timothy. 2000. *Why We Curse*. Philadelphia/Amsterdam: John Benjamins Publishing Company.
Jay, Timothy. 2009. The Utility and Ubiquity of Taboo Words. *Perspectives on Psychological Science* 4 (2). 153–161.
Jay, Timothy & Kristin Janschewitz. 2008. The Pragmatics of Swearing. *Journal of Politeness Research* 4. 267–288.
Jay, Timothy, Krista King & Tim Duncan. 2006. Memories of Punishment for Cursing. *Sex Roles* 55 (1–2). 123–133.
Kany, Charles E. 1960. *American-Spanish Euphemisms*. Berkeley/Los Angeles: University of California Press.
Kristiansen, Gitte & René Dirven (eds.). 2008. *Cognitive Sociolinguistics. Language Variation, Cultural Models, Social Systems*. Berlin: De Gruyter Mouton.
Lechado García, José. 2000. *Diccionario de eufemismos y de expresiones eufemísticas del español actual*. Madrid: Verbum.
López Morales, Humberto. 2005. Sociolingüística del tabú. *Interlingüística*, no. 16. 7–20.
MacWhinney, Brian, Janice M. Keenan & Peter Reinke. 1982. The Role of Arousal in Memory for Conversation. *Memory and Cognition* 10. 308–317.
Martín, Jaime. 1974. *Diccionario de Expresiones Malsonantes Del Español*. Madrid: Istmo.

Montero Cartelle, Emilio. 1981. *El Eufemismo en Galicia (su comparación con otras áreas romances)*. In *Verba*. Anexo 17. Santiago de Compostela: Universidad de Santiago.

Pfaff, Kerry L., Raymond W. Gibbs & Michael D. Johnson. 1997. Metaphor in Using and Understanding Euphemism and Dysphemism. *Applied Linguistics* 18. 59–83.

Pizarro Pedraza, Andrea. 2015. Who said 'abortion'? Semantic variation and ideology in Spanish newspapers' online discussions. *Australian Journal of Linguistics* 35(1). 53–75.

Pizarro Pedraza, Andrea & Barbara De Cock. 2018. Taboo effects at the syntactic level: reducing agentivity as a euphemistic strategy. *Pragmatics: quarterly publication of the International Pragmatics Association* 28(1). 113–138.

Radcliffe-Brown, Alfred R. 1952. *Structure and Function in Primitive Society. Essays and Addresses*. London: Cohen & West.

Richter, Alan. 1993. *Dictionary of Sexual Slang: Words, Phrases and Idioms*. New York: Harper Collins.

Rodríguez González, Félix. 2008. *Diccionario gay-lésbico. Vocabulario general y argot de la homosexualidad*. Madrid: Gredos.

Rodríguez González, Félix. 2011. *Diccionario del sexo y el erotismo*. Madrid: Alianza Editorial.

Senabre, Ricardo. 1971. El eufemismo como fenómeno lingüístico. *Boletín de La Real Academia Española* 51 (192). 175–189.

Stenström, Anna-Brita. 2006. Taboo Words in Teenage Talk: London and Madrid Girls' Conversations Compared. In Mar-Molinero, Clare & Miranda Stewart (eds.), *Language Variation and Change: Historical and Contemporary Perspectives*. Special issue in *Spanish in Context*.115–138.

Thomas, Northcote W. 1911. Taboo. In *Encyclopaedia Britannica*, 11th ed.

Miguel Casas Gómez
1 Lexicon, discourse and cognition: terminological delimitations in the conceptualizations of linguistic taboo

Abstract: This theoretical paper has two basic aims: 1) to make a terminological revision both of concepts such as *taboo, interdiction, euphemism, dysphemism, euphemistic/dysphemistic substitute, euphemistic/dysphemistic use,* generally incorrectly used in lexical research on the subject, as well as of others used in more recent works in the pragmatic-discursive and cognitive field (*orthophemism, X-phemism, quasi-euphemism – quasi-dysphemism* and, above all, *word taboo* and *concept taboo* or *conceptual interdiction*); and 2) to establish the evolution of terminological-conceptual delimitations carried out in the field of interdiction, from lexical and pragmatic-discursive perspectives to the new dimensions of the cognitivist paradigm.

Key words: lexicon, discourse, cognition, taboo, euphemism, dysphemism, euphemistic/dysphemistic substitute, euphemistic/dysphemistic use, orthophemism, X-phemism, word taboo, conceptual interdiction, quasi-euphemism, quasi-dysphemism.

1 Introduction

Whenever we deal with problems pertaining to interdiction and taboo we can either ratify or reconsider some of the formulations proposed in our doctoral thesis (Casas Gómez 1986) and related publications, in the framework of a lexical and pragmatic vision of the phenomenon, such as proposing a more up-to-date perspective of interdiction in line with the communicative and cognitive sphere, as we have done in more recent works.

In the different theoretical approaches to linguistic taboo, we have discovered the existence of numerous confusions among the diverse notions encompassed by this phenomenon. Most of them, very widespread in traditional research,

---

This work is included in the I+D Excellence Project: "Specialized communication and terminography: terminological uses related to current perspectives and contents of lexical semantics" (FFI2014-54609-P).

arise from an exclusively lexical vision of the phenomenon and, above all, from a narrow concept of *euphemism*, limited to the lexical sphere and to a substitutive mechanism. In fact, the *euphemism*, wrongly defined as a lexical substitute, is not always a substitute, nor does it function only at this linguistic level and neither should it be identified with a substitution process.

This study, of a theoretical and partly historiographical nature, has two main aims: 1) to revise those concepts arising from pragmatic-discursive and cognitivist approaches, such as *orthophemism*, *X-phemism*, *quasi-euphemism – quasi-dysphemism*, and, above all, the difference between *word taboo* and *concept taboo*, or, more precisely, *conceptual interdiction*; and 2) to account for an evolution in the development of the epistemological delimitations made in this field, from structuralist and pragmatic-discursive lexical perspectives to the recent dimensions of the cognitivist paradigm, which explain the change from the traditional concept of euphemism as a lexical substitute to euphemism as a cognitive process of the conceptualization of a forbidden reality.

2 Terminological-conceptual clarifications from a lexical standpoint

In a previous paper (Casas Gómez 2005), we carried out a critical revision of the concepts and terms included in this first section. Of all these, for the purposes of this study, we would like to return both to the distinction between *taboo* and *interdiction*, as a starting point for some reflections on the subject of euphemism from a cognitivist standpoint, and to the identification between *euphemism* as a process and *substitute* as a result.

In accordance with the second aim of this work, different authors have observed that *euphemism* is frequently identified with *euphemistic substitute* and that this consists simply of using the former to indicate the term that is used to replace the forbidden word and not the substitution itself, or, more exactly, the linguistic expression itself. This misunderstanding is seen clearly in traditional linguistic definitions or those within the framework of semantic structuralism, such as those by Ullmann (1964: 205), who described it as a "harmless substitute"; Baldinger (1970: 223), who considered that "a través del eufemismo se hace abstracción de la función de síntoma o de señal implicada por la palabra que es reemplazada por el eufemismo" [through euphemism an abstraction is made of the symptom or the signal implied by the word that is replaced by it]; Lamíquiz (1974: 415), who regarded euphemism as the "sustituto léxico que siempre generaliza quitando semas o dando sólo el género próximo" [lexical substitute that always generalises, eliminating semes or giving only the generic term]; or Senabre (1971), who, at the time, went deeper and determined the linguistic concept of euphemism (Casas Gómez 1993 and 1995). Starting from the notion of *syncretism*, which he clearly confuses with the concept of *neutralization*, this author defines it as "sincretismo léxico resoluble, producido en el plano del contenido y al nivel del emisor y del que sólo se manifiesta el término extensivo o no marcado" [resoluble lexical syncretism, produced at the level of the content by the speaker in which only the extensive or unmarked term is manifested] (Senabre 1971: 185).

Euphemism and *dysphemism* are two linguistic processes whose function, with different motivations and purposes, is the substitution or linguistic expression of the abhorrent term or the forbidden reality. However, they are frequently used to indicate, not the linguistic process itself, but rather, the substitute that replaces the forbidden object, which, for the sake of greater precision, we will refer to as *euphemistic* or *dysphemistic* substitute. In this way, in the linguistic norm, for each conceptual area covered by the interdiction, we have lexicalized substitutes, which can be either euphemistic or dysphemistic. However, it is necessary to emphasize that this can be defined only as a speech act or discursive phenomenon, which explains the existence of an unlimited number of euphemistic and dysphemistic uses, created spontaneously and sporadically by users in certain situational contexts, and it is these that really acquire value in this process as situational uses and contextual products of the speech act. In fact, given the general instability[1] and the particular relativity of the phenomenon, euphemism or dysphemism should be, first, understood and, subsequently, recognised as this type of (euphemistic or dysphemistic) use both by the speaker and the hearer. This is a more acceptable interpretation, given the pragmatic and discursive nature of euphemism. Hence, it is impossible to make a categorical affirmation of the existence of euphemisms or euphemism-words, or even of substitutes, euphemistic or dysphemistic forms or expressions, but, rather, of euphemistic or dysphemistic uses in a particular context and situational background, depending on their functions in affective and evocative speech, their intention and their true function as a communicative value.

The linguistic opposite of *euphemism* is *dysphemism*, historically ignored by semanticists and not clearly differentiated from its antonym, although it has recently received greater scholarly attention.[2] Its basis is identical to that

---

[1] A description of the different types of instability of euphemism with examples in various languages can be found in Casas Gómez (1995: 26–32).
[2] In this pragmatic-discursive and cognitive vein, see, among others, the studies by Chamizo and Sánchez Benedito (1994: 78–92 and 2000: 23–65), Chamizo (2004: 45–51), Allan and Bur-

of euphemism as regards the "substitution" or, rather, manifestation and the mechanisms that produce it in the sense that there are no actual euphemistic and dysphemistic resources, although some are appropriate to one attitude or another. However, the motivation and purpose are different, since dysphemism does not seek to break the associations with the forbidden word or reality, but, on the contrary, to intensify them. This means that, although both euphemism and dysphemism are based on the same principle and use the same linguistic devices, the aim of dysphemism is not to attenuate or soften, but to have the opposite effect, the motivation or reinforcement of the forbidden sign or concept.

3 Terminological-conceptual clarifications from a pragmatic-discursive and cognitivist standpoint

To the terms and concepts revised in the previous section, it is necessary to add other, more up-to-date distinctions, such as *orthophemism* as opposed to *euphemism/dysphemism* and *X-phemism*, within the framework of the proliferation of definitions that highlight the pragmatic perspective of the phenomenon[3] and which emphasize its discursive nature and the elements intervening in the euphemistic communicative process. Thus, Allan and Burridge (2006: 31–33) define *euphemism* in relation to *dysphemism* and *orthophemism*. In this sense, a *dysphemism* is "a word or phrase with connotations that are offensive either about the denotatum and/or to people addressed or overhearing the utterance", whereas "*orthophemisms* and *euphemisms* are words or phrases used as an alternative to a dispreferred expression. They avoid possible loss of face by the speaker, and also the hearer or some third party". In this way, they establish a difference between both terms: "An *orthophemism* is typically more formal and more direct (or literal) than the corresponding euphemism" and "a *euphemism* is typically more colloquial and figurative (or indirect) than the corresponding orthophemism".

---

ridge (1991 and 2006), Crespo Fernández (2007 and 2015: 135–186), Díaz Pérez (2012) and Pizarro Pedraza (2013).

3 As an example of this perspective, see our work (Casas Gómez 2012a: 61–63), in which we analyse the characterizations of authors such as Warren (1992: 135), Lechado García (2000: 14), Gómez Sánchez (2004: 45), Armenta Moreno (2009), Edeso Natalías (2009: 147 and 150) and, above all, Crespo Fernández (2007: 82–83).

Along with *orthophemism*, these authors have coined the term *X-phemism*, with reference to the whole group of euphemisms, orthophemisms and dysphemisms and related to the concept of "cross-varietal synonymy", that is "words that have the same meaning as other words used in different contexts. For instance, the X-phemisms *poo*, *shit* and *faeces* are cross-varietal synonyms because they denote the same thing but have different connotations, which mark different styles used in different circumstances" (Allan and Burridge 2006: 29). Therefore, this is a concept which, due to its inclusive character, encompasses the phenomena of *orthophemism*, *euphemism* and *dysphemism* in a kind of "x-phemistic continuum".

This concept of *orthophemism* has recently been incorporated from a cognitive sociolinguistic perspective into the study of taboo and euphemism in the sexual concepts of the city of Madrid carried out by Pizarro Pedraza (2013: 81). This author refers to "formas neutras o directas de nombrar las realidades tabuizadas, que no sean ni eufemísticas ni disfemísticas" [neutral or direct ways of naming tabooed realities, that are neither euphemistic nor dysphemistic], as a phenomenon which is "más estable, al tratarse de la expresión directa o literal del concepto tabuizado, en algún sentido, la expresión formal estandarizada" [more stable, since it is the direct or literal expression of the tabooed concept, in a sense, the standardized formal expression]. And, in the line of the above-mentioned researchers, Cestero Mancera (2015a: 303, no. 28 and 2015b: 80, no. 19) characterizes *orthophemism* as a form of expression consisting in the use of "unidades lingüísticas directas, neutras, literales, formales o estandarizadas, que se utilizan para nombrar conceptos o realidades tabuizadas y que resultan no marcadas" [direct, neutral, literal, formal or standardized linguistic units, which are used to name tabooed concepts or realities and that are unmarked], in her essentially methodological and practical sociolinguistic analyses on taboo, also in the speech of Madrid, albeit in the framework of *PRESEEA* ("Proyecto para el Estudio Sociolingüístico del Español de España y América" [Project for the sociolinguistic study of the Spanish language of Spain and South America]).

As mixed processes for the manipulation of the referent, Crespo Fernández (2007: 211–235) incorporates two axiological types of reference to taboo which combine the affective tendencies of euphemism and dysphemism: the distinction between *quasi-euphemism* "cuando la intención del hablante es de signo eufemístico, pese a materializarse por medio de una locución disfemística" [when the intention of the speaker is of a euphemistic nature, in spite of being manifested in a dysphemistic expression] and *quasi-dysphemism* "cuando la expresión formal eufemística responde a un propósito peyorativo" [when the formal expression of the euphemism responds to a pejorative intention] (2007: 214). This author offers a comprehensive study of these processes as regards their pragmatic nature, formative resources and contextual variants. Even though his terminology, and, above all, his pragmatic characterization appears innovative, his concepts are not, since several authors (Silva Correia 1927: 778–779; Grimes 1978: 17 and 22; Montero Cartelle 1981: 89–90; Casas Gómez 1986: 93–96, and Allan and Burridge 1991: 30–31 and 149–150 and 2006: 39–40, among others) had previously referred to *dysphemisms with positive effects, pejorative* or *damning euphemisms, formal dysphemisms*, or *euphemistic dysphemisms/dysphemistic euphemisms*, in allusion to the fact that "ambas tendencias afectivas, la eufemística y la disfemística, se combinan mutuamente hasta el punto de aparecer eufemismos por su estructura formal con valor peyorativo y disfemismos formales con función eufemística (...) de acuerdo con la intención o el énfasis del que se sirve el hablante a la hora de emitir el vocablo" [both euphemistic and dysphemistic affective tendencies are combined mutually to the point of the appearance of euphemisms for their formal structure with a pejorative value and formal dysphemisms with euphemistic functions (...) according to the intention and the emphasis used by the speaker at the moment of emitting the word] (Casas Gómez 1986: 93). However, we are in complete agreement with Crespo Fernández (2007: 14) in that these authors, although they have considered "los actos de habla con una ilocución de signo contrario a su locución (...), no han profundizado lo suficiente en el fenómeno como hecho en el que se solapan el eufemismo y el disfemismo, siendo, al mismo tiempo, independiente de éstos" [speech acts with an illocution having an opposing sign to their locution (...), they have not gone deeply enough into the phenomenon as a fact in which euphemism and dysphemism overlap, being, at the same time, independent].

In line with the distinction between *taboo* and *interdiction*, we can include a conceptual and terminological delimitation, which is fully integrated in the cognitivist perspective: the distinction between *word taboo* and *concept taboo* or, more precisely, *conceptual interdiction* (Casas Gómez 2000: 84–92).

The origin of the former type of taboo, rooted in ancient thought and still present in advanced societies, has its essence in the belief in an intrinsic or magical power of the word (Malinowski 1962 and Casas Gómez 1996), capable of producing exactly what it designated, an idea which constitutes the original basis of the so-called *linguistic taboo*. For this reason, we prefer to characterize this first type of interdiction in a strict sense as *word taboo* and not *concept taboo*, which is what defines linguistic interdiction in the broadest sense of the word. More exactly, this is word taboo because in this sphere we always have forbidden base terms (rather than taboo realities, what we really have here are taboo words which are fully identified with such forbidden objects). For this reason, we must start from the lexical plane, and, therefore, from the process which is, in general, euphemistic substitution, although it is manifested by the most varied linguistic resources belonging to different linguistic levels.

Unlike word taboo, *concept taboo* or *conceptual interdiction* is not restricted at its base exclusively to a lexical level. In addition, it is not always evident which is the taboo term and which is the dysphemistic one (as happens, for example, in the cases of *cornudo-cabrón* [*cuckold-wimp*], *diablo-demonio* [*devil-demon*], *joder-follar* [*shag-fuck*]); hence the frequent identification of *taboo* with *dysphemism*. Sometimes it even seems that there is no forbidden term, although there is, of course, a forbidden concept or reality, which leads us to consider whether, instead of a forbidden vocabulary (as a base for "substitutions"), we should speak of a conceptual interdiction as the starting point for different euphemistic or dysphemistic formulae. These difficulties arising from the descriptive analysis of interdiction come from the attempt to depart, at all times, not from a forbidden reality, but from a base term, when this term sometimes does not have a counterpart in the real world. Think, for example, of what happens when we try to determine which is the base term in the sphere of *the other world* and *the afterlife* or what occurs in the conceptual area of *toilet*. This means that the limits between the two phenomena are not always clear-cut, and neither is it evident which element works synchronically as a taboo (which can sometimes only be discovered from a diachronic point of view, since speakers are no longer conscious of it) and which are dysphemistic. No doubt it is the expressive capacity, which has a fundamental function in the interdictive process, that explains the fact that, on occasions, the forbidden term is not at our disposal, since the respective euphemistic and dysphemistic uses really express contents about which the supposed base term gives no information.

In fact, all these obstacles arise from a purely lexical concept of euphemism, conceived semantically as a substitute or substitution process. However, the phenomenon under consideration goes beyond the lexical plane in that it is "más complejo de lo que se puede dar a entender con sustitución lexica" [more complex than might be understood by lexical substitution] (Uría Varela 1997: 6). Consequently, this means approaching the problem from a different angle, taking the forbidden conceptual categories as a starting point.

From this onomasiological activity, carried out by the speaker, which starts, not from the supposed forbidden term, but from the prohibited object, speakers *conceptualize* the various *forbidden realities* in different ways, approaching them, depending on a certain pragmatic situation, euphemistically or dysphemistically, by means of a great variety of resources belonging to all linguistic levels. These procedures which may involve substitution, alteration, modulation, modification, composition or inversion, combination and even a whole textual description result in a reinforced or motivated communication (dysphemistic language or speech) or, on the contrary, an attenuated one (euphemistic language or speech). To these modalities of taboo naming we can add orthophemism, which typically involves direct and literal language, as a neuter reference to the forbidden reality.

4 The evolution of terminological and conceptual delimitations in the field of interdiction

According to the clarifications made above, differentiating between *taboo* and *conceptual interdiction* means correcting the lexical limitations produced by the "supposed" substitutions in the euphemistic or dysphemistic field in traditional and structuralist approaches and entering the sphere of conceptualization starting from "contents" (Uría Varela 1997), "meanings"[4] (Pizarro Pedraza 2013) or "forbidden realities" (Casas Gómez 2009, 2012a, 2012b), and, consequently, adopting a cognitivist perspective through which it becomes clear that the euphemistic/dysphemistic phenomenon goes beyond the purely lexical plane, and that it should obviously not be identified with a mere substitution process.

The evolution of the definitions of euphemism, from those authors who start from a lexical vision to those who, more recently, subscribe to the framework of cognitivist perspectives,[5] either from semantics, understood as a cognitivist process of conceptualization of a forbidden reality, or from sociolinguistics, conceived as a communicative strategy, is clearly shown in the linguistic and extralinguistic characterization of the process (Casas Gómez 2009 and 2012a).

These two main phases in the study of euphemism can also be observed in the linguistic treatment that it has received and in the definitions and characterizations of its terms and concepts, as we have attempted to show in the contrast of theoretical-methodological positions described in the first two sections.

---

[4] This author proposes that taboo is manifested along the X-phemistic continuum, in which *euphemism*, *dysphemism* and *orthophemism* are "estrategias de estructuración conceptual (atenuada, intensificada o neutra) de ciertos significados negativos presentes en conceptos categorizados como tabú" [conceptual construal strategies (attenuated, intensified or neutral) of certain negative meanings present in concepts categorized as taboo] (Pizarro Pedraza 2013: 95–96).
[5] A cognitive vision of euphemism and dysphemism from the standpoint of conceptual networks (with examples in Spanish and English) can be found in works by Chamizo (1995: 205–219 and 2004: 45–51), Chamizo and Sánchez Benedito (2000: 67–309), Sánchez Benedito (1995: 339–347) and Crespo Fernández (2013: 99–118). For a recent cognitive model of sociolinguistic analysis of interdictive processes, see Pizarro Pedraza (2013).

In this regard, certain researchers have suggested specific stages in the development of the euphemistic phenomenon. Thus, in a work from a sociolinguistic perspective,[6] Cestero Mancera (2015a: 288–289) starting from the "status quaestionis" on linguistic taboo presented by Martínez Valdueza (1998) and Calvo Shadid (2011), identifies two stages: the first until the 1970s (with studies based on semantic, lexicological, lexicographical and dialectological perspectives) and the second, from that date until the present, in which she rightly different modern-day approaches to the study of taboo and euphemism and, equally aptly, includes the specialists in their corresponding analytical, such as pragmatics, sociolinguistics, cognitive linguistics and, more recently, multi-disciplinary perspectives such as cognitive pragmatics or cognitive sociolinguistics.

Nevertheless, to reach greater precision from a strictly historiographical point of view, we should increase the number of these phases and consider the existence of four major stages which have, to a certain extent, marked the linguistic evolution of the phenomenon and which follow the specific periods of semantic historiographics (historical, "traditional", prestructural and modern), the disciplinary perspectives on which its study has been focused linguistically (lexicology/lexical semantics, lexicography, dialectology, Romance linguistics, pragmatics, discourse analysis or sociolinguistics) and the contrast between methodological trends and paradigms, especially between structuralism and cognitivism. The first, which is related to the birth of *Semasiology* as a science in the nineteenth century, includes classical studies, in the field of historical and traditional semantics, which analysed taboo as an essentially psychological cause of semantic change.[7] The second, which is situated at the origins of modern semantics with structuralism and continues until the late 1970s and early 1980s, has its maximum expression in a collection of works of a semantic, lexicographical and dialectological nature (Martínez Valdueza 1998: 107–112), which, mainly within the framework of Romance linguistics, consist of a largely practical study of "euphemisms" and, exceptionally, "dysphemisms" in

---

6 Arising from López Morales' specific contributions (1990, 1997, 2001 and 2005) on the expression of taboo as the object of sociolinguistic research, there has recently been a proliferation of works from this perspective, such as those by Martínez Valdueza (1995 and 1998: 132–136), Calvo Shadid (2008 and 2011), Pizarro Pedraza (2013), Fernández de Molina Ortés (2014) and Cestero Mancera (2015a and 2015b).
7 See the tradition which starts with Hey (1900) and continues until Ullmann's studies of "traditional" semantics.

different languages.⁸ The third, starting from the 1980s and continuing to the end of the twentieth century, starts with the first reflections that are not only lexical, but also, essentially, pragmatic and discursive on euphemism,⁹ going as far as to call it a "speech act", concluding with statements such as "there are really no euphemisms", not even "euphemistic substitutes", although it is "euphemistic and dysphemistic uses" that really do exist. Finally, the fourth includes studies carried out in the twenty-first century, focusing on the area of linguistic cognitivism, although this phase had already been distinguished at the end of the last century, since it marks a turning point in the evolution of pragmatic discursive works towards communicative and cognitive conceptual approaches.

In order to make these stages clearer, above all the first one, let us turn to historiography as regards the origins of the study of euphemism, which are linked to the birth of *Semasiology* as a linguistic discipline within the German model of the theory of signification and which connect two disciples (Heerdegen and Hey) with opposing theoretical positions (a logical perspective, in the case of the former, and a psychological one in the latter case) of the semasiological school of Latin philology of Reisig (1839), considered to be the intellectual father of the scientific study of meaning from a purely linguistic angle. Therefore, it would seem appropriate to highlight the historiographical fact that, unsurprisingly, innovative questions, such as the relevant contributions made in this sphere by Uría Varela, start from the field of Latin linguistics, since we must remember that *Semantics* (under its original name of *Semasiology*), in general and *euphemism* in particular have their origins in classical philology. However, in this vein, Hey rejected in his studies of semasiology the logical classifications made by authors like Heerdegen,[10] in favour of a psychological perspective, which, in some way, explains why he analysed, among the "causes" of semantic changes, a specific psycho-associative phenomenon like euphemism and its use in Latin (Hey 1900: 515–536).[11]

---

[8] See the research carried out in different languages by, among others, Silva Correia (1927), Mansur Guérios (1956), Kany (1960), Galli de' Paratesi (1973), Widłak (1970), Montero Cartelle (1981), Kröll (1984), Radtke (1980) and Reutner (2009).
[9] See the works by Montero Cartelle, Casas Gómez, Allan and Burridge and Crespo Fernández cited in the bibliography.
[10] For historiographical data regarding the authors belonging to this school, see Casas Gómez (1991: 114–115 and 120–122).
[11] On the subject of taboo, euphemism and dysphemism in the sphere of Latin philology, see also Löfstedt (1959: 181–194). However, the most complete works, at least in the Spanish domain, are those by Montero Cartelle (1973) on "erotic" Latin, and, essentially, Uría Varela (1997).

Within this explanatory framework, I would like to highlight, for its relevance, the innovative scientific advance made, as a starting point in the study of taboo and euphemism, by the work of the latinist Uría Varela (1997: 6). This author was the first to mention, instead of forbidden *terms*, forbidden *"contents"* of certain conceptual spheres and areas of experience, as well as *attenuated communication*, as is reflected in his definition of the euphemistic process. In his definition, starting with some remarks which will be discussed below, Uría Varela warns that euphemism should be considered, not as a systematic phenomenon, but rather, as a discursive one, according to a pragmatic definition of euphemism included in a linguistics of communication as "conjunto de mecanismos lingüísticos que, basándose en una alteración, modulación o sustitución de formas o *contenidos* lingüísticos interdictos, proporcionan al hablante la posibilidad de *comunicación atenuada* de un sector de la experiencia" [a set of linguistic mechanisms which, based on an alteration, modulation or substitution of forbidden linguistic forms or *contents*, provide the speaker with the possibility of *attenuated communication* of one field of experience]. In this regard, he contributed numerous new aspects which have served as filters and links with recent cognitivist considerations, since he was the first to go beyond this exclusively lexical approach to the phenomenon, making this observation in his revision of the definitions of *euphemism* formulated previous to the publication of his monography. In this vein, the most outstanding points in his contribution can be summarized as follows: 1) euphemism cannot always be characterized as a lexical substitute; 2) its functions should not be reduced exclusively to this linguistic plane; and 3) above all, the phenomenon must not be identified at all times as a substitution process. In his arguments he alleges the existence of euphemistic substitutes that are not lexical (gestures), euphemistic processes that are crystallized in the lexicon but do not imply a substitution, such as those used in apologizing formulae or in syntagmatic groups, and others which are neither lexical nor substitutive (intonation or tone of voice), ending by saying that, in this process, together with the possible *substitution*, there can also be a *modulation* of the forbidden term, carried out verbally through apologizing formulae which excuse the utterance (previous or forthcoming) (such as *if you don't mind me saying so, if you'll pardon the expression,* etc.) or through non-verbal, paralinguistic resources such as intonation or tone of voice. Furthermore, he warns of another problem in this domain: "existen realidades interdictas que parecen carecer de término de base, esto es, que sólo tienen expresión eufemística ["o disfemística"], y en las que, por tanto, es impropio hablar, al menos en sincronía, de *sustitución*" [there are forbidden realities that appear to lack a base term, that is, realities which only have a euphemistic [or dysphemistic] expression, and in which it is, therefore, inappropriate, at least in synchrony, to speak of *substitution*]. This difficulty shows that in the area of interdiction, lexical substitution is not the be-all and end-all, and which allows us to focus on the process not from a forbidden term but from a forbidden "content" or reality.

In both phases of our scientific treatment in the study of taboo, we can observe this evolution in terminological-conceptual delimitations. In our initial approaches to the subject, we erroneously identified *euphemism* with *substitute* and limited it to a *substitution process*. In this regard, in our monography on linguistic interdiction, we first maintained a lexical formulation of euphemism as a linguistic process resulting in the neutralization of a forbidden term by means of associative resources of a formal and semantic nature. We also included certain pragmatic components, deriving from their essential reality and their social, contextual and discursive features. From this standpoint, we defined the phenomenon as "un acto de habla, como la actualización discursiva por parte del hablante de unos sustitutos léxicos – habituales o lexicalizados u ocasionales o creativos – que, a través de un conjunto de recursos lingüísticos y paralingüísticos, permiten, en un contexto y situación pragmática determinada, neutralizar léxicamente el término interdicto" [a speech act, being the discourse use by the speaker of some lexical substitutes –habitual, lexicalized, occasional or creative-, which, through a set of linguistic and paralinguistic resources, in a certain context and pragmatic situation, allow the lexical neutralization of the forbidden term] (Casas Gómez 1986: 35–36).

More recently, however, I have disagreed with the views expressed in the studies of this early period. This definition of *euphemism*, at the time it was made, contained some innovative aspects, especially in a pragmatic-discursive sense, but it also had limitations arising both from the linguistic plane taken as the starting point of the analysis and, essentially, from the perspective adopted in the study. The positive features of this characterization centred on two aspects: 1) the formulation of euphemism in the domain of speech, and not of the system, considering it to be a discursive use, a pragmatic aspect integrated in a linguistics of speech; and 2) the manifestation of a whole classification of linguistic mechanisms that are not limited to the lexical level, such as phonetic, morphological, syntactical and other resources belonging to the plane of paralinguistics. However, its main negative aspect was that the proposed definition of euphemism still had the limitation of implicitly characterizing the functioning of euphemism only on a lexical plane (Uría Varela 1997: 5–6), as well as operating by means of a substitution. This limitation becomes evident not only in my consideration of the phenomenon, in which I refer expressly to *substitution* and *lexical* or *euphemistic substitute* or *lexical neutralization* of the *forbidden term*, but also in the conclusions of this work in which *euphemism*, as a substitution process (also applicable to *dysphemism*) is distinguished from the various euphemistic or dysphemistic *substitutes* or *uses*. We could now add to these objections a vital clarification for this new approach to the problem: this definition still starts from the existence of a forbidden term rather than from a reality that is prohibited or conceptually subject to interdiction.

To be honest, I was unable to go any further than my predecessors, in whose teachings of the period a restricted concept of *euphemism*, limited to the lexicon and a substitutive process was endorsed, just as it is in the majority of formulations nowadays. In the same way as semantics began at the level of the word and from the lexicon it was then studied at other levels of analysis, in the field of the euphemism researchers only focused on the lexical angle. In recent years, however, this phenomenon is considered from other standpoints and, above all, from the analysis of other linguistic levels.

Because of all these difficulties arising in the descriptive study of interdiction from a linguistic point of view, we have suggested another approach to the problem starting, not from the base terms, but from forbidden conceptual categories. In this line of analysis, Martínez Valdueza (1998: 125), on linking euphemism and dysphemism with taboo, states that, in research, these processes are usually referred to as "sustitutos del tabú, aunque impliquen distinta finalidad" [substitutes for the taboo, although they imply different purposes], when "estos fenómenos no son meros sustitutos del tabú ni sus funciones ni sus límites coinciden" [these phenomena are not mere substitutes for the taboo nor do their functions and limits coincide]. More recently, Horak (2010: 12) initially takes López Eire (1999: 315) as his starting point, for whom "en un principio y básicamente, el eufemismo es el concepto de un proceso" [in principle and basically, euphemism is the concept of a process], with the aim of characterizing it not as an attenuated expression of a notion, but as a process of attenuation of a tabooed reality (Horak 2010: 62). Even Pizarro Pedraza asks "¿palabras tabú o conceptos tabú?" [taboo words or taboo concepts?] in a section of her thesis, in which she states that "esta asimilación de tabú con expresión léxica no es errónea, sino imprecisa, y es incoherente con ciertas premisas teóricas manejadas en la bibliografía. Se percibe, más o menos sutilmente, que los autores sitúan la interdicción en un plano más profundo que el de las formas" [this assimilation of taboo with lexical expression is not wrong but inaccurate, and it is incoherent with certain theoretical premises dealt with in the bibliography. It is, more or less subtly, perceived that the authors situate interdiction on a deeper plane than that of forms] (Pizarro Pedraza 2013: 71). Likewise, when Cestero Mancera (2015a and 2015b) theoretically characterizes the phenomena involved in the interdictive process in her sociolinguistic studies, she constantly refers, not so much to forbidden terms and lexical substitutes as to taboo concepts and realities: "Lo tabuizado en sociedad son comportamientos y realidades, conceptualizados a través del lenguaje, de manera que lo que resulta interdicto son los conceptos" [It is behaviour and realities that are tabooed in society, conceptualized through the language, so that it is the concepts that are actually forbidden] (2015a: 289). For all these reasons, the specific proposal, within the general framework of linguistic interdiction and based on the above-mentioned linguistic characteristics,[12] of a differentiation between *word taboo*, based on a psychic-internal block on the part of the *speaker*, and *conceptual interdiction*, with external affective or associative motivations, and focusing more on the hearer, in accordance with the pragmatic definitions of the phenomenon which highlight the fact of not offending or making the message more pleasant to the hearer, has led us to this new approach and characterization of the euphemistic-dysphemistic phenomenon towards a discursive and cognitive dimension.

In accordance with these last considerations, what we proposed, more precisely, was a linguistic definition of *euphemism* and *dysphemism* as cognitive processes of conceptualization of a forbidden reality, which, manifested discursively through the use of a group of linguistic mechanisms of lexical substitution, phonetic alteration, modification, morphological composition or inversion, grouping or syntagmatic combinatorics, verbal or paralinguistic modification or textual description, allows the speaker, in a certain context and in a specific pragmatic situation, to attenuate, or, on the contrary, communicatively reinforce a certain forbidden concept or reality.

Thus, this is an approach that starts from cognition (forbidden concept/taboo → euphemism/dysphemism) in order to arrive at discourse (euphemistic/dysphemistic use) and which represents the cognitive nature of interdictive processes and the distinctly discursive character of euphemistic and dysphemistic uses. As Pizarro Pedraza (2013: 84) points out, "hay, por tanto, una diferencia entre los procesos cognitivos, en términos de Casas (eufemismo o disfemismo), y los resultados de estos procesos en el discurso (expresiones eufemísticas)" [there is, therefore, a difference between the cognitive processes, in Casas' terms (euphemism and dysphemism), and the results of these processes in discourse (euphemistic expressions)].

This author in particular refers to our definition of both processes, first proposed from this perspective in 2005, to indicate that its interest "reside en que el autor integra, por un lado, el eufemismo y el disfemismo, y, por otro lado,

---

[12] This basic distinction between *word taboo* and *concept taboo* or *conceptual interdiction* has proved to be vital in research on politically correct language in educational legal texts (Armenta Moreno 2009) or on the interdisciplinary nature of linguistic interdiction (Dávila Romero 2002: 752–755).

las varias facetas de estos fenómenos complejos, como su naturaleza cognitiva, semántica y pragmática, así como la variedad de recursos lingüísticos implicados en su expresión, en todos los niveles de la lengua" [lies in the fact that the author integrates, on the one hand, euphemism and dysphemism, and, on the other, the different facets of these complex phenomena, such as their cognitive, semantic and pragmatic nature, as well as the variety of linguistic resources implied in their expression, at all levels of the language]. She rightly points out, however, that euphemism "no solo sirve para suavizar el tabú, sino cualquier concepto que pueda resultar incómodo o una realidad que se desea embellecer" [serves not only to soften the taboo, but also any concept that may prove uncomfortable or a reality that one wishes to enhance] (Pizarro Pedraza 2013: 83), as occurs, for example, in politically correct language.[13] In fact, in my paper on expressive enhancement as a function of euphemism (Casas Gómez 2012b: 75–76), I observed the widespread use of this intensification mechanism as a discursive value, together with other pragmatic functions. Therefore, as Edeso Natalías also suggested,[14] I widened the linguistic characterization, including, as well as attenuation, aspects such as covering, ennobling and expressive enhancement, as well as the important role of the hearer in the euphemistic or dysphemistic communicative interaction, due to the perlocutive effects that they can cause in the interlocutors.

5 Conclusions

In this paper, we have started from the most relevant identifications or confusions that occur, both in general and specific studies, in the analysis of linguistic taboo. According to a set of epistemological distinctions of a terminological-conceptual nature, some of which are especially significant (such as the delimitation between *word taboo* and *conceptual interdiction*), we have tried to account for an evolution in the theoretical treatment of this topic from the first approaches

---

13 In this regard, politically correct expressions show how euphemism has widened its borders and has occupied spheres that do not completely correspond to its forbidden origin. See, especially, some papers included in the monographic work edited by Reutner and Schafroth (2012) on political correctness.

14 "Existen otra serie de eufemismos que no se atienen a esta definición. O, mejor dicho, que nos obligan a ampliarla, ya que no sólo atenúan los posibles rasgos negativos de su referente sino que, además, acentúan o enfatizan sus rasgos positivos" [There is another series of euphemisms that do not belong to this definition. Or, more exactly, that oblige us to widen it, since they do not only attenuate possible negative traits of the referent, but they also accentuate or emphasize its positive features] (Edeso Natalías 2009: 158).

within the framework of "traditional" or structural lexical semantics to the most modern pragmatic-discursive considerations, and, more recently, the cognitive considerations with regard to the different processes encompassed by the interdictive phenomenon in general.

As constants that can be observed in all these descriptions, we can see both the limitation of the euphemistic phenomenon to the *lexical plane*, as well as to a *substitution process*, and the glaring confusion between *substitute* and *process*, that is, the frequent identification of *euphemism* with *euphemistic substitute*. These descriptions do not extend the result of taboo or interdiction, as would be more appropriate, to the manifestation or linguistic strategy itself. In this new approach to the theoretical treatment of the phenomenon, we have maintained that the analysis of euphemism should depart not from taboo lexical forms (which do not always have a counterpart in the real world) but cognitively, from forbidden conceptual contents and realities, which allow the speaker, in a certain "context" and pragmatic situation, to produce an attenuated, covered, ennobled or enhanced communicative utterance, of a euphemistic nature, or on the contrary, an evocatively reinforced or motivated (often humorously or facetiously) utterance, of a dysphemistic nature. Summing up, this is a revised approach, definition and characterization of the euphemistic-dysphemistic phenomenon towards a cognitive dimension, touching on pragmatic issues which are more appropriate to the relative nature and the essentially discursive function of such linguistic processes.

References

Allan, Keith & Kate Burridge. 1991. *Euphemism and dysphemism. Language used as shield and weapon*. New York & Oxford: Oxford University Press.

Allan, Keith & Kate Burridge. 2006. *Forbidden words. Taboo and the censoring of language*. Cambridge & New York: Cambridge University Press.

Armenta Moreno, Luisa María. 2009. *La interdicción lingüística: estrategias del lenguaje políticamente correcto en textos legales educativos. Selección de leyes educativas (1986–2006)*. Cáceres: Universidad de Extremadura PhD thesis.

Baldinger, Kurt. 1970. *Teoría semántica. Hacia una semántica moderna*. Madrid: Alcalá.

Calvo Shadid, Annette. 2008. *Análisis sociolingüístico sobre el tabú sexual en el español de Costa Rica*. Bergen: Universidad de Bergen PhD thesis.

Calvo Shadid, Annette. 2011. Sobre el tabú, el tabú lingüístico y su estado de la cuestión. *Kañina. Revista Artes y Letras, Universidad de Costa Rica* 35(2). 121–145.

Casas Gómez, Miguel. 1986. *La interdicción lingüística. Mecanismos del eufemismo y disfemismo*. Cádiz: Universidad de Cádiz.

Casas Gómez, Miguel. 1991. Panorama actual de la semántica en la filología latina española contemporánea. *Excerpta Philologica Antonio Holgado Redondo sacra* 1(1). 113–153.

Casas Gómez, Miguel. 1993. A propósito del concepto lingüístico de eufemismo como sincretismo léxico: su relación con la sinonimia y la homonimia. *Iberoromania* 37. 70–90.

Casas Gómez, Miguel. 1995. Sinonimia y eufemismo. *Quaderni di Semantica* 16 (1). 17–46.

Casas Gómez, Miguel. 1996. El poder mágico de la palabra. *Trivium. Anuario de Estudios Humanísticos 8. In memoriam Prof. José Luis Millán Chivite.* 29–52.

Casas Gómez, Miguel. 2000. Tabú de palabra e interdicción conceptual. In Antonio Pamies Bertrán & Juan de Dios Luque Durán (eds.), *Trabajos de lexicografía y fraseología contrastivas,* 79–98. Granada: Método Ediciones.

Casas Gómez, Miguel. 2005. Precisiones conceptuales en el ámbito de la interdicción lingüística. In Luis Santos Río, Julio Borrego Nieto, Juan Felipe García Santos, José J. Gómez Asencio & Emilio Prieto de los Mozos (eds.), *Palabras, norma, discurso. En memoria de Fernando Lázaro Carreter,* 271–290. Salamanca: Ediciones Universidad de Salamanca.

Casas Gómez, Miguel. 2009. Towards a new approach to the linguistic definition of euphemism. *Language Sciences* 31. 725–739.

Casas Gómez, Miguel. 2012a. De una visión léxica y pragmático-discursiva a una dimensión cognitiva en la caracterización extralingüística y lingüística del eufemismo. In Marc Bonhomme, Mariela de la Torre & André Horak (eds.), *Études pragmatico-discursives sur l'euphémisme,* 53–72. Frankfurt am Main, Berlin, Bern, Bruxelles, New York, Oxford & Wien: Peter Lang, Studien zur romanischen Sprachwissenschaft und interkulturellen Kommunikation, Band 83.

Casas Gómez, Miguel. 2012b. El realce expresivo como función eufemística: a propósito de la corrección política de ciertos usos lingüísticos. In Ursula Reutner & Elmar Schafroth (eds.), *Political Correctness. Aspectos políticos, sociales, literarios y mediáticos de la censura política,* 61–79. Frankfurt am Main, Berlin, Bern, Bruxelles, New York, Oxford & Wien: Peter Lang, Studia Romanica et Linguistica, Band 38.

Cestero Mancera, Ana María. 2015a. Estudio sociolingüístico del tabú en el habla de Madrid: propuesta metodológica y primeros resultados. In Ana María Cestero Mancera, Isabel Molina Martos & Florentino Paredes García (eds.), *Patrones sociolingüísticos de Madrid,* 287–348. Frankfurt am Main: Peter Lang.

Cestero Mancera, Ana María 2015b. La expresión del tabú: estudio sociolingüístico. *Boletín de Filología* 50(1). 71–105.

Chamizo, Pedro J. 1995. Eufemismo y redes conceptuales I. In Carlos Martín Vide (ed.), *Actas del XI Congreso de Lenguajes Naturales y Lenguajes Formales,* 205–219. Barcelona: Promociones y Publicaciones Universitarias.

Chamizo, Pedro J. 2004. La función social y cognitiva del eufemismo y del disfemismo. *Panace@* V (15). 45–51.

Chamizo, Pedro J. & Sánchez Benedito, Francisco. 1994. Euphemism and dysphemism: Ambiguity and supposition. *Language and Discourse* 2. 78–92.

Chamizo, Pedro J. & Sánchez Benedito, Francisco. 2000. *Lo que nunca se aprendió en clase. Eufemismos y disfemismos en el lenguaje erótico inglés.* Granada: Comares.

Crespo Fernández, Eliecer. 2007. *El eufemismo y el disfemismo. Procesos de manipulación del tabú en el lenguaje literario inglés.* Alicante: Universidad de Alicante.

Crespo Fernández, Eliecer. 2013. Euphemistic metaphors in English and Spanish epitaphs. A comparative study. *Atlantis. Journal of the Spanish Association of Anglo-American Studies* 35(2). 99–118.
Crespo Fernández, Eliecer. 2015. *Sex in language. Euphemistic and dysphemistic metaphors in Internet forums*. London & New York: Bloomsbury.
Dávila Romero, Raúl. 2002. Reflexiones sobre la interdisciplinariedad en el estudio de la interdicción lingüística. In María Dolores Muñoz Núñez, Ana Isabel Rodríguez-Piñero Alcalá, Gérard Fernández Smith & Victoria Benítez Soto (eds.), *IV Congreso de Lingüística General. Cádiz, del 3 al 6 de abril de 2000. Volumen II. Comunicaciones*, 751–756. Cádiz: Área de Lingüística General, Universidad de Cádiz & Universidad de Alcalá.
Díaz Pérez, Juan Carlos. 2013. *Pragmalingüística del disfemismo y la descortesía*. Madrid: Universidad Carlos III de Madrid PhD thesis.
Edeso Natalías, Verónica. 2009. Revisión del concepto de eufemismo: una propuesta de clasificación. *Revista Internacional de Lingüística Iberoamericana* VII.2 (14). 147–163.
Fernández de Molina Ortés, Elena. 2014. La presencia de eufemismos y disfemismos en el campo semántico del cuerpo humano. Estudio sociolingüístico. *Pragmalingüística* 22. 8–30.
Galli de' Paratesi, Nora. 1973. *Le brutte parole. Semantica dell'eufemismo*, 3rd edn. Torino: Arnoldo Mondadori Editore.
Gómez Sánchez, María Elena. 2004. *El eufemismo político y económico en la prensa diaria: Análisis de ABC y El País (1998)*. Madrid: Universidad Complutense de Madrid PhD thesis.
Grimes, Larry M. 1978. *El tabú lingüístico en México: el lenguaje erótico de los mexicanos*. New York: Bilingual Press.
Hey, Oskar. 1900. Euphemismus und verwandtes im lateinischen. *Archiv für lateinische Lexikographie und Grammatik mit Einschluss des älteren Mittellateins als Ergänzung zu dem Thesaurus Linguae Latinae* 11. 515–536.
Horak, André. 2010. *L'Euphémisme. Entre tradition rhétorique et perspectives nouvelles*. München: LINCOM.
Kany, Charles E. 1960. *American-Spanish euphemisms*. Berkeley-Los Angeles: University of California Press.
Kröll, Heinz. 1984. *O eufemismo e o disfemismo no português moderno*. Lisboa: Instituto de Cultura e Língua Portuguesa.
Lamíquiz, Vidal. 1974. *Lingüística española*, 2nd edn. Sevilla: Universidad de Sevilla.
Lechado García, José Manuel. 2000. *Diccionario de eufemismos y de expresiones eufemísticas del español actual*. Madrid: Verbum.
Löfstedt, Einar. 1959. Taboo, euphemism, and primitive conceptions in language. *Late Latin*. Oslo: Ascheoug. 181–194.
López Eire, Antonio. 1999. Sobre el eufemismo en la Oratoria ática y en la Retórica. In Francesco De Martino & Alan H. Sommerstein (eds.), *Studi sull'eufemismo*, 313–367. Bari: Levante.
López Morales, Humberto. 1990. *Sociolingüística del tabú. El caso de Puerto Rico*. Madrid: MS.
López Morales, Humberto. 1997. Papel del nivel sociocultural y del estilo lingüístico en el uso del eufemismo. In Francisco Moreno Fernández (ed.), *Trabajos de sociolingüística hispánica*, 27–33. Alcalá de Henares: Universidad de Alcalá.
López Morales, Humberto. 2001. Estratificación social del tabú lingüístico: el caso de Puerto Rico. *Estudios de lingüística del español* 13. http://elies.rediris.es/elies13/lopez.htm (accessed 10 June 2016).
López Morales, Humberto. 2005. Sociolingüística del tabú. *Interlingüística* 16(1). 7–20.

Malinowski, Bronisław. 1962. The language of magic. In M. Blank (ed.), *The importance of language*. Englewoods Cliffs, N.J: Prentice-Hall.
Mansur Guérios, Rosario Farani. 1956. *Tabus lingüísticos*. Rio de Janeiro: Organização Simões Editora.
Martínez Valdueza, Pilar. 1995. *El tabú lingüístico: estudio sociolingüístico de Las Palmas de Gran Canaria*. Las Palmas de Gran Canaria: Universidad de Las Palmas PhD thesis.
Martínez Valdueza, Pilar. 1998. Status quaestionis: el tabú lingüístico. *Lingüística* 10. 105–139.
Montero Cartelle, Emilio. 1981. *El eufemismo en Galicia (su comparación con otras áreas romances)*. Santiago de Compostela: Universidad de Santiago de Compostela.
Montero Cartelle, Enrique. 1973. *Aspectos léxicos y literarios del latín erótico (hasta el s. I. d. C.)*. Santiago de Compostela: Universidad de Santiago de Compostela.
Pizarro Pedraza, Andrea. 2013. *Tabú y eufemismo en la ciudad de Madrid. Estudio sociolingüístico-cognitivo de los conceptos sexuales*. Madrid: Universidad Complutense PhD thesis.
Radtke, Edgar. 1980. *Typologie des sexuell-erotischen Vocabulars des heutigen Italienisch: Studien zur Bestimmung der Wortfelder „prostituta" und „membro virile" unter besonderer Berücksichtigung der übrigen romanischen Sprachen*. Tübingen: Narr.
Reisig, Karl Christian. 1839. Semasiologie oder Bedeutungslehre. In *Professor K. Reisig's Vorlesungen über lateinische Sprachwissenschaft. Herausgegeben mit Anmerkungen von Friedrich Haase*. Leipzig: Verlag der Zehnhold'schen Buchhandlung. 286–307.
Reutner, Ursula. 2009. *Sprache und Tabu. Interpretationen zu französischen und italienischen Euphemismen*. Tübingen: Niemeyer.
Reutner, Ursula & Schafroth, Elmar (eds.). 2012. *Political correctness. Aspectos políticos, sociales, literarios y mediáticos de la censura política*. Frankfurt am Main, Berlin, Bern, Bruxelles, New York, Oxford & Wien: Peter Lang, Studia Romanica et Lingüística, Band 38.
Sánchez Benedito, Francisco. 1995. Eufemismo y redes conceptuales II. In Carlos Martín Vide (ed.), *Actas del XI Congreso de Lenguajes Naturales y Lenguajes Formales*, 339–347. Barcelona: Promociones y Publicaciones Universitarias.
Senabre, Ricardo. 1971. El eufemismo como fenómeno lingüístico. *Boletín de la Real Academia Española* 51. 175–189.
Silva Correia, João da. 1927. O eufemismo e o disfemismo na língua e na literatura portuguesa. *Arquivo da Universidade de Lisboa* 12. 445–787.
Ullmann, Stephen. 1964. *Semantics. An introduction to the science of meaning*. Oxford: Basil Blackwell.
Uría Varela, Javier. 1997. *Tabú y eufemismo en latín*. Amsterdam: A. M. Hakkert-Publisher.
Warren, Beatrice. 1992. What euphemisms tell us about the interpretation of words. *Studia Linguistica* 46(2). 128–172.
Widłak, Stanisław. 1970. *Moyens euphémistiques en italien contemporain*. Kraków: Nakładem Uniwersytetu Jagiellońskiego.

Part I: **Construal**

Eliecer Crespo-Fernández
2 The axiological and communicative potential of homosexual-related metaphors

Abstract: Given the crucial role of metaphor in the conceptualization of sexual issues (Kövecses 1988; Zeve 1993; Pizarro Pedraza 2013; Crespo-Fernández 2015), this paper aims to gain an insight into the social and communicative functions that metaphors on homosexuality perform in discourse, with special attention to the conceptualization of verbal mitigation and offence, on a sample of metaphors touching on homosexual issues taken from the Corpus of Contemporary American English (COCA). Following a cognitively based approach to figurative language based on Steen's (2011) discourse-analytical model, homosexual-related metaphors are conceived not only as a matter of language but also as a matter of thought which have a communicative impact and serve a particular purpose in discourse. Evidence from the corpus reveals that metaphor is used for a range of communicative functions which correspond to different axiological categories of taboo naming: to provide a socially acceptable reference to homosexuality and avoid offence (euphemism); to degrade homosexuals as people who do not conform to traditional gender roles (dysphemism); and to display group solidarity or direct the reader's attention towards the homosexual topic in discussion (quasi-euphemism).

Keywords: discourse metaphor; contemporary metaphor theory; taboo of homosexuality; axiology; euphemism; dysphemism

1 Introduction

Homosexuality has traditionally been subject to interdiction and social stigma. Either owing to its association with marginality and epidemics like AIDS or to moral or religious impositions, homosexuals have been targets for every sort of intolerance and oppression through the years and, consequently, same-sex practices linked to the forbidden, the sinful, and therefore remained hidden. In fact, homosexuals have been depicted as sexually outsiders and deviants, even perverts, and excluded from the heterosexual world in that they do not conform to what is (socially and sexually) expected from men according to dominant male heterosexist ideology (Cameron and Kulick 2006; Coates 2013). Although the censorship on homosexuality and, by extension, LGBT (Lesbian Gay Bisexual Transgender) issues, has progressively relaxed, the topic of homosexuality still imposes some restrictions nowadays: it is considered taboo[1] in our western secularised and democratic societies, as – we should not forget – intransigence still holds out in some social and political groups.[2] Needless to say, this homophobic attitude does not only discriminate homosexuals; it also undermines their social status.

Despite the taboo surrounding homosexuality, language users do not only aim at preserving the taboo when they talk about homosexuality and homosexual-related issues; they also use explicit and offensive references to homosexuality to show the paradoxical nature of the taboo which compels people to refer to the concepts, regardless of whether or not they are forbidden. This ambivalence towards the taboo leads to the emergence of an endless set of what Allan and Burridge (2006: 47–48) called *cross-varietal synonyms*, i.e., terms sharing the same denotation but differing in connotation. These onomasiological, i.e., expressive and value-laden, variants (see Pizarro Pedraza, this volume) constitute different modalities of taboo naming between the major axiological[3] categories of *euphemism* i.e., the process whereby the taboo is stripped of its pejorative overtones, and *dysphemism*, i.e., the process which highlights those traits of the taboo especially apt for offence and disrespect.

Metaphor constitutes a potent source for sexual reference. In fact, people resort to figurative language as a means to talk about a wide range of sex-related issues (Kövecses 1988; Deignan 1997; Hines 1999; Crespo-Fernández 2008, 2015; Pizarro Pedraza 2013), including, of course, homosexuality (Zeve 1993; Baker 2002; Rodríguez González 2008; Crespo-Fernández and Luján-García 2017). Considering the crucial role of metaphors in the verbalization of sexual topics, it is the aim of this paper to gain an insight into the social and communicative functions that metaphors on homosexuality perform in discourse,[4] with special attention to the conceptualization of verbal mitigation and offence, through the analysis of a sample of metaphors touching on homosexual issues taken from the Corpus of Contemporary American English. This seems to prove a worthy enterprise. Despite the publication of volumes on such topics as the language, symbols, and communication strategies used by the homosexual community (Chesebro 1981; Ringer 1994), to the best of my knowledge the only study so far exclusively devoted to the use of metaphor in homosexual parlance (Zeve 1993) has not considered the euphemistic or dysphemistic potential of metaphorical language.

I start from the hypothesis that homosexual-related metaphors perform a variety of communicative functions in discourse: not only that of softening or avoiding the use of a taboo term but also attracting people's interest, displaying in-group solidarity, or disparaging homosexuals, among others. I must make it clear that I am not concerned here with metaphors used exclusively by the homosexual community ("metaphors by Gays and for Gays", as Zeve [1993: 3] remarks);[5] rather, I adopt here a more comprehensive view: it is my intention to look at metaphors touching on homosexual issues as employed by any language user in a variety of discourse genres. In this regard, Zeve's (1993) binary model, which distinguishes between *metaphors of disruption*, i.e., those that denounce heterosexual judgments about gays, and *metaphors of redefinition*, i.e., those which explore gay identity, seems unable to account for the diversity of homosexual-related metaphors in everyday discourse. In fact, the metaphors on homosexuality found in the database consulted perform a wider range of communicative functions, as we will see in the course of the analysis.

This paper is structured as follows. I will first provide some theoretical considerations regarding the axiological value of metaphor, the concept of X-phemism and the discourse-analytical model of metaphor. Then I will outline the corpus and the methodology used in this research. In the third section I will analyze the homosexual metaphors encountered in the corpus. Finally I will present some concluding remarks.

2 Axiology and X-phemism

The study of word axiology necessarily involves looking at the positive and negative connotations attached to the lexical units, which, in turn, leads to considering the X-phemistic functions that language units perform in discourse. In order to explain the axiological and communicative functions of homosexual-related metaphors in discourse, I will follow here Allan and Burridge's (2006) approach to the study of language and taboo. These scholars proposed the term X-phemism to explain the union set of the major axiological categories of taboo naming: euphemism and dysphemism. They insightfully defined X-phemism in relation to the notion of *face* (i.e., public self-image the speaker wants for him or herself in society), initially proposed by Brown and Levinson (1987). In this light, euphemism and dysphemism are considered in terms of the degree of face affront which is caused by any verbal expression in communication. In Allan and Burridge's (2006: 32) own words: "[D]ysphemism is a word or phrase with connotations that are offensive either about the denotatum and/or to people addressed or overhearing the utterance", whereas euphemism is used to "avoid possible loss of face by the speaker, or also the hearer or some third party". From this perspective, euphemism can be considered as the use of polite and mild-sounding words to avoid a possible loss of face both to the speaker and hearer, whereas dysphemism deliberately affronts the hearer's face. Allan and Burridge suggested a further modality to refer to the taboo, *orthophemism*, which provides, usually through literal language, an axiologically neutral reference to the taboo topic.

It is worth noting that the boundaries between euphemism and dysphemism are fuzzy in real discourse (Casas Gómez 2012: 48–52). In fact, the locution (i.e., the form of words) does not always coincide with the illocution (i.e., the aim of a speaker in making an utterance). I will refer to these axiological categories – which basically correspond with Allan and Burridge's (2006: 39–40) "dysphemistic euphemism" and "euphemistic dysphemism" – as *quasi-euphemism* and *quasi-dysphemism*. The former category consists of those words and expressions which, despite their dysphemistic locution, are used positively, as a means to display friendship, in-group identity, or intimacy. The latter category includes those items which are intentionally offensive despite their euphemistic disguise.

We can also distinguish different X-phemistic types on the basis of the communicative functions they serve (Crespo-Fernández 2015: 47): *consolatory* (used to mitigate the death of a loved one); *protective* (to avoid offence); *provocative* (to attract someone's interest); *underhand* (to deceive and misrepresent); *uplifting* (to upgrade and magnify); *cohesive* (to display in-group identity); *complimentary* (to praise); *dirty* (to stimulate your partner sexually); *ludic* (to defuse the seriousness of taboo topics); and *derogatory* (to make a socially acceptable criticism).

After having delimited the key concepts in the present research, namely axiology and the modalities of X-phemism used to talk about taboo topics, I will now proceed to present the analytical framework on which this study is based.

3 The discourse-analytical approach to cognitive metaphor

The theoretical assumptions on which this study relies are derived from Steen's (2011) discourse-analytical model of metaphor, a cognitive approach to *discourse metaphor*[6] based on Lakoff's [1979] (1993) contemporary theory of metaphor. The approach to metaphor proposed by Lakoff and his followers argues that metaphor is a device that structures our conceptual system, providing, at the same time, a way to make sense of our experience and a particular understanding of the world. From this perspective, metaphor is defined as "a cross-domain mapping in the conceptual system" (Lakoff 1993: 203), that is, a mapping or set of conceptual correspondences from a source domain (a concrete domain of experience) to a target domain (a more abstract domain, homosexuality in this case). For instance, *pansy* is an instantiation of the conceptual metaphor MALE HOMO-SEXUALS ARE FLOWERS, in which the mapping projects attributes of the source domain of FLOWERS like delicateness, softness, or vulnerability onto the taboo target domain of HOMOSEXUALITY.

In order to understand the role of metaphors in real-world discourse, a more comprehensive and socially-oriented approach to metaphor than that originally proposed by Lakoff must be adopted. Over the past decade, different cognitively-based studies have explored the communicative dimension of metaphor in use, which necessarily involves exploring the links between body, language, culture, and cognition (Kövecses 2006; Steen 2011; Sharifian 2011, among others). Steen's (2011) discourse-analytical model of metaphor provides a three-dimensional view of metaphor which accounts for the communicative impact of metaphors in communication: "[M]etaphor may be theoretically defined as a matter of conceptual structure, but in empirical practice it works its wonders in language, communication, or thought" (2011: 59). Steen argues for the existence of three dimensions of metaphor which perform different functions in discourse: *naming* (linguistic function, i.e., formal dimension of metaphor); *framing* (conceptual function, i.e., mental processes of metaphor use); and changing (communicative function, i.e., interactive force of metaphors in discourse). This model allows us to gain an insight into the deliberate use of metaphors in real-life communication and thus understand how their axiological value and persuasive force project in discourse. As Steen (2011: 59) points out, "metaphor may manifest itself in communication when it is used deliberately, and then it is a matter of conscious thought by challengeable metaphorical models with a predominantly social function, as an official, contested, implicit or emerging metaphorical representation of some aspect of the world". What this discourse-analytical approach suggests is that discourse metaphor is necessarily linked to social and cultural issues, and related to its deliberate vs. non-deliberate use in communication.

Following Steen's discourse-analytical model, I depart from the notion of discourse metaphor as a basic tool to conceptualize reality with a socio-cultural dimension which makes it possible to analyze the deliberate use of homosexual-related metaphors in real-life language, their axiological values, and communicative functions. It is evident that most metaphors are not used unconsciously; rather, speakers deliberately exploit the perspective of the source domain as a means to talk about the target domain (Steen 2011: 50–51, 59). In the metaphorical expression *pansy*, the qualities of softness and delicateness are highlighted for persuasive purposes: the man referred to as 'a pansy' will be seen as soft and delicate, attributes commonly associated with femininity and, by extension, with homosexuality. This view serves the speaker's offensive intention. In this regard, homosexuality metaphors are conceived not only as a matter of language but also as a matter of thought which have a communicative impact and serve a particular, i.e., X-phemistic, purpose in discourse. This approach to metaphor supports Casas Gómez's (2012: 43) definition of euphemism and dysphemism as "two cognitive processes of conceptualisation, with countervalent effects (having the same base and resources but different aims and purposes), of a certain forbidden reality". From this viewpoint, it is evident that X-phemism goes beyond a mere substitution strategy at the lexical level. Indeed, those approaches which reduce euphemism and dysphemism to lexical substitution processes are too limiting, as Casas Gómez (2009, 2012, and this volume) insightfully argues;[7] rather, X-phemism can be considered as a process of conceptual make-up which emerges as a linguistic manifestation of our cognitive system and performs a specific communicative intention in a context of use.

Having introduced the theoretical framework for metaphor analysis this study relies on, I will now present the corpus and describe the methods used to analyze the data.

4 Corpus and methodological issues

The homosexual-related metaphors which constitute the corpus for the present study have been retrieved from the Corpus of Contemporary American English (henceforth COCA), created by Mark Davies at Brigham Young University (Davies 2009–). This choice is not random. In the first place, the COCA is an extensive and updated corpus: it contains a total of about 520 million words from 220,225 texts which range from 1990 to 2015. In the second place, the texts come from a variety of sources, namely spoken, fiction, magazine, newspaper, and academic. In the third place, the language data are contextualized, which is of crucial importance for the analysis of metaphor in use. The COCA database therefore provides a significant, representative, and updated collection of homosexual-related metaphors in naturally-occurring contexts in a variety of discourse types and genres.

The methodology followed in this research paper corresponds to the adoption of a "bottom-up" approach to analyze the metaphorical occurrences obtained: first, certain language data are selected; second, that data are classified and interpreted in context; and third, some conclusions are reached from the data collected. As it is virtually impossible to detect every single homosexual-related metaphorical occurrence in a database of the size of the COCA, I opted for concentrating on exhaustive search of a restricted number of words and expressions concerning the topic of homosexuality in the different text categories and genres.

For the sake of constructing an updated sample, I only included homosexual-related metaphors over a two-year period (2014–2015), which implies a corpus size of 39,730,594 million words.

As metaphors are not always easy to find in natural discourse, I relied on the Metaphor Identification Procedure (MIP) developed by the Pragglejaz Group (2007: 3). This procedure consists of the following steps: first, establishing the meaning of the word in the context in which it appears; second, determining the more basic contemporary meaning that the word has; and third, deciding whether the contextual meaning of the examined word contrasts with the basic meaning but can be understood in comparison with it. If so, the word is taken to be metaphorical. Let us take the term *chick* in (1) as an example of how the procedure for metaphor identification has been applied in the analysis of the corpus:

(1) *He took another slow sip of his drink, leaned back on the low lounge-style sofa and let out a deep sigh. Virat threw his head back and laughed. "Bastard, you're sighing. I swear, Chintu, you're such a **chick**". "Shut up, Bhai. That was a man-sigh".* (FIC, BK: BollywoodAffair 2014)[8]

- Step 1. *Chick* is perceived to have a homosexual-related meaning in (1): it alludes to a young or boyish-looking gay man. *Chick* here is one of the realizations of the metaphor MALE HOMOSEXUALS ARE YOUNG BIRDS, a more specific version of the general HUMAN IS ANIMAL metaphor. On account of the small size of birds, this metaphor conveys the idea that gays are weak and defenceless.[9]
- Step 2. The word *chick* has a more basic contemporary meaning: It literally designates 'the young of a bird, esp. of a domestic fowl' (*Collins English Dictionary*).
- Step 3. The contextual meaning of the term ('young gay man') contrasts with its more basic meaning ('young bird') but can be understood by some form of familiarity with it: both chicks and male homosexuals are weak, vulnerable, and delicate according to heteronormative assumptions of masculinity. This is why the word *chick* is identified as metaphorically used in (1).

After having collected all the metaphorical units related to homosexuality, I grouped them according to the source domain they belong to. Then I examined their X-phemistic value, that is, in an axiological scale related to the degree of face-affront and emotional load (Herrero Ruiz 2009: 252–260) from lower-level magnitude (euphemism) to higher-level magnitudes (dysphemism). In order to account for the communicative force of metaphors in action, I necessarily had to look at the context in which the metaphor in question occurs. The word's lexical surrounding is provided by the COCA database, as the keyword can be observed both in its immediate context (KWIC view) or in its expanded context. Contextual information is of great relevance in that it provides the X-phemistic quality of a given lexical unit. After all, as Allan and Burridge (2006: 51) argue, the euphemistic or dysphemistic force of a given word or expression ultimately depends on the context in which it occurs.

Before moving to the analysis of the homosexual-related metaphors encountered in the sample, I must admit that this study does not claim to be complete. I have adopted a qualitative approach to language data, as I am concerned with the way metaphor is used to reason about homosexuality on the basis of a small sample of language data. This choice implies that some metaphors used in homosexual discourse have not appeared in the corpus and therefore have not been analyzed. In any case, I believe that the sample consulted may add valuable insights into the way homosexual-related metaphors are used in everyday American English.

5 Analysis and discussion

As stated in the Introduction, the analysis carried out for this research paper is not limited to metaphors used by gays and lesbians; rather, it focuses on the metaphors on homosexuality used by any language user regardless of his or her sexual orientation. The metaphorical expressions encountered in the corpus (62 in total) are drawn from the domains of CONTAINERS, JOURNEYS, WOMEN, and ANIMALS. These metaphors, grouped according to the source domain they belong to, are shown in quantitative terms in Figure 1:

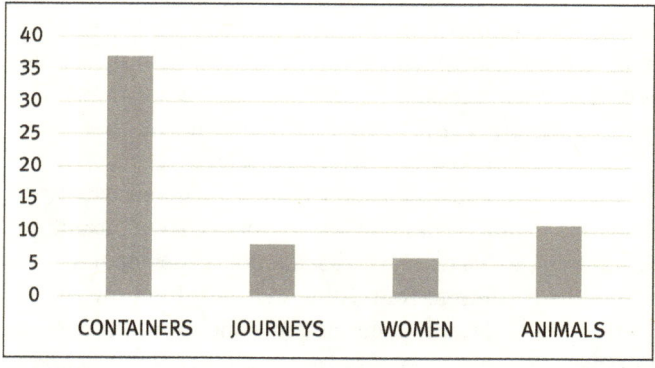

Figure 1: Source domains for homosexuality metaphors (n= 62)

The first noticeable quality is that over a half of the linguistic metaphors encountered in the corpus (37 out of 62, which makes up almost 60 % of the total number of metaphorical occurrences found) fall under the source domain of CONTAINERS. The source domains of ANIMALS (11), JOURNEYS (8), and WOMEN (6) are less quantitatively relevant. These metaphors perform euphemistic, dysphemistic, and quasi-euphemistic functions in discourse, as we will see in what follows.

5.1 The CLOSET metaphor

As shown in Figure 1, the CLOSET metaphor, used by both homosexuals and heterosexuals alike, is used pervasively in the corpus consulted.[10] This metaphor is an instantiation of the CONTAINER metaphor, an ontological metaphor whereby an entity is seen as consisting of three parts: an exterior, an interior, and a boundary.[11] When applied to homosexuality, the inside of the container metaphorically describes traditional society as a closed and bounded space, which implies oppression and difficulty in getting out to the exterior (i.e., the outside of the container) where the homosexual person can live his sexual identity free from prejudices or censorship. Lakoff's (1987: 283) "Spatialization of Form Hypothesis" applies here. In his own words, "this view requires a metaphorical mapping from physical space into a conceptual space. Under this mapping, spatial structure is mapped into conceptual structure". According to this theory, our experience of space (closet as a bounded space) is used metaphorically to reason about the taboo of homosexuality.

The metaphor can be formulated as follows: REVEALING ONE'S HOMOSEXUALITY IS COMING OUT OF THE CLOSET. The notion of the CLOSET depicts homosexuality in terms of isolation and social rejection. These entailments of the CLOSET metaphor – which constitute what Kövecses (2002: 104) refers to as the "metaphorical entailment potential" – that are mapped onto the taboo target domain of homosexuality lead us to consider this metaphor as one of disruption. Indeed, the CLOSET metaphor, following Zeve (1993: 4–7), was originally chosen and used by male homosexuals in order to denounce unfair social judgments about gays: this metaphor disrupted the heterosexual assumptions that non-heterosexual behavior is a deviation from the norm and that gays are perverts and sexual outlaws. However, it later became a metaphor of redefinition and used positively by homosexuals as an exploration of gay consciousness and sexual awareness: "The closet no longer disrupts the Straight view of a Straight world in which anyone who doesn't conform is a pervert; the closet becomes a familiarized and personalized space which provides a positive marker of identification for gays. It redefines Gays as the owners of their space" (Zeve 1993: 5). Fitzgerald, however, maintains that the notion of the closet is not positive for gay identity; rather, it symbolizes the stigma and exclusion of gay people in society and therefore should be avoided: "[B]oth gays and nongays are guilty of using the closet metaphor to symbolise and justify exclusion and exclusiveness" (1993: 217). The redefinition of the metaphor as SOCIETY IS A CLOSET IN WHICH HOMOSEXUALS ARE LOCKED UP by virtue of the metaphorical entailment potential of this metaphor pointed out above seems to justify Fitzgerald's view.

The notion of the closet has provided different socially acceptable – hence euphemistic – alternatives to refer to homosexuality. The expression "come out of the closet", meaning 'to reveal one's homosexual condition', is the most popular in standard English:

(2) "I believe I was the first student to **come out of the closet** at the school", says Minter, who later attended Texas State University. (MAG, *Austin American Statesman* 2015)

If coming out of the closet means revealing one's condition as homosexual, *closeted* qualifies those homosexuals who have not revealed their sexual identity. Significantly enough, all the occurrences of this adjective found over the two-year period consulted (25) have this homosexual-related meaning. Consider example (3) in which a homosexual person overtly defines himself as *closeted*. This adjective has a quasi-euphemistic value: it signals the speaker's sexual identity and attracts people's attention to his homosexual condition:

(3) *I was more **closeted** in my life when I was younger. By the time I started to do work where people knew who I was, I just never made the choice to hide, you know, that I was gay.* (SPOK, *CNN Showbiz* 2014)

The CLOSET metaphor has a range of linguistic manifestations in which the original expression "to come out of the closet" is abbreviated to *out* (4), *outing* (5), and *come out* (6):

(4) *"If one is **out** there who straight out plans not to issue a marriage license to a same-sex couple, I have not met them", said Daughtrey.* (NEWS, *Atlanta Journal Constitution* 2015)
(5) *The hysteria surrounding the Lawrence storyline made other cartoonists extremely cautious about introducing new gay characters or **"outing"** existing characters.* (ACAD, *Journal of American Culture* 2014)
(6) *The reason that people are able to **come out** publicly, or assume a gay public identity when singing in the DGMC is because they are doing it in a group. Few*

people would ever stand on a stage alone and say "I am gay"? In a group, there is safety and unity, and a sense of doing this i.e., claiming a gay identity with your brothers. (ACAD, *Journal of American Culture* 2015)

It is worth noting that in examples (4–6), euphemism combines with quasi-euphemism: on the one hand, ellipsis provides the metaphorical item with an extra-euphemistic effect by way of shortening of the original expression; on the other hand, the use of individual words involves some kind of familiarity with the topic under discussion. *Out, outing,* and *come out* are not used as "pure" euphemisms. Although these words are lexical alternatives to publicly refer to homosexuality without a threat to the speaker's face, they do not perform a real mitigating function; rather, they are close to the in-group words used by the homosexual community. In this regard, these items can be considered to be halfway between euphemism and quasi-euphemism, that is, between the protective and cohesive X-phemistic types respectively.

The use of abbreviated forms with a quasi-euphemistic value is evident in the rhymed expression *out and proud*, used to identify those who have revealed their sexual identity and are proud of it:

(7) *Jane praised Ellen for paving the way for her to take a stand and pursue her Hollywood career as an* **out and proud** *lesbian!* (SPOK, *CNN Showbiz* 2014)

The expression *out and proud* does not serve euphemistic purposes in (7): it is used as a celebration by the community of gays, lesbians, bisexuals, and transgenders in their self-characterization.

5.2 The CRUISING metaphor

The CRUISING metaphor, more precisely defined as CRUISING IS SEARCHING FOR A SEXUAL PARTNER, first recorded in 1904 according to the *Oxford English Dictionary*, derives from the more general JOURNEY metaphor, which is based on the SOURCE-PATH-GOAL image schema (Lakoff 1987: 275) whereby a sexual encounter may be understood as a process with a starting (i.e., a source), a time span (i.e., a path), and an end-point (i.e., a destination). This schema does not apply in the same way in all sex-related metaphors: by the addition of profiling and a trajectory-landmark relation (Lakoff and Johnson 1999: 33), the focus can be on the destination or on the motion itself (see Crespo-Fernández 2015: 96–102). For instance, in (8) below the focus is on the act of walking around the streets in search of casual homosexual partners, which is understood as a journey:

(8) *I told her what I knew about his short, wild life, his uncontrollable drinking, his turbulent existence as a gay man in those times (...). And I think of him **cruising** for sailors when he says, "Under thy shadow by the piers I waited".* (FIC, *Paris Review* 2015)

In (9) the SOURCE-PATH-GOAL schema is more clearly used for euphemistic purposes. The context contributes to the mitigating function of *cruising*. The generic nature of the term *stuff* introduces an element of intentional vagueness (see Grondelaers and Geeraerts 1998; Chamizo Domínguez, this volume) which contributes to the euphemistic force of this metaphor:

(9) *"Can I park on the drive, maybe up near the road?" "I'd rather you didn't. There's stuff up there. (...) Night stuff. Gay stuff. **Cruising**. That kind of stuff".* (FIC, *New England Review* 2015)

In examples (8) and (9) the folk knowledge people have of cruises yields a euphemistic reference to homosexual encounters: first, a cruise is a pleasurable experience; second, a euphemism for homosexual practices allows passengers to visit a number of places en route for short periods of time. These characteristics of cruises are mapped onto the target domain of homosexual encounters to show casual sex as a pleasurable activity in which the voyage itself is equated with the act of looking for sexual partners, and the ports where the passengers stop correspond to the lovers. These entailments of the metaphor provide evidence for the fact that the metaphorical utilization of the source domain is partial (Kövecses 2006: 214): whereas some of its components are highlighted, as just commented, others are left out, namely the element of passivity which characterizes passengers of a cruise ship, who can just go where the ship takes them.

Obviously enough, cruising implies motion. In the occurrences of the JOURNEY metaphor, the notion of movement from one place to another plays an important role. Stychin (2005: 85–90) understands the movement implied in the JOURNEY metaphor as a search for a gay space and identity, as a movement towards a new life style in which homosexuals can freely live their sexual orientation. In this respect, *to cruise* is a verb that maps MOTION (as source domain) onto CHANGE (as target domain) by virtue of the primary metaphor CHANGE IS MOTION. From this perspective, the JOURNEY metaphor fulfils a quasi-euphemistic purpose in that it serves as a metaphor for homosexual identity.

5.3 The WOMAN metaphor

Effeminacy is the dysphemistic basis of those metaphors which associate homosexuality with women: gays and effeminate men are downgraded by ascribing to them some qualities that come to be stereotypically associated with women like delicacy, beauty, or innocence. The metaphor MALE HOMOSEXUALS ARE FLOWERS employs the negative connotations of flowers as symbols of femininity as the raw material for dysphemism. In fact, the metaphorical entailments that the source domain of FLOWER gives rise to (flowers are delicate, beautiful, soft, silky, etc.) are mapped onto the target domain of MALE HOMOSEXUALITY to refer to gays disparagingly. The term *pansy*, originally a floral name for women, is a realization of the FLOWER metaphor detected in the corpus in which effeminacy is used as the source of offence. Consider the following example in which *pansy* appears in a juxtaposition of homophobic terms of abuse:

(10) *She penned a series of melodic quips, literally saying that Ibn Zaydun "has an ass that loves the cocks of Persian breeches", including the verse: You are a **pansy**, a bugger, a fornicator, a cuckold, a swine and a thief.* (MAG, *History Today* 2015)

Given that effeminacy is the dysphemistic basis of the FLOWER metaphor, as already commented, the underlying metaphor is MALE HOMOSEXUALS ARE WOMEN. In this way, it is not only male homosexuals that are degraded; this metaphor implicitly undermines women insofar as females become material for the dysphemistic language against gays (Rodríguez González 2008). In this way, both male homosexuals and women are considered, according to the heteronormative social order, as "inferior" beings. This implicitly reinforces heteronormative assumptions of masculinity whereby both gays and women are considered as marginal groups.

Nancy boy exploits for offensive purposes the same metaphorical entailments as the floral metaphor. *Nancy*, originally a woman's name, maps onto the target domain of homosexuality those female-related attributes (delicacy, beauty, etc.) which suggest lack of virility. *Nancy boy* is, from this perspective, an instantiation of the metaphor MALE HOMOSEXUALS ARE WOMEN. Consider in (11) how this phrase is figuratively used as a disparaging term for 'an effeminate or homosexual boy or man' (*Collins English Dictionary*):

(11) *What Olly Williams saw was a boy who was "looking for a brother." And that's what Olly and Greg became. "There's love there – you can use that word with*

*Tom without being a **nancy boy**. If he loves you, he's a brother. That's it.* (MAG, *Esquire* 2014)

The dysphemistic effect of using two source domains like FLOWERS and WOMEN in (10) and (11) can be explained in terms of the Great Chain of Being, i.e., "a hierarchy of things and corresponding concepts from a lower source to a higher target or from higher source to a lower target" (Kövecses 2002: 126). This model allows us to draw a connection between the target domain of MALE HOMOSEXUALS and the source domains of WOMEN and FLOWERS, i.e., a lower form of life than humans in the chain of being. This association implicitly reinforces heteronormative assumptions of masculinity whereby both gays and women are considered as marginal groups.

5.4 The ANIMAL metaphor

By virtue of the ontological metaphor PEOPLE ARE ANIMALS homosexuals and homosexual practices are associated with animals and animal behaviour. This metaphor is also an instance of The Great Chain of Being metaphor: it proceeds from a lower, i.e., non-human, source domain (ANIMALS) to a higher, i.e., human, target domain (HOMOSEXUALS). The metaphorical representation of people as animals is inherently negative (see Hines 1999: 17–19; Allan 2007; Crespo-Fernández 2015: 136–153 for examples). The dysphemistic nature of this conceptualization can be seen in the association between men and small birds in example (1) in which the word *chick* is used for insulting purposes. The same happens in (12) below in which *pussy* (literally 'a furry catkin, esp. that of the pussy pillow', *Collins English Dictionary*) is used to insult a male for being effeminate:[12]

(12) *The filmmaker behind Representation turns a critical lens on American masculinity. Man up! Grow a pair! Don't be a **pussy**! That's the message boys still get from coaches and peers, movies and video games, and all too often their own fathers.* (MAG, *Mother Jones* 2105)

Although the metaphorical representation of male homosexuals as animals is dysphemistic in origin, the axiological value of the metaphor shifts in some occurrences found in the corpus. Take the case of *bear*:

(13) *I'm a little sluttier than the average **bear**. I really am, a little sluttier. I can be honest about that. Like I'm no stranger to Plan B, I'll say that. I'm not like what is that, like I know what that is.* (SPOK, *Inside Amy Schumer* 2104)

In (13) the folk knowledge people possess about bears as wild, big, and hairy animals is mapped onto homosexuals and specifically used to designate hairy and strong homosexual males in gay speech. *Bear* is not therefore used as a dysphemism but as a quasi-euphemism: it has been adopted by the homosexual community and used as a sign of in-group identity. *Bear* is, following Zeve (1993), an example of a metaphor of redefinition: the result of gay experience and culture. Of course, no offence is meant in (13) towards homosexuals, as the negative aspects of the domain of WILD ANIMALS (bears are aggressive and dangerous animals) are disregarded in this particular use of *bear*.

The term *bareback* from the equine imagery is closely related to the PEOPLE-ARE-ANIMALS metaphor. Its original, non-sexual meaning 'to ride without a saddle' has led to the meaning 'to practise unprotected sex' (*Collins English Dictionary*) in homosexual jargon. The analogy that is established between riding without a saddle and practising anal penetration without protection seems evident. The underlying metaphor, TO COPULATE IS HORSE RIDING, implies that one of the sexual partners is the horse whereas the other is the rider who "mounts" him:

(14) *I would be so high, it would be nothing for me to be with 15, 20, 25 men in a night. It was never a part of my agenda to practice safe sex. You know, it's always about **barebacking** (...). You know, wearing condoms is the rare thing when you're high on crystal meth.* (SPOK, Ind_Oprah 2014)

When applied to sexual encounters, *barebacking* is dysphemistic because of two reasons: first, it conceives a sexual relation as a purely animal activity in which those involved are represented as irrational beings; second, one of the sexual partners is in a position of dominance over the other, who is "mounted" and therefore represented as inferior. In spite of this, *barebacking* does not carry negative connotations in (14). It is used by a homosexual person with no intention to hide or mitigate the topic of anal sex whatsoever; rather, like *bear* in (13), it belongs to the category of quasi-euphemism: it provides a sense of in-group cohesion in that it designates a practice which is characteristic of the homosexual community.

6 Final remarks

The analysis of metaphors for homosexuality in naturally-occurring contexts of use has shown that metaphor is a valuable tool to verbalize the taboo of homosexuality and reason about it in particular terms. Evidence from the corpus reveals the use of a set of conceptual metaphors drawing on the source domains of CONTAINERS, JOURNEYS, WOMEN, and ANIMALS to understand and conceptualize homosexuals and homosexual-related issues. Regarding frequency of occurrence, it is worth noting that the CLOSET metaphors are the most quantitatively relevant in the corpus (almost 60 % of the total number of metaphorical items found fall under this conceptualization), whereas those which take ANIMALS, JOURNEYS, and WOMEN as source domains are less frequent. Metaphor is used for a range of communicative purposes which correspond to different axiological categories of taboo naming: to criticize and degrade male homosexuals as people who do not conform to conventional gender roles (dysphemism); to provide a socially acceptable way to refer to one's homosexual condition and thus avoid offence (euphemism); and to display in-group solidarity or attract people's interest on the topic in discussion (quasi-euphemism). As a result, different types of X-phemistic types have been detected, namely, the so-called protective (in some occurrences of the CLOSET and CRUISING metaphors), derogatory (WOMAN and ANIMAL metaphors), and cohesive (ANIMAL and CLOSET metaphors).

In addition, metaphor plays a relevant role in constructing dominant hetero-normative discourse. The use of metaphorical items such as *nancy boy* (MALE HOMOSEXUALS ARE WOMEN) reveals that some men have an ideologically biased view of homosexuals: they consider them as effeminate and therefore as part of a marginal social group in accordance with the heteronormative social order they contribute to maintain and reinforce through metaphor. From this viewpoint, the present study contributes to understanding the heterosexual response to homosexuality and homosexual behaviour.

In conclusion, this research shows the value judgments and views concerning homosexuality which are conveyed through figurative language in an updated sample of homosexual-related metaphors in present-day American English. The analysis carried out, however, does not exhaust the topic of homosexual metaphor. A number of issues require further attention. First, it would be interesting to look at the metaphors on homosexuality used exclusively by gays and lesbians and see whether these speakers have a distinctive use of metaphorical language. Second, it would be of value to compare how homosexuality metaphors are used in different cultures and languages and, in doing so, explore to what extent the differences in the use of metaphor contribute to maintain or reproduce heteronormative gender roles in different societies.

Acknowledgments: I would like to thank the editor for her valuable remarks on an earlier draft of this chapter.

References

Allan, Keith. 2007. The pragmatics of connotation. *Journal of Pragmatics* 39. 1047–1057.
Allan, Keith & Kate Burridge. 2006. *Forbidden words: Taboo and the censoring of language.* Cambridge: Cambridge University Press.
Amnesty International. 2015. Human rights facts and figures for 2014. https://www.amnesty.org/en/latest/news/2015/02/annual-report-201415-facts-and-figures/ (accessed 4 May 2016).
Baker, Paul. 2002. *Polari: The lost language of gay men.* London & New York: Routledge.
Brown, Penelope & Stephen Levinson. 1987. *Politeness. Some universals in language use.* Cambridge: Cambridge University Press.
Cameron, Deborah & Don Kulick. 2006. Heteronorms. In Deborah Cameron & Don Kulick (eds.), *The language and sexuality reader*, 165–178. London & New York: Routledge.
Casas Gómez, Miguel. 2009. Towards a new approach to the linguistic definition of euphemism. *Language Sciences* 31. 725–739.
Casas Gómez, Miguel. 2012. The expressive creativity of euphemism and dysphemism. *Lexis: Journal in English Lexicology* 7. 43–64.
Chesebro, James W. (ed.). 1981. *Gayspeak: Gay male & lesbian communication.* New York: Pilgrim Press.
Coates, Jennifer. 2013. The discursive production of everyday heterosexualities. *Discourse & Society* 24. 536–552.
Collins English Dictionary. Complete and unabridged. 2003. 6th edn. Glasgow: Harper Collins Publishers.
Crespo-Fernández, Eliecer. 2008. Sex-related euphemism and dysphemism: An analysis in terms of Conceptual Metaphor Theory. *Atlantis. A Journal of the Spanish Association of Anglo-American Studies* 30(2). 95–110.
Crespo-Fernández, Eliecer. 2015. *Sex in language. Euphemistic and dysphemistic metaphors in Internet forums.* London & New York: Bloomsbury.
Crespo-Fernández, Eliecer & Carmen Luján-García. 2017. Anglicism and word axiology in homosexual language". *RESLA. Revista Española de Lingüística Aplicada.* 30(1). 74–102.
Davies, Mark. 2009–. *The corpus of contemporary American English: 450 million words, 1990-present.* http://corpus.byu.edu/coca/ (accessed 27 April 2016).
Deignan, Alice. 1997. Metaphors of desire. In Keith Harvey & Celia Shalom (eds.), *Language and desire: Encoding sex, romance and intimacy*, 21–42. London & New York: Routledge.
Evans, Vyvyan. 2013. Metaphor, lexical concepts, and figurative meaning construction. *Journal of Cognitive Semiotics* 5(1–2). 73–107.
Fairclough, Norman. 1992. *Discourse and social change.* Oxford: Blackwell.
Fitzgerald, Thomas K. 1993. *Metaphors of identity: A culture-communication dialogue.* Albany, NY: State University of New York Press.
Grondelaers, Stefan & Dirk Geeraerts. 1998. Vagueness as a euphemistic strategy. In Angeliki Athanasiadou & Elzbieta Tabakowska (eds.), *Speaking of emotions: Conceptualisation and expression*, 357–374. Berlin & New York: Mouton de Gruyter.
Herrero Ruiz, Javier. 2009. *Understanding tropes: At the crossroads between pragmatics and cognition.* Frankfurt am Main: Peter Lang.
Hines, Caitlin. 1999. Foxy chicks and playboy bunnies: A case study in metaphorical lexicalization. In Masago K. Hiraga, Chris Sinha & Sherman Wilcox (eds.), *Cultural,*

psychological and typological issues in cognitive linguistics, 9–23. Amsterdam & Philadelphia: John Benjamins.

Kövecses, Zoltán. 1988. *The language of love. The semantics of passion in conversational English*. London: Bucknell University Press.

Kövecses, Zoltán. 2002. *Metaphor: A practical introduction*. Oxford: Oxford University Press.

Kövecses, Zoltán. 2006. *Language, mind, and culture. A practical introduction*. Oxford: Oxford University Press.

Lakoff, George. 1987. *Women, fire, and dangerous things. What categories reveal about the mind*. Chicago & London: The University of Chicago Press.

Lakoff, George. 1993 [1979]. The contemporary theory of metaphor. In Andrew Ortony (ed.), *Metaphor and thought*, 2nd edn., 202–251. Cambridge: Cambridge University Press.

Lakoff, George & Mark Johnson. 1999. *Philosophy in the flesh: The embodied mind and its challenge to western thought*. New York: Basic Books.

Land, Victoria & Celia Kitzinger. 2005. Speaking as a lesbian: Correcting the heterosexist presumption. *Research on Language and Social Interaction* 38(4). 371–416.

Oxford English Dictionary. 1992. 2nd edn. Oxford: Oxford University Press.

Pizarro Pedraza, Andrea. 2013. *Tabú y eufemismo en la ciudad de Madrid. Estudio sociolingüístico-cognitivo de los conceptos sexuales*. Madrid: Universidad Complutense PhD thesis.

Pragglejaz Group. 2007. "MIP: A method for identifying metaphorically used words in discourse". *Metaphor and Symbol* 22(1). 1–39.

Ringer, R. Jeffrey (ed.). 1994. *Queer words, queer images: Communication and the construction of homosexuality*. New York & London: New York University Press.

Rodríguez González, Félix. 2008. The feminine stereotype in gay characterization. A look at English and Spanish. In María de los Ángeles Gómez-González, J. Lachan McKenzie & Elsa M. González-Álvarez (eds.), *Languages and cultures in contrast and comparison*, 221–245. Amsterdam & Philadelphia: John Benjamins.

Sharifian, Farzad. 2011. *Cultural conceptualizations and language*. Amsterdam & Philadelphia: John Benjamins.

Steen, Gerard. 2011. The contemporary theory of metaphor: Now new and improved!. *Review of Cognitive Linguistics* 9(1). 26–64.

Stychin, Carl. 2005. *Governing sexuality. The changing politics of citizenship and law reform*. Oxford & Portland: Hart Publishing.

Zeve, Barry. 1993. The Queen's English: Metaphor in gay speech. *English Today* 9(3). 3–9.

Notes

1. The distinction between *taboo* and *linguistic taboo* seems necessary. Whereas the taboo is the prohibition or restriction of any practice or behavior which is believed to be harmful, embarrassing or shameful to the members of a social group, the linguistic taboo is the term which is, depending on the speaker's intention, either avoided and replaced by a euphemism or maintained as a dysphemism.
2. Homosexuality is still severely punished in many countries of the world. According to Amnesty International (2015), 78 countries have laws in force that criminalize

non-heterosexual relationships between adults. This association records human rights abuses against LGBT people: simply because of their sexual identities, they are not only imprisoned or forced to undergo psychiatric treatment but also raped or tortured (Land and Kitzinger 2005: 371–372).

3. When applied to linguistic research, axiology is related to the (positive or negative) values that lexical units acquire in communication.
4. In this research I follow Fairclough's (1992) three-dimensional concept of discourse, i.e., discourse as a piece of text; discourse as an instance of discursive practice; and discourse as an instance of social practice. Within the general view of discourse as a context-embedded process of communication, Fairclough's approach allows to relate specific language characteristics to particular social situations and communities.
5. In fact, the existence of a common language use in the homosexual community which came to be known as "Gayspeak" (see Chesebro 1981), is difficult to maintain. The homosexual community is so heterogeneous and diverse both socially and demographically that the idea of a unique discourse style whereby lesbians and gay men signal their identity is rather naive.
6. Following Evans (2013: 75) by *discourse metaphor* I understand those instances of figurative language which "arise in language use to address particular and often specific communicative needs and functions" whereas *conceptual metaphors* are "independent of language but influence certain types of language use".
7. See Casas Gómez (this volume) for a comprehensive overview of the evolution in the theoretical treatment of X-phemism from the early descriptions within the framework of structural lexical semantics to the more recent definitions of X-phemistic processes from a cogntive standpoint.
8. In the examples the metaphorical items are highlighted in bold and the text category to which the quotations from the COCA belong is indicated in brackets: ACAD: Academic journals; FIC: Fiction; MAG: Popular magazines; NEWS: Newspapers; SPOK: Spoken. The specific source of the quotation is also given.
9. These characteristics are also attributed to young, attractive, and sexually appealing women by virtue of the metaphor WOMEN ARE BIRDS (see Crespo-Fernández 2015: 142–143). Hence, in this materialization of the BIRD metaphor the domain of WOMEN conflates with the ANIMAL domain to target male homosexuality dysphemistically. The same conflation between domains applies to the FLOWER metaphor (see 5.3).
10. The CLOSET metaphor has been borrowed by other languages via English. For example, in Spanish it appears both as a pure, i.e., non-adapted, anglicism, and as a calque in *salir del armario*, a word-for-word translation of *come out of the closet*. It is worth noting that the individual words of this expression (*come*, *out*, *outing*, and *closet*) have been borrowed as pure anglicisms (Crespo-Fernández and Luján-García 2017: 84).
11. The SPATIAL-CONTAINMENT schema does not only apply to homosexuality. It also provides the conceptual basis to refer to a wide range of sex-related issues, like female genitalia, anal sex, sexual excitation, and coition (Crespo-Fernández 2015: 104–107).
12. It is worth noting that *pussy* is also used as a slang word for a lesbian who adopts a feminine role (Allan 2007: 1049).

Ivana Moritz
3 Metonymy-based euphemisms in war-related speeches by George W. Bush and Barack Obama

Abstract: In the last two decades, the USA has taken part in conflicts that have not always been supported by the public. Two recent presidents, George W. Bush and Barack Obama had to deliver war-related speeches, and have been in positions to euphemize different topics for different reasons. A particular contextual situation is occasionally a trigger for the creation of new euphemisms as well as new taboo topics, so the presidents make use of euphemisms to avoid addressing certain topics and to achieve their rhetorical and political goals.

The paper attempts to show that euphemistic expressions are not merely rhetorical figures, that they have cognitive grounding.

Euphemistic expressions were extracted from transcripts of war related speeches, grouped according to concepts euphemized, and further subdivided according to cognitive mechanisms underlying their formation – conceptual metaphor and metonymy.

Metonymy-grounded euphemistic expressions were analyzed more thoroughly, their number outreaching the number of metaphor-grounded euphemistic expressions. The analysis also included looking into the choice of the preferred metonymic vehicle for particular examples, following Radden and Kövecses' (1999) principles for selecting metonymic vehicles.

Furthermore, the paper draws inferences regarding most frequently euphemized topics in the speeches, and also attempts to determine the aims of euphemism usage in presidential war-related speeches.

1 Introduction

Political discourse is one of the most complex and most elaborate types of discourse and is known to be rich in rhetorical figures, including euphemistic expressions, which have been studied as rhetorical figures, but recently also occasionally explained in the light of cognitive linguistics. Euphemistic expressions are words or expressions used instead of concepts belonging to taboo, concepts that are too direct, too embarrassing, or communicatively, contextually or situationally inadequate for different reasons. Taboo topics are more or less universal in all societies, and the most common ones are: *death, sex, physiological functions,* and *bodily effluvia*. Nevertheless, these are not as common in political discourse as in everyday communication. Politicians and participants in political discourse create taboos and euphemistic expressions in existing contextual and political situations, and they are the ones who determine which concepts belong to taboo at a given moment and, therefore, also create euphemistic expressions in a current piece of text or speech as well as define concepts that can be communicated directly. In other words, euphemistic expressions are formed, altered and interpreted within a communicative situation; in order to recognize a euphemistic expression in an instance of political discourse one has to be familiar with language dynamics of political discourse, as well as with political, historical and social factors (Allan and Burridge 1991, Kuna 2007).

Euphemism has been considered a mere rhetorical device, and therefore rarely submitted to cognitive analysis. Traditional definitions of euphemism as found in contemporary and online available dictionaries have more or less been on the level of rhetorical terms, including expressions like *used instead of words for something bad, embarrassing* (English Oxford Living Dictionaries)[1]; *used to avoid uttering unpleasant or offending words* (Cambridge Dictionary[2], Merriam Webster[3]); *mild and indirect expressions* (TheFreeDictionary[4]), *with the aim of being polite* (Literary Devices[5]), *saving own or listener's face* (English Works[6]) and *avoiding taboo topics* (TheLingSpace[7]).

Due to the war situations in the last two decades in the USA, the Presidents were in numerous delicate situations day after day, where they had to address the nation regarding the war events, and, where there is war there are injuries, death and other concepts not easy to communicate. George W. Bush and Barack Obama were two presidents of the USA in war times in different positions and of different viewpoints. Just as political discourse in general, their speeches on war are also packed with euphemistic expressions.

The present study attempts at answering the questions: *What are the most commonly euphemized topics in war related speeches by the two recent presidents of the USA – George W. Bush and Barack Obama? What are the cognitive mecha-*

---

[1] https://en.oxforddictionaries.com/definition/euphemism
[2] http://dictionary.cambridge.org/dictionary/english/euphemism
[3] https://www.merriam-webster.com/dictionary/euphemism
[4] http://www.thefreedictionary.com/Euphemism
[5] https://literarydevices.net/euphemism/
[6] http://www.englishworks.com.au/euphemisms/
[7] http://thelingspace.tumblr.com/post/143132629704/taboo-language-and-euphemisms-companion-post

nisms underlying them? Do the euphemistic expressions function as taboo concealers or do they perhaps serve a different purpose?

The research does not aim at comparing, explaining and drawing general inferences on the complete political rhetoric and discourses of George W. Bush and Barrack Obama. The euphemisms and euphemistic expressions discussed in the present chapter are only a minor part of a vast amount of different conceptual, linguistic and rhetorical phenomena in their speeches.

2 Euphemism and conceptual metonymy

As already stated, research into the combination of euphemism, political discourse and cognitive linguistics, particularly metonymy, is very rarely found in literature. Political discourse, due to its nature and goals, is (in)famous for being rich in rhetorical figures, including euphemistic expressions, but that is exactly what they have been – only rhetorical figures. There is a lack of cognitive and conceptual insight into euphemism, in other words, it is difficult to find answers to the following questions: *Where do euphemistic expressions come from?* and *Why is that so?*

Ways of euphemism formation and creation are versatile as confirmed by many authors, among others Allan and Burridge (1991), Kuna (2007), Burridge (2006), Warren (1992), for example: shortening (*jeez* for *Jesus*), circumlocution (*solid human waste* for *feces*), remodeling (*heck* for *hell*), external and internal borrowing (*perspire* for *sweat; cupid's measles* for *syphilis*) and semantic change, including metaphorization and metonymization (*give life* for *die, be in Iraq* for *war in Iraq*).

Euphemistic expressions based on conceptual metonymy in political speeches on war by George W. Bush and Barack Obama have proved to be ubiquitous. Out of most commonly euphemized topics (data obtained by manually collecting euphemistic expressions from the mentioned speeches) in war-related speeches by both presidents, *death* is the only topic (among the first three most frequently euphemized topics – *war, army and soldiers* and *death and dying*) in part euphemized by means of conceptual metaphor LIFE IS A PRECIOUS POSSESSION, and its entailments TO DIE IS TO GIVE LIFE and TO DIE IS TO LOSE LIFE:

(1) Thousands and thousands of young men and women **lost their lives** during that war (G.W. Bush).

(2) *It lives on in memories of your fellow soldiers, sailors, airmen and Marines who* **gave their lives** *(B. Obama)*[8].

The focus of this chapter though is conceptual metonymy as a cognitive mechanism underlying the formation of euphemistic expressions in speeches related to war by George W. Bush and Barack Obama.

Conceptual metonymy functions within an ICM (Idealized Cognitive Model) (Lakoff 1987), a conceptual domain or a frame, it involves a 'for' relationship among vehicle and target concepts. The function of conceptual metonymy is mental access to a certain concept based on associations or contiguity, where metonymic processes highlight, elaborate or expand the meaning of the vehicle concept, giving it a different perspective. The mentioned metonymy-related processes and relationships are all interconnected by the notion of *contiguity*, physical or mental:

(3) *America will help the Iraqis so they can* **protect their families** *and secure their free nation* (G.W. Bush) (CAUSE FOR EFFECT – PROTECTION FOR WAR).
(4) *We also know the service does not end with the person* **wearing the uniform** (Barack Obama) (PART FOR WHOLE – UNIFORM FOR SOLDIERS).

Example (3) is an instance of mental contiguity within the metonymic process, since the vehicle (PROTECTION) and the target (WAR) do not exist nearby each other in physical reality. An example of physical contiguity is illustrated in (4), since UNIFORM and SOLDIER do coexist in physical reality.

According to Panther (2005:357), the basic criterion for recognizing metonymy is not "'addition' or 'substitution' but the degree of conceptual prominence of the target meaning", it is, therefore a means of semantic elaboration or enrichment, as evident in examples of euphemistic expressions from the corpus, for example:

(5) *The rest are forming and not yet ready to participate fully in* **security operations** (G.W. Bush) (EFFECT FOR CAUSE – SECURITY FOR WAR).

---

[8] For more see: Moritz, Ivana. 2017. Sacrificed, lost or gave life for their country: Cognitive analysis of euphemisms for death in Bush and Obama's war speeches. In Alessandro Capone & Vahid Parvaresh (eds.), *The Pragmeme of Accommodation: The Case of Interaction around the Event of Death*, 300–318. Cham: Springer International Publishing.

*(6) America, our allies and the world were acting as one to destroy al Qaeda's terrorist network and **to protect our common security** (B. Obama)* (CAUSE FOR EFFECT – PROTECTION FOR WAR).

The meaning of the target concept (WAR) is modified by being attributed semantic details and shades implicated by the meanings of vehicle concepts (*security operation, to protect our common security*) with the aim of euphemizing literal meaning of the concept *war*. Croft (2002) puts it differently by claiming that in the process of metonymization the secondary domain becomes primary. Vehicle meaning is constantly conceptually present; it is not erased by the target concept, not even in euphemistic expressions, in this case, metonymic linguistic expressions.

3 Corpus and methodology

The corpus this research was conducted on were the transcripts[9] of the speeches directly or indirectly related to war by the two most recent former presidents of the United States of America George W. Bush (in office 2001–2009) and president Barack Obama (in office 2009–2017). The aim of the corpus study was to detect most commonly euphemized topics in war related speeches by the two presidents and to compare them taking into account presidents' respective political ideologies. The main idea was to see whether the most commonly euphemized topics by both presidents were the same or different and whether they were euphemized in the same way, i.e. by using the same underlying cognitive mechanisms for the formation of euphemistic expressions. The paper analyses only three most frequently euphemized concepts in the speeches by both presidents: WAR, ARMY AND SOLDIERS and DEATH AND DYING.

Out of 331 speech transcripts, given by George W. Bush, 221 are directly or indirectly related to war(s). The total number of euphemistic expressions analyzed in war-related speeches by George W. Bush is 3581, out of which 2731 are euphemistic expressions for WAR, 685 for ARMY AND SOLDIERS, and 165 are euphemistic expressions for DEATH AND DYING. Additionally, he also euphemizes, for instance, WEAPONS (*equipment, components, means, tools*), KILLING (*ethnic cleansing, clearing, removing*), BOMBS (*IEDs*).

---

9 www.presidentialrhetoric.com (a site providing information and resources on the study of presidential rhetoric, data retrieved August 15 2015)

In contrast to George W. Bush, Barack Obama delivered only 15 speeches related to war in the period from 2009 to 2013, and later on, in his second term, the number of war-related speeches by Barack Obama significantly decreases, probably due to the fact that the wars ended or were in the process of coming to an end, and total number of euphemistic expressions extracted from the transcripts is 495, much less than from the speeches by George W. Bush. Out of this number, 328 euphemistic expressions are for WAR, 115 for ARMY AND SOLDIERS, and 52 euphemistic expressions for DEATH. Therefore, the comparison and conclusions reached in this research are only rough ones, based on the mentioned data. Additional topics Barack Obama euphemizes in smaller numbers are for example: PROBLEM (*challenge*), REFUGEES (*displaced citizens*), KILL (*do away with*, *bring to justice*), ATTACKS (*incidents*).

Table 1. *Number of euphemistic expressions based on conceptual metonymy in war-related speeches by George W. Bush and Barrack Obama*

	George W. Bush	Barack Obama
Number of speeches	221	15
Total number of euphemisms	3622	495
WAR	2722 EFFECT FOR CAUSE 688 CAUSE FOR EFFECT 322 PART FOR WHOLE 461 WHOLE FOR PART 1301	328 WHOLE FOR PART 167 EFFECT FOR CAUSE 322 CAUSE FOR EFFECT 25
ARMY AND SOLDIERS	685 DEFINING PROPERTY FOR CATEGORY 556 PART FOR WHOLE 129	115 DEFINING PROPERTY FOR CATEGORY 87 PART FOR WHOLE 28
DEATH	165 CAUSE FOR EFFECT 106	52 CAUSE FOR EFFECT

Euphemistic expressions were manually extracted from the texts, then grouped by the topic euphemized. They were recognized by semantic analysis of sentences and expressions, i.e. by elaborating on the literal and figurative meanings of euphemistic expressions and by trying to replace figurative euphemistic expressions with the respective literal expressions. The ones successfully replaced qualified as euphemistic expressions. WAR, ARMY AND SOLDIERS and DEATH AND DYING were three most frequently euphemized topics, i. e. euphemistic expressions used instead of these lexemes appeared in highest numbers. Euphemistic expressions euphemizing other various concepts, appearing in lower frequency, were not studied in detail for the purpose of the present analysis.

The formation of many of the euphemistic expressions from the corpus could also be explained in a more traditional way, for instance, by stating that saying *conflict* instead of *war* is litotes, that *defend freedom* instead of *war* is either particularization or circumlocution, or that *sacrifice* instead of *death* is elevation (Burridge 2006). This should, though, be observed as a completely different level of analysis, since all the mentioned examples and the examples from the corpus analyzed in the paper can be explained in cognitive terms, and when analyzing them in this direction, they all come down to either conceptual metaphor or conceptual metonymy.

4 George W. Bush and metonymy-based euphemistic expressions

In the next section, we analyze three most commonly euphemized topics in war-related speeches by George W. Bush – WAR, ARMY AND SOLDIERS and DEATH AND DYING. The euphemistic expressions are also categorized according to general and more specific instances of conceptual metonymies.

4.1 WAR

4.1.1 EFFECT FOR CAUSE

WAR is the lexeme most commonly replaced (as shown in Table 1.) by euphemistic expressions in war related speeches by George W. Bush. He frequently uses lexemes denoting expected effects of war like *safety, freedom* and *liberty* instead of the lexeme *war* itself. The cognitive mechanism taking part in the formation of these euphemistic expressions is conceptual metonymy EFFECT FOR CAUSE. The number of euphemistic expressions whose formation is based on conceptual metonymy EFFECT FOR CAUSE is 688.

According to Panther and Thornburg's (2007:257) the taxonomy of EFFECT FOR CAUSE metonymy, which shows the hierarchical structure of metonymy (from high-level metonymies to specific subtypes), RESULTANT STATE FOR ACTION and RESULTANT EVENT FOR ACTION (the examples of which are found in the corpus) are on the third, most specific level of the structure (1. EFFECT FOR CAUSE→ 2.

RESULTANT SITUATION FOR CAUSING SITUATION → 3. RESULTANT STATE FOR ACTION & RESULTANT EVENT FOR ACTION).

A more specific metonymy, RESULTANT STATE FOR ACTION is the cognitive mechanism underlying euphemistic expressions containing lexemes *security*, *freedom* and *liberty* or their variants. These three concepts, as results of *war*, were highlighted via metonymic mappings within the ICM WAR. For example:

*(7) One year ago, military forces of a strong coalition entered Iraq to enforce United Nations demands, to **defend our security**, and to liberate that country from the rule of a tyrant.*

*(8) In this war, we have lost good men and women who left our shore to **defend freedom** and did not live to make the journey home.*

*(9) Many of you here today were also involved in **the liberation of Afghanistan**.*

The lexeme *liberty*, as a vehicle concept within conceptual metonymy EFFECT FOR CAUSE conveys at least two meanings when it comes to euphemistic expressions from the corpus. The first meaning is the dictionary[10] one, where *liberty* is 'personal freedom from physical and moral restrictions', as in:

*(10) By **serving the ideal of liberty**, we are bringing hope to others, and that makes America more secure.*

On the other hand, as illustrated in example (10) *liberty* does not refer to personal freedom, but to armed liberation of a country. This phenomenon goes along the lines of Brdar-Szabó and Brdar's (2011:232) examples where metonymic vehicles CAPITAL CITY and STATE can 'map' or refer to the same metonymic target, in their case GOVERNMENT or one of its institutions. This is a sort of metonymic chain, a group of metonymic vehicles united by the same metonymic target. More than one metonymic vehicle is activated simultaneously with the activation of one or more metonymic targets, and, according to the authors, this is very common in language. The lexeme *liberty* and its two meanings in this case represent two metonymic vehicles, both lexemes with the same root, but with different semantic properties, referring to the same metonymic target war.

---

10 http://dictionary.cambridge.org/dictionary/english/liberty
https://en.oxforddictionaries.com/definition/freedom
http://www.dictionary.com/browse/liberty?s=t

4.1.2 CAUSE FOR EFFECT

President George W. Bush frequently uses euphemistic expressions containing lexemes *defense* and *protection* in his war related speeches. In this way he actually refers to the causes leading to war, using conceptual metonymy CAUSE FOR EFFECT, i.e. its more specific instances DEFENSE FOR WAR and PROTECTION FOR WAR as cognitive mechanisms for formation of euphemistic expressions. They appear 322 times in the corpus. For example:

(11) Our government has taken unprecedented measures to **defend the homeland**.
(12) I'm honored to be with so many courageous men and women who have stepped forward to **protect our nation**.

4.1.3 PART FOR WHOLE

The cognitive mechanism responsible for the formation of euphemistic expressions of this kind is conceptual metonymy SUBEVENT FOR EVENT, which can also be analyzed as PART OF THE SCENARIO FOR WHOLE SCENARIO, more specifically BE IN IRAQ FOR WAR IN IRAQ, and CONFLICT FOR WAR, both manifestations of high-level conceptual metonymy PART FOR WHOLE, all elaborated by Peirsman and Geeraerts (2006).

The *presence* in Iraq is the highlighted aspect in these examples, not the whole, more complex event of the war itself. If we observe war as a more complex event or scenario, the presence in the war is an inevitable part of the event. The concept is schematized, and by that, the details that would enable complete understanding of the complex concept and scenario of war are prevented from being evoked. As a part of this linguistic expression of the conceptual metonymy SUBEVENT FOR EVENT or PART OF THE SCENARIO FOR WHOLE SCENARIO, WAR is the vehicle, and PRESENCE (BE IN IRAQ) is the target in the mapping within the domain or ICM WAR. For example:

(13) I'm often asked why we'**re in Iraq** when Saddam Hussein was not responsible for the 9/11 attacks.

Another lexical realization of conceptual metonymy SUBEVENT FOR COMPLEX EVENT or PART OF SCENARIO FOR WHOLE SCENARIO – is conceptual metonymy CONFLICT FOR WAR. Conflict is a part of every *war*, every war begins with a conflict. The vehicle in this case is CONFLICT, and the target unit is WAR.

There are 141 euphemistic expressions containing the lexeme *conflict* in the corpus. For example:

(14) *Their refusal to do so will result in a **military conflict**, commenced at a time of our choosing.*

President George W. Bush frequently uses lexemes such as *strategy* and *tactics* to refer to war, and the number of these euphemistic expressions in the corpus is 280. Originally French, the lexeme *strategy*[11] has its source in military terminology, and both *strategy* and *tactics*[12] are used in political, business and informal registers. Barcelona (2003) analyzes conceptual metonymy STRATEGY (IN A CONFLICT) FOR CONFLICT, and considers it a subtype of metonymy PART FOR WHOLE, since STRATEGY is a part of the ICM WAR. Via STRATEGY listeners approach the whole ICM WAR. For example:

(15) *Therefore, the United States has adopted a new policy, a forward **strategy of freedom** in the Middle East.*
(16) *As the enemy shifts the tactics, we are **shifting our tactics**, as well.*

4.1.4 WHOLE FOR PART

The most common euphemistic expression for war in the corpus by George W. Bush by far is *work* and concepts and expressions belonging to the ICM WORK. It appears in the form of numerous various lexical units listed below, and the total number of examples is 1301.

The formation mechanism underlying this euphemistic expression is conceptual metonymy GENERAL FOR SPECIFIC, i.e. metonymy WHOLE FOR PART. In this realization of the mentioned conceptual metonymy WORK is a more general concept, and the target concept WAR is the more specific concept, metonymic vehicle. For the parties directly taking part in the war (president and military officers), war is a part of work.

According to Langacker's (1991, 2008) network model, WORK is the most schematic structure within conceptual metonymy WORK FOR WAR, and the lexemes appearing in euphemistic expressions are the structures elaborating or representing the schema. WORK is the general concept, and the expressions with

---

11 http://www.oxforddictionaires.com/definition/english/strategy?q=strategy
12 http://www.oxforddictionaries.com/definition/english/tactic?q=tactics

lexemes belonging to the conceptual frame of WORK are much more specific in their meaning than the lexeme *work* itself. The lexemes taking part in the elaboration process of euphemistic expressions for WAR, with metonymy WORK FOR WAR as underlying formation mechanisms are: *operation, job, objective, campaign, mission, duty, calling, undertaking, task, action, responsibility, ambition, stake, succeed, assignment, execution* and their forms. For example:

(17) *Admiral Kelly, captain Card, officers and sailors of the USS Abraham Lincoln, my fellow Americans: Major combat* **operations** *in Iraq have ended.*

(18) *Setting an artificial timetable would send the wrong message to the Iraqis, who need to know that America will not leave before the* **job** *is done.*

4.2 ARMY AND SOLDIERS

4.2.1 DEFINING PROPERTY FOR CATEGORY

The second most frequently euphemized topic in war related speeches by George W. Bush is ARMY AND SOLDIERS. Mentioning the expression *army* in front of his people (listeners) might be too direct or too harsh for the president because most certainly some of his listeners belong to soldiers' families or have already lost beloved ones who were soldiers or their family members have been injured or hurt in any other way. Also, the connotations to the lexemes *army* and *soldiers* imply weapons, fighting, danger, injuries and even death. Therefore he resorts to euphemistic expressions formed on the basis of conceptual metonymy DEFINING PROPERTY FOR CATEGORY, more specifically its subtype FORCE FOR ARMY. FORCE is one of the properties characterizing the ARMY, and serves as a vehicle within this metonymic mapping, where ARMY is the target.

(19) *American and coalition* **forces** *are sacrificing for the security of free nations.*

4.2.2 PART FOR WHOLE

The most common euphemistic expression George W. Bush uses instead of the concept SOLDIER is *uniform*, as it appears in the corpus 129 times. This manifestation of conceptual metonymy is a subtype of conceptual metonymy PART FOR WHOLE. UNIFORM, as a part of the whole invokes the expressions SOLDIER. The examples from the corpus are not direct manifestations of the metonymy UNIFORM FOR SOLDIER, but, in most cases, they are paraphrases, for instance, *women and men wearing uniforms, serve our country in uniform*, that distinguish soldiers from civilians and present them as special people who deserve to wear the uniform. For example:

(20) I want to thank everybody in **uniform** *who is here today – thank you for your service, your sacrifice and your love of America.*

4.3 Death and dying

The third most common topic of euphemization in war related speeches by George W. Bush is DEATH AND DYING. The largest number of examples was formed with the help of conceptual metonymy SACRIFICE FOR DEATH[13], which is a linguistic manifestation of high-level metonymy CAUSE FOR DEATH. The examples appear 106 times in the corpus, out of the total of 165 euphemistic expressions for DEATH. The cause of death in this case is sacrifice for homeland.

Through *sacrifice*, the president presents death as something purposeful, meaningful, as something almost positive. Death is one the universal taboos, and is a specifically delicate taboo topic when used by politicians in the times of war. George W. Bush is particularly sensitive when it comes to this topic, since he was in an ungrateful position during his presidential term where he had to justify joining the war, and since every war brings death, he had to justify the deaths of numerous American soldiers to their families and the nation. For example:

(21) American and coalition forces are **sacrificing** *for the peace of Iraq and for the security of free nations.*

---

13 The rest of the euphemistic expressions for death from the corpus were formed with the help of conceptual metaphor LIFE IS A PRECIOUS POSSESSION, for more see Moritz, Ivana. 2017. Sacrificed, lost or gave life for their country: Cognitive analysis of euphemisms for death in Bush and Obama's war speeches. In Alessandro Capone & Vahid Parvaresh (eds.), *The Pragmeme of Accommodation: The Case of Interaction around the Event of Death*, 300–318. Cham: Springer International Publishing.

5 Barack Obama and metonymy-based euphemism

5.1 WAR

The lexeme most commonly replaced by euphemistic expressions in the period from 2009 to 2013 in war related speeches by Barack Obama was also *war* itself, just the same as with George W. Bush. It must, however, be mentioned that the previous president was the one who started wars in Iraq and Afghanistan, and Barack Obama was the one who, at least according to his own words, was trying to end them.

5.1.1 WHOLE FOR PART

WAR is most commonly euphemized as WORK and the lexemes belonging to the ICM WORK by Barack Obama. It appears in the form of numerous and diverse lexical units, for example: *duty, mission, job, objective, work, accomplish, focus, operate, effort, action, success, responsibility, campaign, task, professionalism, goal, obligation*. Out of 328 analyzed euphemistic expressions for war, 167 were formed with the help of conceptual metonymy WHOLE FOR PART, i.e. its subtype WORK FOR WAR, which is described in more detail in 4.1.4. For example:

(22) *You have endured tour after tour after tour of* **duty**.

The issue observed as a difference between the examples based on conceptual metonymy WORK FOR WAR by the two presidents is the fact that Barack Obama refers to WAR as WORK in the context of its ending, which is also a characteristic of his foreign policy, for example:

(23) *Let me say this as plainly as I can: by August 31, 2010, our* **combat mission** *in Iraq will end.*
(24) *And so I want to be very clear: We sent our troops to Iraq to do away with Saddam Hussein's regime – and you* **got the job done**.

Also, by euphemizing WAR using the lexemes belonging to the umbrella concept WORK, he characterizes it as something that must be done (see (24)), especially by the president, however, he also stresses the fact that *war* is not easy, that it is tedious, and that it brings about serious consequences (25):

(25) *I opposed the war in Iraq precisely because I believe that we must exercise restraint in the use of military force, and always consider the long-term consequences of our **action**.*

5.1.2 Effect for cause

Barack Obama frequently uses expected effects or results of war instead of the term *war* itself. The cognitive mechanism taking part in the formation of these euphemistic expressions is conceptual metonymy EFFECT FOR CAUSE, (See 4.1.1. for more details), particularly SECURITY FOR WAR and SAFETY FOR WAR. The number of euphemistic expressions analyzed is 104. For example:

(26) *Tonight, I'd like to talk to you about the end of our combat mission in Iraq, the ongoing **security challenges** we face, and the need to rebuild our nation here at home.*
(27) *In the midst of all these challenges, however, my single most important responsibility as President is to **keep** the American people **safe**.*

5.1.3 Cause for effect

President Obama in his war related speeches also frequently uses euphemistic expressions containing lexemes *defense* and *protection* instead of the lexeme *war* itself, actually talking about the causes leading to war, using conceptual metonymy CAUSE FOR EFFECT as a cognitive mechanism for the formation of these euphemistic expressions. The number of euphemistic expressions is 57.

The cognitive mechanism underlying euphemistic expressions containing the lexeme *defense* or one of its forms (conceptual metonymies DEFENSE FOR WAR and PROTECTION FOR WAR) is also frequently used by the president George W. Bush, as described in 4.1.2, and there are 32 of them in Barack Obama's corpus. For example:

(28) ***In defense of our nation** we will never waver; in pursuit of al Qaeda and its extremist allies, we will never falter. America, our allies and the world were acting as one to destroy al Qaeda's terrorist network to **protect our common security**.*

When talking about protection, George W. Bush is more aggressive than Barrack Obama, and his speeches give away frustration and determination to do anything to protect the state and the nation:

*(29) The only way to **protect** our people is by early, united, and decisive action.*

President Obama has seen his own role as the protector of the state and nation in the transitional period, in which the end of the war is approaching and the role of American army is changing:

*(30) I have long said, we will retain a transitional force to carry out three distinct functions: training, equipping, and advising Iraqi Security Forces as long as they remain non-sectarian; conducting targeted counter-terrorism missions; and **protecting our ongoing civilian and military efforts** within Iraq.*

5.2 Army and soldiers

5.2.1 Defining property for category

The number of euphemistic expressions whose formation is based on conceptual metonymy DEFINING PROPERTY FOR CATEGORY, more specifically FORCE FOR ARMY in the corpus is 87. This conceptual metonymy, as well as the euphemistic expressions based on it is described in more detail in 4.2.1. For example:

*(31) Initially, this **force** will likely be made up of 35–50,000 U.S. troops.*

5.2.2 Part for whole/uniform for soldiers

The most common euphemistic expressions Barack Obama uses instead of the expression *soldier* is *uniform*. This euphemistic expression is formed with the help of high-level conceptual metonymy PART FOR WHOLE. UNIFORM as a part invokes the concept SOLDIER as a whole. In order to avoid the rough and common connotation of the expressions and give them more importance, Barack Obama uses the lexeme *uniform*, again, this is not a direct metonymy UNIFORM FOR SOLDIERS, but a paraphrase. He uses these euphemistic expressions 28 times. For example:

*(32) We also know the service does not end with the person **wearing the uniform**.*

5.3 Death and dying

In Barack Obama's war related speeches, DEATH AND DYING is also the third most commonly euphemized topic. The majority of the examples in the speeches is based on conceptual metonymy SACRIFICE FOR DEATH, which is a linguistic expression of the high-level conceptual metonymy CAUSE FOR EFFECT. The cause of death in this case is sacrifice for the homeland, and the number of euphemistic expressions in the corpus is 29. For example:

(33) You've seen buddies of yours injured and you remember those who have made the ultimate sacrifice.

6 Why these vehicles?

A plausible answer to this question: authors Langacker (1993) and Radden and Kövecses (1999) claim the existence of cognitive and communicative principles applied in the process of the selection of metonymic vehicles, in other words, the selection of the vehicle in certain cases of metonymy is motivated or restricted by cognitive and communicative principles. The first one to introduce cognitive principles was Langacker (1993:199), explaining metonymy functions: "Metonymy allows an efficient reconciliation of the conflicting factors: the need to be accurate, i.e. of being sure that the addressee's attention is directed to the intended target; and our natural inclination to think and talk explicitly about those entities that have the greatest cognitive salience for us." Metonymic euphemistic expressions perfectly fit in Langacker's inferences on metonymy – they can certainly be used to direct listeners' attention to the intended target, and this proved to be particularly useful in presidential speeches and political discourse in general.

Cognitive principles of the selection of metonymic vehicle by Langacker (1993) are: HUMAN OVER NON-HUMAN, WHOLE OVER PART, CONCRETE OVER ABSTRACT, VISIBLE OVER NON-VISIBLE. They function according to three general factors of conceptual organization that frequently interact and overlap: human experience, perceptive selection and cultural tendencies (Radden and Kövecses 1999).

Radden and Kövecses (1999) elaborate on the cognitive principles of the selection of metonymic vehicles. Principles governed by *basic human experience* include *perspective selectivity* and *cultural tendency* and the ones (from the lengthy list) violated by the two presidents are: IMMEDIATE OVER NON-IMMEDIATE and OCCURENT OVER NON-OCCURENT.

According to the same authors there are at least two communicative principles governing the selection of the preferred metonymic vehicle: CLEAR OVER OBSCURE and RELEVANT OVER IRRELEVANT.

Cognitive motivation is stronger if more cognitive principles are applied, although, as a rule, one example of metonymy does not undergo more than one cognitive principle (Radden and Kövecses 1999). Nevertheless, there are examples where the selection of the vehicle is motivated by more than one principles, particularly when the speaker has expressional needs, or when it is required by the social situation. A speaker might wish to achieve a rhetorical effect by deliberately violating one or more principles, and it is frequently done, particularly in political discourse.

The existence of the listed cognitive and communicative principles lets us conclude that through the selection of a certain metonymic vehicle we can manipulate people, in other words, the principles can be used to achieve rhetoric effects. By violating these principles, the speakers, in this case the presidents, create euphemistic expressions. Almost every example from the corpus is an instance of the violation of at least one of these principles, thus diverting attention from objective and relevant facts, accordingly creating euphemistic expressions and taboos.

George W. Bush and Barack Obama systematically violate the mentioned principles. For example, by using *security, liberty* or *safety* instead of *war*, they both violate the IMMEDIATE OVER NON-IMMEDIATE principle, where *war* is certainly a more immediate experience for those directly or indirectly involved (maybe by only being Americans) than *security, liberty* or *safety*, them being further away in temporal, or even in physical terms. Euphemistic expressions based on conceptual metonymies FREEDOM FOR WAR or LIBERTY FOR WAR indicate the violation of the principle INITIAL OR FINAL OVER MIDDLE, FREEDOM and LIBERTY being concepts coming after the war, and WAR being obviously the central event. The two presidents also bring about more irrelevant concepts to the fore, violating the principle RELEVANT OVER IRRELEVANT, by mentioning *defense, conflict, strategy* instead of *war*, as part of their metonymic expressions. Furthermore, the cause of death, *sacrifice* in this case, is by all means much less relevant than the event of death, particularly in the context of war speeches and war victims, and, especially when the presidents address American people or families of the deceased. *War*, an event that was unfortunately for many really happening, is overshadowed by *protection*, a concept not directly and physically occurring for the civilians of the USA, who were not directly threatened by the dangers of war. The presidents violate the principle OCCURRENT OVER NON-OCCURRENT in the case of conceptual metonymy PROTECTION FOR WAR. Some concepts are less central in comparison to the concept of *war* itself, like, for example, BEING IN IRAQ compared to WAR

IN IRAQ (conceptual metonymy BE IN IRAQ FOR WAR IN IRAQ), FORCE as one of the army's properties compared to ARMY itself (conceptual metonymy FORCE FOR ARMY), and, previously mentioned SACRIFICE compared to DEATH itself (conceptual metonymy SACRIFICE FOR DEATH). The cognitive principle violated in these instances is CENTRAL OVER PERIPHERAL. Likewise, saying *to be in Iraq* instead of *war in Iraq*, or labeling army as *force*, is simply using more obscure expressions, thus violating the cognitive principle CLEAR OVER OBSCURE. *Work* is a much more general term than *war* when it comes to the domain of work of the USA president, war being considered a part of their *work*, and the cognitive principle violated in this case is SPECIFIC OVER GENERIC. Both presidents also violate the cognitive principle HUMAN OVER NON-HUMAN by constantly referring to soldiers as *women and men in uniforms*, shifting the focus from people to objects they wear.

7 Why euphemism in *war* speeches?

Political activity does not exist without the use of language, and political language is a powerful means of getting public support, particularly in the times of crises. Conveying a message successfully is a task requiring great skill in many fields (McNair 2011). Gradečak-Erdeljić and Varga (2009: 2) claim that political discourse is one of the most productive sources of new expressions of different levels of lexical complexity, from lexemes, to complex idiomatic structures. Therefore, it is a particularly fertile ground for the use of rhetoric figures that aim at creating "political reality", simplifying complex concepts or situations, personifying and illustrating abstract political concepts, emphasizing "our" positive characteristics and concealing certain aspects (e.g. metonymy) (Reisigl 2006).

Our corpus confirms many authors' statements on political discourse, it is extremely rich in rhetorical figures, not only at the linguistic level, but in cognitive structures as well, where we can (at least partially) decipher speakers' underlying conceptual frames, attitudes and political commitment.

Due to the fact that George W. Bush and Barack Obama belong to different political ideologies, conservative and progressive, and following Lakoff's (2002) thesis stated in *Moral Politics*, that conservatives and progressives employ different cognitive mechanisms (conceptual metaphors) when thinking about life, politics, moral and values, it is to expect that the two presidents also use different linguistic expressions, including euphemistic expressions, to communicate their messages. However, the research shows that it is not the case, at least when it comes to euphemistic expressions in war related speeches – both of them euphemize the same topics, using the same cognitive mechanisms for their creation, and employing them in almost the same proportions (as shown in Table 1.).

Metonymy-based euphemistic expressions reveal a lot about the messages George W. Bush and Barack Obama want to communicate. In order to avoid mentioning *war* itself, they frequently speak about *security, freedom, liberty,* some of the possible results of war, since they sound more acceptable, making it easier to accept war and imagine its possible outcomes. Also, by talking about the results of war, George W. Bush attempts to justify joining the war, to convince the listeners that he made the right decisions by declaring the war. FREEDOM and LIBERTY are concepts with great significance in American society, and are considered also legal human rights (e.g. 'freedom of speech'), therefore it is not unusual that they are taken advantage of to push the reality to the background. Freedom is taken as a self-implied justification for all negative effects of a political or armed conflict. Another typical example of justification of war is the usage of causes, like *defense* and *protection* instead of *war* itself. The weightiness and the seriousness of war are greatly downsized in conceptual terms by saying, for example, 'our troops *are* in Iraq', instead of 'our troops *are fighting the war* in Iraq'.

Using the lexemes *strategy* and *tactics,* two terms with a great role within the concept of war, the presidents try to make an impression of a good and serious commander in chief, and if strategy and tactics are well thought through and frequently spoken of, a message of a well-organized war will be transmitted. *War* is present as a part of presidents' *work*, as their and their soldiers' duty, something that must be done and cannot be avoided. By doing so, they try to decline the responsibility for joining and taking part in the war, and to present the war as something out of their control.

Also, the presidents attempt to soothe and embellish the expression *army*, by calling it *force*, which conceals the function of the army, featuring much more than the force itself, and also serving the purpose of encouraging the nation and motivating it for patriotism. Also, *women and men wearing the uniform* is much less direct and milder, more dignified and less dangerous sounding than the expression *soldier*. *Uniform* is a symbol of every soldier[14]. Presidents try to ingratiate soldiers and their families, because they make a huge sacrifice, and also to present them to public in an idealized way.

By saying *sacrifice* instead of *death*, DEATH is presented as something purposeful, meaningful, as something almost positive. In general, DEATH is one of the most frequently euphemized topics, being particularly delicate when politicians talk about war, and the presidents feel obliged to justify many deaths to

---

[14] And many other professions, but is used in this context as a prototypical symbol of army.

the nation and the families. DEATH in George W. Bush's speeches is an abstract concept, and in accordance with his republican ideology, war is sacred, hence also the sacrifice for the homeland. However, this is not a plausible explanation for Barack Obama's usage of this euphemistic expression. Life is the most precious thing people possess, and those who give life for their homeland are the greatest heroes. The presidents, by using euphemistic expressions, do not only soften the reality of the concept of *death*, but also attempt to comfort the families of the victims, as well as to sympathize with them.

All the mentioned topics of euphemization are systematically avoided in the speeches related to war by George W. Bush and Barack Obama, and, by persistent occurrence of euphemistic expressions instead of the original lexemes themselves, we can conclude, that they are more frequently euphemized than used literally, in their original form. For example, in the short speech *War message* by G. W. Bush from 19th March 2003, the lexeme *war* appears once in the title and twice in the text, both times in the context of the enemy, which opens up a completely new topic for discussion on the relation of euphemism with *us-them* rhetoric strategy in political discourse suggested by van Dijk (2006), whereas euphemistic expressions for *war* appear as follows: *freedom* – 2 examples, *conflict* – 3 examples, *work* and the lexemes belonging to the ICM WORK – 7 examples. In the similar manner, the lexeme *army* is used only once in the text, whereas *force*, as a euphemistic expression for *army* is used 7 times. Through the use in this fashion, the topics euphemized are becoming, or might become taboo topics, if they already are not something that should not openly be talked about.

In the same manner, Barack Obama, in his *The Plan for Afghanistan: Address at West Point* uses the lexeme *war* 15 times, whereas euphemistic expression for *war* appear at least 42 times. Also, *army* is used only twice, and *force(s)* 15 times. When it comes to *death and dying*, Barack Obama only uses *sacrifice* twice, and G. W. Bush does not mention death in any form in the speech taken as a sample.

Gradečak-Erdeljić (2005) presents a study on metonymic mapping PART OF SCENARIO FOR WHOLE SCENARIO demonstrating the way euphemism functions in discourse. Examples *body count* and *air support* demonstrate that metonymy as a cognitive mechanism underlying euphemistic expression "redirects recipients' attention from the message sent to marginal aspects of the scenario representing a political situation (287)", just as is the case in the present corpus.

Gradečak-Erdeljić and Milić (2011:163–164) also research into euphemism in the light of conceptual metonymy, particularly a very productive conceptual metonymy when it comes to the formation of euphemistic expressions in political discourse – PART OF SCENARIO FOR WHOLE SCENARIO. Their conclusion is that both politicians (speakers) and listeners (message recipients) in cases like this depend on individual selection of conceptual parts of the scenario, in other words, the purpose of metonymy in euphemization is highlighting or concealing literal meaning of the target concept, which, along with the results of the present study, partly resolves the issue of the purpose of euphemism usage in presidential war speeches.

8 Conclusions

Conceptual metonymy is omnipresent in all contexts, discourses and linguistic situations and the present analysis is based on the characteristics of the context and the messages it transmits, which is crucial in political discourse, where it is used for political purposes with the aim of influencing the audience or affirming their viewpoints. Being a cognitive process and a conceptual and linguistic phenomenon, and having the capacity of highlighting, elaborating and enhancing the meaning of the target concept, conceptual metonymy makes a perfect cognitive mechanism for the formation of euphemistic expressions.

The metonymic processes in this corpus divert attention from the relevant concepts such as WAR, ARMY AND SOLDIERS and DEATH AND DYING and highlight, push forward, elaborate on, expand, or change perspective to their contextually, situationally or personally more appropriate aspects: LIBERTY, SECURITY, PROTECTION, WORK, FORCE, UNIFORM, SACRIFICE.

In this way, under the influence of the context and the message aspiring to be transmitted, the presidents in question make these topics taboo by almost never saying out loud *war, army* or *death* when giving their own (previously written) speeches. The reasons for *tabooization* of these topics are, therefore, the same as the reasons for euphemization. They are not particularly original or new, nor are they surprising since we are dealing with political discourse here. It can be assumed, that, if looking into detail into war speeches from any other period in history, or any other leading politician, there would be found at least some chunks aimed at justifying speaker's own decisions or keeping their self-respect and respect from the public.

The research has also shown the surprising fact that both presidents, though belonging to different political, moral and life ideologies, as well as trying to achieve different political and presidential goals, euphemize the same topics almost in the same way and in the same proportion in their speeches: *war, army and soldiers* and *death*.

References

Allan, Keith & Kate Burridge. 1991. *Euphemisms & Dysphemism: Language Used as a Shield and Weapon*. New York & Oxford: Oxford University Press.
Barcelona, Antonio. 2003. The case for a metonymic basis of pragmatic inferencing: Evidence from jokes and funny anecdotes. In Klaus-Uwe Panther & Linda L. Thornburg (eds.), *Metonymy and Pragmatic Inferencing, 81–102*. Amsterdam: John Benjamins B.V.
Brdar-Szabó Rita & Mario Brdar. 2011. What do metonymic chains reveal about the nature of metonymy? In Réka Benczes, Antonio Barcelona & Francisco José Ruiz de Mendoza Ibáñez (eds.), *Defining Metonymy in Cognitive Linguistics*, 217–248. Amsterdam: John Benjamins Publishing Company.
Burridge, Kate. 2006. Euphemism and Political Correctness. In Keith Brown (ed.), *The Encyclopedia of Language and Linguistics. Volume 10*. 2nd edn., 452–455. Oxford: Elsevier.
Croft, William. 2003. The role of domains in the interpretation of metaphors and metonymies. In René Dirven & Ralf Pörings (eds.), *Metaphor and Metonymy in Comparison and Contrast*, 161–205. Berlin & New York: Mouton de Gruyter.
Gradečak-Erdeljić, Tanja. 2005. Euphemisms in the language of politics or how metonymy opens one door but closes the other. In Piotr Cap (ed.), *Pragmatics today*, 287–299. Frankfurt am Main: Peter Lang.
Gradečak-Erdeljić, Tanja& Goran Milić. 2011. Metonymy at the crossroads. A case of euphemisms and dysphemisms. In Réka Bencses, Antonio Barcelona & Francisco Jose Ruiz de Mendoza Ibanez (eds.), *Defining Metonymy in Cognitive Linguistics: Towards a consensus view*, 147–165. Amsterdam & Philadelphia: John Benjamins Publishing Company.
Gradečak-Erdeljić, Tanja&Mirna Varga. 2009. Jezik kao izvozni proizvod. Engleski eufemizmi u hrvatskom političkom diskursu. In Jagoda Granić (ed.), *Jezična politika i jezična stvarnost*, 339–348. Zagreb: HDPL.
Kuna, Branko. 2007. Identifikacija eufemizama i njihova tvorba u hrvatskom jeziku. *Flumensia* 19 (1). 95–113.
Lakoff, George. 2002. *Moral Politics. How Liberals and Conservatives Think*. Chicago: The University of Chicago Press.
Lakoff, George. 1987. *Women, Fire and Dangerous Things. What Categories Reveal about the Mind*. Chicago & London: The University of Chicago Press.
Lakoff, George, Mark Johnson. 1980. *Metaphors We Live by*. Chicago & London: The University of Chicago Press.
Langacker, Ronald W. 2008. *Cognitive Grammar. A Basic Introduction*. Oxford: Oxford University Press.
Langacker, Ronlad W. 1991. *Concept, Image and Symbol. The Cognitive Basis of Grammar*. Berlin: Mouton de Gruyter.
Langacker, Ronald W. 1993. Reference-point constructions. *Cognitive Linguistics* 4 (1). 171–202.
McNair, Brian. 2011. *Introduction to Political Communication*. London and New York: Routledge.
Moritz, Ivana. 2017. Sacrificed, lost or gave life for their country: Cognitive analysis of euphemisms for death in Bush and Obama's war speeches. In Alessandro Capone & Vahid Parvaresh (eds.), *The Pragmeme of Accommodation: The Case of Interaction around the Event of Death*, 300–318. Cham: Springer International Publishing.

Panther, Klaus-Uwe. 2005. The role of conceptual metonymy in meaning construction. In Francisco J. Ruiz de Mendoza Ibáñez and M. Sandra Peña Cervel (eds.) *Cognitive Linguistics. Internal Dynamics and Interdisciplinary Interaction*, 353–386. Berlin: Mouton de Gruyter.

Panther, Klaus-Uwe& Linda L. Thornburg. 2007. Metonymy. In Dirk Geeraerts & Hubert Chuyckens (eds.), *The Oxford Handbook of Cognitive Linguistics*, 236–263. New York & Oxford: Oxford University Press.

Peirsman, Yves & Dirk Geeraerts. 2006. Metonymy as a Prototypical Category. *Cognitive Linguistics* 17 (3). 269–316.

Radden, Günter & Zoltán Kövecses. 1999. Towards a Theory of Metonymy. In Klaus-Uwe Panther & Günter Radden (eds.), *Metonymy in Language and Thought*, 17–59. Amsterdam: John Benjamins B.V.

Reisigl, Martin. 2006. Rhetorical Tropes in Political Discourse. In Keith Brown (ed.), *The Encyclopedia of Language and Linguistics, Volume 10, 2^{nd}edn*, 596–605. Oxford: Elsevier.

Truszczyńska, Anna. 2003. Conceptual Metonymy – The Problem of Boundaries in the Light of ICMs. *Poznań Studies in Contemporary Linguistics* 38. 221–237.

Van Dijk, Teun Adrianus. 2006. Politics, Ideology and Discourse. In Keith Brown (ed.) *Encyclopedia of Language and Linguistics*. 728–740. Amsterdam: Elsevier.

Warren, Beatrice. 1992. What Euphemisms Tell us About the Interpretation of Words. *Studia Linguistica* 46 (2). 128–172.

Pedro J. Chamizo-Domínguez
4 Ambiguity and vagueness as cognitive tools for euphemistic and politically correct speech

> And as Plain Man he continued to splash solemnly about in the Vocabulary of Ambiguity.
> (C. K. Ogden and I. A. Richards)

> In the present day mistiness is the mother of wisdom.
> (Cardinal Newman)

Abstract: This contribution will deal with two topics closely related and intermingled, namely, euphemism and political correctness since both share the salient features of ambiguity and vagueness. In order to achieve my purpose, this paper is divided into three main sections as well as into an introduction. Section 1 is devoted to establishing a workable distinction between ambiguity and vagueness and to showing how both have cognitive effects (Grondelaers and Geeraerts 1998). This means that ambiguous and/or vague sentences play a fundamental, cognitive role (Tuggy 2006) when the speaker intends to be politically correct. Section 2 is focused on presenting three paradigmatic instances of dysphemism, ambiguity and vagueness, as well as showing how a given text or utterance can be dysphemistic from a cognitive point of view in spite of the fact all the terms used in it are instances of euphemisms in other contexts. Finally, section 3 is devoted to analysing how politically correct language achieves its purposes thanks it is either ambiguous or vague, or even both. And it is the case that ambiguity and vagueness are usually achieved by means of both (supposed) synonymic substitution and indirect speech acts. Both mechanisms are exemplified by appealing to actual cases, namely, the recommendations found in the guidelines of a learned society and several sings in which smoking is prohibited.

Key words: Political (in)correctness, euphemism, dysphemism, ambiguity, vagueness, censorship/prohibition.

1 Introduction: Key concepts

Speakers can achieve euphemistic effects by means of several linguistic mechanisms such as metaphors, diminutives, learned words, borrowings, allusions, and many others (Burridge 2012: 72–78). For their part, euphemisms themselves fulfil several relevant social functions (Chamizo Domínguez 2004, 2005) such as conveying dignity to a (menial) profession, being polite or respectful, or attenuating a painful topic, typically death (Bultnick 1998; Crespo Fernández 2011, 2013). Vagueness and ambiguity are two paradigmatic mechanisms that have cognitive effects and that (Grondelaers and Geeraerts 1998), when they are consciously used, allow the speakers to be euphemistic as well as achieve other additional effects such as being witty (Nerlich and Clarke 2001). In fact, Gricean maxims of Quality and Manner (Grice, [1975] 1989: 27) have to be necessarily violated by the speaker in such cases. The maxim of Quality is violated from the very moment that the synonym chosen instead of the forbidden word (or the orthophemism, in its case) has not the same exact referential meaning and, consequently, it does not have the same cognitive meaning. On its part, the maxim of Manner is violated from the very moment that both ambiguity and vagueness entail a violation of the submaxim, which recommends the avoidance of ambiguity. Among the social functions of euphemisms political correctness nowadays stands out. I will argue in this contribution that most of the political correct expressions or terms become so because they are euphemistic and they are euphemistic just because they are ambiguous or vague, to the extent that euphemism has been called "the main tool of political correctness" (Halmari 2011: 828). If so, the identification of euphemisms, as well as what political correct language might be, will depend on an adequate contextual interpretation of texts or utterances (Casas Gómez 2009).

Although the borderline between ambiguity and vagueness is not always clear (Dunbar 2001: 9–10, Tuggy 2006: 168–172) as well as in many cases it is not clear whether polysemy resides either in one particular lexical item or in its context (Taylor 2012: 220–226), (lexical) ambiguity generates in the fact that a given word (or syntagm) is polysemous (e.g. *lesbian* works as a euphemism because this noun may mean either 'from Lesbos' or 'dyke'). Syntactic ambiguity originates in the fact that a sentence can have several different meanings because its structure (e.g. a former President of the Spanish Government, the socialist Felipe González, referred to the two chiefs of the parliamentary opposition as "Anguita y Aznar son la misma mierda", which, in Spanish, can mean either "Anguita and Aznar are the same shit" or "Anguita and Aznar are the shit itself"). For its part, vagueness originates in the fact that the meaning of a given word or syntagm (hyponym) is included in the meaning of another word or syntagm (superordinate term) and people may use a superordinate term for avoiding (inconvenient) hyponyms (e.g. *restroom* works as a euphemism for *loo* because the first word can mean any room for resting as well as 'toilet' or 'bathroom'), or vice versa. The result is no other than the emergence of a vague proposition, which occurs when "there are possible states of things concerning which it is intrinsically uncertain whether, had they been contemplated by the speaker, he would have regarded them as excluded or allowed by the proposition." (Peirce 1902: 748).

The concept of political correctness has been used according to many senses (Reutner 2013). Consequently, the nominal syntagms *politically correct language* and *politically incorrect language* cover not only topics related to ethnic groups or sexual options but also many other topics such as toponymy (Wochele 2013) or diseases (Drescher 2013). In fact, political correctness may be considered "as a brainwashing programme and as simple good manners" (Allan and Burridge 2006: 90).[1] In any case, the core of my argument in the following pages will be that politically correct language has to be euphemistic and, as any euphemistic language, has to be ambiguous or vague as well (Halmari 2011).

2 Instances of dysphemisms and euphemisms

To start with, let us consider three excerpts, one quote from a 20th century British writer and two quotes from two contemporary Spanish singers:

(1) *The Professor of Gynaecology. He began his course of lectures as follows: Gentlemen, woman is an animal that* micturates *once a day,* defecates *once a week,* menstruates *once a month,* parturates *once a year and* copulates *whenever she has the opportunity. –I thought it a prettily-balanced sentence* (Maugham 1949: 15. My emphasis).

(2) *Me gusta todo de ti: /tus pezones como lilas, / tu alcancía* carmesí, */ tus ingles y tus axilas [I love everything about you: / Your nipples like lilacs, / Your* crimson *moneybox, / Your groin and your underarms]* (Serrat Teresa 1998. My emphasis).

(3) *Nada sabe tan dulce como su boca, / tan sólo* alguna cosa que no se nombra *[Nothing tastes as sweet as her mouth, /* Just something which cannot be named/is not named*]* (San José Sánchez 1986. My emphasis).

All the three texts share the following features:
1. They have been written by males and refer to women; (1) refers to woman in general while (2) and (3) refer to two specific women.

---

[1] Paradoxically, the syntagm *politically correct* is "politically correct" used to refer to what is "conforming in behaviour or language to dogmatic opinions" (Holder 2003: 306).

2. They deal with topics traditionally included under the label of taboo, topics such as bodily effluvia and pudenda (Allan and Burridge 2006: 144–174).
3. Taboo or inconvenient terms have been substituted by their respective, convenient terms which work as euphemisms.

In spite of these shared features, their cognitive effects are pretty different. (1) can be (nowadays) considered as derogatory with regard to women and even an instance of a macho chauvinist text, as well as factually false, while (2) and (3) probably do not. If so, one can ask about what makes (1) derogatory while (2) and (3) can be considered commendatory, complimentary or axiologically neuter at least.

All the verbs used to refer to bodily effluvia or sex in (1) are paradigmatic examples of euphemisms to the extent that *defecate* and *copulate* are verbs typically used in (euphemistic) medicalese instead of vulgar *shit* and *fuck*, respectively (Allan 2001: 165); whose "dignity comes from the Greek or Latin roots of the words used" (Allan and Burridge 2006: 62).[2] This means that the derogatory flavour of (1) cannot be attributed to the use of any dysphemism.

Perhaps the aforementioned derogatory flavour of (1) could be explained by hyperboles such as "defecates once a week", but hyperboles – as the rest of the figures of speech – are neither dysphemistic nor euphemistic by themselves; in fact they can be both (Burridge 2012: 75 and 78). Moreover, the professor's humorous tenor can be explained by arguing that, given he was teaching his first lesson, he was trying to achieve the *captatio benevolentiae* on the part of his students, as well as providing the adequate cognitive context for allowing some implicatures in the future.

The use of the noun 'animal' for referring to women is another plausible candidate in order to explain why (1) has acquired its derogatory flavour. But the professor could argue in his own defence he was speaking as a "scientist" and, as such and from a medical/biological point of view, human beings, whether they are male or female, can be considered as animals. Not even the use of the noun

---

[2] What is said about the English language can be said about almost any other modern European language. In the case of Romance languages, and given that most of their vocabulary derives from Latin, learned words or expressions work as euphemisms in spite of the fact that both a given learned word and a given common word can derive from the same Latin word. Consequently, one can translate into Spanish Maugham's quote and maintain all the learned words used in the original English text: "El catedrático de ginecología. Comenzó sus clases de la siguiente manera: Caballeros, la mujer es un animal que *micciona* una vez al día, *defeca* una vez a la semana, *menstrúa* una vez al mes, *partea* una vez al año y *copula* cada vez que tiene la oportunidad. –Pensé que se trataba de una frase muy bien equilibrada" (My translation).

'animal', if one disregards any other consideration, can be regarded as derogatory by itself, even if it is used for naming a woman.[3] In fact, it can be even a eulogy, as shown in the fact that Ava Garner was defined as "The World's Most Beautiful Animal" in the advertising campaign of the movie *The Barefoot Contessa* (1954).

In my opinion, what makes (1) derogatory, inconvenient or politically incorrect are three things: 1) its explicitness, since it plainly refers to bodily effluvia and sexual functions; 2) the text itself as a whole and not because any of its parts separately considered; and 3) the intentions the reader attributes to the professor and/or to S. Maugham.

By contrast, (2) and (3) can be considered as eulogistic. And what makes eulogistic both cases is that female pudenda are ambiguously and vaguely referred to. Indeed, in (2) female pudenda are referred to by means of a metaphor which is not usual. In fact, as far as I know, this metaphoric/euphemistic use of the noun *alcancía*[4] can be considered as a hapax legomenon; so, what allows us to state that it stands for *vagina* or *pussy* is the fact that it occurs together with other parts of the human body. In any case, *alcancía* works as a euphemism in this case because the author of the song converted this word in a polysemous one and, consequently, a sentence such as "Me gusta tu alcancía carmesí" is ambiguous since it can be understood either as "I love your crimson moneybox" or as "I love your crimson vagina/pussy".

As far as (3) is concerned, its euphemistic flavour can be explained by the fact that the periphrasis "alguna cosa que no se nombra" stands for *vagina* or *pussy* as well. But now we are not dealing with an instance of ambiguity originated in the fact that a given word is polysemic, but with an instance of vagueness originated in the fact that "something which is not named" is vague enough as to have the possibility of meaning anything. Not to mention that the original Spanish sentence is ambiguous since it can mean both "something which is not named [because it is not necessary since it is well-known, implicit, or assumed]" and "something which cannot be named [because it is forbidden, taboo, or inconvenient]".

---

3 Since the noun *animal* is used by our Professor together with the technical verbs *micturate, defecate, menstruate, parturate,* and *copulate,* he also could argue he only was aiming "to communicate the vocabulary and syntax of a contemporary scientific language" (Kuhn [1962] 1996: 136) as it is used in lectures and textbooks.
4 In addition, the noun *alcancía* has some archaic and/or dialectal flavour in Spain, although this is not the case in many American Spanish speaking countries.

3 Prohibiting is not politically correct

Politically correct language can be characterised by a paradox which is pretty difficult to be solved. On the one hand, although the term *political correctness* probably originated in the English translation of Mao's *The Little Red Book*, in its current conception, the phenomenon of political correctness, either as some kind of externally imposed censorship or as self-censorship about what is socially permissible or inconvenient to say by an individual, became to be widespread throughout western countries in the sixties of the 20th century, the same decade (1960–1970) in which the paradoxical motto "Il est interdit d'interdire (it is forbidden to forbid)" also became trendy (Hughes 2006: 348, 2010: 60). On the other hand, and as a consequence of my previous remark, politically correct language has to avoid terms such as *prohibit, forbid, censor, prohibition,* or *censorship*. In other words, in the same decade two phenomena, which seem to be opposed and very difficult to reconcile, emerged. This leads to the paradoxical Gordian knot that could be summarized as follows: "in the interests of political correctness it is politically incorrect to prohibit, but political correctness itself demands the prohibition, avoidance or (supposed) synonymic substitution of some words". One of the ways to cut this Gordian knot is by means of some calculated ambiguity and or vagueness of the message, so as to get two main issues: 1) the substitution of terms considered as dysphemistic and/or insulting (and even orthophemistic) by a given social group by other terms which the social group in question considers more "adequate"; and 2) the avoidance of terms which literally mean prohibition or censorship. The first method basically consists in the substitution of politically incorrect terms by supposed synonyms which are considered euphemistic just because they are ambiguous or vague. The second method basically consists in using indirect speech acts instead of direct speech acts.

3.1 Synonymic substitution

Vagueness in politically correct language is typically achieved by means of suggesting the substitution of a given term by another which is considered a plausible synonym of the term which has to be avoided. This leads us to the subject of synonymy. Let us consider one instance of this subject, where (supposed) politically incorrect connotations of several terms are intended to be avoided by prescribing their substitution for terms which (supposedly) have positive cognitive connotations.

The website of *The British Sociological Association* (*BSA*, hereinafter), under the epigraph "Language and the BSA: Sex and Gender" and with the praiseworthy purpose of "assist[ing] BSA members in avoiding sexist language by showing people some of the forms it takes and by suggesting non-sexist alternatives", includes a list of terms considered sexist and offers an alternative list of non-sexist substitutes. In this list there is one term which fits into my argument. It is about the adjective *seminal*, which is considered sexist by the authors of the aforementioned website, and, consequently to be avoided. Since *seminal* is to be avoided, two alternative substitutes are suggested, namely *classical* and *formative*. In order to shorten my paper I will focus on the case of *classical*.

In view of the fact that the BSA does not provide any account for explaining or justifying the reason that makes sexist the adjective *seminal*, one can imagine that the *ultima ratio* for such interdiction could be explained by appealing to its etymology, since the English adjective derives from the Latin noun *semen*. And, in view of the fact that the semen is something which is produced by the males of the different animal species, its derivatives have to be "guilty" of machismo. But it is the case that, in Latin, *semen* means firstly and generally *seed*, so that the meaning of "the impregnating fluid of male animals; the seed or sperm" (*OED*), is only a metonymic specification of the general meaning of the Latin noun *semen*.[5] Suggesting that *classical* can substitute *seminal* brings two matters up that are intermingled: 1) the matter of synonymy; and 2) the matter of vagueness.

The BSA can propose that *classical* substitutes *seminal* because it is tacitly assumed they are synonymous, i.e., they can be substituted one by another because both have the same (or similar, at least) meaning in whatever contexts, so that sentences in which the substitution is carried out do not change their truth values (Chamizo Domínguez 2009). I will argue that, if this substitution is possible in order to get some euphemism or some political correctness, it is not due to the fact that both adjectives are synonymous, but just to the fact they are not. Really, the adjective *seminal* has two salient meanings: 1) a literal meaning as "of or pertaining to the seed; of the nature of seed"; and 2) a figurative meaning as "having the properties of seed; containing the possibility of future development. Also, freq[uently] used of books, work, etc., which are highly original and influential; more loosely: important, central to the development or understanding of a subject" (both *OED*). Although it is not stated anywhere at the BSA website, I assume that *seminal* is to be avoided only if it is used according to its second sense, not according to its first sense. Prohibiting the use of *seminal* according

---

[5] Although not included either in the *OED* or in the *Merriam-Webster*, the noun *semen* is also used in English according to its Latin meaning by botanists in their sociolect. So, for instance, the official website of the *American Botanical Council* defines *semen* as "the seed of a plant, usually removed from the fruit, and may or may not contain the seed coat."

to its first sense as well would be obviously foolish.[6] Consequently, it is allowed to assume they refer to the figurative sense of the adjective in question. Consequently, the adjective *classical* has to be understood according to its meaning "of the first rank or authority; constituting a standard or model; especially in literature" (*OED*) and not according to any other meaning. If so, we can substitute, *salva veritate*, *seminal* for *classical*, since such substitution has to be symmetric so that the speaker says what s/he exactly wants to say. And so, because a literary or philosophical work can be classical but not necessarily seminal. For instance, Aristotle's *Metaphysics* can be considered a classical work on the doctrine about the composition of sublunary world, i.e. that all sublunary matter is composed of earth, air, fire, and water. But Aristotle's *Metaphysics* cannot be considered the seminal (i.e. original/ground-breaking) work on this topic, since Aristotle himself states very often that such doctrine was established earlier by Empedocles. So, for instance, in the following text: "'Ἀναξιμένης δὲ ἀέρα καὶ Διογένης πρότερον ὕδατος καὶ μάλιστ' ἀρχὴν τιθέασι τῶν ἁπλῶν σωμάτων,'Ἵππασος δὲ πῦρ ὁ Μεταποντῖνος καὶ Ἡράκλειτος ὁ Ἐφέσιος, Ἐμπεδοκλῆς δὲ τὰ τέτταρα, πρὸς τοῖς εἰρημένοις γῆν προστιθεὶς τέταρτον" (*Metaphysics*, 984a 8–9).[7]

Accordingly, one can say that while the sentence (4) is false (or inaccurate at least), (5) is true:

(4) *Aristotle's seminal four element theory was accepted until 17–18th centuries*
(5) *Aristotle's classical four element theory was accepted until 17–18th centuries.*

By contrast, if one replaces the name *Aristotle* with the name *Empedocles*, both sentences are (or can be) true. And so because something, which is seminal, uses to be (or at least may be) classical, but something, which is classical, is not necessarily seminal.[8] Consequently, if someone is obliged to replace *seminal* with

---

[6] Although it is at no time specified by *BSA*, it is reasonable to think that its zeal for political correctness goes not so far as to forbid the use of *seminal* in collocations as *seminal fluid*; since, in this case, we would not be speaking of a matter of synonymy. And so because, if one substitutes *seminal fluid* for *classical fluid*, we are not in the face of a matter of a euphemistic synonym but in the face of a jocular situation. In fact, *seminal fluid* is considered as an orthophemism with regard to *spunk* or *spoof* (Allan and Burridge 2006: 151).
[7] The authoritative English translation by Sir William David Ross reads as follows: "Anaximenes and Diogenes make air prior to water, and the most primary of the simple bodies, while Hippasus of Metapontium and Heraclitus of Ephesus say this of fire, and Empedocles says it of the four elements (adding a fourth – earth – to those which have been named)." (Aristotle, [1924] 2014).
[8] Although not included in other dictionaries, the *Collins English Dictionary* also lists the sense of "rudimentary or unformed". This new sense also fits Empedocles in very well, since, as far as

classical when s/he wants to mean that something is highly original, influential, important, and capable of later developments or something like this, s/he would probably be betraying his/her thought.

3.2 Indirect speech acts

Eventually, an accomplished example of being sat on the fence is the resort to indirect speech acts in order to prohibit and being politically correct at once. This is what typically happens in signs in which something is "kindly" or "mildly" prohibited (Suhr and Johnson 2003), or, conversely, something is recommended in advertising (Wenzhong and Jingyi 2013). Let us focus on the case of no smoking signs. Let us start by considering the following sign:

Figure 1: Explicitness as political incorrectness.

Figure 1 is a paradigmatic example of both political incorrectness and explicitness, or to put it the other way round, its explicitness is the reason of its political incorrectness, if we accept that prohibiting is prohibited and, consequently, politically incorrect since May 68. The Canadian City of Surrey (British Columbia) Government's zeal for making explicit that smoking is not allowed in certain places brings them to minimise the possibilities of misunderstanding their message. Consequently, they make clear:
1. That smoking is prohibited in a given building.

---

we know according to the texts that exist, he did not develop his four element theory. And, again, it would make false *Aristotle's seminal four element theory was accepted until 17–18th centuries*, since Aristotle left us a very fastidious four element theory.

2. The (minimum) distance from any opening of the building within which smoking is prohibited.
3. Since the prohibition of smoking is general, it implicitely includes not only tobacco, but also other smokable products such as marijuana or herbal blends.
4. The maximum amount of the penalty with which violators will be punished.

Having said that and according to the principle that what is not forbidden is allowed, the use of chewing tobacco or snuff would be allowed by the Government of the City of Surrey inside or within 7.5 meters of any opening of the building in question. In order to avoid such kind of objections, other signs are more explicit with regard to the point about what actions are included under a no smoking prohibition.

Figure 2: Explicitness as political incorrectness.

Indeed, possible objections to Figure 1 are avoided in Figure 2, since it is explicitly prohibited both smoking, which includes marijuana or herbal blends, and the use of tobacco products, which includes chewing tobacco and snuff in addition to cigarettes, pipe tobacco, and cigars. Not to mention that the zeal of the Government of the State of Iowa for making explicit this prohibition goes so far as to substitute the mere and easy adverb *always* for the periphrasis "24 hours per day, 7 days per week".[9]

---

[9] In fact, this periphrasis seems to be more typical of a mall sign or a petrol station than of a sign published by the Government of a State.

4 Ambiguity and vagueness as cognitive tools — 89

In any case, the explicitness of figures 1 and 2 is just what makes them impolite or politically incorrect since both include direct speech acts of prohibitions. In order to be polite by honouring the motto "it is forbidden to forbid" and forbid in fact at once, speakers appeal to ambiguity. Let us consider some instances of this:

(6) *Thank you for observing our no smoking policy.*
(7) *Benzene is found in gasoline and cigarettes.*

Figure 3: Vagueness as political correctness.

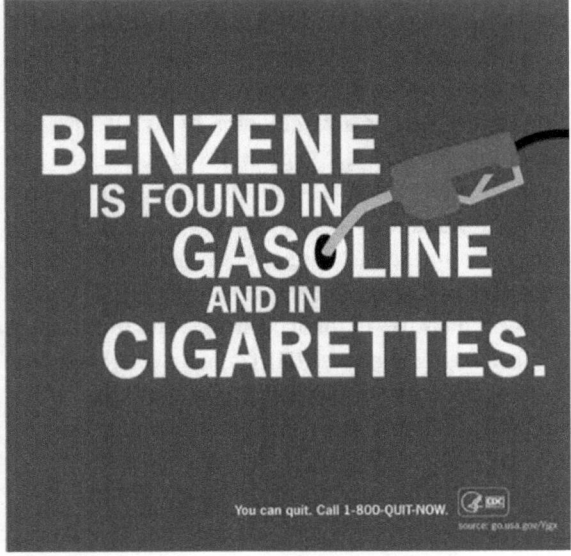

Figure 4: Vagueness as political correctness.

In (6) impolite and politically incorrect, but explicit and direct utterances, *No smoking* or *Smoking is prohibited* have been substituted by a sentence in which both ambiguity and vagueness occur. Ambiguity originates in the fact that, instead of the noun *prohibition* or any of its synonyms, we find the noun *policy*.[10] As a result of this, *policy* works as a euphemism because, in this case, this noun does not mean what usually means, i.e. a principle of action adopted or proposed by an organization, group, or individual, but *prohibition* or *banning*. As well as it probably works as a "purr word", or word in which its positive emotive meaning prevail over its referential meaning (Leech 1974: 50 and ff.) with regard to *regulation* or *rule*. Vagueness originates in the fact that someone thanks the reader for not smoking, instead of an explicit proscription of smoking; that is to say, while the implication of (6) is an act of gratitude, its implicature is the prohibition of smoking. But, since any implicature can be cancelled if the hearer/reader cannot be or wants not to be cooperative (Grice [1975] 1989), the reader of Figure 3 can interpret (6) according to what it literally means and the implicature will cease to have the desired effect. In this case the hearer/reader will understand that someone acknowledges or shows gratitude for the fact that people do not smoke, not that smoking itself is prohibited.

In (7) the ambiguity of the message in order to achieve a euphemistic effect is going beyond any previous examples, if we assume that, who wrote it, tried to politely mean "Smoking is discouraged" (Lee and Pinker 2010). In (7) not even *no smoking* is written or alluded to, it only states that benzene can be found in both gasoline and cigarettes. But this assertion is, in fact, an ambiguous euphemistic substitute of an advice, recommendation, counsel, or suggestion. In fact, if someone argues that smoking is inadvisable on account of the fact that tobacco smoke contains benzene and this compound is a carcinogen, by using an *a pari* argument, one can argue that gasoline (or gasoline vapour) is carcinogen as well and, consequently, the use of gasoline should be also discouraged, since, when refuelling, gasoline vapour can be inhaled and it is in fact, even if it is in small quantities. Needless to say one can counterargue that smoking is not necessary whereas the use of gasoline is not only necessary but also unavoidable nowadays. But, given I am not speaking about the virtues of tobacco smoke and the hazards of gasoline vapours or vice versa, what is clear is that (7) is an assertion that describes a truth of fact. And, from the truth of fact described in (7), its author pretends that the reader understands that smoking is not recommended and not

---

10 If Yahweh were politically correct when He gave Moses the Ten Commandments, he should have said, for instance, *Thank you for observing my no murdering policy* instead of the impolite *You shall not murder*.

that the use of gasoline is not recommended. In other words, the ambiguity of the recommendation or prohibition under the shape of an assertion is what makes (7) politically correct as opposed to other less acceptable (from the political correctness point of view) or inacceptable signs such as "Smoking is not recommendable".

Sometimes, resorting to polite politically correct signs such as (7) seems to be not enough in order to make clear that something is not recommendable probably because of the ambiguity itself of (7). In such cases, messages which are polite and impolite at once can be found, as happens in this sign published by the Authorities of the State of Washington:

(8) *Smoking is prohibited within 25 feet of all building entrances. Thank you for not smoking.*

Figure 5: Political correctness and incorrectness at once.

This sign refers to the *Washington Clean Air Act*, which establishes that 1) "Smoking is prohibited within a presumptively reasonable minimum distance of twenty-five feet from entrances, exits, windows that open, and ventilation intakes that serve an enclosed area where smoking is prohibited so as to ensure that tobacco smoke does not enter the area through entrances, exits, open windows, or other means" (*RCW* 70.160.075) and 2) "Any person intentionally violating this chapter by smoking in a public place or place of employment, or any person removing, defacing, or destroying a sign required by this chapter, is subject to a civil fine of up to one hundred dollars" (*RCW* 70.160.070).[11] Things being so, one can wonder why, if something is obliged by law, someone has to thank for it. And vice versa, one thanks for something that people are not obliged to do or refrain from doing, not for something that people are obliged to abstain from. Furthermore, given the fact that people will be fined if they violate the order in question. Unless the sentence "thank you for not smoking" has become an empty phrase or, at the most, fulfils a mere phatic function.

Finally, politeness and political correctness seem to be applicable to the speakers of some languages and not to the speakers of other languages. This is the case of Figure 6.

Figure 6: Political correctness in English and incorrectness in Spanish.

In Figure 6,[12] the ambiguous and polite English version ("This is a smoke-free facility. Thank you for not smoking") becomes the explicit (and consequently "impolite") explanation of a prohibition: "En este edificio es prohibido fumar" [literally, "It is forbidden to smoke in this building"]. Should one think that who

---

11 *RCW* is the acronym of *Revised Code of Washington*. Available at: http://app.leg.wa.gov/rcw/default.aspx?cite=70.94 (Accessed 7 May 2016).
12 I do not know whether this sign has been factually used somewhere. In fact, I found it at the website of a sign company: http://www.safetysign.com/products/p7270/bilingual-this-is-a-smoke-free-sign (Accessed 7 May 2016).

wrote the Spanish version thought that politeness (or political correctness) had nothing to do with Spanish speakers?[13] Is not this a case of an ethnic and/or linguistics insult? And to add insult to injury even the Spanish sentence is ungrammatical, since, in correct Spanish, it should be either "En este edificio está prohibido fumar" or "En este edificio se prohíbe fumar". Not to mention that the addition "Gracias por no fumar" makes no sense when joined to an explicit prohibition, as it happens in Figure 5.

4 Conclusions

Among the various linguistic mechanisms that euphemistic and/or politically correct language use to achieve their cognitive goals (e.g. diminutives, terms loaned from a foreign language or a specific sociolect such as medicalese or legalese, periphrases or circumlocutions, and so on) this contribution focused on analysing ambiguity and vagueness. Ambiguity and vagueness are so relevant in order to achieve a euphemistic or politically correct speech that one can find dysphemistic and/or politically incorrect texts where all the words used in them are adequate candidates to be considered euphemisms (and even technical terms in a given sociolect) when they are considered by themselves or in any other context.

These considerations have been put to the test in two particular case studies. The first case study is focused on the guidelines of a learned society where some synonyms are suggested in order to avoid other (factual or supposed) dysphemistic or politically incorrect words. Since it is the case that suggested words are less precise than the banned ones are, the sentences or utterances in which such words are used have necessarily to be less precise, and, for this very reason, vaguer. And, from this very moment, these words/sentences become acceptable.

The second case is focused on the analysis of a series of signs in which smoking is prohibited. Among these signs, the politically correct ones are those prohibitions that are not directly expressed, but suggested by means of an indi-

---

13 This recalls me the case of *Friedhof Große Hamburger Straße* (the oldest Jewish cemetery in Berlin), where, among other notorious members of the Jewish Community of Berlin, the philosopher Moses Mendelssohn (1729–1786) was buried. All the historical, religious, or cultural, significant information for understanding what this historical site symbolises is written in Hebrew and German, except the list of prohibitions (e.g. "Men and married women have to cover their heads inside the burial ground" or "It is forbidden to eat, drink, or smoke inside the burial ground"), which is written in English as well.

rect speech act or by an implicature, counting on the fact that the hearer will be cooperative and will interpret certain assertions as polite orders, rules, or prohibitions. In both cases what makes acceptable (or more tolerable than the explicit prohibition would be) the sign in question is just the fact of achieving a message as vague as possible.

In short, far from being an obstacle to communication, "ambiguity is in fact a *desirable* property of communication systems" (Piantadosi, Tily & Gibson 2012: 281. Original italics) and, when the speaker intends to be euphemistic and/or politically correct, ambiguity is not only desirable, but unavoidable as well in most cases.

5 References

Allan, Keith. 2001. *Natural Language Semantics*. Malden: Blackwell.
Allan, Keith and Kate Burridge. 2006. *Forbidden Words. Taboo and the Censoring of Language*. Cambridge: Cambridge University Press.
American Botanical Council. Available at: http://abc.herbalgram.org/site/PageServer?pagename=Terminology (Accessed October 2016).
Aristotle. [1924] 2014. *Metaphysics*. Translated by W. D. Ross. Adelaide: The University of Adelaide Press. Available at: https://ebooks.adelaide.edu.au/a/aristotle/metaphysics/index.html (Accessed 20 November 2016).
British Sociological Association. Language and the BSA: Sex and Gender. Available at http://www.britsoc.co.uk/about/equality.aspx Accessed 30 October 2016.
Bultnick, Bernhardt. 1998. *Metaphors We Die By: Conceptualizations of Death in English and their Implications for the Theory of Metaphor*. Antwerp: Universitet Antwerpen.
Burridge, Kate. 2012. Euphemism and Language Change: The Sixth and Seventh Ages. *Lexis* 7. 65–92.
Casas Gómez, Miguel. 2009. Towards a new approach to the linguistic definition of euphemism. *Language Sciences* 31. 725–739.
Chamizo Domínguez. 2004. La función social y cognitiva del eufemismo y del disfemismo. *Panace@*, 15. 45–51. Available at: http://www.medtrad.org/panacea/IndiceGeneral/n15_tribuna-ChamizoDominguez.pdf (Accessed 20 November 2016).
Chamizo Domínguez. 2005. Some theses on euphemisms and dysphemisms. *Studia Anglica Resoviensia* 25. 9–16.
Chamizo-Domínguez, Pedro José. 2009. Linguistic Interdiction: Its status quaestionis and possible future research lines. *Language Sciences* 31. 428–446.
Collins English Dictionary. Available at: http://www.collinsdictionary.com/dictionary/english (Accessed 2 October 2016).
Crespo-Fernández, Eliecer. 2011. Euphemistic Conceptual Metaphors in Epitaphs from Highgate Cemetery. *Review of Cognitive Linguistics* 9 (1). 198–225.

Crespo-Fernández, Eliecer. 2013. Euphemistic Metaphors in English and Spanish Epitaphs: A Comparative Study. *Atlantis. Journal of the Spanish Association of Anglo-American Studies* 35 (2). 99–118.

Drescher, Martina. 2013. La gestion des tabous dans la communication sur le VIH/sida en Afrique francophone. In Ursula Reutner & Elmar Schafroth (eds.), *Political Correctness*, 389–402. Berlin: Peter Lang.

Dunbar, George, 2001. Towards a Cognitive Analysis of Polysemy, Ambiguity and Vagueness. *Cognitive Linguistics* 12 (1). 1–14.

Fergusson, Rosalind. 1986. *The Penguin Dictionary of English Synonyms and Antonyms*. Harmondsworth: Penguin.

Grice, Herbert Paul. [1975] 1989. Logic and Conversation. In *Studies in the Way of Words*, 22–40. Cambridge (Mass.): Harvard University Press.

Grondelaers, Stefan & Dirk Geeraerts. 1998. Vagueness as a euphemistic strategy. In Angeliki Athanasiadou & Elzbieta Tabakowska (eds.), *Speaking of Emotions: Conceptualisation and Expression*, 357–374. Berlin & New York: Mouton de Gruyter.

Halmari, Helena. 2011. Political correctness, euphemism, and language change: The case of 'people first'. *Journal of Pragmatics* 43 (3). 132–151.

Holder, Robert W. 2003. *A Dictionary of Euphemisms. How Not To Say What You Mean*. Oxford: Oxford University Press.

Hughes, Geoffrey. 2006. *An Encyclopedia of Swearing: The social history of oaths, profanity, foul language, and ethnic slurs in the English-speaking world*. New York: M. E. Sharpe.

Hughes, Geoffrey. 2010. *Political Correctness. A History of Semantics and Culture*. Oxford-Malden: Wiley-Blackwell.

Kuhn, Thomas S. [1962] 1996. *The Structure of Scientific Revolutions*. Chicago: The University of Chicago Press.

Lee, James J. and Steven Pinker. 2010. Rationales for Indirect Speech: The Theory of the Strategic Speaker. *Psychological Review* 117 (3). 785–807.

Leech, Geoffrey. 1974. *Semantics*. Harmondsworth: Penguin.

Maugham, William Somerset. 1949. *A Writer's Notebook*. New York: Doubleday & Company.

Merriam-Webster Dictionary. Available at: http://www.merriam-webster.com/ (Accessed 25 October 2016).

Nerlich, Brigitte & David D. Clarke. 2001. Ambiguities We Live By: Towards a Pragmatics of Polysemy. *Journal of Pragmatics* 33 (1). 1–20.

OED. 1989. *The Oxford English Dictionary*. Edited by J. A. Simpson & E. S. C. Weiner. Oxford: Clarendon Press.

Peirce, Charles Sanders. 1902. Vague. In J. M. Baldwin (ed.). *Dictionary of Philosophy and Psychology*, 748. New York: MacMillan.

Piantadosi, Steven T., Harry Tily & Edward Gibson. 2012. The communicative function of ambiguity in language. *Cognition* 122. 280–291.

Reutner, Ursula. 2013. Descamando un camaleón conceptual: un análisis del empleo del término *políticamente (in)correcto* en el diario español *El País*. In Ursula Reutner & Elmar Schafroth (eds.). *Political Correctness*, 123–156. Berlin: Peter Lang.

San José Sánchez, Víctor Manuel. 1986. Nada sabe tan dulce como su boca. In *Para la ternura siempre hay tiempo*. Madrid: Sony-Columbia.

Serrat Teresa, Joan Manuel. 1998. Me gusta todo de ti (pero tú no). In *Sombras de la China*. Barcelona: BMG Ariola.

Suhr, Stephanie & Sally Johnson. 2003. Re-visiting 'PC': Introduction to Special Issue on 'Political Correctness'. *Discourse & Society* 14 (1). 5–16.
Taylor, John R. 2012. *The Mental Corpus. How Language is Represented in the Mind*. Oxford: Oxford University Press.
Tuggy, David. 2006. Ambiguity, polysemy, and vagueness. In Dirk Geeraerts, (ed.). *Cognitive Linguistics: Basic Readings*, 167–184. Berlin & New York: Mouton de Gruyter.
Wenzhong, Zhu & Li Jingyi. 2013. A Pragmatic Study on the Functions of Vague Language in Commercial Advertising. *English Language Teaching* 6 (6). 103–112.
Wochele, Holger. 2013. *Fiume* oppure *Rijeka*, *Gand* (*Guanto*) o *Gente*, *Hermannstadt* o *Sibiu*? Correttezza politica e uso di esonimi. In Ursula Reutner & Elmar Schafroth (eds.). *Political Correctness*, 241–248. Berlin: Peter Lang.

Part II: **Cultural Conceptualization**

Réka Benczes, Kate Burridge, Keith Allan, Farzad Sharifian
5 Old age revolution in Australian English: Rethinking a taboo concept

Abstract: We age from the moment we are born. This is a completely natural process, and yet ageing is now a matter of strong taboo. No one wants to evoke it too vividly, and the fall-out is a flourishing of verbal vanishing creams and linguistic makeovers in the form of euphemism. And yet, as baby boomers are reaching retirement age and wish to remain active for many more decades, they are redefining the concept of ageing considerably (Kalache 2012). This redefinition is all the more relevant in Australia, which has the third highest proportion of people aged over 65 in the world.

Using a web-based database of Australian newspapers (http://www.factiva.com) 1987 to 2014 (1987 being the year when the term "successful ageing" entered gerontological literature), we searched for words and expressions related to ageing to support our main hypothesis that ageing is undergoing a major reconceptualization in Australian English.[1] Our findings strongly suggest that this reconceptualization of ageing is manifested in: 1) the emergence of novel conceptual categories (the degree of entrenchment of *successful ageing* as compared to *healthy ageing* in Australian English; 2) category extension (analysis of the phrase *older Australians*, which is producing dynamic growth rates in the media as compared to the more established *seniors*); and 3) novel conceptual metaphors and cultural schemas (as manifested in the naming practices of aged care facilities).

Keywords: ageing, euphemism, cognitive linguistics, taboo, conceptual metaphor, conceptual metonymy, cultural schema, reconceptualization

1 Introduction

There are certain things in life speakers and writers would rather not evoke too vividly and growing old has become one of these – probably not surprisingly, given the end of the ageing process is death. Even those with strong religious beliefs are not usually in a hurry to meet their maker. And those who are lucky

---

[1] For a full list of these terms, see http://artsonline.monash.edu.au/lsc/the-cultural-model-of-ageing-the-australian-conceptualisation-of-the-third-age/

https://doi.org/10.1515/9783110582758-006

enough to live to become old have to face some unpleasant potential consequences of old age, such as infirmity, loss, dependence and increasing alienation (a growing problem for the elderly whose social networks are more fragmented and harder to maintain).

Technology has intensified the negative associations, and anxieties, surrounding the ageing experience by feeding a fairy tale that perpetual well-being and ever-lasting youth are within our grasp. Fresh medical breakthroughs routinely rescue people from death. There are products of modern science – pain relief, tranquillisers, the pill, fertility drugs, Viagra, hormone replacement therapy, Botox, hair dyes – that have made it possible to control some aspects of ageing. Digitally altered images of designer bodies feed the fairy tale, as do the big companies who profit from modern health preoccupations. Advances in cosmetic surgery – face lifts, tummy tucks, breast enhancements, pectoral and calf implants, penile reconstruction – have meant we can change the way we look and function. Ironically, the increased life expectancy that modern medicine now affords us has considerably added to the negative perceptions of old age. These days ageing is disparaged also from the point of view of the burden that old people place on society at large – a longer life means more exposure to disease and ill-health and this means greater encumbrances on relatives and on already stretched resources. It all makes the reality of ageing bodies that much harder to bear.

Australia has additional historical factors that reinforce a negative view of old age because of a long-standing tradition of the country perceiving itself as a "youthful society". This still seems to be strong in people's conceptualizations. Within the scope of our research project on language and ageing, we have interviewed several older Australians who are considered as role models in society. One of them told us that in Australia older people in general are shunned, because "culturally Aussies don't like you being old".[2] Davison (1993) was one of the first Australian researchers to draw attention to this phenomenon. In tracing the roots of Australian ageism to the late nineteenth and early twentieth centuries, he attributes it to three main factors.[3]

First, Australia's association as a "youthful" society: Australia – especially colonial Australia – was used to thinking of itself (and being thought of) as a "young society", especially in contrast with Britain, "the Old Country" (as it was commonly referred to), and of course the high percentage of young people in early

---

[2] We conducted eleven interviews with Australians who were either nominated for or won the Senior Australian of the Year award. The interviews were carried out in Australia in 2016.
[3] See Benczes et al. (2017) for an elaboration of these three factors.

colonial Australian society strengthened this view (in the 1850s, at the height of immigration, the proportion of people aged 65 or more was around 1%). Second, the early introduction of the old age pension (in 1909): as Davison explains, "[a]t the heart of the case for the Old Age pensions was the idea that old people deserved recognition, not on account of their dignity or wisdom or rights *as old people*, but as a delayed reward for what they had contributed to their country *in their youth*. It thus simultaneously confirmed the moral claim of the old for state support while reinforcing the belief that it was the young who had most to contribute to the progress of the nation" (pp. 20–21; emphasis as in original). Finally, changes in religious views: Darwinism challenged the traditional view of old age (as a reward for a virtuous life) by conceptualizing life as a struggle, and old people were the least well equipped for this struggle. To this we might also add the waning power of the Christian faith generally in English-speaking societies like Australia; religion provided a reason for living and also for dying, but without such religious conviction, the fear of a meaningless end has intensified the taboos surrounding the subject of death, and the process leading up to it – that of growing old.

2 Talking about "growing old"

The question necessarily arises, therefore, how do we talk about ageing if it is considered to be such a sensitive subject? One of the most common strategies is to use euphemism.[4] Very broadly, euphemistic expressions are sweet-sounding, or at least inoffensive, alternatives for those that speakers or writers prefer not to use in executing a particular communicative intention on a given occasion (Allan and Burridge 1991; 2006). In their primary function, they are characterized by avoidance language and evasive expression, and we create them using a variety of different linguistic devices (cf. Allan 2012; Burridge 2012). These fall into three overarching mechanisms: analogy (generalizing forms to new situations), distortion (modifying forms in some way) and borrowing (incorporating forms from elsewhere). None of these processes are mutually exclusive, and many expressions involve at the same time a number of different devices. For instance, euphemistic expressions such as *at the evening of one's days* and *the autumn* or *the winter of one's life* for "old" are metaphorical, long-winded and hyperbolic,

---

[4] See Pizarro Pedraza (this volume) for an elaboration on the relationship between social identity and semantic variation within the scope of sexual concepts.

as are the expressions *mutton dressed up as lamb* and *long in the tooth*. *No spring chicken* is an example of metaphor and understatement. *Past it* illustrates a general-for-specific euphemism and also omission (leaving out *one's prime* from the end of the phrase).

Time typically blows the cover of any euphemistic disguise, and there are internal forces at work in language change to ensure that the majority of expressions are doomed to be short-lived. One is semantic pejoration. Taboo areas of the lexicon perpetually generate a narrowing and deterioration of meaning. As the euphemistic expressions become sullied by the disagreeable concepts they designate, the negative associations reassert themselves and undermine the euphemistic quality of the word, and the next generation of speakers grows up learning the word as the direct term (orthophemism). Jespersen once described this as "the usual destiny of euphemisms" – the "innocent word" becomes "just as objectionable as the word it has ousted and now is rejected in its turn" ([1905] 1962: 230). This promotes an ever-changing chain of vocabulary replacements for words denoting taboo concepts, something Steven Pinker once referred to as the "euphemistic treadmill" (though the image of an ever-grinding lexical mill is perhaps a more accurate one). As Pinker (2002: 213) remarks, people have concepts, and not words, in their heads. When a concept that has a negative connotation is given a new name, the concept tarnishes the name over time; therefore, the effect of the new name wears off rather quickly, which means that new euphemisms need to be constantly generated. In other words, the referent ultimately remains the same; it is the word form that changes. Few euphemisms that have degraded in this way into taboo terms come back from the abyss, even after they have lost their taboo sense (cf. Allan and Burridge 1991; 2006).

In the case of "old age", the pejoration can be rapid. As society's prejudiced perceptions foment, the euphemistic value is diluted and the negative connotations quickly reattach themselves, requiring the formation of a new euphemism. *Senile* "belonging to old age" dates from the 1600s; Samuel Johnson's dictionary has entries such as "a senile maturity of judgment", but the word soon started to deteriorate and, with the exception of disease names such as *senile dementia*, is now dysphemistic. *Senility* has suffered a similar fate, evident in Charles Lamb's now striking description "he is yet in green and vigorous senility" (*Essays of Eli*, first published 1823); here the clash of meaning renders the quotation extremely odd. A further example is *geriatrics* ("the branch of medicine / social science to do with the health of old people"). The adjective *geriatric* started life in the 1920s also as an orthophemistic description; though both the adjective and noun retain a neutral sense within medical jargon, in everyday usage they were already contemptuous terms by the 1960s.

It is also true to say that some euphemisms are simply so fleeting that they never linger long enough to become unfit for use. Many expressions simply shuffle off the lexical coil before they have a chance to deteriorate: expressions to do with "old age" such as *ultra-mature, chronologically gifted, experientially enhanced, dynamic maturity, seasoned citizen, golden ager* were short-lived; few would have them as part of their active vocabulary these days. Unlike other euphemisms that maintain a low profile, these obscure and disguise disagreeable reality by doing something clever or humorous with the language; these creations refuse to take the back seat normally reserved for the regular face-saving euphemisms (to draw on Dwight Bolinger's image for anaphora; 1980: 96). The life expectancy of these more attention seeking euphemisms is very often short, and so they escape the chronic contagion generally associated with euphemism. Speakers and writers constantly strive to enhance expression and supply new and exciting ways of communicating. This sort of emotional extravagance drives change at all linguistic levels, but especially the lexicon, and in particular, it is the culturally potent words that fray the fastest. Many euphemisms involve slang, and the mark of slang is that it will quickly date. The point of these expressions is to startle, to amuse and to shock – they have to stand out, and so they have to be novel.

The word *age* and its derived forms *ageing* and *aged* offer yet another prospect for the duration of a euphemism. *Age* refers literally to "length of life, period of existence". When it entered English from French some time during the 14th century it had already acquired the meaning "period of human life", but had soon narrowed to "the end part of life". From the beginning of the 18th century, the term *age* could refer quite generally to "old age", "senility" (as a quotation from the *Oxford English Dictionary* illustrates: "the moroseness and peevishness of age"). Since the 1400s, the central sense of *aged* has been "the latter part of life", and since the 1550s *ageing* has also been used to refer to "the process of growing old". From birth we are ageing and yet the meaning is always "old". These three terms have narrowed but have so far resisted contamination; in most contexts they are now orthophemistic; in other words, the direct terms, being neither sweet-sounding, evasive, overly polite (euphemistic), nor harsh, blunt, offensive (dysphemistic). For instance, a University of New England study found that elderly people in Australia preferred to be seen as "citizens who were ageing" as opposed to "old people", because they did not feel old (Pountney 1998). Thus, like *elderly* (which has been in the language since the early 1600s), *aged* and *ageing* have in common that they allude to taboo topics in a very remote way; their association lacks any sort of precision, and it is perhaps this that allows them to remain unobtrusive and escape the corrosion of expressions such as *senile* and *geriatric*.[5]

3 The "longevity revolution" and the reconceptualization of ageing

In the past two decades or so, we have been witnessing a "longevity revolution" (former Director of the WHO's Health of the Elderly program, Alexander Kalache's term). According to the Australian Bureau of Statistics,[6] the median age (the age at which half the population is older and half is younger) of the Australian population has increased from 33.4 years in 1994 to 37.3 years in 2014. It is projected that over the next 40 years, the proportion of the population over 65 years will almost double to around 25 %.

Why are these changes occurring in the population? Researchers often mention low fertility rates and medical breakthroughs as significant factors. However, a big part of the ageing picture is the baby boom generation – the statistical "pig in the python" as it is sometimes described. The boomers are now reaching retirement age and would like to remain active and productive for many more decades. By doing so, they are reshaping how we think about ageing and old age considerably. In Alexander Kalache's (2012) words, "Never before have we seen a cohort hitting the age of 65 who are so well informed, so wealthy and in such good health ... [we] are ... *redefining what it means to age*. We are witnessing the emergence of a 'gerontolescence', a new period of transition" (emphasis added).

Is there, however, a reconceptualization taking place in Australia? Davison (1993), while pointing out the inevitable ageing of the Australian population and the inherent ageism of Australian society, emphasized that "[w]hether Australia will grow gracefully and kindly depends, not only on the brute facts of demography and economics, but upon *how we think about older people, and how we conceptualise the process of getting older*" (p. 1; our emphasis).

---

[5] Cf. McGlone, Beck and Pfiester (2006) write about "pragmatic stealth and mindlessness-inducing qualities" (p. 279), claiming that familiar euphemisms remain polite over long periods precisely because they come to offer routine and unexciting ways of indirectly mentioning taboo topics. Yet familiarity effects cannot provide the whole story here, since expressions have to survive in the first place in order to become routine.

[6] Source: http://www.abs.gov.au; accessed: 30 June 2015.

Generally speaking, Australian society is aware of the change in people's attitudes to ageing, which has been exacerbated by the so-called "new aged" (McCallum 1997) – the baby boomers. According to the Australian Longitudinal Study of Ageing (2006), the majority of the 2,000 people aged over 65 that participated in the study enjoyed an active and high-quality life, and the respondents had "a strong sense of psychological well-being [...] maintained well into advanced old age" (p. 65). McCallum (1997) remarked on this phenomenon very aptly: "There's a new mood among Australia's aged. They've slipped out of grey, ill-fitting clothes into bicycle pants and Reeboks. They've occupied Australia's beach resorts and are a significant political force in those communities and nationally. ... Rather than being described as 'over the hill', they can be now characterised as 'storming the hill', taking the high ground and holding on to it" (ibid.). This change in attitude, however, has brought about an onomasiological problem with it: how can this new outlook on old age be expressed with the right words? Note McCallum's (ibid.) ponderings on the inadequacy of the language to express this change: "The old-age pensioner name tag is now as ill-fitting as the discarded grey clothes."

Thus, our main hypothesis is that ageing is indeed undergoing a major reconceptualization in Australian English, and that this process can be best analysed within a cognitive linguistic framework of the euphemistic (figurative) language used in connection to ageing. Cognitive linguistics has been especially successful in the description and analysis of cultural conceptualisations (Sharifian 2011) and figurative language use (Benczes 2006a), including euphemisms (e.g., Benczes 2006b; Gradečak-Erdeljić 2005; Portero Muñoz 2011). It is very much hoped that this current paper can open up further avenues into the investigation of taboo domains such as ageing within a cognitive linguistic paradigm.

Based on this assumption we also wish to argue that this reconceptualization of ageing will be manifested in 1) the emergence of novel conceptual categories, 2) category extension, and 3) novel conceptual metaphors and cultural schemas.

3.1 Novel conceptual categories

The year 1987 can be considered as a milestone in gerontological literature, as this was the year when the term "successful ageing" (Rowe and Kahn 1987) entered gerontological terminology to denote the idea that an ever-increasing number of older people were leading an active and healthy lifestyle and were still contributing to society. However, there has been much disagreement in gerontological literature on what "successful ageing" implies (see Baltes and Carstensen 1996;

Depp et al. 2010; Peel et al. 2005), depending on what aspects (physical, psychological, social, spiritual, etc.) are being focused on.

In their classic article, Rowe and Kahn (1987) defined successful ageing in adults primarily as the absence of physical and cognitive disabilities, and the ability to engage with society and to be productive in their own eyes and the eyes of others. Yet more recent data, drawing especially on studies based on the incorporation of older adults, imply that those affected consider subjective qualities, such as emotional well-being and social and community involvement, more important than objective ones, such as physical and mental health (Depp and Jeste 2009; Depp et al. 2010; Lamond et al. 2008).

Thus, *successful ageing* has become a novel conceptual category, a subordinate-level category of *ageing*. There are major implications of this subcategorization. First, ageing is no longer a general process that affects everybody similarly. Rather, it is now perceived as something over which people can exercise some control. There are various ways to age, such as *successful ageing* or *positive ageing*, and it is an individual's choice to decide what "type" of ageing s/he will pursue. Second, the category of *successful ageing* evokes a COMPETITION frame, where the adversary is ageing, and we can fight ageing by overcoming its negative effects. People who manage to do so are *successful agers*. The problem with this conceptualization is that it also suggests that those who are not successful in overcoming the negative effects of ageing[7] are "losers" who "didn't try hard enough" (Horin 2012).[8] Yet "trying hard enough" to *combat* ageing or *halt* the ageing process (verbs that routinely show up with *ageing* in language) has to start quite early on, in middle age.[9] According to the longest ongoing study of adult development, the Grant Study (or Harvard Study of Adult Development), which has followed the lives of 724 white American males for more than seventy years,

---

[7] Rowe and Kahn (1987) contrasted successful ageing with "usual ageing" – the latter referring to the condition when there is a high risk of acquiring some sort of chronic disease. Successful agers are healthy people who have a low risk of becoming chronically ill. There is hardly any reference to *unsuccessful ageing* in the gerontological literature (which implies that it is not a conventionalised term); where there is, it is understood as a collection of qualities and attitudes, such as self-absorption, moodiness, rigid opinions, fears associated with money, obsession with life's inequities and lack of intimate friends (Hardin 1990). Note that the expression has not shown up at all in the newspaper database we used in our study.

[8] Source: http://www.hms.harvard.edu/psych/redbook/redbook-family-adult-01.htm; accessed: 13 July 2015.

[9] While *ageing* is orthophemistic in its use (see above, section 2), the verbs that often accompany it imply that we conceptualize ageing as an adversary in a competition – as evidenced in *fight ageing* or *conquer ageing* among others. This conceptualization is in harmony with the COMPETITON frame evoked by *successful ageing* (as pointed out in the present paper – see below).

midlife lifestyle choices are key to ageing happily (that is, successfully). Factors such as regular exercise, moderate consumption of alcohol, non-smoking, level of education and the quality of the marital relationship significantly influence how we age.

To what degree, however, is *successful ageing* lexicalized in Australian English? Our data suggest that it is not a well-entrenched conceptual category. Using a web-based database of Australian newspapers (http://www.factiva.com), we searched for the term "successful ageing" from 1987 (which was the year of its introduction) to 2014. Interestingly, *successful ageing* first appeared in the Australian media only in 1993, but even after its first appearance it remained at a relatively low frequency, occurring on average twice per year in the investigated period (1987 to 2014).

Nevertheless, this does not mean that Australian English does not have subordinate categories of ageing. According to our results, Australian English prefers *healthy ageing* over *successful ageing*. Although the expression first appeared only in 1994, a year later than *successful ageing*, it had a yearly average frequency of 8.8 in the period of 1987–2014, which is four times higher than that of *successful ageing*. What might be the reason for this preference of *healthy ageing* over *successful ageing*? We believe that the underlying motives are most probably linked to different cultural schemas. The concept of "success" has a long tradition in American cultural history (see e.g. Banta 2015); according to the American myth of success (Weiss 1969), every American has the right to "mold his own life" (p. 1). The key to reaching one's goals and being successful is through self-improvement – the origins of which McGee (2005) traces to the Puritan notion of "calling" (and the conflation of spiritual and material values that came when the "divinely ordained vocation or calling" shifted to "the secular sphere of everyday work"; p. 26). Success, however, is a less central schema in Australian culture than it is in the United States, which means that ageing will be less likely conceptualized within the COMPETITION frame of winners and losers. Although *healthy ageing* also emphasizes a pro-active attitude to ageing via a cause-for-effect metonymy such that by eating healthily, staying fit, etc. we will age healthily,[10] there is a less direct individual responsibility involved as compared to *successful ageing*. Responsibility in the case of *healthy ageing* is distributed more evenly throughout

---

10 The Australian government's webpage on aged care has a dedicated tab on "Healthy and active ageing" (http://www.myagedcare.gov.au/healthy-and-active-ageing; accessed 06 April 2016), which emphasizes the importance of both physical and social activity as a means to promote general well-being in old age.

the whole of society – a notion most probably rooted in the long-standing tradition of the Australian welfare state.[11]

Supporting this positive ageing model is the enthusiastic take up of the expression *third age* during the 1980s and 1990s, and the subsequent flourishing of "Universities of the Third Age" (U3A) around Australia. Beginning in Melbourne in 1984, the Australian U3A movement has always based itself on the British "self-help" model. As a "grassroots" initiative, it was originally driven by retired community supporters and it continues to receive little or no support from external sources. As U3A members emphasize, "experts of every kind retire, thus, there should be no need for older learners to have to rely on paid or unpaid Second Age teachers" (Swindell 2009: 6). There are now 300 independent U3A organizations listed in Australia with more than 100,000 members.[12]

The label *third age* emerged from Peter Laslett's (1989) influential book, *A Fresh Map of Life: The Emergence of the Third Age*, which addressed the challenges of an ageing population in the world's developed countries. Laslett's point was that medical, social and economic changes had created a new "third age" (first age = immaturity and dependence; second age = maturity and independence; third age = personal fulfilment; fourth age = final dependence and death). The expression still connotes activity, vigour, freedom, control and achievement. Given that most people are unfamiliar with Laslett's work and the four ages, the "third age" has come to stand for "old age", with "youth" and "middle age" being the two other ages. It is of course not clear where exactly middle age falls, and where old age begins. Age-related terms shift around much like the labels for those body parts speakers prefer not label – the taboos surrounding ageing create the same instability. A further factor contributing to the ambiguity with respect to the start of "old age" is a protracted adolescence. As Richardson (2001) explains, people in the West reach adulthood only at the age of 35. This – as a consequence – also pushes out the borders of "middle age", which is now sometimes referred to as *middlescence* and can range from our mid-thirties to the sixties.[13]

---

11 Note that other synonymous expressions for *healthy ageing* – such as *active ageing* and *positive ageing* – are also very rarely used in Australian newspapers. We found – in sum – a total of four instances of the former and nine instances of the latter in the period 1987–2016.
12 https://www.u3aonline.org.au; accessed 17 May 2016.
13 See, for instance the following *Financial Times* quote from 1975: "Somewhere between the ages of 35 and 60 some – but not all – men go through what is variously termed a 'mid-life crisis', the 'male metapause syndrome', 'middlescence'" (quoted in the *OED*).

3.2 Category extension

An example of category extension is the expression *older Australians*, which was coined most likely to replace the worn-down *seniors*. The label *seniors* is still used in Australian official contexts for the 50+; for example, the Australian government's official website for Australians over 50 is http://www.seniors.gov.au; but there is hardly any use of the word *seniors* on the website of Australia's foremost governmental agency dedicated to the 50+ (and there are not many 50-somethings who are happy to be described as *seniors* or even *senior citizens*). The Council on the Ageing's (COTA) website (http://www.cota.org.au) prefers to use either *older Australians* and *people over 50* instead. In the media, there is also an increasing preference for *older Australians*.[14] Even though the token frequency of *seniors* is distinctively higher in the period of 1987 to 2014 as opposed to *older Australians* (see Figures 3 and 4), with nearly twice as much tokens, the average annual growth rate of *seniors* is only 17 %, as compared to that of *older Australians*, which is 41 %.

---

14 Note that *old Australians* is typically used to refer to English-speaking people who were born in Australia (and usually have an Anglo-Saxon background). It is very rarely used in the sense of "elderly Australians": in the Factiva database we found only 5 such instances (and two of these appeared in headlines, which could have been a rational decision to economize on the longer *older Australians*).

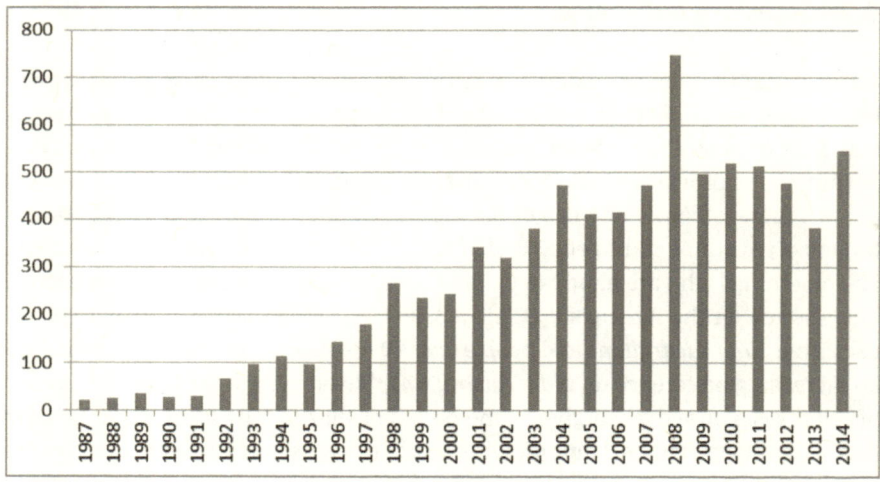

Figure 3: Number of tokens of *seniors* in major Australian newspapers, per year, 1987–2014.[15]

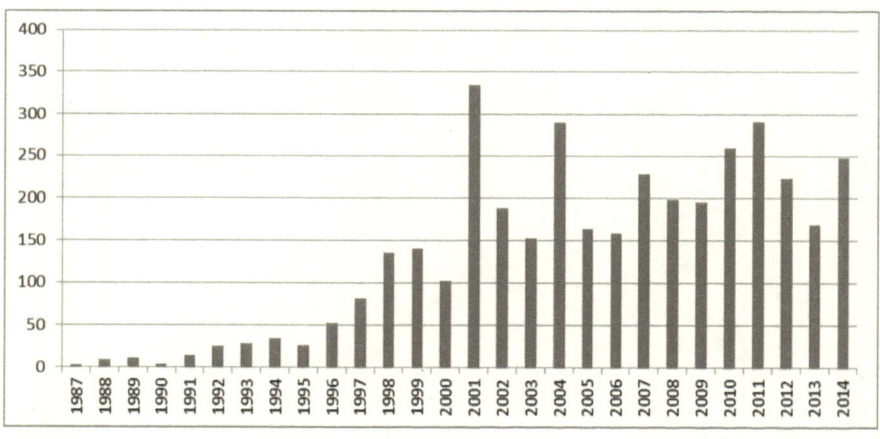

Figure 4: Number of tokens of *older Australians* in major Australian newspapers, per year, 1987–2014.[16]

---

15 Source: own compilation. The figures come from an online database of searchable, indexed newspapers, http://www.factiva.com; accessed: 03 July 2015.
16 Source: own compilation. The figures come from an online database of searchable, indexed newspapers, http://www.factiva.com; accessed: 03 July 2015.

Both *seniors* and *older Australians* describe a subcategory of people, yet why is the latter nowadays more favoured than the former? We believe that this preference for *older Australians* can be attributed to a number of semantic properties. First, *seniors* and *older Australians* differ in the number of features they contain: while *older Australian* focuses on a single feature, *seniors* includes a number of features, which are not necessarily positive. In other words, *older Australians* singles out Australians only along the dimension of age, while *seniors* represents an entrenched category characterised by additional features.

Second, *older Australians* (as a comparative construction; compare earlier expressions like *the longer living* and *the longer lived*) blurs the entry age of "senior citizenship" by overgeneralization, which is achieved via a whole-for-part metonymy. Ageing can be considered as a scale, which corresponds to the whole. In this respect, everybody is an *older Australian* on the ageing scale, yet we use this generic concept to refer to the end part of the scale, "old Australians". By doing so, the category of "old Australians" becomes included in the far more general and larger category of "older Australians", which can be used to refer to anybody who is past the period of full employment and the responsibilities of parenting. What is happening here, therefore, is that the boundaries of the original category of "old people" have become substantially extended.

This boundary extension can also be accounted for by a blend-based analysis (see Radden and Dirven 2007: 147–148 for a blend-based analysis of scalar and complementary adjectives). As explained by Langacker (1987), premodification is a valence relation of correspondence, i.e., a composite structure where the component structures share certain features. Scalar adjectives such as *old* require the existence of an implied norm to which the figure is matched against – somebody who is *old* falls beyond this implied norm (see Allan 1986, Allan 2001: 262f). However, the comparative suffix in *older Australians* implies that there is no fixed norm to which the figure is matched against. Consider the following sentence: "Jack is older than Jill". Here, the blend can be analysed as a mirror network (Fauconnier and Turner 2002), where one mental space includes a scale on which Jack's age is located somewhere. In the other mental space, we have the same scale, with Jill's age located somewhere lower than Jack's age in the previous mental space. In the blend the two scales are projected onto one another and Jack's age falls higher than Jill's; hence we can say that "Jack is older than Jill".

However, in the case of *older Australians*, the situation is different. We have a simplex network (Fauconnier and Turner 2002), where one mental space contains a general scale of human lifespan. In the other mental space we have a group of individuals – Jack, Jill, etc. In the blend, the elements (Jack, Jill) correspond to various ages on the human lifescale. Accordingly, Jack corresponds to the 90-year-old mark on the scale, Jill to the 80-year-old mark, etc. In the blend we have a group of people whose age is understood in relation to one another's – thus, Jack will be an "older Australian" as compared to an 80-year-old Jill, who will also be an older Australian as compared to a 70- or 60-year-old. Importantly, the scale is open on both ends: a 100-year-old can just as well be an "older Australian" as a 60-year-old who has just retired from full employment.

This open-endedness on the lower end of the scale has a very significant implication: just as adolescence is pushing into middle age – thereby offsetting the start of middle-age, so is middle age pushing into "old age", and hence offsetting – or even perhaps stalling – the onset of old age. This blur between the boundaries of "middle age" and "old age" is very aptly illustrated by the growing popularity of the adjective *grey* in relation to older people – such as *grey market*, *grey power* or *grey vote*. The *greying of Australia* was for some time a catch phrase in reference to the rising population of "ageing" or "aged Australians" who remain active well past retirement, and *grey* is still accepted and used even within the community of older people – consider, for example, the coinage *grey nomads* ("someone who is 55 or older and is taking a long term camping trip around Australia"),[17] which is used in the name of the webpage maintained for and by older people seeking to travel around the country.[18]

3.3 Novel conceptual metaphors and cultural schemas

We investigated the naming practices of aged care facilities in Melbourne, by comparing the naming strategies of 2013 with those of 1987 (Benczes and Burridge 2015). The justification for the selection of 1987 as the base is twofold: 1) this was the year when Rowe and Kahn (1987) introduced the concept of "successful ageing" in gerontological literature; 2) a twenty-five year span is adequately long to investigate subtle changes in naming customs within such a euphemistic area as ageing. The 1987 data come from the Melbourne Yellow Pages of that year, from the sections listed under "Nursing Homes" and "Retirement Communities and Homes." There was no separate "Aged Care" section in the volume. It was hypothesized that the 2013 sample would show a much greater degree of euphemistic

---

17 Source: https://en.wiktionary.org/wiki/grey_nomad (accessed 11 April 2016).
18 See, for instance the following quote: "If you are one of the growing army of grey nomads discovering, or hoping to discover, the joys of the open road in this wonderful country, then this site is for you. Whether you are a baby boomer travelling indefinitely, choosing to spend the winter months up north, or simply enjoying a few short trips a year, you are part of the growing grey nomad community in Australia." Source: http://www.thegreynomads.com.au/ (accessed 11 April 2016).

usage as compared to the 1987 data by using a wider array and a larger proportion of appealing names.[19]

The data did indeed justify the hypothesis. Regarding the 2013 sample, there was a wide selection of names typically centred on either the FAMILY metaphor, which conceptualized the facility as an upper-class family home, as in the case of *manor, hall*, or *gardens* (e.g., Trinity Manor, Broughton Hall, Kew Gardens), or the VACATION metaphor, which viewed the facility as a holiday resort, as in the case of *lodge, view*, or *villa* (e.g., Edwards Lodge, Princeton View, Villa Franca) – or even used foreign-sounding names for achieving the same effect (e.g., Casa Serena, Embracia). These two conceptualizations cater to essentially two different needs or requirements when it comes to an aged care facility. The FAMILY frame emphasizes community and permanence, while the VACATION frame stresses individuality and transience. These metaphorical frames were mostly missing in the 1987 data, where the vast majority of the facilities (82%) were *nursing homes*, which evoked the HOSPITAL frame. Within this frame, the aged are conceptualized as invalids, who need constant care.[20]

4 Conclusions

The "longevity revolution" has seen positive ageing models focus on productive and optimistic ways that people can intervene in the ageing process. With the attention well and truly away from loss, dependence and infirmity, the message is now that with a few simple lifestyle choices people stand a good chance of carrying on fruitfully to *a ripe old age*. In his account of educational initiatives for the elderly, Swindell (2009) put it, "these models have the potential to transform western societies deeply ingrained, condescending mindset that ageing inevitably equates with poor health, decline, and expensive reliance on social services, into a socially acceptable and more accurate understanding of the realities of ageing" (p. 1).

The initial data supports this, and bears out our hypothesis that ageing is currently undergoing a major reconceptualization in Australian English and that this process can be best analysed within a cognitive linguistic framework of the

---

[19] For a full list of the data, see Benczes and Burridge (2015).
[20] The prevalence for *nursing home* in the 1987 data can be explained by the fact that prior to the 1997 Aged Care Act, *nursing home* was the generally used term for a live-in facility. It is rather its disappearance from use in the 2013 data that is noteworthy – signalling that in the past three decades *nursing home* has become a tarnished name.

euphemistic (figurative) language used in connection to ageing. Such research indicates that this reconceptualization manifests itself in three major forms: 1) novel conceptual categories; 2) category extension; and 3) novel conceptual metaphors and cultural schemas.

Regarding novel conceptual categories, we looked at the entrenchment of *successful ageing* as compared to *healthy ageing* in Australian English, and according to the data the latter is significantly more entrenched than the former. Though both target personal intervention and the positive ways individuals can choose to involve themselves in the ageing experience, the difference in preference might be explained by differences in cultural schemas: Australian English attaches less importance to success and competition than American English does. Furthermore, *healthy ageing* implies that the responsibility for one's health (and thus indirectly the way one ages) is not carried entirely by the individual but also by others in the community – so the preference might be rooted in Australia's long-standing tradition of welfare policies.

As for category extension, we analysed the expression *older Australians*, which is manifesting very dynamic growth rates in the media as compared to the more established *seniors*. The analysis of the expression has demonstrated that *older Australians* leaves the lower end of the human lifescale open, thus blurring the entry point of "old age". Anybody can be "older" – even a five-year old is older than a three-year old (compare *fuller figure*, a euphemism used in the fashion industry for larger sizes in women's clothes).

Novel metaphors can be observed in the naming practices of aged care facilities of the Melbourne region. In the 2013 sample, we found an abundance of names evoking either the FAMILY metaphor or the VACATION metaphor. These two conceptualizations place the negative associations of old age (such as decrepitude, dependence and loneliness) into the background by focusing on the traits that are associated with healthy and successful ageing – such as emotional well-being, active lifestyle, and social and community involvement.

There is undoubtedly a change taking place in how people speak and think about ageing in Australian English. Negative associations are being replaced by more positive concepts such as good health, independence, active engagement and personal fulfilment. Accordingly, it is possible that the current expressions and euphemisms that we use to talk about ageing (including *healthy ageing* and *older Australians* among others) are not just by-products of the euphemistic treadmill and will eventually be tarnished by the concept (and thus need replacement), but do in fact change for the better how we think about ageing. Therefore, euphemistic usage might eventually become orthophemistic, eradicating in the process many of the taboo associations of old age and ageing.

Acknowledgements: We wish to thank our two anonymous reviewers and Andrea Pizarro Pedraza for the very helpful comments. This research was supported under Australian Research Council's *Discovery Projects* funding scheme (project number DP140102058).

References

Allan, Keith. 1986. Interpreting English comparatives. *Journal of Semantics* 5. 1–50.
Allan, Keith. 2001. *Natural Language Semantics*. Oxford & Malden, MA: Blackwell.
Allan, Keith. 2012. X-phemism and creativity. *Lexis: E-Journal in English Lexicology* 7: 5–42.
Allan, Keith and Kate Burridge. 1991. *Euphemism and Dysphemism: Language Used as Shield and Weapon*. New York: Oxford University Press.
Allan, Keith and Kate Burridge. 2006. *Forbidden Words: Taboo and the Censoring of Language*. Cambridge: Cambridge University Press.
Australian Longitudinal Study of Ageing, The. 2006. Adelaide: Flinders University. Downloaded from: http://www.flinders.edu.au/sabs/fcas-files/Documents/StudyOfAgeing[1].pdf (accessed 24 May 2016).
Baltes, Margaret M. and Laura L. Carstensen. 1996. The process of successful ageing. *Ageing and Society* 16. 397–422.
Banta, Martha. 2015. *Failure and Success in America: A Literary Debate*. Princeton, NJ: Princeton University Press.
Benczes, Réka. 2006a. *Creative Compounding in English: The Semantics of Metaphorical and Metonymical Noun–Noun Combinations*. Amsterdam & Philadelphia: John Benjamins.
Benczes, Réka. 2006b. Analysing metonymical noun–noun Compounds: The case of *freedom fries*. In Réka Benczes and Szilvia Csábi (eds), *The Metaphors of Sixty*, 46–54. Budapest: Eötvös Loránd Tudományegyetem.
Benczes, Réka and Kate Burridge. 2015. Current attitudes to ageing as reflected in the names of Australian aged care facilities. *Names: Journal of Onomastics* 63 (2). 96–114.
Benczes, Réka, Kate Burridge, Farzad Sharifian & Keith Allan (2017). 607–24. Ageing and Cultural Linguistics: What naming practices can reveal about underlying cultural conceptualisations. In Farzad Sharifian (ed.), *Advances in Cultural Linguistics*. New York: Springer.
Bolinger, Dwight. 1980. *Language – the Loaded Weapon: The Use and Abuse of Language Today*. London & New York: Longman.
Burridge, Kate. 2012. Euphemism and language change. *Lexis: E-Journal in English Lexicology* 7. 65–92.
Davison, Graeme. 1993. *Old People in a Young Society: Towards a History of Ageing in Australia*. Lincoln Papers in Gerontology 22. Melbourne: Lincoln Gerontology Centre, La Trobe University.
Depp, Colin A. and Dilip V. Jeste. 2009. Definitions and predictors of successful aging: A comprehensive review of larger quantitative studies. *FOCUS* 7 (1). 137–150.
Depp, Colin A., Ipsit Vahia & Dilip V. Jeste. 2010. Successful aging: Focus on cognitive and emotional health. *Annual Review of Clinical Psychology* 6. 527–550.

Fauconnier, Gilles and Mark Turner. 2002. *The Way We Think: Conceptual Blending and the Mind's Hidden Complexities*. New York: Basic Books.

Gradečak-Erdeljić, Tanja. 2005. Euphemisms in the language of politics or how metonymy opens one door but closes the other. In Piotr Cap (ed.), *Pragmatics Today*, 287–299. Frankfurt am Main: Peter Lang.

Hardin, Paula Payne. 1990. Successful and unsuccessful aging: What makes the difference? Paper presented at the Annual Meeting of the American Association for Adult and Continuing Education (Salt Lake City, UT, 28 October–3 November 1990). http://eric.ed.gov/?id=ED326654 (accessed 07 April 2016).

Horin, Adele. 2012. Ageing disgracefully: Get real. *Sydney Morning Herald*. 21 April 2012.

Jespersen, Otto. 1962 [1905]. *Growth and Structure of the English Language*. Oxford: Basil Blackwell.

Kalache, Alexander. 2012. How the baby boomers are reinventing old age. *The Huffington Post*. 4 April 2012.

Lamond, Amanda J., Colin A. Depp, Matthew Allison, Robert Langer, Jennifer Reichstadt, David J. Moore, Shahrokh Golshan & Theodore G. Ganiatis. 2008. Measurement and predictors of resilience among community-dwelling older women. *Journal of Psychiatric Research* 43 (2). 148–154.

Langacker, Ronald W. 1987. *Foundations of Cognitive Grammar. Vol I: Theoretical Prerequisites*. Stanford, CA: Stanford University Press.

Laslett, Peter. 1989. *A Fresh Map of Life: The Emergence of the Third Age*. Cambridge, MA: Harvard University Press.

McCallum, John. 1997. Fictional ageing crisis obscures health facts. *The Australian*. 10 January 1997.

McGee, Micki. 2005. *Self-Help, Inc.: Makeover Culture in American Life*. New York & Oxford: Oxford University Press.

McGlone, Matthew S., Gary Beck & Abigail Pfiester. 2006. Contamination and camouflage in euphemisms. *Communication Monographs* 73. 261–282.

Peel, N. M., R. J. McClure & H. P. Bartlett. 2005. Behavioral determinants of healthy aging. *American Journal of Preventive Medicine* 28 (3). 298–304.

Pinker, Steven. 2002. *The Blank Slate: The Modern Denial of Human Nature*. New York: Penguin.

Portero Muñoz, Carmen. 2011. Noun–noun euphemisms in the language of the late 2000s' global financial crisis. *Atlantis* 33 (2). 137–157.

Pountney, Michelle. 1998. Ageism out for baby boomers. *Herald Sun*. 26 February 1998.

Radden, Günter and René Dirven. 2007. *Cognitive English Grammar*. Amsterdam & Philadelphia: John Benjamins.

Richardson, S. 2001. *The Young West: How We Are All Growing Older More Slowly*. San Diego, CA: University of California Press.

Rowe, John. W. and Robert L. Kahn. 1987. Human aging: Usual and successful. *Science* 237. 143–149.

Sharifian, Farzad. 2011. *Cultural Conceptualisations and Language: Theoretical Framework and Applications*. Amsterdam & Philadelphia: John Benjamins.

Swindell, Rick. 2009. Educational initiatives for the elderly. U3A Online. [https://www.u3aonline.org.au/content/educational-initiatives-elderly; accessed 30th November 2017]

Weiss, Richard. 1969. *The American Myth of Success: From Horatio Alger to Norman Vincent Peale*. New York: Basic Books.

Magdalena Zawrotna
6 Taboo subjects as insult intensifiers in Egyptian Arabic

Abstract: The chapter aims at analysing the conceptual basis underlying insult intensifiers in Egyptian Arabic, with the focus on three domains: FAMILY, SEXUALITY and RELIGION, all of which are strongly tabooed in the community in question. Additionally, two other aspects of the problem are discussed; first the level of intensity provided by a reference to the three domains is examined by means of questionnaire, where educational (sociolinguistic) differences among speakers are taken into account, and then the phenomenon of grammaticalization of the words (primarily nouns) used as intensifiers is discussed with reference to Bolinger's (1972) theoretical perspective. The study reveals that insult intensifiers are diverse in terms of conceptual background and that references to various domains provide different levels of intensity. Also, in terms of grammaticalization, the analysed words tend to present different levels.

Key words: taboo, intensifiers, Egyptian Arabic, insults

1 Introduction

This study analyses the conceptual basis underlying the reference made by Egyptians to such semantic domains as FAMILY, SEXUALITY and RELIGION when intending to intensify insults. According to Stewart (1996: 166), such words as *abu* 'father', *'aḫ* 'brother, *dīn* 'religion' function as common insult intensifiers in Egyptian Arabic (henceforth EA); when inserted into an abusive phrase, they maximize the pragmatic effect of it. These words are semantically rooted in tabooed domains and therefore considered either as sacred (FAMILY, RELIGION) or as forbidden (SEXUALITY). Maledictions, curses and insults[1] referring to symbolic actions taken by the speaker as well as the abusive terms of address are intensi-

---

[1] A typology of curses and other insults can be found in Stewart (2014).

fied by the insertion of taboo words[2] in various types of grammatical constructions. In the current chapter, the focus will be on the following types:

(1) *aḷḷāh yiḫrib bētak* 'may God destroy your house'[3] >
 aḷḷāh yiḫrib bēt ahlak 'may God destroy the house of your family' or
 aḷḷāh yiḫrib bēt dīnak 'may God destroy the house of your religion'

(2) *yilʿan šaklak* '(may God) curse your appearance' >
 yilʿan abu šaklak '(may God) curse the father of your appearance'

(3) *yilʿan ummak* '(may God) curse your mother' >
 yilʿan abu ummak '(may God) curse the father of your mother' or
 yilʿan dīn ummak '(may God) curse the religion of your mother' or
 yilʿan mayyitīn ummak '(may God) curse your mother's ancestors'

(4) *ibn il-kalb* 'son of a dog' >
 ibn dīn kalb 'son of the religion of a dog'

(5) *haṭallaʿ ʿēnak* 'I will take your eye out' >
 haṭallaʿ mayyitīn ummak or 'I will get the ancestors (the dead) of your mother out of their place (i.e. the grave)'
 haṭallaʿ dīn ummak 'I will get the religion of your mother out of its place'

Intensification in these examples is obtained by inserting words (intensifiers) to fixed expressions. The intensifier enters into an attributive relation with one of the nouns in the construction (Arabic: *'iḍāfa*), corresponding more or less to the concept of possession. The intensifiers used here can be either unspecified for definiteness, as in: *yilʿan abu ummak* '(may God) curse the father of your mother' or bear the possessive pronoun (definiteness) as in *aḷḷāh yiḫrib bēt ahlak* 'may God destroy the house of your family'.

Intensifiers in abusive expressions represent a few more or less related semantic concepts: *bēt* 'house', *abu* 'father', *mayyitīn* 'ancestors' and *dīn* 'religion'. They slightly differ in terms of the conceptual background and represent

---

[2] Not only insults are intensified this way, Stewart also sees the example *allāh yibārik fī-ʿumrak* 'may God bless your life' as an emphatic form of *allāh yibārik fīk* 'may God bless you' and claims that ʿumrak 'your life', another tabooed word, has been substituted for "you" (Stewart 2007: 16).
[3] Unless stated otherwise, the examples were obtained through fieldwork between 2013 – 2016 or found online, on the Facebook profiles of the study participants (for details see section 4).

various levels of tabooisation. This yields a question regarding the possible difference in the degree of intensification they provide. Are *haṭallaʿ dīn ummak* 'I will get the religion of your mother out of its place' and *haṭallaʿ mayyitīn ummak* 'I will get the ancestors (the dead) of your mother out of their place' equally strong maledictions? An attempt to answer this question will be made in section 4.

Another problem addressed in this chapter is the fact that such expressions are usually marked by a high level of desemanticisation (also referred to as "semantic bleaching"), where the emotional layer is more salient than the meaning. I will try to determine whether or not such utterances as *anīk dīn ummak* 'I will fuck the religion of your mother' are still felt to belong to the category of *sabb ad-dīn* 'blasphemy' classified as seriously sinful in Islamic culture. Despite the social stigmatisation, such expressions are found among the basic techniques of forming insults. Perhaps the connection between "religion" and the word has been lost, which raises the question of the level of grammaticalization they undergo. Semantic bleaching (Sweetser 1988) can also be observed in such lexemes as *nēk* 'fucking' and *fašḫ* 'being spread wide' (referring to a woman's legs during sexual intercourse), both of which can be used to intensify the effect of not only insults but also compliments and utterances conveying positive attitudes:

(6) *di ṣūra ḥilwa nēk!* 'this photo is fucking beautiful'
(7) *waḥšāni fašḫ!* 'I miss you like fuck'

The goal of the chapter is to better understand the problem of intensifiers in EA, as well as their semantic background and its consequences. For this purpose, after analysing in section 2 some theoretical problems related to the two research questions mentioned, in section 3 three semantic domains: FAMILY, RELIGION and SEXUALITY are discussed. In sections 4 and 5 the focus is, respectively, on the level of intensity provided by specific domains and the problem of grammaticalization.

In terms of methods, a model of cognitive linguistics is applied to the analysis of the semantic background of a group of popular expressions. The level of intensification is examined by means of questionnaire, where educational (sociolinguistic) differences among speakers are taken into account. Finally, I examine the chosen lexical items for grammaticalization employing the diagnostic tool proposed by Bolinger (1972).

2 Theoretical aspects of intensifiers and research questions

Labov states that "[a]t the heart of social and emotional expression is the linguistic feature of intensity" (Labov 1984: 43). The author claims, that there is no closed set of devices used to mark the utterance for intensity, it usually involves using a group of adverbs such as *very, so, really, extremely,* or other examples of less common expressions. Apart from these explicit markers there are a number of other methods, involving specific prosodic contour (Labov 1984: 43), intonation and stress, syntactic devices such as word order, and extralinguistic means, referred to as peripheral systems. According to Labov, "the peripheral systems are the primary means of conveying social and emotional information, and the grammatical mechanism is the primary means for conveying referential and cognitive information" (Labov 1984: 43). Expressing emotional states prompts the use of peripheral codes: prosody, vocal qualifier, and gestures rather than grammatical or lexical means. When it comes to intensifiers, the information coded is not semantic in nature; it is, rather, the emotional load. What are intensifiers then? According to Bolinger (1972: 17), an intensifier is "any device that scales a quality, whether up or down or somewhere between the two". They are linguistic devices employed to modify expressions by amplifying the emotional load and adding emphasis, and there are indications that they might be devoid of any semantic references themselves, except for their source domains, which may or may not play a role. Labov, for instance, calls them "cognitive zeroes", referring to the fact that they have zero representational content (Labov 1984:43). However, their semantic basis consists of a rather considerable number of domains; in each language they are slightly different due to their socio-cultural sensitivity.

There is a number of ways to lexically convey the rise in intensity. Feodorov (2009) mentions the idea of FORCE as a major domain, from which intensifiers are derived. And indeed, the most common EA intensifiers used in various context are:

(8) '*awi* 'very' (< *qawi* 'strong')
(9) *gāmid* 'strongly', 'hard'

According to Feodorov (2009: 104), other types of meaning that generate grammaticized intensifiers include: the idea of "completeness" indicating the UPPER LIMIT (as in EA *'āḫir ḥāga* 'the last thing'), and the idea of LARGE QUANTITY. This is obviously a common feature of many languages; in Arabic especially frequent are the following two methods: increase by means of repetition and by reference to numbers. Also, the cognate accusative (*al-mafʿūl al-muṭlaq*)⁴ construction is employed to intensify the meaning. When greeting, blessing or consoling a friend or a relative, usually more then one polite formula is used at a time. The employed strategy is based on the scheme MORE OF FORM IS MORE OF CONTENT (Lakoff and Johnson 1979: 127).

Quantity is often enlarged in EA by means of repetition; this is one of the main features of the EA style, both in speech and in the written form. Repetitions serve the function of intensifying the message, strengthening the effect and giving the utterance an exuberant character. They are based on flouting the Maxim of Quantity and appear in many different grammatical and lexical structures. Repetitions are used when the utterance is felt not to be expressive enough (e.g. *baḥibbik baḥibbik baḥibbik* 'I love you, love you, love you') to intensify and maximise the effect of an utterance. This is also seen in a specific type "root repetition" e.g. *allāhumma farriğ humūm al-mahmumīn* 'oh, God, drive away the troubles of the troubled', where the root *h-m-m* expressing 'trouble' is repeated for more intense effect. Repetition is also a method encountered in curses and maledictions as well:

(10) *yiḫrib bētak* '(may God) destroy your house' >
 *yiḫrib bētak wi l-bēt illi gamb bētak*⁵ 'may God destroy your house, and the house next to your house!'

An exceptionally interesting example is the root-echo response in curses (cognate curse) and blessings. However, these were described thoroughly in two brilliant articles by Devin Stewart *Root-echo Responses in Egyptian Arabic Politeness Formulae* (1996) and *Impoliteness Formulae: The Cognate Curse in Egyptian Arabic* (1997). Therefore, we are not going to go any deeper in this subject⁶.

Some expressions, especially blessings, curses and maledictions are intensified by numerical multiplication, which aims to intensify their effect, e.g. positive politeness, as curses and maledictions, when used jokingly, are a means of marking intimacy⁷. The numbers appearing in curses, as in (12) and (13), often the multiplications of 60, seem to confirm the thesis regarding the magical origin of such maledictions. Also, the combination of both repetition and multiplication with numbers is encountered as in (14).

---

4 Cognate accusative or "the absolute object" – a construction in Arabic based on the root repetition, usually used to add emphasis.
5 The example was found in Stewart (1997).
6 In Stewart (2014) there is a discussion of the same problem in Morrocan Arabic.
7 This refers to the "joke" strategy of positive politeness in Brown and Levinson's (1978: 102) politeness theory.

(11) *alf salāma 'alēk* '(may God multiply) your soundness a thousand times'
(12) *gatak nīla* 'go to hell' >
    gatak sittīn nīla 'go to sixty hells'
(13) *ġūri fi dahya* 'go to hell' >
    ġūri fi sittīn dahya 'go to sixty hells'
(14) *salamtak milyūn salāma* 'your health a million times ("healths")'

In her elaboration on conceptual basis of intensifiers Feodorov notices:

> One of the means to express graded values by the help of relatively grammaticized intensifiers, which is used in several languages, has most particularly drawn our attention: it refers to the presence of semes which have a spatial origin, expressing relational, bipolar meanings: up/down, above/below, full/empty, high/low. The role that this type of meanings play in expressing graded values may be comprehended if seen in the light of George Lakoff's approach to certain metaphors that have, in his opinion, a basis in the human experience (Feodorov 2000: 106).

This subtype includes among other things: reaching the upper limit, filling (increasing the level), exceeding the upper limit (Feodorov 2000: 106). It is met both in positive and negative types of content:

(15) *da magnūn āḫir ḥāga* 'he's extremely mad'

Woidich (in press) sees *āḫir ḥāga* 'the last thing' as referring to the end or the top of a scale or the extreme positions in a row. The author also gives some interesting examples of '*āḫir ḥāga* being combined with other types of intensification, e.g. numerical multiplication:[8]

(16) *āḫir talat ḥagāt* (lit.) 'last three things'
(17) *āḫir talatīn ḥāga* (lit.) 'last thirty things'

Feodorov also mentions a different grammaticized means of conveying intensity:

> [A] certain entity can be a central, less central or marginal member of a given class. One of the most common ways of expressing graded values is the reference to a prototype, in comparative structures where one of the members is the prototype of the class. There exists a relatively narrow domain of elements to which reference is made in terms of prototypical qualities (Feodorov 2000: 107).

---

[8] I would like to express my deep gratitude to Professor Manfred Woidich for allowing me the access to the text before it is printed.

According to the author, such domains might comprise legendary figures, natural elements, and animals. Also the three domains analysed in this chapter (FAMILY, RELIGION and SEXUALITY) should be regarded as central values/concepts in the Egyptian society. It is important to note, that they, at the same time, constitute a strong taboo in the discussed community[9].

Among many other terms, taboo terms are found to be an inexhaustible source of intensifiers. The most commonly encountered are adverbs modifying adjectives, as in very many languages. There is, however, a large portion of linguistic means of conveying intensity specific to one or a few languages only. In English, the most extensively analysed are wh-questions intensified by inserting such expressions as: "the hell", "the fuck" after the wh-item. Among other broadly studied examples of intensifiers are exclamations, curses, swear-words, insults, maledictions, and name-calling, which are all known for the use of taboo terms, e.g. "damn!", "fuck!", "shit!" (Hoeksema and Napoli 2008: 349). Taboo-based intensifiers may include the reference to such topics as religion and the supernatural, body and sexuality, death and disease, dirt and bodily excretions (Andersson and Trudgill 1990). As Vogel (2014: 1) puts it: "Taboo emerges from the extremities of human value systems", and the value of "extremity" is found to be effective in amplifying the emotional load of utterances. Many of the intensifiers are terms to which, as a result of mental processing, such categories as 'sacred' or 'unclean' are applied. Also, numerous intensifiers evolve from the notion of fear. Feodorov gives examples of Classical Arabic adjectives conveying the concept of admiration as being semantically based on 'fear', among them: *rāʾiʿ* 'imposing', 'great' and *hāʾil* 'extraordinary', both originally: 'frightening' (Feodorov 2000: 106). However, 'death' is most often employed to intensify the positive content rather than negative, as can be seen in the already mentioned: *baḥibbik mōt* 'I love you like hell (death)'.

We do not have space here to delve into the mental mechanisms which translate the power of fear, sacredness and uncleanliness associated with taboos to the power that drives the processes of emotional intensification in language, we shall however consider some issues concerning the lexical input involved. One of the goals of this work is to examine what types of meanings generate intensifiers in languages such as EA. As mentioned above, they derive from various semantic categories, including strongly tabooed ones such as: bodily excretions, foods, death (Allan and Burridge 2006), disease, religion, scatological and sexual terms (Napoli and Hoeksema 2009: 625).

---

[9] The same, along with the domain DISEASE, can be found in other communities too, see: Ruette (this volume).

In section 1 of this chapter (introduction), two research question have been mentioned, the problem of assessing the level of intensity provided by certain terms and grammaticalization. Below, some theoretical aspects of them are discussed.

According to Labov (1984: 44), intensity is a gradable value operating on a continuous scale centred around zero. It is therefore inappropriate to mark the feature of intensity as (+) in an element of the binary opposition. Aggravation and mitigation in intensity are both a matter of a degree (a position on an ordinal scale). However, how do we assess the level of intensity of expressions containing intensifiers and what kind of value do the words need to possess to become intensifiers? The thesis here is that tabooness is what gives the word intensity, and that different levels of tabooness would result in different levels of intensity. Therefore, after discussing the conceptual domains in section 3, a study based on questionnaire will be presented followed by an attempt to answer this question.

Another problem I address here is grammaticalization; this will probably be best explained based on such common intensifiers as *mōt* 'death' or *nēk* 'fuck' / *fašḫ* 'spreading wide (legs)'. We can see that both are based on highly tabooed themes: DEATH and SEXUALITY. Both of them are used as intensifiers in many contexts, including overtly positive ones as in the following examples:

(18) *hināk fi'lan ṭawāf fašḫ* 'there is a fucking good *tawaf* (part of the pilgrimage)'
(19) *di ṣūra ḥilwa fašḫ!* 'this photo is fucking beautiful'
(20) *šufna 'arabiyya gamda nēk* 'we saw a fucking great car'
(21) *waḥišni mōt* 'I miss you like hell (like death)'

Mōt is also used with verbs as in (22). The idea of death as the EXTREME POINT is visible in other examples of intensification; in (23) the verb *yimūt* 'to die' replaces more logically expected, but less emotionally loaded *yiḥibb* 'to love':

(22) *baḥibbik mōt* 'I love you like hell'
(23) *bamūt fīki* 'I adore you' (lit. 'I am dying about you')

(24) is yet another example where the verb *yimūt* 'to die' is employed to express the extreme intensity of a feature/ action/ state:

(24) *bamūt min il-bard* 'I'm dying from cold'

The function of using such strong taboo-based intensifiers extends beyond the borders of linguistic expression; a large proportion of them are used as positive politeness strategies to convey intimacy by asserting common grounds and a small distance between speakers. This transposition of tabooness into intensity is visible in other examples too, where it intensifies the praise:

(25) *da fašīḫ* 'this is fucking cool'

The expressions used in praise for example *fašīḫ!* 'fucking cool' or intensifying positive politeness as in *waḥšāni fašḫ/ mōt* 'I miss you like hell' are usually marked by a high level of semantic bleaching. This way, such expressions as *nēk!* 'fucking' and *fašḫ!* 'spreading wide' have been reduced to the function of an intensifier: "fuck!".

Woidich sees *mōt* 'death' as belonging to the class of intensifying adverbials (Woidich, in press) since it occurs without article after definite noun phrases as in the example quoted by the author:

(26) *il-banāt il-ḥilwa mōt* 'the terribly nice girls'

Hoeksema and Napoli (2008: 352) see the role of the lexical meaning of taboo terms used in constructions conveying intensity as insignificant: "If anything, these constructions show the victory of connotation over denotation. The fact that taboo terms have a certain rude quality about them is more relevant than their meaning. This is quite obvious when we consider the many constructions where *fuck* may be used instead of *hell*. Semantically, the two words are rather different, apart from their taboo status". It appears that the same can be said about *fašḫ* and *mōt*. Hoeksema and Napoli claim that such versatility of taboo terms in the ability to appear in different types of context may only be explained on the assumption that "some constructions have a special emphatic status in the language, and show a tendency to employ taboo terms to express that status" (Hoeksema and Napoli 2008: 372). The more the terms are used in certain constructions, the more they are likely to spread to other constructions.

According to Woidich (1995: 259) the change in meaning is due to metaphorical and metonymic processes. The process of grammaticalization starts with the reanalysis of the grammatical structure through the speaker-hearer channel. The interpretation of uttered content on the side of the hearer may be slightly different from the intended by the speaker. "Hearers tend to reanalyze the syntactical structure of a sequence abductively according to an underlying semantic or pragmatic structure (rebracketing). Reanalysis brings about morphosyntactic changes, e.g. the switching of certain items from major categories to minor categories" (Woidich 1995: 259). The last note is particularly important. According to Woidich the reanalysis characteristic of items undergoing grammaticalization involves the loss of morphological markers and syntactic relations assigned to the categories of nouns or verbs (tense, aspect, modality, person-number marking, articles, inflection). This leads to their transition to the secondary categories: adjectives, particles or prepositions (Woidich 1995: 260). As they lose their autonomy, says Woidich (1995: 260), "their syntactic or pragmatic behaviour becomes predictable". Therefore, our assumed definition of grammaticalization would involve the transition of words belonging to major lexical categories into minor categories. Such a definition is adopted in Woidich (1995) as well as in McMahon (1994). Verbs, nouns and adjectives undergoing the process become prepositions, adverbs, auxiliaries, and finally – affixes. Such a view encompasses also the "unidirectional conceptualization from concrete to abstract" (Feodorov 2000: 99) and is in accordance with Heine and Reh's definition of grammaticalization as "evolution whereby linguistic units lose in semantic complexity, pragmatic significance, syntactic freedom, and phonetic substance, respectively" (Heine and Reh 1984: 15).

As Woidich points out, grammaticalization of a word might yield divergence, i.e. the occurrence of variants of the same lexical item with different grammatical characteristics (Woidich 1995: 260), which provides us with an insight into linguistic processes. The effect might be the coexistence of homonymic expressions coming from the same root (compare EA: *qawi* 'strong' and *'awi* 'very'). However, it might also happen that the grammaticized word retains some reflexes of the original meaning and "details of its lexical history may persist and be reflected in constraints on its grammatical distribution" (Woidich 1995: 260).

3 Taboo intensifiers in insults: qualitative analysis

In this section a group of expressions containing taboo intensifiers will be analysed. The data under examination come both from everyday life (material gathered during several pieces of field research in Cairo between 2013 – 2016 and online sources (Facebook accounts of the participants in the study). In the analysis, reference will be made to Egyptian culture, which is crucial to the understanding of values ascribed to certain categories.

In terms of insult intensifiers Arabic dialects have developed a number of techniques. However, in Boudot-Lamotte (1974), only four out of the sixteen types mentioned refer to concepts other than taboo, they are: the adjective *l-āḫor* 'other' (sing. masc.), *l-oḫra* 'other' (sing. fem.), the Turkish prefix *baš* 'pasha', the intensive form *faʿʿāl, faʿʿāla* as well as curses forming rhythmic couplets.

Since the major topic of this chapter is to examine taboo words serving as insult intensifiers, we shall now proceed to analysing the types of culturally sensitive themes in EA[10].

It will be useful to reflect on the fact that one of the main domains where taboos are employed is adjuration, which incidentally, also has the function of intensifying the utterance. Adjuration is an important feature of the oral communication in Egypt. In the system of etiquette it plays a role of intensifying the positive politeness, reinforcing and confirming speaker's intentions and expressing his/her sincerity. The most frequent examples of adjuration serving as intensifiers are: *wa-ḷḷāhi* 'by God'[11] or *wa-ḷḷāhi l-'aẓīm* 'by God, the greatest', *wa-n-nabi* 'by the Prophet', *wa-ḥyat rabbina* 'by the life of our Lord', *wa-ḥyātak* 'by your life', *wa-ḥyat ummi/ abi* 'by the life of my mother / father', *wa-ḥyat aġla ḥāga 'andak* 'by the life of your most precious possession'[12]. These examples are sometimes felt not to be expressive enough to convey speaker's emotional excitation and so a repetition is used: *wa-ḷḷāhi wa-ḷḷāhi* 'by God, by God'. Exaggeration is also expressed though adjuration: *wa-n-nabi nāwilni l-mallāḥa* 'for the Prophet's sake (please) pass me the salt container'[13]. Adjuration in its function of reinforcing the message and strengthening positive politeness is usually found in examples where the sincerity of speaker's intentions might be subject to doubt; this might include blessings. However, in such cases as condolences, where speaker's sincerity is out of question, adjuration usually does not occur.

In adjuration as well as in other types of speech marked for intensity, central values of the Egyptian culture are referred to. Notions of family (mother, father, ancestors) and faith (religion, God) are among them. On the other hand, body and sexuality are associated with slightly different set of concepts, encompassing fear, desire and repulsion. Let us now see, how these values are applied to linguistic usage.

3.1 Family

Stewart discusses the example *yiḫlī dār ummak* "May He [God] empty out your mother's house!" in the Bedouin dialect of the Marazig in southern Tunisia as containing an intensifier: *umm* 'mother' and explains that such terms as 'mother',

---

10 A short list of taboo domains in the Egyptian culture can be found in Stewart (2007: 4).
11 A discussion of the many functions of *wa-llahi* can be found in Mughazy (2003).
12 More examples can be found in Rosenbaum (2012).
13 The example was found in Abdel-Samad (1990).

'father', 'grandfather', 'family' are common in their function of curse intensifiers in many dialects of Arabic (Stewart, 2014: 7).

In Egypt, referring to the interlocutor's family is in fact referring to his/her root/origin. This central point of human identity is represented by mother, father and ancestors. Expressions such as *illi gabūk* 'those who brought you into the world' and *illi ḫallifūk* 'those who begot you/gave birth to you' are often used in curses, which emphasise the importance of the relation between a human and his/her origin. The family as a basic social unit is considered a sanctity and the symbolic violation of it provides a semantically active basis for insults. Also, *yiḫrib bētak* '(may God) destroy your house' can be understood as a metonymic insult to the interlocutor's family, in such case, *bēt* 'house' would refer to people living in the mentioned house. Addressing his/ her family instead of the actual person serves as intensifier:

(27) *ya gamza* 'you shoe' >
    ya-bn ig-gazma 'you son of a shoe'
(28) *ḥumār* 'donkey' >
    ibn il-ḥumār 'son of a donkey'
(29) *kalb* 'dog'>
    ibn il-kalb 'son of a dog'
(30) *'arṣ* 'pimp'>
    ibn il-'arṣ 'son of a pimp'
(31) *ya 'abīṭ* 'you stupid' >
    ya-bn il-'abīṭa 'you son of a stupid (woman)'

Abu 'father' represents values, which might be also understood metaphorically. A man can be a "father" of some kind of a value, therefore, the possessor of it. This is often used both in creating insults as in (32), (33), (34) and (37) as well as in intensifying them (36), (37), (38), and (39).

(32) *lissa mikallimāk min 'ašar minits ya-bu barabīr wi maraddetš, kalb!* 'I just called you ten minutes ago, you father of a snot, and you didn't answer, dog!'
(33) *ya mundass ya-bu ažinda* 'oh bribed (the one who was pushed in), oh agent (father of agency)'
(34) *wi di zayy ya-bu barbūr wi ya-bu šaḫḫa?* 'How is that, father of a snot and father of a piss?'
(35) *abu l-'āhira* 'father of a prostitute'
(36) *'abīṭ* 'stupid' >
    abu l-'abīṭa 'father of a stupid woman'

(37) *yilʿan abūk* '(may God) damn your father'[14] >
   yilʿan abūk wi abu abūk 'may (God) damn your father and the father of your father'
(38) *yiʿlan ummak* '(may God) damn your mother' >
   yilʿan abu ummak '(may God) damn your mother's father'
(39) *yilʿan šaklak* 'may your appearance be cursed' >
   yilʿan abu šaklak 'may (the father of) your appearance be cursed'

Notice, that in (37) it is said *yilʿan abūk wi abu abūk* 'may (God) damn your father and the father of your father', and not *abūk wi giddak* 'your father and your grandfather', which might be an indication, that the curse is not really addressed at the interlocutor's grandfather or even father, but it as addressed at the very person involved in the conversation, but intensified in this particular way. The same situation can be seen in (38), the insult is addressed not to the interlocutor's family, but to the interlocutor himself/herself with a certain amount of intensity added.

'Mother' is considered a metaphor of the beginning (of everything), not only the origin of a human race, but also all things on earth. In fact, the very word 'mother' (*umm*) in certain contexts can express negative emotions, e.g. *ya umm iš-šuġl!* 'this damned work!' (literally: 'oh, mother of the work'). This way, the very core of the annoying work is addressed. Referring to the interlocutor's mother is a method of intensifying the insult targeted at that person. The sanctity of the mother is most frequently tarnished by the suggestion of her loose morals or allusions to her intimate body parts or sex life. Below are some examples of insult intensifiers based on the reference to mother:

(40) *mitnāk* 'fucked' >
   ibn il-mitnāka 'son of a fucked woman'
(41) *ḥarāmi* 'thief' >
   ibn il- ḥaramiyya 'son of a thief'
(42) *anīkak* 'I will fuck you' >
   anīk ummak 'I will fuck your mother'
(43) *yiḫrib bētak* '(may God) destroy your house' >
   yiḫrib bēt ummak '(may God) destroy the house of your mother'

Insult, curses, maledictions, and exclamations intensifiers may refer to ancestors:

---

14 A version with a euphemistic metathesis *yinʿal* is also possible (Stewart 2014: 10).

(44) *ya umm iš-šuġl...* 'this damned work...' >
   mayyitīn umm iš-šuġl... (as above, *mayyitin* 'ancestors' adds emphasis)
(45) *yilʿan ummak* 'may your mother be cursed' >
   yilʿan mayyitīn ummak 'may your mother's ancestors be cursed'

It is however important to remember that tabooisation is not necessarily an inherent characteristics of a word (Andersson and Trudgill 1990), and, as Vogel argues "being taboo is not an immediately predictable consequence of literal content" (Vogel 2014: 2). That's why *abu* 'father' and *umm* 'mother' can be used as taboo intensifiers (especially in crude language), but their synonyms: *wālid* 'father', *walda* 'mother' cannot. While it is common to say *ummak wisḫa* 'your mother is dirty' or *ya-bn il-wisḫa* 'oh, son of a dirty woman' as an intensified form of *ya wisiḫ* 'oh, dirty'/ *inta wisiḫ* 'you are dirty', it would be unacceptable to say **walditak wisḫa* 'your mother is dirty'.

3.2 Body and sexuality

Among the frequently used intensifiers are heavily obscene terms e.g. *fašḫ* 'being spread wide' (referring to a woman's legs during sexual intercourse) and *nēk!* 'fuck!', 'fucking'. In the process of losing their meaning, these expressions have been reduced to the function of intensifiers and, as mentioned before, can be used both in a positive and negative context.

(46) *šufna ʿarabiyya gamda nēk* 'we saw a fucking great car'

The word *ṭīz* 'ass' is a very rare example of an insult intensifier based on body part terms. It is employed in this function probably due to the fact that this particular word is often used as a vulgar substitute of almost any other lexical item.

(47) *yilʿan ummak* '(may God) curse your mother'>
   yilʿan ṭīz ummak '(may God) curse the ass of your mother'

3.3 Religion

Religion is a source of strongly tabooed words, which, when used in curses or blessings magnify the force of the utterance. On the lexical level, when the word *dīn* 'religion' is used to intensify the insult, it directs the power of e.g. curse onto the religion of the interlocutor (which is usually the religion of the speaker too). Therefore, instead of wishing for someone to be burnt in hell, one might say:

(48) *yiḥra' dīnak* '(may God) burn your religion!'

Below, there is another way of intensifying insults with the word *dīn* 'religion':

(49) *yiḫrib bētak* '(may God) destroy your house' >
yiḫrib bēt dīnak '(may God) destroy the house of your religion'
(50) *yil'an ummak* '(may God) curse your mother' >
yil'an dīn ummak '(may God) curse the religion of your mother'
(51) *yil'an abūk* '(may God) curse your father' >
yil'an dīn abūk '(may God) curse the religion of your father'
(52) *ibn kalb* 'son of a dog' > *ibn dīn kalb* 'son of the religion of a dog'

Having read all these examples, it is possible to ask the following question: why is the reference to taboo needed in insult intensifiers? A probable answer would be that insult and curses belong to a very specific linguistic area, in which an action of some external agent (usually God, though rarely explicit) is called for. They therefore originate in linguistic magic and involve a higher level of emotional involvement than other utterances. Thus, when intensifier is used, it should be equally emotionally intense as the phrase to which it is added.

4 Gradation of intensity

In the previous section conceptual domains have been discussed, let us now proceed to the first question: how are these intensifiers different from one another in terms of the degree? Do those semantic domains contribute to the level of intensity in the same way?

For this purpose, a questionnaire was conducted among a group of young people. 60 participants aged 20–35 from Cairo and Alexandria took part in the study. They were asked to evaluate the vulgarity/offensiveness/stigmatization[15] of a group of expressions and place them on the scale stretching from 1 (neutral)

---

15 The participants were asked to use their own words to describe the analysed words, which was futher generalized into the three values mentioned.

up to 5 (unmentionable), and as far as 6 (unknown)[16]. The sixth level was added after the observation that some tabooed expressions are completely excluded from usage in certain social circles, to the effect that a part of the people belonging to such circles might be completely unaware of their existence.

To render the analysis even more fine-grained and to ensure that a broad spectrum of Egyptians was included, some social variables were taken into consideration while choosing the participants in the enquiry. The chosen group was divided into three sub-groups based on their education (1 – high private, 2 – high public, 3 – secondary or lower); each numbering 10 males and 10 females. This division roughly mirrors the social stratification of Egypt[17].

The expressions chosen for the enquiry were pairs such as: *kalb* 'dog' versus *'ibn il-kalb* 'son on a dog', *wisiḫ* 'dirty' versus *'ibn il-wisḫa* 'son of a dirty woman', *ya 'umm il-...* 'this damned...' versus *dīn 'umm il–...* '(the religion of) this damned...', *yil'an mayyitīn 'ummak* '(may God) curse the ancestors of your mother' versus *yil'an dīn 'ummak* '(may God) curse the religion of your mother' and *mitnāk* 'fucked' versus *'ibn il-mitnāka* 'son of a fucked woman'. Obviously, it was expected that in all expressions containing intensifiers, the feature of intensity would have a greater value than in those without them.

---

[16] The full scale included: 0 – neutral; 1 – slightly vulgar or insulting, used without or with a minimum level of redress in all life situations; 2 – vulgar or insulting, used with a minimum level of redress in all life situations except in the social media; 3 – vulgar or insulting, used with minimum level of redress in all life situations except in the social media and in conversations with older people (including parents, grandparents, other relatives); 4 – vulgar or insulting, used with a high level of redress (only in same-gender company); 5 – unmentionable; 6 – unknown to the speaker.

[17] This criterion was adopted because in Egypt education is strongly correlated with social class and the aim of the study was to obtain a wide perspective. Egyptian society is a strongly stratified one, class divisions being associated with financial status, which results in a division in terms of the level of education and lifestyles. Social stratification involves divisions along two axes — localised-cosmopolitan and traditional-modern (De Koning 2009) — resulting in the existence of refined and popular classes, with the middle class somewhere in between, and with education as the most decisive factor determining class membership. The class system is characterised by a relatively low social mobility, despite the fact that since the Nasserite revolution in 1952, Egypt assumed a policy of equal opportunities and free education for all (De Koning 2009:49), therefore these differences tend to be visible in language. This led to the formation of a middle class, whose hallmark was university education (de Koning 2009:47). Since the 70s, the declining quality of state education has given rise to the growth of private education, expensive and available only to the affluent stratum of the society. Their graduates are fluent in English and often in other foreign languages, which makes them culturally closer to the West.

6 Taboo subjects as insult intensifiers in Egyptian Arabic — 133

1a) kalb 'dog'

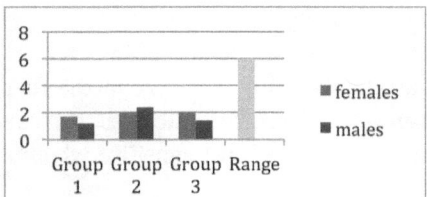

1b) ibn kalb 'son of a dog'

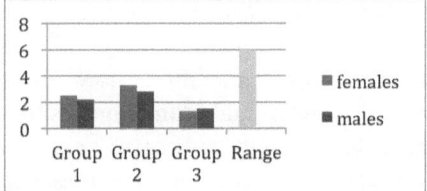

2a) wisiḫ 'dirty'

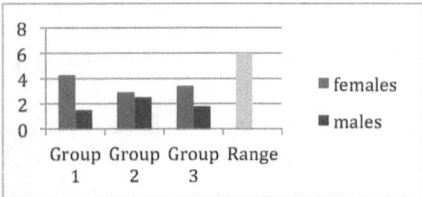

2b) ibn il-wisḫa 'son of a dirty woman'

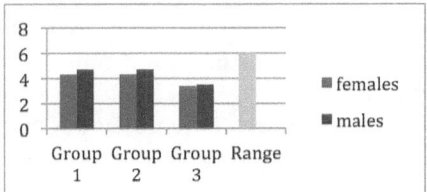

3a) umm il-... 'this damn...'

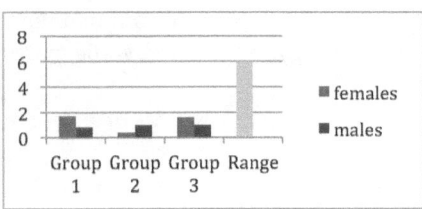

3b) dīn umm il–... '(the religion of) this damn...'

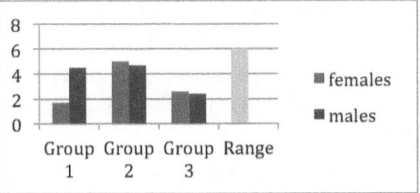

4a) yilʿan mayyitīn ummak 'may the ancestors of your mother be cursed'

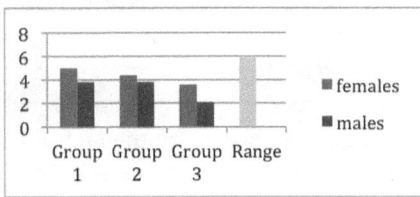

4b) yilʿan dīn ummak 'may the religion of your mother be cursed'

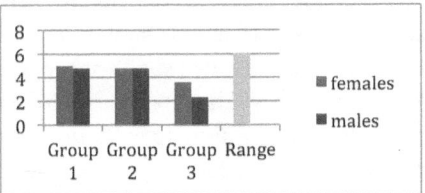

5a) mitnāk 'fucked'

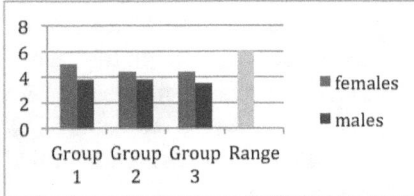

5b) ibn mitnāka 'son of a fucked woman'

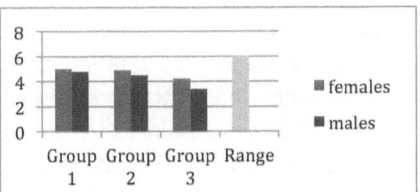

Figure 1: Intensity assessment – results of the questionnaire.

The results presented in Figure 1 reveal the following:

Case 1a) *kalb* 'dog' and 1b) *ibn il-kalb* 'son on a dog'

Both are counted as rather mild insults often used in family setting and not really vulgar. *Ibn il-kalb* is however seen as slightly more offensive in the first two groups, for males and females, however, women tend to evaluate it as more insulting. Also in both cases group 2 appears to be the most sensitive when it comes to the offensiveness of those expressions.

Case 2a) *wisiḫ* 'dirty' and 2b) *ibn il-wisḫa* 'son of a dirty woman'

Here again the overall view shows that *ibn il-wisḫa* is seen as more offensive than *wisiḫ*. Interestingly, the difference is visible mainly in males.

Case 3a) *umm il-...* 'this damned...' and 3b) *dīn umm il-...* '(the religion of) this damned...'

The greatest difference, however, can be observed in the case of *ya umm il-...* and its counterpart intensified by the addition of the tabooed *dīn* (*dīn umm il-...*) with the latter being highly stigmatized due to its religious connotations. The expression *ya umm il-...* is, on the contrary, viewed as light and inoffensive.

Case 4a) *yilʻan mayyitīn ummak* '(may God) curse the ancestors of your mother' and 4b) *yilʻan dīn ummak* '(may God) curse the religion of your mother'

Both of them are seen as equally (and highly) vulgar by females, while males perceive *yilʻan mayyitīn ummak* as stronger.

Case 5a) *mitnāk* 'catamite (fucked)' and 5b) *ibn mitnāka* 'son of a whore (fucked woman)'

The observed (not very significant) difference in the level of vulgarity of 5a and 5b concerns only males. The difference is much slighter in females, which is probably due to the fact, that both these words are already strongly tabooed and reach almost the top of the vulgarity scale (5). Therefore, the use of the intensifier does not make much difference.

The comparison of such concepts as FAMILY, and RELIGION as a way of intensifying insults reveals a great power of *dīn* 'religion' to render the expression highly offensive, vulgar, and socially unacceptable. This is supported by the fact, that all of these were counted by the participants in the study as *sabb ad-dīn* 'blasphemy'. There are, however, socio-pragmatic issues interfering with the interpretation – the addition of *dīn* is a risky endeavour because there is an explicit religious ban on using the *sabb ad-dīn*. Among the three analysed groups, group 2 was the most sensitive to religious rules and the social ostracism (in the case of not observing them), therefore they are cautious not to use such intensifiers. An example of this is a mild expression of anger: *ya umm il-...* (e.g. *ya umm iš-šuġl* 'this damned work'), which is used frequently by all groups. However, modified with *dīn* 'religion', *dīn umm iš-šuġl* it becomes a blasphemy.

To sum up, it is possible to conclude, that *dīn* 'religion' represents the level of intensity considerably higher than the examples referring to the domain: FAMILY. Therefore, answering the first research question, there exists a significant difference in the level of intensity depending on the semantic concept the speaker refers to. This thesis is confirmed in all social groups examined here despite the occurring class and gender differences.

In this limited study, intensifier pertaining to the domain SEXUALITY were not included, because of syntactic differences – in the studied material there were not enough number of examples where such words as *nēk* 'fuck', *fašḫ* 'spreading wide' or *ṭīz* 'ass' could be easily integrated into a similar construction.

5 Level of grammaticalization

To assess the level of grammaticalization of the examined lexical items, Bolinger's approach is employed. Additionally, participants' responses evaluating the studied expressions were analysed to see if they were aware of the word's semantics.

The degree of grammaticization varies from item to item and the ability to apply to different words is an indicator of a high level of grammaticalization (Bolinger 1972). There is a large group of words that are semantically empty, which allows them to appear in great variety of lexical contexts. These are devoid of the semantic content, instead they have acquired grammatical role and became function words. On the other hand, with other examples, there is the reduction of semantic features: some of the intensifiers retain certain semantic features, which impedes their connectivity – they might occur in some types of lexical contexts but not other types.

According to this rule, a high level of grammaticalization is visible in words such as *mōt* 'death' and *nēk* 'fuck', which apply to various types of context. This, however, only means that there has been a loss of connection between the lexical form and its referent (e.g. there is no "death" involved in the presented examples – 21, 22, 23, 24, 26). It does not mean the loss of the tabooness or vulgarity of these words. Therefore, in polite settings euphemistic expressions are employed, as in *mōz* 'bananas' (instead of *mōt* 'death') or *kēk* 'cake' for *nēk* 'fuck' (Woidich, in press).

In the studied material, the most common expressions, such as *ibn il-kalb* 'son of a bitch' are characterised by a high degree of desemanticisation. This thesis is supported by the fact that they can be used affectionately, e.g. by parents talking to their children. Also, *ibn il-kalb* 'son of a bitch/dog' can have a non-human referent: *ṭaʿmu ibn il-kalb* 'it tastes horrible' (it tastes like a son of a bitch/ dog). Inserting *ibn* 'son' serves as a relatively grammaticized intensifier in such constructions as: *ya ʿabīṭ* 'you stupid' > *ya-bn il-ʿabīṭa* 'you son of a stupid woman'; the construction can be applied to a large variety of cases in which *ibn* 'son' appears to be desemanticized, though not completely. *Ibn* 'son' itself itself might serve as an insult in some cases, e.g. *ya-bn il-...* 'you son of...' without anything added to it. It indicates vulgarity and the intention to offend, which may be used in euphemistic variants such as *ya-bn il-ēh* 'you son of what?' or *ya-bn il-lazīna* 'you son of those'. Also such variants are in use as: *ibn in-naṣḥa* 'son of a wise woman' or *ibn iz-zakiyya* 'son of an intelligent woman' (for a stupid person), *bint in-nās iṭ-ṭayyibīn* 'daughter of nice people' (for a wrong-doer).¹⁸

A slightly different level of grammaticalization is represented by *ummak* 'your mother'/ *abūk* 'your father'/ *ahlak* 'your family' in such expressions as: *kuss ummak* 'your mother's cunt', *kuss ahlak* 'your family's cunt'. In those, the abusiveness of the expression is transferred to *ummak* 'your mother' / *ahlak* 'your family', therefore it licences such uses as in: *rigl ummak* 'your mother's leg' *tīt ahlak* 'your family's beep'. This last example is however restricted to a small number of examples when compared with *ibn* 'son'.

Highly grammaticized are the insults with *abu* 'father', where the lexeme has lost its semantic content to the degree that it can be used in such examples as: *ya mundass ya-bu ažinda* 'oh bribed (the one who was pushed in), oh agent (the father of agency)' (*ažinda* 'agency' was an insult during the 25 January Revolution), *abu barbūr* 'father of a snot' or *abu šaḥḥa* 'father of a piss'. Obviously none of "agency", "snot" or "piss" is something that can possibly possess a father.

One might understand curses that make reference to the recipient's family literally as insulting his/her ancestors. However, Stewart argues:

> Even if, originally, the idea of the ancestor's curse having an effect on the descendant may have been prevalent, in current usage, "your father" is merely an emphatic form of reference to "you"; in Egypt the term *ahlak* ("your family") is used in a similar fashion, as in *yiḥrib bēt ahlak* ("May God destroy your family's house!"), which implies, "May God make you destitute!" (Stewart 2014: 11).

This, however, is levelled by the evidence from the questionnaire – many of the respondents, when asked why they see *ibn kalb* 'son of a dog' as stronger than *kalb* 'dog' explained that cursing or insulting their parents feels more painful. Therefore, we cannot postulate that there is no connection to the literal meaning in the analysed examples.

---

18 *Bint* 'daughter' is much rarer, but technically possible.

The word *dīn* 'religion', similarly to the discussed above, can be applied as an intensifier in different types of context (e.g. *haṭallaʿ dīn ummak* 'I will get the religion of your mother out of its place', *allāh yiḫrib bēt dīnak* 'may God destroy the house of your religion'). It is, however, restricted to utterances expressing negative content. As explained above, participants in the study were asked to describe the studied group of expressions with their own words after evaluating their level of intensity. With the expressions involving religion most of them were explicit about their sinfullness (they were using the word *ḥarām* 'forbidden' referring to a religious ban).

In the examples above, *dīn* 'religion' is at a highly advanced stage of grammaticalization, which means it has lost the connection with the original meaning; only the tabooed character and emotional value are preserved. We therefore observe, that with many of the studied insult intensifiers, there is a discrepancy between what we evidence from the analysis of word occurrences in context and what the participants in the study declare. This however can be explained by referring to the fact, that the loss of semantics does not involve the loss of tabooness, so the strongest intensifiers are in fact not the ones retaining their literal meaning or its reflexes, but the ones based on the strongest taboo. Since *sabb ad-dīn* 'blasphemy' is banned by Islam, the violation of this ban is what gives the strength to the intensifiers based on this scheme.

6 Conclusion

Vocabulary referring to the taboos can serve as a source of linguistic intensifiers, which might involve a change of morphological category of words. This process is due to the specific character of taboo terms: there is the value of intensity that can be extracted from them and understood as separate from their semantics. This involves losing their meaning but retaining the gradation of intensity according to the level of tabooness ascribed to specific domains of life. This causes differences in the level of intensity to such an extent that the use of some of them is considered a sin (*sabb ad-dīn* 'blasphemy'). Although this mental process of translating emotions into linguistic representation is universal to humans, the obtained forms are highly culture-specific (see: Kuzio, this volume) and tell us a great deal about the perception of reality maintained in a community. In Egypt, the reference to such sanctities as family or religion is commonly found to serve as intensifier, but this might not be true for other communities.

If we assume, that the conception of the world held in a specific culture manifests itself in the grammar, taboo intensifiers used with insults will appear a natural way of amplifying the emotional load of the abusive utterances, which are already marked by a strong level of intensity. In fact, the use of "normal" or more common intensifiers, such as *'awi* 'very' or *giddan* 'very' with this group of utterances would be interpreted as unnatural or ironical; they might even be considered as minimizers, because, since their level of intensity would be lower than needed, it would probably give raise to an implicature.

References

Abdel Samad, Fatma. 1990. *Politeness strategies in spoken British English and spoken Egyptian Arabic. A contrastive Study*. Cairo: Cairo University dissertation.
Allan, Keith & Kate Burridge. 2006. *Forbidden Words. Tabu and the Censoring of Language*. Cambridge: Cambridge University Press.
Andersson, Lars & Peter Trudgill. 1990. *Bad language*. Oxford: Basil Blackwell.
Bolinger, Dwight. 1972. *Degree Words*. London, The Hague & Paris: Mouton.
Boudot-Lamotte, Antoine. 1974. L'expression de la malédiction et de l'insulte dans les dialectes arabes maghrébins. *Arabica 21*. 53–71.
Brown, Penelope & Stephen C. Levinson. 1978. *Politeness. Some universals in language usage*. Cambridge: Cambridge University Press.
De Koning, Anouk. 2009. *Global Dreams: Class, Gender and Public Space in Cosmopolitan Cairo*. Cairo: The American University of Cairo Press.
Feodorov, Ioana. 2000. On the grammaticalization of intensifiers in Arabic. *Analele Universitati București, Limbi clasice și orientale* XLIX. 99–108.
Heine, Bernd and Mechthild Reh. 1984. *Grammaticalization and reanalysis in African languages*. Hamburg: Buske.
Hoeksema, Jack & Donna Jo Napoli. 2008. Just for the hell of it: A comparison of two taboo-term constructions. *Journal of Linguistics* 44. 347–378.
Labov, William. 1984. Intensity. In Deborah Schiffrin (ed.), *Meaning, form, and use in context: Linguistic applications*, 43–70. Washington: Georgetown University Press.
Lakoff, George & Mark Johnson. 1979. *Metaphors we live by*. Chicago: The University of Chicago Press.
McMahon, April. 1994. *Understanding language change*. Cambridge: Cambridge University Press.
Mughazy, Mustafa, A. 2003. Discourse particles revisited: The case of wallahi in Egyptian Arabic. In Dilworth B. Parkinson & Samira Farwaneh (eds.), *Perspectives on Arabic Linguistics XV*. Amsterdam & Philadelphia: John Benjamins.
Napoli, Jo Donna & Jack Hoeksema. 2009. The grammatical versatility of taboo terms. *Studies in Language* 33(3). 612–643.
Piamenta, Moshe. 1979. *Islam in everyday Arabic speech*. Leiden: E. J. Brill.
Rosenbaum, Gabriel, M. 2012. Oaths in modern spoken Egyptian Judeo-Arabic with a comparison to oaths taken by Christians and Muslims. *Folia Orientalia* 49. 449–466.

Stewart, Devin. 1996. Root-echo responses in Egyptian Arabic politeness formulae. In Alaa Elgibali (ed.) *Understanding Arabic. Essays in contemporary Arabic linguistics in honor of El-Said Badawi.* Cairo: The American University in Cairo Press.

Stewart, Devin. 1997. Impoliteness formulae: The cognate curse in Egyptian Arabic. *Journal of Semitic Studies* 42. 327–360.

Stewart, Devin. 2007. Recounting God's blessings: Linguistic prophylaxis and self-representation in Arabic autobiography. *Al-'Arabiyya* 40–41. 197–219.

Stewart, Devin. 2014. Cognate and analogical courses in Morrocan Arabic: A comparative study of Arabic speech genres. *Arabica* 61. 697–745.

Sweetser, E. 1988. Grammaticalization and Semantic Bleaching. *Proceedings of the Fourteenth Annual Meeting of the Berkeley Linguistics Society.* 389–405.

Vogel, Carl. 2014. Taboo semantics. Paper presented at the 5th IEEE International Conference on Cognitive Infocommunications, Vietri sul Mare, Italy.

Woidich, Manfred. 1995. Some cases of grammaticalization in Egyptian Arabic. *AIDA II Proceedings.* 259–268.

Woidich, Manfred. On some intensifiers in Egyptian Arabic slang (in press).

Mohsen Bakhtiar
7 Emotion concepts in context: Figurative conceptualizations of *hayâ* 'self-restraint' in Persian

Abstract: This paper investigates the role of bodily, cognitive, social-cultural, and discourse-pragmatic factors in the formation of the cultural model of *hayâ* in Persian by broadening Kövecses's (1990) account of emotion concepts. The analysis of the data collected from the Persian newspaper *Keyhan* indicates that *hayâ* together with a set of key concepts (EFFAT 'chastity', ÂBERU 'face/public image', and GHEIRAT 'moral vigilance') form a key cluster and jointly regulate social interactions in Iranian culture. *Hayâ* is shown to be a figuratively constructed emotion concept. Conceptual metaphors are employed to measure the existence and sufficiency of the emotion, to represent the sanctity and vulnerability of *hayâ*, and to highlight the protective, segregative, and prohibitive functions of *hayâ*. This research shows that adding formal and socio-pragmatic properties of emotions to the cognitive analysis contributes to discovering characteristic features and cognitive functions of culturally significant emotions which might not be identified if emotions are merely seen as individual feeling states (Kövecses 1990) or social constructs (Lutz 1988).

Keywords: *Hayâ*, metaphor, emotion, Iranian culture, taboo

1 Introduction

The concept of SHAME has been extensively researched from various perspectives across cultures and languages (Abu-Lughod 1996; Díaz-Vera and Manrique-Antón 2015; Gilbert and Andrews 1998; Holland and Kipnis 1995; Jamieson 2000; Li et al. 2004; Myers 1979; Sharifian and Jamarani, 2011; Tissari 2006). In individualistic cultural contexts, shame is experienced when one has done something bad or wrong (when one has violated norms and standards) in his/her own eyes or in the eyes of others. Moreover, shame typically involves being negatively evaluated by others and occurs more frequently in the presence of others (Benedict 1946; Lewis 1992). This construal of shame is close to what is referred to as *khejâlat* or *sharmandegi* 'feeling ashamed' in Persian. The following expressions conventionally denote shame in Persian:

(1) *Az khejâlat ab shodam/az khejâlat ghermez shod*
    'I melted with shame/He blushed of shame.'
(2) *Az khejâlat dus dashtam zamin dahan baz kone.*
    'I felt so ashamed I wished the earth had opened its mouth for me.'
(3) *Az sharmandegi nemitunest saresho boland kone.*
    'He/she was so ashamed that he couldn't raise his head.'
(4) *Aragh e sharm ruye pishunish neshest.*
    'The sweat of shame appeared on his/her forehead.'

Sweating, blushing, lowering the head, and hiding/disappearing figuratively represent the physiological and behavioral responses associated with *khejâlat/sharmandegi* 'shame' in Persian. Some of these responses such as blushing, lowering of the head, and hiding are similarly associated with shame in Western culture (Holland and Kipnis 1995; Tissari 2006).

This paper studies the conceptual organization and contextual use of the concept of HAYÂ, which is closely related to shame. *Hayâ* may be defined as an emotion that operates to prevent the self from causing or feeling (further) shame. "*Hayâ* is a self-regulating force constituting a main component of religious faith in Islam" (Pasandideh 2004: 3). Main religious sources providing guidance for Muslims' individual and social behavior (i.e., the Quran and *hadith* 'religious sayings') underscore the significance of *hayâ* in preventing sins, promoting self-esteem, and preserving chastity (Khadem Pir 2015: 131–134).

Hayâ sets up a barrier between the self and what is considered as taboo, offensive, shameful, and unpleasant, eventually leading to censoring or amending one's speech or behavior. In psychological accounts, *hayâ* is defined as an inhibiting as well as an impelling force aroused when one faces situations in which a social or religious taboo is violated or is prone to transgression (Pasandideh 2004). It inhibits one from violating taboos and simultaneously impels the person to amend/mind their speech or behavior (Pasandideh 2004: 30–31). Unlike *sharmandegi* 'feeling ashamed', *hayâ* is considered a capability which is voluntarily applied, functioning to regulate social behavior. *Sharm* is another synonym for *hayâ*, which also conventionally collocates with it (*sharm va hayâ* 'shame and hayâ'). *Sharm* is closer in meaning to shame. Words referring to shame in Persian are derived from *sharm*, such as *sharm-sâr* 'ashamed', *sharm-âvar* 'shameful', *bi-sharm* 'shameless'. Feeling shame after one has broken a norm or value would indicate the existence of *hayâ* in a person, which shows one's awareness of culturally specified codes of behavior and more importantly, one's attempt to avoid violating norms. It should be noted that physiological and behavioral responses associated with shame exhibit *hayâ* only when a social or religious norm is involved and this type of shame should be distinguished from the manifestations of shame which result from personality disorder. Therefore, shame is regarded as a moral virtue when it leads to adjusting one's behavior to the specified norms of conduct. The same criterion (refraining from violating taboos) could be the basis for distinguishing behavioral manifestations that jointly realize *hayâ*, shyness and timidity.

Hayâ is associated with a set of emotions and feelings such as fear, respect, and shame (Pasandideh 2004), which result from the interaction of *hayâ* with certain core cultural values. I argue that *hayâ* together with *effat* 'chastity', *âberu* 'face or public image', and *gheirat* 'moral vigilance') constitute a cluster which places restrictions on the speech and behavior of Iranians.

This paper explores the role of the body, cognitive processes (metaphor, metonymy, and categorization), related concepts, social-cultural factors, and discourse-pragmatic elements in the formation of the cultural model of *hayâ* in Persian by broadening Kövecses's (1990) account of emotion concepts. I attempt to show that unraveling the complex structure of emotion concepts requires paying attention to various factors that play a role in characterizing different aspects of emotion concepts.

2 Causes of *hayâ*

Hayâ emerges when one perceives the physical or non-physical presence of an observer (Pasandideh 2004: 19). The perceived observers and the particular emotions they may trigger in an individual could be the basis for categorizing different types of *hayâ* (ibid: 20–22): a) *Hayâ az khod* '*hayâ* toward the self' (self as observer) b) *Hayâ az digari* '*hayâ* toward the other' (the other as observer) c) *Hayâ az khodâ* '*hayâ* toward God' (God as observer) d) *Hayâ az moghaddasât* '*hayâ* toward sanctities' (sanctities as observers).

Due to the contagious nature of taboos, a wide variety of people, objects, places, and events can indirectly play the role of observers. Refraining from holding celebrations or listening to music in the month (Safar in Arabic calendar) the Prophet passed away, or avoiding drinking in one's parents' house since they pray in the house (even when they are away), are examples of how *hayâ* is applied through perceiving the presence of non-physical observers.

As Pasandideh's (2004) research demonstrates, the observers perceived in a particular situational context trigger a number of emotions which result in the emergence of *hayâ* and its expressive responses:

a) Abhorrence of committing sins and violating social norms and values: This may originate in the senses of *kerâmat e nafs* 'self-esteem' and *vejdân* 'conscience'.
b) Fear of being criticized or punished by a socially or religiously more powerful observer or by an observer in one's social group or community.
c) Fear of jeopardizing or losing one's *âberu* 'face or public image'.
d) Respect to the observer: Class, gender, and age are among the main social factors determining the emergence and intensity of *hayâ* in relation to others.

Hayâ is a major means of maintaining respect among individuals, particularly when one has the right or capability to respond to the other's disrespectful or offensive behavior, but one applies *hayâ* to hold back what he/she could have done or said in response. Parents, women, relatives, neighbors, elders, teachers and clerics are among the classes of individuals one may avoid criticizing or confronting openly.

Assessment is the key to activating *hayâ* (Pasandideh 2004: 113). Assessing the degree of unpleasantness of a particular behavior, the consequences of demonstrating the behavior, and social and religious status of the perceived observer(s) determine the emergence, intensity, and physiological and behavioral effects of *hayâ*.

3 Data and methodology

Hayâ is a key concept in Iranian culture. According to Wierzbicka (1997: 15), key words in a culture are "words which are particularly important and revealing in a given culture". She proposes that for the identification of key concepts it should be established that the word in question is common, frequently used in a particular semantic domain, and is at the center of a whole phraseological cluster. Moreover, a key word is expected to appear frequently in proverbs and other modes of language use (Wierzbicka 1997: 16). In addition to these criteria, two formal properties of Persian language provide evidence as to the significance of *haya* in Iranian culture. First, Persian marks many of its culturally salient concepts with two prepositions, *bâ/bi* 'with/without', that appear in compound adjectives as prefixes. These two prepositions are major means of categorizing individuals in Iranian culture in terms of perceived existence or lack of cultural values in individuals. While compound adjectives including *bâ* (e.g., *bâhayâ*) are used to compliment and admire a person for possessing a particular moral or religious value, those adjectives constructed with *bi* (e.g., *bihayâ*) are regarded as offensive and often used as swearwords. Second, in Persian, the relationship between core cultural values and their most related concepts is manifested through lexical collocations such as *haya va effaf* 'haya and chastity', *hojb va haya* 'covering/inhibiting and *haya*', *hejab va effâf* 'veiling and chastity'.

To examine the pragmatic use of *hayâ*, 150 statements containing the word *hayâ* were collected from the online version of the Persian newspaper *Keyhan* by searching the word *hayâ*. *Keyhan* is a state-funded newspaper which reflects the viewpoints of political-religious conservatives in Iran. The data cover a period of over two years and a half from 28/09/2013 to 18/05/2016. Lexical collocates (e.g., *hayâ va âberu* '*hayâ* and face', and *hojb va hayâ* 'covering/inhibiting and *hayâ*') and the wider linguistic context surrounding *hayâ* were examined manually to discover the characteristic properties (modesty, mindfulness, and being concealed) as well as the major conceptual domains (EFFAT 'chastity', GHEIRAT 'moral vigilance', and ÂBERU 'face/public image') that interact with it. This was carried out by grouping collocations in terms of whether they denoted a feature of *hayâ* or a major domain interacting with it. Next, metaphorical uses of *hayâ* were identified using Metaphor Identification Procedure (Pragglejaz Group 2007). Criteria for identifying linguistic metaphors in this study are (a) a contrast between the contextual meaning of a word or phrase and its basic meaning, which is more concrete and physical and (b) understanding the contextual meaning based on a comparison with its basic meaning. Almost all metaphorical conceptualizations of *hayâ* are based on a similarity created between the abstract concept of HAYÂ and more concrete or physical conceptual domains. The identified metaphors are grouped into three main categories: metaphors which are responsible for the figurative measurement of *hayâ*, those indicating the functions of *hayâ*, and metaphors highlighting the sanctity and vulnerability of *hayâ*. The conceptual metaphors suggested for each category of linguistic expressions represent the most frequently occurring metaphors in the data.

The analysis of metonymy is limited to the role it plays in linking *hayâ* to its emotional responses in social interactions as there are no cases of the EMOTIONAL RESPONSE FOR EMOTION metonymy in the data.

4 Cognitive structure of *hayâ*

In Persian dictionaries, *hayâ* is defined as *tobeh* 'repentance', *sharm/khejâlat* 'shame, feeling ashamed', or refraining from doing something due to the fear of being criticized (Dehkhoda online dictionary). The expression *hayâ kardan* 'exercising or applying *hayâ*' has two slightly different contextual meanings. In one of its usages, the expression is conventionally used to criticize a person who has violated social norms and values. In this sense, *hayâ kardan* contextually means that one should be ashamed of what he/she has done and cease doing or talking about it:

(5) *Ruhe payame rahpeimai e 22 Bahman be amrika in ast ke bayad **az tahrimha aleihe iran hayâ konad*** (Keyhan, 15/02/2014).

'The gist of the message sent through the 11 February demonstration [the anniversary of founding the Islamic Republic in 1979] to the U.S government is that it should **be ashamed of imposing sanctions on Iran**'.

However, in some contexts, where one is already mindful of the consequences of breaching norms and values, the meaning of *hayâ kardan* seems to be closer to 'avoiding an unpleasant act', where feeling shame might be conceptually less prominent:

(6) *Vey bar zedde ali aliehesalam ta'abire zanande va namonasebi bekar mibord. Be hamin jahat, barkhi az raviane hadis az naghl e anha **hayâ kardeand*** (Keyhan, 19/04/2016).

'He would use unpleasant words to describe Ali (the first Shiite Imam). Therefore, some of the *Hadith* 'religious saying' narrators **have avoided** retelling them'.

Hayâ is characterized by avoidance, shame, concealment, politeness, indirectness, modesty, and mindfulness. A large number of adjectives in Persian represent such characteristics of *hayâ*: *Mahjub* 'covered' (modest), *makhuz be hayâ* 'held back by *hayâ*', *sar be zir* 'head-toward-down' (modest), *cheshm pâk* 'pure-eyed', *afif* 'chaste', *oftâdeh* 'fallen' (modest), *khishtandâr* 'self-controlled', *najib* 'decent', and *kam ru* 'shy'.

Lack of *hayâ* is characterized by rudeness, impudence, exposure, audacity, mindlessness, and assertiveness. The following adjectives exhibit the perceived lack of *hayâ* in an individual. *Vaghih* 'impudent', *porru* 'rude', *rok* 'outspoken', *biâberu* 'lacking honor', *dahan darideh* 'foul mouthed', *bimolâhezeh* 'inconsiderate/mindless, and *nânajib* 'indecent'.

Given the linguistic and non-linguistic usages of *hayâ*, three main prototypical cognitive models, among many others available to the speakers, can be suggested for this emotion concept:

1. A social or religious value is subject to violation > *hayâ* comes into existence > *hayâ* exerts force upon the self to hold it back > the self overcomes the force of *hayâ* > the self violates the taboo.

This prototype characterizes behaviors that are described as shameless and against moral values.
2. A social or religious value is violated by the self > the self feels shame/embarrassment > *hayâ* comes into existence >*hayâ* holds back the self > the self quits the act > the self amends his/her behavior.
   This prototype may illustrate situations in which *hayâ* and shame are closely interrelated, where feeling shame suggests the existence of *hayâ* in the person. Although a norm or rule is broken, the person attempts to correct his/her conduct in compliance with expected behavioral principles.
3. Self is subject to violating a social or religious value > the self feels fear/anxiety/resentment/embarrassment > *hayâ* comes into existence > *hayâ* holds back the self > the self avoids violating the value > *hayâ* is manifested in behavior.

Given the skeletal emotion schema (cause of emotion-emotion-response) suggested by Kövecses (2000), the control aspect involved in *hayâ* can be understood both as a physical force applied to the causal part of the schema, where *hayâ* exerts its force to hold back the self (to cause control, which is the inherent responsibility of *hayâ*) and as a physical force exerted by the self to resist the force of *hayâ* (to control the controlling cause). In the case of *hayâ*, being emotional can be translated into 'being in control.' A person avoids violating norms and values when he/she is overcome by the force of *hayâ* and he/she violates taboos when one resists and overcomes the force of *hayâ*. The expression *hefz e hayâ* 'preserving *hayâ*' and *hayâ ra kenâr gozâshtan* 'putting *hayâ* aside' represent the two forms of control involved.

5 Lexical collocates of *hayâ*

Lexemes collocating with *hayâ* specify the characteristic properties of the concept as well as major domains which interact with, and structure, *hayâ*. Lexical collocates of *hayâ* extracted from the data are as follows: *Hayâ va sharm* '*hayâ* and shame', *hayâ va iman* '*hayâ* and faith', *hayâ va âberu* '*hayâ* and public image/face', *hayâ va gheirat* '*hayâ* and moral vigilance', *hayâ va effat* '*hayâ* and chastity', *hojb va hayâ* 'covering/inhibiting' and *haya*', *hayâ va din* '*hayâ* and religion', *haya va nejâbat* '*hayâ* and decency', *aghl va hayâ* 'common sense and *hayâ*', *hayâ va salâmat* '*hayâ* and [moral] health', and *hayâ va hejab* '*hayâ* and veiling'.

Based on the above list, exercising *hayâ* is assumed to be indicative of religious faith, moral health, common sense, decency, chastity, and *âberu* 'face'.

The word *hojb* 'covering/inhibiting', however, can be taken as a characteristic feature of *hayâ*. The word *gheirat* 'moral vigilance' can be seen as an emotional cause of *hayâ*. The other collocate of *hayâ* is *sharm* 'shame'. Being ashamed of one's wrongdoings is indicative of the existence of *hayâ*, and one's will to quit the unpleasant behavior. This latter psychological state is assumed to be motivated by *hayâ*.

Effat 'chastity', *âberu* 'face/public image', *hayâ*, and *gheirat* 'moral vigilance' seem to minimally form a conceptual cluster functioning to place restrictions on speech and behavior of Iranians. The reason for grouping these concepts is that a barrier or cover between the self and the other is the chief property defining the concepts of EFFAT, ÂBERU, and HAYÂ. *Gheirat*, however, is included in the cluster since it is a broad regulating force activated when social norms and values are violated, which is demonstrated through a form of anger or indignation. Fear of being criticized or punished, which is one of the causes of observing *hayâ*, could be attributed to one's awareness of the existence of *gheirat* in others and the consequences of its operation. Below, I explain each of these concepts.

5.1 *Effat* 'chastity'

Refraining from *harâm* 'forbidden', piety, being covered or concealed, and self-control are the meanings provided for *effat* in Persian dictionaries (www.vajehyab.com). *Effat* as a defining feature of Iranian women mostly applies to restrict the speech and behavior of women in relation to men. However, men are also expected to display *effat* when communicating with women by casting down the gaze. *Effat* is a subcategory or a more specific form of *hayâ*, meaning that showing *effat* is demonstrating *hayâ* as well. Whereas *effat* is tailored to harness illegitimate sexual desire in men and women, *hayâ* encompasses a wider range of taboos, including sexual desire.

Example (7) presents *hayâ* and *effat* as essential features of the wise relying on an interpretation of Quranic verses. The verb phrase *ejtenâb az zeshtihâ* 'avoiding obscenities' provides the clue as to the function that *hayâ* and *effat* have in common.

(7) *Hamchenin dar in ayat bayan shod e ke osulan kheradmandan kesani hastand ke **ahle haya va effat bude va az zeshtiha ejtenab mikonand*** (Keyhan, 27/08/2016).
'Also, these [Koranic] verses express that the wise are those who **tend to observe *hayâ* and *effat*, and avoid obscenities**'.

The sufficiency of *effat* in women is estimated by monitoring their conducts when encountering *nâmahram* men (men in whose presence a woman should cover up): women are not supposed to arouse the sexual feelings of *nâmahram* men intentionally (i.e. by controlling their gaze), nor use heavy make-up, nor go out with and touch *nâmahram* men, nor talk and laugh provocatively (flirtatiously) (https://rasekhoon.net, 20/04/2015). Besides, keeping virginity until marriage and observing *hejab* 'veiling' in the presence of *nâmahram* men are other important properties that define the conceptual category of EFFAT. Such features can form a prototype for an *afif* 'chaste' woman.

5.2 *Âberu* 'face or public image'

Âberu "embodies the image of a person, a family, or a group, particularly as viewed by others in the society" (Sharifian 2007: 36). Zaborowska (2014: 125) maintains that "*âberu* is a veil covering the human face, protecting his personality from disclosure and guarding his moral character in the eyes of others." In almost all social interactions, Iranians attempt to preserve their own *âberu* as well as that of their family or social group by virtue of presenting a socially pleasant image of their speech, behavior, appearance, and possessions. A major part of this attempt necessarily involves concealing or restricting aspects of speech and behavior which might threaten one's public image. "Loss of *âberu* is regarded as a great misfortune and makes it difficult to function in a group because it is associated with shame and embarrassment" (Zaborowska 2014: 14). Hence, showing *hayâ* by means of avoiding violating social norms and values is to demonstrate that one possesses *âberu*, that is, a *bâhayâ* person (a person possessing *hayâ*) is *bââberu* 'possesses *âberu*' and conversely, a *bihayâ* person (a person lacking *hayâ*) is *biâberu* 'lacks *âberu*'. The main emotion triggering *hayâ* in connection with *âberu* is fear, i.e. the constant fear of losing *âberu* propels the person to observe *hayâ*. *Tars e az âberu* 'fear of losing *âberu*' is a relatively common phrase in Persian used to express the main reason why people may opt to remain passive to the face-threatening acts of others:

(8) *Polis: Ghrobanian e tajavoz **az tars e âberu** va tahdid e mojreman shekayat nemikonand* (www.yjc.ir, 15/04/2015).
'Police: victims of rape do not file complaints against the perpetrators **for the fear of [losing] âberu** and of being threatened by them'.

Closely connected with *âberu* is the word *ru* 'face' in Persian which represents both the figure and image of a person (Zaborowska 2014: 120). It also expresses shame, shyness, embarrassment, and *hayâ*. Two adjectives *kam ru* literally 'little-face' [shy/timid] and *por ru* literally 'full-face' [rude] denote shyness and lack of *hayâ* respectively. Given the common behavioral responses associated with both shyness and *hayâ*, such as hiding the face, lowering the gaze, shrinking, and so on, *hayâ* may be mistakenly taken for shyness. However these two are not the same. Whereas shyness denotes the incapability of a person in showing proper behavior in communicative situations, *hayâ* is regarded as a capability, and a moral virtue, which is voluntarily applied to restrict the self in relation to taboo behavior in the presence of an observer.

5.3 *Gheirat* 'moral vigilance'

Gheirat may be defined as a monitoring device or alarm system in the minds of Iranians. It is a complex concept with a variety of functions. Transgressing taboos typically activates the feeling of *gheirat* in Iranians. In relation to taboo areas, *gheirat* operates to protect one's values against threat, insult, and injury, which is realized as a form of anger or indignation (Bakhtiar 2015). *Gheirat* is socially expected to exist in both men and women with the difference that it is considered as an essential feature of men and a relatively peripheral property of women.

Perceived passivity or non-existence of *gheirat* in men is highly insulting and may seriously injure his *âberu* 'face/public image'. The behavioral responses associated with *gheirat* range from verbal fighting to physical fighting, and even to murdering the perpetrator. Example (6) demonstrates the relationship between *hayâ* and *gheirat*. Here, insensitivity or inattentiveness of some Iranian politicians toward the West's alleged interference in Iran's domestic affairs (lack of *gheirat*) is believed to have caused the open violation of political norms (lack of *hayâ*). The adverb *bimahâbâ* 'daringly/fearlessly' describes the manner with which the principle of *hayâ* is violated.

(9) ***che bihaya hastand anan ke bimahaba va ba bigheirati** amalan parcham e biganegan ra bar sar dar e khanehaye khod nasb mikonand (Keyhan, 21/02/2016).*
    'How ***bihayâ* [shameless]** are those, who daringly and without any ***gheirat***, practically put up the flag of aliens on top of their house doors'.

6 Metaphors of *hayâ*

This section deals with the analysis of frequently occurring conceptual metaphors in the data set.

6.1 Figurative measurement of *hayâ*

Many examples in the data figuratively conceptualize the existence, lack, sufficiency, insufficiency, intensity, and preserving *hayâ*.

HAYÂ IS A POSSESSED OBJECT: Adjectives containing *bâ* and *bi* along with a number of other Persian expressions manifest the HAYÂ IS A POSSESSED OBJECT metaphor:

(10) *Bazi **be hadi bahayâ** hastand ke ba hameye nadari va bicharegi hazer nistand niaz e khod ra ezhar konand (Keyhan, 19/07/2014).*
'Some people are **so bâhayâ/possess so much of hayâ** that they do not want to express their need despite all their poverty and desperation'.

(11) *che **bihayâ** hastand anan ke bimahaba v aba bigheirati amalan parchame biganegan ra dar sar dare khanehaye khod nasb mikonand (Keyhan, 21/02/2016).*
'How **bihayâ (shameless)** are those who rudely and without any *gheirat* (sensitivity to taboo violations) practically put up the flag of aliens on top of their house doors'.

The other expressions realizing the metaphor in the data are *hayâ dashtan* 'having *hayâ*' and *vojoud e hayâ* 'the existence of *hayâ*.'

HAYÂ IS A VALUABLE COMMODITY: Verbal objects modifying the verbs *be kharj dâdan* 'spending' and *hefz kardan* 'preserving' typically denote valuable objects or entities. For that reason, VALUABLE COMMODITY seems to be a proper source domain for the metaphors of this category. This metaphor highlights the significance of *hayâ* as a moral virtue.

(12) *Agar ma **hayâ be kharj midahim** va hochigari nemikonim anha ham reayat konand (Keyhan, 04/05/2014).*
'If we **spend hayâ** [observe *hayâ*] and do not raise a ruckus, they should also observe it'.

HAYÂ IS A SUBSTANCE IN A CONTAINER: The intensity of *hayâ* is figuratively conceived as a SUBSTANCE IN THE BODY (conceived as the metaphorical container), as in *ahamiat e taghviate hayâ* 'the significance of reinforcing *haya*', *mazerrât e kahesh e hayâ* 'the disadvantages of the decrease of *hayâ*', *sharm va hayâye andak* 'a low (amount of) shame and *hayâ*'.

(13) *Az ghena beparhizid ke **hayâ ra kam mikonad*** (Keyhan, 06/04/2016).
'Refrain from singing as it **lowers *hayâ***'.

Intense forms of *hayâ* in the above examples are thoroughly positively viewed, which is in contrast with the rather negative evaluation of the intense forms of shame in English (Tissari 2006: 152). Moreover, while increasing intensity in many of prototypical emotion concepts such as anger, love, and sadness can lead to loss of control over one's emotions (Kövecses 1990, 2000), an increase in the intensity of *hayâ* results in gaining more control over socially or religiously negatively viewed emotions such as lust, anger, and conceit.

In addition to the body in general, the mouth, heart and stomach also play the role of metaphorical containers for *hayâ*.

(14) *Besyari az anha **sharm ra khorde o hayâ ra ghei kardeand** va ba anasore zede enghelab hamkari mikonand* (Keyhan, 17/05/2016).

'Many of them have **eaten shame and vomited *hayâ*** and are cooperating with the anti-revolution camp'.

(15) *Kesi ke **hayâ dar ghalb o delash vojud dashte bashad** az gonahan duri mijooyad* (Keyhan, 07/04/2014)

'Anyone who **has *hayâ* in his heart and *del*** (heart/stomach) will keep distance from sins'.

Example (14) is an idiom which is used to describe people who openly break norms and values. The idiom based on the HAYÂ AND SHAME ARE FOOD metaphor (a specific-level realization of the HAYÂ IS A SUBSTANCE IN A CONTAINER metaphor) conveys speaker's extreme dissatisfaction with the addressee's inattentiveness to moral prohibitions. What may have motivated the use of the mouth as the container for shame is that the mouth is the organ of speech (INSTRUMENT FOR ACTION); shame as the content of the container (the mouth) controls the quantity and quality of one's speech and prevents one from uttering face-threatening speech. The expression *hayâ ra ghei kardan* 'vomiting *haya*' in (14) provides the inference that the stomach is the metaphorical container for *hayâ* (the content). Also, in (15) the heart and *del* 'heart/stomach' are seen as the containers. In Persian, the word *del* 'heart/stomach' "refers to the area of the body below the chest and above the pelvis, roughly similar to the area described in English by abdomen" (Sharifian 2008: 249). This area of the body is figuratively viewed as "the seat of emotions, feelings, and desires" (Sharifian 2008: 251). *Hayâ* figuratively exists in *del* so as to restrict or control desires which do not conform to cultural values. Therefore, vomiting the content of the stomach (*hayâ*) is to deliberately get rid of the barrier *hayâ* sets up on the way of breaking a norm or value.

HAYÂ IS A PHYSICAL LOCATION: PHYSICAL LOCATION evoked by the prepositional phrase *be dur az* 'far away from' is a significant source domain for measuring the deviation of one's speech and behavior from expected social and religious values, exemplified by *be dur az hayâ/adab/ensâniat/javânmardi/ensâf/efâf* 'far away from *hayâ*/politeness/humanity/chivalry/fairness/chastity. Moreover, the metaphorical spatial distance between one's act or speech and moral values determines the reaction of observers (people or government officials) to taboo violations:

(16) *Moteasefane bad az tazakorat e mokarrar e mardom va mas'ulan, hamchenan barkhi az forushgahha lebashaye mardane va zanane ra dar mankanhaye* **be door az haya va efaf e eslami-irani** *tarvij o tabligh mikonand* (Keyhan, 02/03/2014).

'Unfortunately, despite repeated admonishments of people and officials, some clothes stores are still displaying men and women's clothes in mannequins which are **far away from Islamic-Iranian *hayâ* and chastity**'.

In Iranian society, representations of nudity (e.g., mannequins, sculptures, and statues exposing female head, bodily curves, and private parts) are believed to cause shame on a par with actual nudity, motivated by the REPRESENTATIONS OF TABOO FOR TABOO conceptual metonymy. In this case, *hayâ* operates to avoid causing shame. Therefore, shop keepers are required to veil mannequins exposing the body and bodily curves (www.dailymail.co.uk, 24/09/2009).

6.2 Metaphors representing the sanctity and vulnerability of *hayâ*

A group of metaphors focus on the sanctity and vulnerability of *hayâ*, revealing the ways in which human conducts posit threats to the existence and normal functioning of this moral value.

HAYÂ IS A HOLY SPACE/BOUNDED REGION: The word *harim* in Persian dictionaries is defined as "a holy place or territory which must be protected" (Dehkhoda Online Dictionary). *Harim* frequently appears in such verb phrases as *pâsdâri az harim e hayâ* 'guarding the space or territory of *hayâ*' and *reâyat e harim e hayâ* 'observing/respecting the space or territory of *hayâ*'. These expressions seem to be verbal metaphors forming the HAYÂ IS A HOLY SPACE/BOUNDED REGION conceptual metaphor. Example (17) shows an elaborated form of this metaphor, where scenes featured in a TV series are seen as being destructive to social-religious norms, which demand respecting and obeying parents through exhibiting *hayâ*:

(17) *Osyangari dar barabare valedein va **shekaste shodan e harim e haya va sharm** ra mitavan nemunehayi az nokate manfie in serial onvan kard* (*Keyhan*, 16/02/2014).
'Rebelling against parents and **breaking the space of *hayâ* and shame** are among the negative points of the TV series'.

SOCIAL AND RELIGIOUS PROHIBITIONS ARE OPPONENTS OF HAYÂ: In many examples, social-religious prohibitions violated by individuals are metaphorically pictured as OPPONENTS OF HAYÂ. OPPONENT is a well-known source domain in the metaphorical conceptualization of emotions, which can be seen as an instantiation of the master metaphor EMOTION IS FORCE (Kövecses 2000: 61). Some particular acts and behaviors such as disrespecting parents, begging, dressing immodestly in public, and representing taboos in the media and novels (e.g., prostitution, drug addiction, and cheating in married life) are verbally shown to be attacking (*morede hajme gharâr dâdan*), targeting (*neshâne raftan*), and obliterating (*az bein bordan*) *hayâ*. Other phrases such as *defâ az harim e hayâ* 'defending the territory of *hayâ*', *herâsat az harim e hayâ* 'guarding the territory of *hayâ*' also provide further evidence for taking social-religious prohibitions as metaphorical opponents of *hayâ*:

(18) *Chegune mitavan paziroft arzeshhaye akhlaghi va engarehaye dini nazire **haya va efaf va nejabat**, be bahaneye film va sinema va ghesseguyi ingune mored e hajme gharar girad?* (*Keyhan*, 11/05/2014).
'How can it be accepted that moral values and religious assumptions, such as **hayâ, chastity, decency, get attacked** like this on the pretext of cinema, movies, and story-telling'.

(19) *Inha pusheshhayi hastand ke **hayâ va effat ra neshane miravand*** (*Keyhan*, 31/01/2016)
'These are forms of dressing which **target *hayâ* and chastity**'.

6.3 Metaphors representing the protective and segregative functions of *hayâ*

The most important psychological function of *hayâ* (i.e., setting up barriers between the self and taboos) is extensively reflected in Persian conceptualizations of *hayâ* through various metaphors employing BARRIER, COVER, CURTAIN or CLOTHES as their source concepts. The expression *pardehdari* literally meaning 'curtain-tearing', for instance, refers to the deliberate infringement of social-religious norms and values. The adjective *mahjub* literally meaning 'covered' is also a compliment term based on the same generic metaphor used to describe a modest person who properly observes *hayâ* and refrains from transgressing cultural-religious red lines.

HAYÂ IS A COVER/BARRIER: In example (20), *hayâ* is conceptualized as a CURTAIN (HAYÂ IS A CURTAIN); removing curtains corresponds to ignoring all elements restricting or regulating one's social behavior in a Muslim country. Likewise, in (21), based on the HAYÂ IS A COVER/BARRIER metaphor, putting the screen or cover aside corresponds to disregarding one's previous considerations for not reacting to a dishonest behavior (e.g., because of considering the *âberu* 'face/public image' of the person):

(20) **Bardashte shodan e kheili az pardehaye hayâ** *va tarvije bihayâee va addisazi e ravabet e nasalem az mazerrat e shabakehaye ejtemaeest* (*Keyhan*, 12/01/2016).
'**Removing many of *hayâ* curtains**, propagating shamelessness, and normalizing immoral relationships are some of the disadvantages of social media'.

(21) *Ama ou **hayâ ra kenar nahad** va chehreye vaghei e in jemaat ra neshan dad* (*Keyhan*, 14/05/2016).
'But he **put *hayâ* aside** and revealed the real face of these people'

Physiological and expressive responses associated with an emotion metonymically refer to it (Kövecses 1990, 2000). Blushing, perspiring, shrinking, maintaining physical distance with the other, casting down the gaze, silence, lowering the voice, walking modestly, setting the intonation in compliance with *hayâ*, covering up hair and the body (observing *hejab*), standing up when an elder or a respectable person enters into a place, and folding legs in front of elders are other physiological and behavioral responses which can designate *hayâ* through the EMOTIONAL RESPONSE FOR EMOTION conceptual metonymy. However, linguistic representations of the responses associated with *hayâ* occur non-metonymically, as the causing emotion (*hayâ*) is also realized in the same linguistic context.

7 Summary of the findings

Some of the *hayâ* metaphors are similar to metaphors of shame in English. The conceptual metaphors SHAME IS A VALUABLE COMMODITY, SHAME IS DOWN, SHAME IS A COVER/CLOTH, SHAME IS A FLUID, SHAME IS AN OBSTACLE (Tissari 2006) can be compared with HAYÂ IS DOWN (a metonymy-based metaphor), HAYÂ IS A VALUABLE COMMODITY, HAYÂ IS A COVER, HAYÂ IS A FLUID IN A CONTAINER metaphors. A major difference between the metaphors is that the metaphorical source domains of *hayâ* provide a largely positive evaluation of the concept, whereas the metaphorical source domains of shame in English depict a rather negative image of shame.

Metaphors of *hayâ* in Persian and those of shame in English (Tissari 2006) both employ THE BODY and THE HEART as metaphorical containers. However, Persian presents two more metaphorical containers for *hayâ* (DEL 'HEART/STOMACH' and the MOUTH). Moreover, while the substance in the metaphorical container is negatively characterized in English (Tissari 2006: 152), the fluid in the metaphorical containers for *hayâ* is positively viewed. Whereas shame is seen as NUDITY in English (Holland and Kipnis 1995), *hayâ* is conceived of as a COVER. This contrast highlights the protective function of *hayâ* in Iranian culture.

Data analysis indicates that the protective, segregative, and prohibitive functions of *hayâ* are shown via the HAYÂ IS COVER/CURTAIN conceptual metaphors. The source domain COVER is also used in the metaphorical conceptualization of other cluster members associated with *hayâ* (*âberu* 'public image' and *effat* 'chastity'). These functions originate from a fundamentally religious outlook which believes in segregating men and women, and separating public and private realms in order to preserve social order and reduce moral corruption.

The conceptual link between *hayâ* and shame in social interactions is facilitated by the SHAME FOR HAYÂ metonymy, whereby physiological and behavioral manifestations of shame such as blushing and lowering the gaze provide mental access to *hayâ*. Furthermore, demonstrations of modesty (walking modestly, lowering the head, not being talkative, and downgrading one's own achievements) also metonymically refer to *hayâ*. This conceptual association highlights one of the main functions of *hayâ*, which is creating modesty. *Hayâ* and modesty also get connected through COVER metaphors. Observing *hejab* is a chief manifestation of COVER metaphors in social-physical reality and is illustrative of modesty.

The conceptualizations of *hayâ* in Persian demonstrate similarities to the conceptualizations of shame in collectivist cultures. Some of the emotional causes (fear of losing one's *âberu* 'face/public image' and respect to the other), physiological and behavioral responses (lowering the head, blushing, and hiding the face) and functions (prohibitive and protective functions) characterizing *hayâ* similarly characterize shame in Tagalog (Palmer and Brown 1998), Thai (Ukosakul 2003), Dalabon (Ponsonnet 2014), the Mediterranean cultures (Abu-Lughod 1996), Chinese (Li et al. 2004) and Indian (Menon and Shweder 1993).

Whereas shame in some cultures is mostly experienced in face-to-face interactions such as *hiya* in Tagalog (Plamer and Brown 1998), *kunta* in Pintupi (Myers 1979), *swira* in Kakabila (Jamieson 2000), *yer(mu)* in Dalabon (Ponsonnet 2014), *lajya* in Orissa (Menon and Shweder 1993), *hayâ* can also emerge in private and under the influence of objects, places and events functioning as observers. The other point distinguishing *hayâ* from similar concepts in other cultures is the overwhelming role of religion in shaping the structure and defining the functions of *hayâ*. *Hayâ* is shown to be predominantly guided by religious assumptions that underscore the necessity for controlling such desires as lust, anger, conceit, self-displaying, and covetousness, which damage self-esteem and disrupt social order. Compared to the concept of shame in the aforementioned cultures, *hayâ* seems to have a wider scope of application. This is due to the large number of social and religious prohibitions as well as a large number of non-physical or non-human elements which can take on the role of observer.

8 Conclusion

The analysis of *hayâ* in linguistic and nonlinguistic contexts indicates that *hayâ* is a constituent element of a key conceptual cluster which regulates and restricts the individual and social behaviors of Iranians. The cultural model of *hayâ* is shown to be formed through the interaction of bodily, cognitive, social-cultural, and discourse-pragmatic factors. Moreover, studying the concept of HAYÂ supports Kövecses' view that emotions are mostly figuratively conceived (Kövecses 2000: 85).

Various approaches view emotions as social constructs (Lutz 1988), discourse models (Rosaldo 1980; Rafael 1988), and as individual feeling states formed through universal bodily experiences and cognitive processes (Kövecses 1990, 2000). There are also approaches which relate the emergence of emotions to a combination of factors such as social actions, discourse models, and figurative meaning-making devices (Palmer and Brown 1998). The present research finds that the complex structure of emotion concepts and key cultural concepts may be more illuminated when sufficient attention is given to various bodily, cognitive, social-cultural, and discourse-pragmatic factors and views emotions as being jointly formed through the collaboration of all these factors. This goal is achieved by providing a detailed, context-based analysis of metaphors which are shown to be crucial to comprehending the meaning of emotion concepts and concepts representing core cultural values. Considering the immediate linguistic context and the discourses surrounding the key concept of HAYÂ proves to be useful in systematically identifying the range of related emotion concepts as well as broader conceptual domains which interact with and structure it, contributing to discovering the cognitive-cultural functions of the concept. Besides, since the cultural underpinnings of metaphors are emphasized in both Cultural Linguistics (Sharifian 2015) and in recent approaches to metaphor in Cognitive Linguistics (Deignan 2005; Kövecses 2015), a context-based metaphor analysis preserves the interdisciplinary nature of the investigation and takes into account the objectives of both Cultural Linguistics and Cognitive Linguistics.

The results of the research can be used to compare taboo-avoiding strategies across cultures and language. Moreover, exploring taboo areas can provide a basis to investigate the cultural roots of political conflicts across the globe.

References

Abu-Lughod, Lila. 1996. Honor and shame. In Michael Jackson (ed.), *Things as they are: New directions in phenomenological anthropology*, 51–69. Bloomington, IN: Indiana University Press.
Bakhtiar, Mohsen. 2015. Cognitive model of *gheirat* in Persian. *Cognitive Linguistic Studies* 2 (2). 257–288.
Benedict, Ruth. 1946. *The chrysanthenum and the sword*. Boston: Houghton-Mifflin.
Cohen, Dov., Joseph Vandello & Adrian K. Rantilla. 1998. The sacred and the social: cultures of honor and violence. In Paul Gilbert & Bernice Andrews (eds.), *Shame: interpersonal behavior, psychopathology, and culture*, 261–282. New York: Oxford University Press.
Deignan, Alice. 2005. *Metaphor and corpus linguistics*. Amsterdam: John Benjamins.
Díaz-Vera, Javier E & Teodoro Manrique-Antón. 2015. Better shamed before one than shamed before all: Shaping shame in Old English and Old Norse texts. In Javier Díaz-Vera (ed.), *Metaphor and metonymy across time and cultures: Perspectives on the sociohistorical linguistics of figurative language*, 225–264. Berlin: Mouton de Gruyter.
Gilbert, Paul & Bernice Andrews. 1998. *Shame: Interpersonal behavior, psychopathology, and culture*. New York: Oxford University Press.
Holland, Dorothy & Andrew Kipnis. 1995. The not-so-egotistic aspects of American self. In James A. Russell, Jose M. Fernandez-Dols, Antony S. R. Manstead & J. C. Wellenkamp (eds.), *Everyday conceptions of emotion*, 181–202. Dordrecht: Kluwer.

Jamieson, Mark. 2000. It's shame that makes men and women enemies: The politics of intimacy among the Miskitu of Kakabila. *The Journal of the Royal Anthropological Institute* 6 (2). 311–324.

Khadem Pir, Ali. 2015. Khastgah va avamel va asar e sharm va haya dar negah e ghoran va hadis [The origin, factors, and effects of shame and *haya* from the viewpoint of the Quran and tradition]. *Basirat va Tarbiat e Eslami [Quarterly Insight and Islamic Training]* 12 (32). 127–153.

Kövecses, Zoltan. 1990. *Emotion Concepts*. New York: Springer.

Kövecses, Zoltan. 2000. *Metaphor and Emotion: Language, Culture, and Body in Human Feeling*. Cambridge: Cambridge University Press.

Kövecses, Zoltan. 2015. *Where metaphors come from: Reconsidering context in metaphor*. Oxford: Oxford University Press.

Lewis, Michael. 1992. *Shame: The exposed self*. New York: The Free Press.

Li, Jin, Lianqin Wang & Kurt W. Fischer. 2004. The organization of Chinses shame concepts. *Cognition and Emotion* 18 (6). 767–797.

Lutz, Catherine A. 1988. *Unnatural emotions: Everyday sentiments on a Micronesian Atoll and their challenge to Western theory*. Chicago: The University of Chicago Press.

Menon, Usha & Richard A. Shweder. 1993. Kali's tongue: cultural psychology and the power of shame in Orissa, India. In Shinobu Kitayama and Hazel R. Markus (eds.), *Emotion and culture*, 241–284. Washington, DC: American Psychological Association.

Myers, Fred R. 1979. Emotions and the self: A theory of personhood and political order among Pintupi Aborigines. *Ethos* 7 (4). 343–370.

Palmer, Gary B. & Rick Brown 1998. The ideology of honour, respect, and emotion in Tagalog. In Angeliki Athanasiadou, & Elzbieta Tabakowska (eds.), *Speaking of emotions: Conceptualisation and expression*, 331–355. Berlin/New York: Mouton de Gruyter.

Pasandideh, Abbas. 2004. *Pazhuheshi dar farhang e haya [A survey on the culture of haya]*. Ghom: Darolhadis.

Ponsonnet, Maïa. 2014. *The language of emotions: The case of Dalabon (Australia)*. Amsterdam: John Benjamins.

Pragglejaz Group. 2007. MIP: A method for identifying metaphorically used words in discourse. *Metaphor and Symbol* 22 (1). 1–39.

Rafael, Vincente L. 1988. *Contracting colonialism: Translation and Christian conversion in Tagalog society under early Spanish rule*. Ithaca: Cornell University Press.

Rosaldo, Michelle. 1980. *Knowledge and passion: Ilongot notions of self and social life*. Cambridge: Cambridge University Press.

Sharifian, Farzad. 2007. L1 cultural conceptualizations in L2 learning: The case of Persian speaking learners of English. In Farzad Sharifian & Gary B. Palmer (eds.), *Applied Cultural Linguistics: Implications for Second Language Learning and Intercultural Communication*, 33–51. Amsterdam: John Benjamins.

Sharifian, Farzad. 2008. Conceptualizations of *del* 'heart-stomach' in Persian. In Farzad Sharifian, René Dirven, Ning Yu & Susanne Niemeier (eds.), *Culture, body and language. Conceptualizations of internal body organs across cultures and languages*, 248–265. Berlin: Mouton de Gruyter.

Sharifian, Farzad & Maryam Jamarani. 2011. Cultural schemas in intercultural communication: A study of the Persian cultural schema of *sharmandegi* 'being ashamed'. *Intercultural Pragmatics* 8 (2). 227–251.

Sharifian, Farzad. 2015. Cultural linguistics. In Farzad Sharifian (ed.), *The Routledge handbook of language and culture*, 473–492. London & New York: Routledge.
Tissari, Heli. 2006. Conceptualizing shame: Investigating uses of the English word shame, 1418–1991. In R. W. McConchie, Olga Timofeeva, Heli Tissari & Tanja Saily (eds.), *Selected Proceedings of the 2005 Symposium on New Approaches in English Historical Lexis*, 143–154. Somerville, MA: Cascadilla Proceedings Project.
Ukosakul, Margaret. 2003. Conceptual metaphors underlying the use of Thai 'face'. In Eugene Casad & Gary B. Palmer (eds.), *Cognitive Linguistics and Non-Indo-European Languages*, 275–303. Berlin: Mouton de Gruyter.
Zaborowska, Magdalena. 2014. A contribution to the study of the Persian concept of *aberu*. *Hemispheres* 29 (1). 113–125.

Moses Gatambuki Gathigia, Daniel Ochieng Orwenjo
and Ruth Wangeci Ndung'u

8 A Cognitive Linguistics approach to menstruation as a taboo in Gĩkũyũ

Abstract: The taboos concerning bodily effluvia are generally motivated by our distaste and concern about pollution. Menstruation, for example, one of the bodily effluvia, is a physiological characteristic of the female human experience. However, cultural and social factors influence the way people conceptualize menstruation and, therefore, the meaning of menstruation may differ across different cultures. It is against this background that the chapter is anchored. Since the sanctioning of taboo does not originate in the object itself, but in society (Bobel and Kissling 2011), the study identifies the metaphors of menstruation in Gĩkũyũ and interprets them using the Conceptual Metaphor Theory (CMT). To achieve this objective, a purposive sample of 60 speakers of Gĩkũyũ was interviewed. The study collected 29 metaphors of menstruation in Gĩkũyũ. The study also identified four conceptual metaphors of menstruation in Gĩkũyũ: MENSTRUATION IS A PERIOD; MENSTRUATION IS A VISITOR; MENSTRUATION IS AN INDISPOSITION; MENSTRUATION IS A COLOUR; and MENSTRUATION IS A VALUABLE POSSESSION. The study concludes that metaphor is an integral component of the way people conceptualize and embody menstruation in Gĩkũyũ.

Key Words: Menstruation, metaphors, Gĩkũyũ, cognitive linguistics

1 Introduction

Cognitive Linguistics (CL) is an approach to the study of language that looks at the nature of language, the mind, and their relationship with sociophysical (embodied) experience (Evans and Green 2006). CL emerged in the 1970's as a reaction against the dominant generative paradigms, and specifically the Generative

---

Gĩkũyũ is a language in the Central Bantu branch of the Niger – Congo family spoken primarily by the Agĩkũyũ of Kenya (Guthrie 1971: 43)

Grammar and the Montague Grammar[1], which were then dominant in the disciplines of linguistics and philosophy (Ruiz de Mendoza 1997). In CL, metaphor is regarded as one of the several kinds of *idealised cognitive models* (or ICM)[2]. ICMs result from the activity of a number of structuring principles, like image-schematic reasoning, argument-predicate relations, and metaphoric and metonymic mappings. Indeed, Langacker (1997:241) argues that cognitive and cultural considerations are so closely connected that metaphor stands out as the main device in cultural construction[3]. Similarly, Indurkhya (1992:111) notes that "[T]he world we see in our mind's eye is a world that is not 'given' but is constructed by our cognitive apparatus... the conceptual organization of the world is brought about by an interaction between the cognitive agent and the environment, a process in which each participant is actively involved". Accordingly, our conception of the target domain as expressed in a source-domain pairing is grounded in our knowledge and experience of how the reality expressed by the source domain is culturally understood (Crespo-Fernández 2008). Thus, since socio-cultural considerations play a crucial role in the conceptualization of phenomena (Langacker 1997), metaphors can help us see how human beings organize knowledge about menstruation, a taboo subject, in Gĩkũyũ (Gathigia and Ndung'u 2011).

The word *taboo* has its roots in the "Tongan word *tabu* and became a part of the English lexicon at the end of the eighteenth century" (Allan and Burridge 2006:2). The Tongan culture of Polynesia, as well as many other cultures, believed that certain objects, actions, and words could expel harmful power onto people (Strazny 2005:1073). According to Allan and Burridge (2006: 1), a taboo is a "proscription of behaviour that affects everyday life". Generally, the taboos concerning the bodily effluvia are motivated by our distaste and concern about pollution. In many cases, people find the bodily effluvia revolting mainly because of health reasons (Allan and Burridge 2006:162). What is considered a taboo and

---

[1] Montague grammar is a theory of semantics, originally developed by the logician Richard Montague (1930–1971) and later modified and extended by linguists, philosophers, and logicians. Classical Montague grammar had its roots in logic and the philosophy of language; it quickly became influential in linguistics, and linguists have played a large role in its evolution into contemporary formal semantics (Partee 1975).

[2] According to Lakoff (1987: 68), ICMs are the way in which "human beings organize knowledge". Therefore, ICMs may be postulated as cognitive structures whose purpose is to represent reality from a certain perspective.

[3] Metaphor is defined as a cross-domain mapping (Lakoff 1993: 203), or as "a cognitive mechanism whereby one experiential domain is partially 'mapped', that is, projected, onto a different experiential domain, so that the second domain is partially understood in terms of the first one" (Barcelona 2000:3).

how each taboo is perceived depends on the cultural norms of a given society[4]. These cultural norms determine what is acceptable and what must be avoided (Strazny 2005: 1073). We are, therefore, constantly censoring our everyday language in all situations. Taboos surround topics such as: "bodies and their effluvia (sweat, snot, feces, menstrual fluid, etc.); the organs and acts of sex, micturition and defecation; diseases, death and killing (including hunting and fishing); naming, addressing, touching and viewing persons and sacred beings, objects and places; food gathering, preparation and consumption" (Allan and Burridge 2006: 1). According to Agyekum (2002), there is evidence in many societies that menstruation is dangerous and / or offensive, and that is why its being perceived as taboo can be considered universal.

Menstruation, a phenomenon unique to all females, is the periodic discharge of blood, mucus, and cellular debris from the uterine mucosa (Drakshayani and Venkata 1994). The view of menstruation as something bad results in "othering" (Grove and Zwi 2006). That is, those who "other" (for example, cultures, societies and males) secure their own identity by making themselves "normal", whilst secluding the other group; in this case, menstruating women (Grove and Zwi 2006). Despite the fact that menstruation is a natural process of the female body, it is considered to be undesirable and dirty. Since cultural and social factors influence the way people experience and interpret menstruation, the present study was undertaken to study the metaphors used regarding menstruation among the Agĩkũyũ in Kenya. Second, there is limited research regarding the aspect of menstruation and the implications different cultural and social beliefs may have on the Agĩkũyũ. The Agĩkũyũ speak Gĩkũyũ. Gĩkũyũ is a language in the Central Bantu branch of the Niger–Congo family spoken primarily by the Agĩkũyũ of Kenya. Kikuyu (technically, Gĩkũyũ) belongs to the Kamba-Kikuyu subgroup of Bantu and is spoken in the area extending from Nairobi to the southern and southwestern slopes of Mt. Kenya, in Kenya. The genetic mode of classifying languages places Gĩkũyũ in Zone E, group 50. It is language number 51 (Guthrie, 1967). Gĩkũyũ is spoken by about 6.8 million (17 % of Kenya's population) and the Agĩkũyũ constitute the largest ethnic group in Kenya (National Bureau of Statistics, 2009).

---

[4] Akmajian et al. (2004) stated that what counts as taboo is defined by culture and not by anything inherent in the language itself.

2 Methodology and Theoretical Paradigm of the Study

This study is a qualitative analysis of responses which a purposive sample of 60 speakers of Gĩkũyũ gave to the interview question: "There are words that Gĩkũyũ speakers use to mention menstruation. Name any polite words in Gĩkũyũ that are used to avoid mentioning menstruation and explain why each of the words is used." We followed the notational convention of Lakoff and Johnson (1980); the mnemonics "TARGET DOMAIN IS SOURCE DOMAIN" which suggests meanings are achieved through a mapping from the source domain to the target domain in the conceptual system.

The study adopted the principles of the Conceptual Metaphor Theory (CMT, hereafter). The CMT, the dominant paradigm in metaphor studies, was developed by Lakoff and Johnson (1980). Other scholars (for example, Lakoff and Turner 1989; Gibbs 1994; Kövecses 2000, 2002) have also extensively contributed to the CMT. The CMT aims at systematically inferring conceptual representations and organisation from linguistic expressions. In other words, the CMT approach assumes that language is a window into cognition, and that linguistic expressions in part reflect cognitive processes and structures (Lakoff and Johnson 1980). Lakoff and Johnson (1980:153) put it clearly that "Metaphors are primarily a matter of thought and action and only derivatively a matter of language". The CTM assumes that there is a process of *mapping* between closely related concepts based on some particular correspondences[5]. Thus, a particular pattern is "mapped" in Lakoff and Johnson's words, or "projected" in Turner's words, (1996) from a source conceptual domain into a target domain. The source domain is the conceptual domain from which the metaphor is drawn, and the target domain is the conceptual domain to which the metaphor is applied (Knowles and Rosamund 2006)[6]. The relevance of the CMT is the fact that it deepens our understanding of the pervasiveness of metaphor in our language and cognitive system.

The application of the CMT was significant in the discussion of the mapping of the source domain to the target domain of metaphors of in Gĩkũyũ. For example, the embodiment thesis made it possible for us to explain and accommodate metaphorical expressions of menstruation in Gĩkũyũ. As postulated by the MIP pro-

---

[5] In this theory, the sets of systematic correspondences between the source and the target are referred to as "mappings" (Lakoff and Johnson 1980, Kövecses 2002; Deignan 2005; Charteris-Black 2004, 2005).

[6] [R]esearch on metaphor is now as multidisciplinary, and interdisciplinary, as perhaps any topic being studied in contemporary academia (Gibbs 2008: 4).

cedure, this implies that human beings find phenomena they can *see, hear, feel, taste and / or smell* easier to understand and categorize than phenomena they cannot. Thus, the MIP procedure helped in the identification of the metaphorical expressions of menstruation in Gĩkũyũ while the CMT assisted in the analysis of metaphorical expressions in terms of the different kinds of conceptual mappings. For example, MENSTRUATION is the Target Domain (TD), while A VISITOR is the Source Domain (SD). The conceptual mappings of the TD corresponding with the SD are "blood" corresponding to "a person," "expected" corresponding to "unexpected," "definite duration of stay" corresponding to "indefinite duration of stay" and "presence is concealed" corresponding to "presence visible to all."

It is important to add that since the study had a target group of 60 respondents, we expected to collect various metaphorical expressions for analysis. However, we only identified 29 metaphors related words for menstruation in Gĩkũyũ (cf. Table 1) (most of the words were repeated by the respondents).

3 Results and Discussion

The study collected 29 metaphors with the target domain MENSTRUATION (cf. Table 1). From the analysis of the corpus, the study identified five different conceptual metaphors that contribute to the understanding of menstruation in Gĩkũyũ.

Table 1: Metaphors of Menstruation

No	GĨKŨYŨ	GLOSS	CONCEPTUAL DOMAIN
1	Kahinda ka mweri	a monthly period	A PERIOD
2	Kĩmakia thinwa	the one that frightens the full moon	A PERIOD
3	Mũgeni	a visitor	A VISITOR
4	Kuura	to rain	A PERIOD
5	Mweri	a month	A PERIOD
6	Kũona	to see	A COLOUR
7	Thakame ya mũirũ	dark-red blood	A COLOUR
8	Kũona muirũ	to see something that is dark-red	A COLOUR
9	Kahinda	a period	A PERIOD
10	Thikũ	days	A PERIOD

Table 1 (continued)

No	GĨKŨYŨ	GLOSS	CONCEPTUAL DOMAIN
11	Gũthũka	to be bad	AN INDISPOSITION
12	Gũtunĩha / utũne	to be red	A COLOUR
13	Kũrĩo nĩ mahĩndĩ	to be eaten by bones	AN INDISPOSITION
14	Mambura	of rain	A PERIOD
15	Kũraga ikenye	to break an egg	A VALUABLE POSSESSION
16	Kwĩnenũra	to keep on changing the colour	A COLOUR
17	Gũkũrĩra	something that is ripe or mature	A PERIOD
18	Kahinda ga atumia	a period of women	A PERIOD
19	Gũita	to pour	A PERIOD
20	Ithaga rĩa mũndũ wanja	a woman's jewel	A VALUABLE POSSESSION
21	Thakame ya mweri	monthly blood	A PERIOD
22	'Mnyesho'	rain	A PERIOD
23	Kũrũara	to be sick	AN INDISPOSITION
24	Mũrata	a friend	A VALUABLE POSSESSION
25	Maũndũ ma atumia	things of the women	A PERIOD
26	Mũgongo	the back	AN INDISPOSITION
27	Mathĩna ma mweri	monthly difficulties	A PERIOD
28	Kuma gwa itumbĩ rĩa mũtumia.	the release of the woman's egg	A PERIOD
29	Chirũ	a feminine visitor	A VISITOR

From a quantitative point of view, the conceptual metaphors MENSTRUATION IS A PERIOD accounts for 52% of the metaphorical euphemisms, MENSTRUATION IS A VISITOR (7%), MENSTRUATION IS A COLOUR (17%), MENSTRUATION IS AN INDISPOSITION (14%), and MENSTRUATION IS A VALUABLE POSSESSION (10%) as indicated in Figure 1 below:

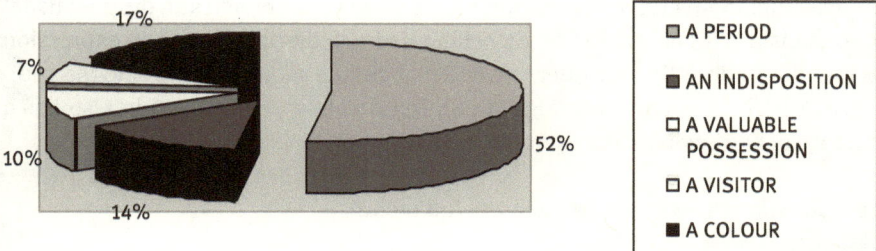

Figure 1: Conceptual Metaphors of MENSTRUATION in Gĩkũyũ

The next section discusses the five different conceptual metaphors that contribute to the understanding of menstruation in Gĩkũyũ.

3.1 MENSTRUATION IS A PERIOD

The theme of periodicity focuses on the timeline of menstruation as a monthly event that lasts for a short period of time. The underlying notion of all the metaphorical expressions included in this conceptual mapping is based on the fact that a period and the act of seeing the salient colour red or darkish red are temporary and therefore, the target domain is conceptualized as a temporary event. For example:

(1) *Kahinda* – 'a period',
(2) *Mweri* – 'a month',
(3) *Kahinda ka mweri* – 'a monthly period',
(4) *Thakame ya mweri* – 'monthly blood',
(5) *Thikũ* – 'days'.

The monthly phase of the menstrual cycle (see metaphors 2, 3 and 4) is a resemblance that has the support from etymology since the words *moon* and *menses* are derived from the same Latin word *mensis*. It is argued that ideally, women should achieve this by menstruating from 3 to 7 days in synchrony with the moon, which periodically "dies" and is "reborn". This is because the hormones in a female's body cause the womb to actively shed the lining that was built up in the previous menstrual cycle.

A submapping for menstruation which may be interpreted as a dysphemistic[7] euphemism is (6) below. In Cognitive Linguistics, a dysphemism is an expression with connotations that are offensive either about the subject matter or to the audience or both (Allan and Burridge 2006). In (6) below, the expression also has a nuance of euphemism. For example, menstruation is:

(6) *Kĩmakia thinwa* – 'to frighten the full moon'.

Since the sudden appearance of the full moon scares people, menstruation gets the connotation of a biological appearance that is scary. This is an expression that is typical of the Gĩkũyũ.

Particularization is used in (7) below to conceptualize MENSTRUATION in Gĩkũyũ. Particularization is a semantic process that involves description of a particular instance. It is sometimes used as a synonym for *detailing* and *specialization* as natural language users resort to semantic narrowing to eliminate the taboo senses (Gathigia and Ndung'u 2011). This metaphor is particularized since for it to be effective, the term 'women' must be employed. For example,

(7) *Kahinda ga atumia* – 'a period of women',

Metaphor (8) is also used for menstruation. This is based on the fact that the ripe unfertilized ovum is released through the vagina after a period of time, since menstruation is typically induced in women by hormonal changes associated with an unfertilized ovum.

(8) *Gũkũrĩra* – 'something which is ripe or mature'.

Menstruation is also likened to rain in this conceptual mapping. Rain expressions are subsumed in the metaphors to do with periodicity. This is aptly captured by Feirrman (1990), who notes that rain has its proper times, like the moon. Fertility is invoked when he postulates that women are said to be more fertile after menstruation, and after the rain you sow the seed. According to Knight (1985: 671), there is cyclical renewal which links menstrual blood and rain. Knight argues that women should achieve this by menstruating in synchrony with the moon, which periodically "dies" and is "reborn." Knight adds that the health of an individual

---

[7] According to Allan and Burridge, speakers resort to dysphemism to talk about people and things that frustrate and annoy them, that they disapprove of and wish to disparage, humiliate and degrade (Allan and Burridge 2006).

presupposes the ability to reduplicate, within the body itself, these rhythms of periodic renewal.

Menstruation is, therefore:

(9) *Kuura* – 'rain',
(10) *Mambur*a – 'of rain'.

In (9) and (10) above, the metaphor of rain is used since the menstrual blood is perceived to come out in drops like rain. Metaphor (9) above, is also homonymous to bleeding, which, when interpreted from the context of our target domain becomes relevant. Metaphors (9) and (10) have the connotation of menorrhagia. Menorrhagia is a medical term for menstrual periods with abnormally heavy or prolonged bleeding. The metaphor of rain is also relevant in the sense that it equates menstruation and rain in terms of their unpredictability.

Employment of loan words to avoid mentioning a tabooed term is an effective way of euphemizing. In menstruation, the lexical process of borrowing is also used as a correspondence for menstruation as it is evidenced in (11) below:

(11) *Mnyesho* – 'for rain'.

The term (11) is a loan word from Kiswahili which means 'to rain'. The word is normally used when a lady is experiencing a heavy menstrual flow.

In (12), the metaphor of 'pouring' may be understood in the context of sexual intercourse (Murphy 2001). That is, menstruation is:

(12) *Gũita* – 'to pour'.

'To pour' may, therefore, be the end point of an ovum since it has not been fertilized. In Gĩkũyũ, metaphorical expression (12) may be seen as a woman's way of ridding herself of impurities that may be bad for her if kept in her body. According to Allan and Burridge (2006), many cultures often associate the loss of blood with injury and loss of strength. This chapter, therefore, interprets the target domain of menstruation as an instance of pouring.

3.2 MENSTRUATION IS A COLOUR

Some metaphors for menstruation are based on colour associations. These metaphors may be considered to be metonymical since the part (the colour of the menstrual blood) represents the whole (menstruation). According to Langacker

(1999), metonymy is distinguished from metaphor in Cognitive Linguistics as an intra-domain mapping and metaphor as a cross-domain mapping. However, many definitions demonstrate that there is conceptual mapping in both metaphor and metonymy, with the difference that metaphor is a cross-domain mapping whereas metonymy is a mapping within a single conceptual domain (Lakoff and Turner 1989) or intradomain phenomenon in Deignan's (2005) terms, However, Radden (2000) argues that the distinction between metaphor and metonymy is notoriously difficult, in that metonymy and metaphor form a continuum with fuzzy cases. Goossens (1995) coins the term "metaphtonymy" to indicate the interaction between metaphor and metonymy. Therefore, metaphor and metonymy can be viewed as one continuum (Goossens 1995).

The colour metaphors in this conceptual domain connect the colour associations of everyday things or occurrences with menstruation. This act of seeing the red or dark colouration is an experience a woman undergoes for a few days every month. This is what motivates the usage of the following expressions for menstruation:

(13) *Kũona or kũona mũirũ* – 'to see or to see something that is dark-red',
(14) *Kwĩnenũra* – 'to keep on changing the colour of the blood',
(15) *Utune* and *gũtunĩha* – 'to be red'.

In Gĩkũyũ, the colour motif (15) is used for menstruation since it is understood that as the menstrual blood flows out, one cannot clearly discern the dominant colour as it keeps on changing from darkish red to a bright reddish colour. Secondly, the usage of the metaphorical expression (11) is also based on the fact that unlike other blood, menstrual blood does not coagulate (Allan and Burridge, 2006). The metaphorical expression (15) directly mentions the colour "red" leaving little room for differing interpretations. These terms (13–15) despite implying periodicity have both orthophemistic and euphemistic connotations.

3.3 MENSTRUATION IS AN INDISPOSITION

According to Agyekum (2002:375), the source concept INDISPOSITION for MENSTRUATION refers to expressions that "semantically denote that the menstruating woman cannot perform her normal domestic duties, including sex". The indisposition plays a large role in the negative views of menstruation and the euphemisms that result. There is a set of oppositions between MENSTRUATION IS AN INDISPOSITION as tabulated below:

Table 2: Mappings of MENSTRUATION IS AN INDISPOSITION

MENSTRUATION	AN INDISPOSITION
Predictable	Unpredictable
Untreatable	Treatable
It is a sign of good health	It is a sign of ill-health
Brings forth new life	Takes away existing life

This conceptualization accounts for four sub mappings (14 %) of the total metaphorical euphemistic expressions for MENSTRUATION as discussed below:

(16) *Kũrĩo nĩ mahĩndĩ* – 'to be eaten by bones',
(17) *Kũrũara* – 'to be sick',
(18) *Gũthũka* – 'to be bad'.

Metaphorical expression (16) *kũrĩo nĩ mahĩndĩ* ('to be eaten by bones') is frequently used to allude to menstruation. Many women will offer up phrases like *nĩndĩrarĩo nĩ mahĩndĩ* (I am being eaten by bones') as a reference for menstruation. Menstruation itself can be painful to the point of indisposition. The pain in the joints or bones is often accompanied by menstrual cramps what is technically referred to as *dysmenorrhea*. Metaphor (17) shows how menstruation causes discomfort such that people views the target domain as an illness. Though this conceptualization implies a negative value judgment of menstruation but not enough to elicit feelings of revulsion or antipathy, Gĩkũyũ speakers view it as euphemistic. Metaphorical expression (18) is associated with the soiling of clothes when one is menstruating giving a picture of indisposition. This metaphor may also be said to have a biblical allusion since the Bible, particularly Leviticus 15:35; 20: 18; 12:2, marks menstruation as unclean and taboo, which resulted in women being temporarily set apart from the community. According to Kenyatta (1938), menstruation is seen as a process which defiles women making them unclean. Agĩkũyũ men were particularly advised to avoid sleeping with such a woman since she was perceived to be unclean and sick. Unlike the Agĩkũyũ, Buckley (1982) discovers field-notes recording myths, descriptions of ritual and statements from female informants among the Yurok which looked at menstruation as a source of sacred power.

3.4 Menstruation is a Visitor

This conceptual metaphor accounts for 7% of the total metaphorical euphemisms for menstruation. Table 3 below displays the mappings of MENSTRUATION IS A VISITOR:

Table 3: Mappings of MENSTRUATION IS A VISITOR

MENSTRUATION	A VISITOR
Blood	A person
Expected	Unexpected
Definite duration of stay	Indefinite duration of stay
Presence is concealed	Presence visible to all

Metaphorical expressions (19) and (20) below illustrate the conceptual metaphor MENSTRUATION IS A VISITOR:

(19) *Mũgeni* – 'a visitor'.
(20) *Chirũ* – 'a female visitor' (Chirũ is the short form of the Wanjiru, one of the nine daughters of Gĩkũyũ, the founder of the tribe according to the Gĩkũyũ myth. The name Chirũ is used when a speaker wants to avoid giving the actual name of a female visitor).

The notion of visitation as expressed in (19) and (20) is presumably motivated by the temporary nature of menstruation. The metaphors look at the target domain as a visitor who should not be scorned but should be treated with love. The metaphors appear to be a sexual interpretation of menstruation. According to Allan and Burridge (1991), by conceptualizing the target domain as a visitor, the female is in other circumstances relishing the visitor to the vagina to be a male. In (20) above, the conceptualization is an evidence of the personification of the female name 'Chirũ'. The term was used when a speaker didn't want to be specific. A girl would jokingly say 'Chiru has come' implying that menstruation had started. The male equivalent is 'Kamau'. The name Kamau is also used in Gĩkũyũ when one does not want to be specific.

3.5 MENSTRUATION IS A VALUABLE POSSESSION

This conceptual metaphor accounts for 10 % of the metaphorical euphemisms for menstruation in Gĩkũyũ. There are correspondences between the source and the target domains as tabulated below:

Table 4: Mappings of MENSTRUATION IS A VALUABLE POSSESSION

MENSTRUATION	A VALUABLE POSSESSION
A sign of fertility	A sign of wealth
It is expected that every woman undergoes the process	Not every lady has a valuable possession
One menstruates for a period of time, until menopause	A valuable possession can be lifelong

This conceptualization looks at the target domain as a form of a woman's precious thing. That is, menstruation is a positive aspect of a female's life as shown in the examples below:

(21) *Ithaga rĩa mũndũ wa nja* – 'a woman's jewel'.

The euphemism (21) is normally used by girls as a form of endearment. Metaphorical expression (21) may be considered novel or non-conventional. Non-conventional metaphors are, according to Lakoff and Johnson (1980:139), "imaginative and creative". Similarly, as Allan and Burridge (2006: 2) note, taboo and censoring of language motivate language change by "promoting the creation of highly inventive and often playful new expressions, or new meanings for old expressions, causing existing vocabulary to be forgone".

Menstruation in Gĩkũyũ is also considered a precursor to the real life of a girl. A metaphor which expresses the notion of endearment using an archaism is:

(22) *Kũraga ikenye* – 'to break an egg'.

This is a technical and archaic phrase for menstruation; a girl's first monthly period. Menarche is a landmark feature of female puberty and signals reproductive maturity. A big part of the first menstruation is that is symbolizes the transition from girlhood to womanhood. That is, menstruation is depicted as something that portrays the fertility and societal recognition of the female. So, when a girl starts menstruating, we say that she has been broken or marked, that is, she has come of age. In other words, the girl has broken the first egg. *Ikenye* could therefore be equivalent to being cut or circumcised for boys. The Agĩkũyũ view menarche or the first menstruation, as a positive aspect of a girl's life. In Gĩkũyũ, menarche is marked by certain rituals as the girl is prepared for adulthood. In other words, it is a physical marker of feminine maturity. Further, it symbolizes aspects such as future childbearing ability and passage into womanhood and femininity.

4 Discussion

The objective of this study was to identify the metaphors of menstruation in Gĩkũyũ and interpret them through the Conceptual Metaphor Theory (CMT). It was found that metaphor is a useful cognitive mechanism of conceptualizing menstruation in Gĩkũyũ since the analysis identified 29 metaphorical expressions. According to McGlone (2007: 113), metaphor provides a way to "piggyback" our understanding of abstract concepts on the structure of concrete concepts. Past studies also corroborate the finding that metaphor is a basic and indispensable linguistic feature of human understanding (Kövecses 2002).

Second, the chapter notes that the metaphors used to refer to menstruation are well accounted for in terms of the Conceptual Metaphor Theory (CMT) as propounded by Lakoff and Johnson (1980). The presence of 29 instantiations of MENSTRUATION confirms the fact that a single idea can also be explained by a number of metaphorical expressions (Charteris-Black 2004). As Cienki (2005:1) notes, metaphor provides "a tool for reasoning about one thing in terms of the other."

The findings of the present study reveal that menstruation is a verbal taboo among the Agĩkũyũ speakers of Kenya and considers the cognitive strategies behind this phenomenon within the aegis of Conceptual Metaphor Theory. The use of euphemisms is found to be the most popular verbal Taboo Avoidance Technique (TAT) (Agyekum 2002) among the Agĩkũyũ and the euphemisms used for menstruation are interpretable within the Conceptual Metaphor Theory. One of the major findings of this study is the fact that euphemisms for menstruation among the Agĩkũyũ follow two basic models: (1) negative (indisposition, and period) and (2) positive (a special thing and fertility and the arrival of a protective visitor or a jewel). The negative conceptualizations of MENSTRUATION are clearly evident in the mappings of MENSTRUATION IS A PERIOD. Both conceptualizations view menstruation as something discomforting and therefore undesirable. Positive conceptualizations of MENSTRUATION include MENSTRUATION IS A VALUABLE POSSESSION, and MENSTRUATION IS A VISITOR. These conceptualizations view MENSTRUATION as something desirable, something to be appreciated and looked forward to because it comes with good results such as blessings and fertility. This is in line with the findings of Agyekum (2002) in his study on the euphemisms used for MENSTRUATION among the Akan of Ghana. He refers to the negative model as the "pollution theory" of menstruation and asserts that it views menstruation as "something messy, revolting, and polluted – something to be avoided" (p. 367). This view, according to him, ignores the importance of menstruation to the female gender and other members of the community and is attributable to "a cultural truism used in male dominated, gender asymmetrical societies" (p. 368). The present study shares these views and interpretations. Additionally, we take the view that changing patterns in the use of the euphemisms and drastic changes in the current generation's knowledge of them reveal much about societal changes in the Agĩkũyũ speech community. These changing patterns reflect the general societal changes that have taken place over a time. For instance, Njoroge and Mukwhana (2015) report that older Agĩkũyũ women would view MENSTRUATION IS RAGS or MENSTRUATION IS SKIN among other things because in the olden days, sanitary pads had not been in use in the community and women would use old, sometime dirty rags instead. They state:

> Before the advent of present day sanitary towels, girls traditionally used rags and skins but because of the technological changes that have brought sanitary towels, the concepts of skins and rags are used as euphemisms for the period that a woman has her menstruation. Only elderly Kikuyu women use these terms to describe the menstruation period (p. 191).

That we did not have any such "aged" euphemisms in our data which was collected principally among modern day Agĩkũyũ speakers is therefore indicative of the changing trends and patterns in the ways MENSTRUATION is cognitively conceptualized in this speech community.

Yet, other studies have adopted a monolithic negative view of menstruation, completely ignoring the dual perspective and obfuscating the positive, productive and healthy perspectives on this phenomenon. Such studies, like that of Kissling (1996) adopt a contrary view of menstruation as the one taken in this study. In her study, Kissling examines the communicative strategies used by teenage adolescent girls use to discuss menstruation, and "to avoid the inherent embarrassments of such a discourse" (p.293). She identifies strategies such as circumlocution, euphemism and omission to seek and share information about menstruation with each other. Having earlier argued in this paper that the conceptualization of menstruation as a physiological experience varies across cultures and languages, and given that societies in themselves are dynamic and ever evolving, we adopt the view that only an eclectic approach to the menstruation phenomenon can be insightful enough to reveal the underlying cognitive intricacies that manifest themselves at the surface level as speech communities such as Agĩkũyũ talk about their daily experiences regarding menstruation.

5 Conclusions

This chapter set out to interrogate how the Agĩkũyũ people cognitively conceptualize MENSTRUATION as a physiological process among women. This was done with the premise that menstruation is a tabooed word in this community, like in many communities around the world. Accordingly, the central focus of the chapter was to unpack the euphemisms that the Agĩkũyũ use to refer to this physiological process and the cognitive mechanisms and process that underlie their use of such euphemisms. Ultimately, within a Cognitive Linguistics framework, the findings of the present study provide useful insights into the conceptual organization of the world among the Agĩkũyũ and how such organization is constrained by their environment, culture, and traditions.

Based on the findings and discussion above, this study concludes that metaphor is so pervasive in the conceptualization of menstruation that it appears to play an indispensable role in our understanding of it. Second, the study concludes that metaphors of menstruation in Gĩkũyũ are well accounted for in terms of the Conceptual Metaphor Theory. That is, the metaphors of menstruation can be categorized into the following conceptual domains: MENSTRUATION IS A PERIOD; MENSTRUATION IS A COLOUR; MENSTRUATION IS A VISITOR; MENSTRUATION IS AN INDISPOSITION; and MENSTRUATION IS A VALUABLE POSSESSION.

This chapter has demonstrated that the menstruation is tabooed among the Agĩkũyũ just like in many other communities and that the euphemisms used instead of the dysphemistic expressions are analyzable from a cognitive linguistics perspective. Secondly, it has also been demonstrated that use of such euphemisms is socially and culturally constrained. The discussions in this paper, in these respects, provide useful insights into the nexus between culture, language and cognition. Such an interface is a rich ground for further research not only for linguistics, but also for anthropologists, and cognitive psychologists. For instance, an investigation into the anthropological dimensions of MENSTRUATION taboo, and how this dimension interacts with the underlying cognitive and linguistic processes would yield useful data and very rich insights into taboo among African communities such as the Agĩkũyũ. Additionally, it would be insightfully interesting to study euphemisms associated with other body effluvia among the Agĩkũyũ within the same paradigms and frameworks of the current study.

References

Agyekum, Kofi. 2013. Menstruation as a verbal taboo among the Akan of Ghana. *Journal of Anthropological Research* 58 (3). 367–87.
Akmajian, Adrian, Demers, Richard, Farner, Ann & Harnish Robert. 2004. *Linguistics: An introduction to language and communication*. New Delhi: Prentice Hall.
Allan, Keith & Burridge, Kate. 1991. *Euphemism and dysphemism: Language used as a shield and weapon*. Oxford, UK: Oxford University Press.
Allan, Keith & Burridge, Kate. 2006. *Forbidden words. Taboo and the censoring of language*. Cambridge: Cambridge University Press.
Barcelona, Antonio. (ed.). 2000. *Metaphor and metonymy at the crossroads*. Berlin and New York: Mouton de Gruyter.
Bobel, Chris & Kissling, Elizabeth. 2011. Menstruation matters: Introduction to representations of the menstrual cycle. *Women's Studies* 40 (2). 121–126.
Buckley, Thomas. 1982. Menstruation and the power of Yurok women: Methods of cultural reconstruction. *American Ethnologist* 9. 47–60.
Charteris-Black, Jonathan. 2004. *Corpus approaches to critical metaphor analysis*. London: Palgrave Macmillan.
Charteris-Black, Jonathan. 2005. *Politicians and rhetoric: The persuasive power of metaphor*. Basingstoke & New York: Palgrave-MacMillan.
Chamizo Domínguez, Pedro. 1998. *Metáfora y conocimiento*. Anexos de Analecta Malacitana. Málaga: Universidad.
Crespo-Fernández, Eliecer. 2006. Metaphor in the euphemistic manipulation of the taboo of sex. *Babel A. F.I.A.L* 15. 27–42.
Crespo-Fernández, Eliecer. 2008. Sex-related euphemism and dysphemism. An analysis in terms of conceptual metaphor theory. *Atlantis, Journal of the Spanish Association of Anglo-American Studies* 30 (2). 95–110.
Drakshayani, Devi & Venkata Ramaiah. 1994. A study on menstrual hygiene among rural adolescent girls. *Indian Journal of Medical Sciences* 48 (6). 139–43.
Deignan, Alice. 2005. *Metaphor and corpus linguistics*. Amsterdam: John Benjamins.
Feierman, Steven. 1990. *Peasant intellectuals: Anthropology and history in Tanzania*. Madison: University of Wisconsin Press.
Gathigia, Moses, & Ndũng'ũ, Ruth. 2011. *A cognitive linguistics analysis of Gĩkũyũ euphemisms*. Saarbrücken: VDM Verlag Publishing House Ltd.
Gibbs, Raymond. 1994. *The poetics of mind: Figurative thought, language, and understanding*. New York: Cambridge University Press.
Gibbs, Raymond. 2008. *The Cambridge handbook of metaphor and thought*. Cambridge: Cambridge University Press.
Goossens, Louis. 1995. *By word of mouth: Metaphor, metonymy, and linguistic action in a cognitive perspective*. Amsterdam/Philadelphia: John Benjamins Publishing Company.
Grove, Natalie & Zwi, Anthony. 2006. Our health and theirs: Forced migration, othering, and public health. *Social Science & Medicine* 62. 1931–1942.
Guthrie, Malcolm. 1971. *Comparative Bantu: An introduction to the comparative linguistics pre-history of Bantu languages*. Farnborough: Greyg Press.
Indurkhya, Bipin. 1992. *Metaphor and cognition: An interactionist approach*. Dordrecht: Kluwer Academic Publishers.

Kenyatta, Jomo. 1938. *Facing Mount Kenya: The tribal life of the Gĩkũyũ*. Nairobi: Heinemann Educational Books.
Kissling, Elizabeth. 1996.Bleeding out loud: Communication and menstruation. *Feminism and Psychology* 6 (4). 481–504
Knight, Chris. 1985. Menstruation as medicine. *Social Science & Medicine* 21 (6). 683–671
Knowles, Murray & Rosamund, Moon. 2006. *Introducing metaphor*. London/New York: Routledge.
Kövecses, Zoltán. 2000. *Metaphor and emotion: Language, culture and the body in human feeling*. Cambridge: Cambridge University Press.
Kövecses, Zoltán. 2002. *Metaphor: A practical introduction*. Oxford: Oxford University Press.
Lakoff, George. 1987. *Women, fire and dangerous things. What categories reveal about the mind*. Chicago: The University of Chicago Press.
Lakoff, George. 1993. The contemporary theory of metaphor. In A. Ortony (Ed.), *Metaphor and thought* (2nd ed.), 202–251. Cambridge: Cambridge University Press.
Lakoff, George & Johnson, Mark. 1980. *Metaphors we live by*. Chicago: University of Chicago Press.
Lakoff, George & Johnson, Mark. 1999. *Philosophy in the flesh. The embodied mind and its challenge to Western thought*. New York: Basic Books.
Lakoff, George & Mark Turner. 1989. *More than cool reason*. Chicago: University of Chicago.
Langacker, Ronald 1997. Constituency, dependency, and conceptual grouping. *Cognitive Linguistics* 8. 1–32.
Langacker, Ronald.1999. *Grammar and conceptualization*. Berlin/New York: Mouton de Gruyter.
McGlone, Matthew. 2007. What is the explanatory value of a conceptual metaphor? *Language & communication* 27. 109–126.
Murphy, Peter. 2001. *Studs, tools and the family jewels: Metaphors men live by*. Madison and Winsconsin: The University of Winsconsin.
National Bureau of Statistics. (2009). *Population demographics*. Nairobi: Government Press.
Njoroge, Rita. 2005. Euphemisms on body effluvia in Kikuyu. *International Journal of Humanities, Social Sciences and Education* 2 (1). 189–196.
Partee, Barbara. 1975. Montague grammar and transformational grammar. *Linguistic Inquiry* 6. 203–300.
Radden, Günter. 2000. How metonymic are metaphors? In A. Barcelona (Ed.), *Metaphor and Metonymy at the crossroads: A cognitive perspective*, 93–109. Berlin/New York: Mouton de Gruyter.
Ruiz de Mendoza, Francisco. 1997. Cognitive and pragmatic aspects of metonymy. *Cuadernos de Filología Inglesa* 612. 161–178.
Rodd, Rosemary 1987. The challenge of biological determinism. *Philosophy* 62. 84–93.
Strazny, Philipp. 2005. Politeness. *Encyclopedia of Linguistics*, Vol. 2, 866–67. New York & Oxon: Fitzroy Dearborn.
Turner, Mark. 1996. *The literary mind*. New York: Oxford University Press.
World Health Organization. 1983. *Programming for adolescent health and development*. WHO Technical Report Series.

Anna Kuzio
9 The socio-cognitive aspects of taboo in two cultures: A case study on Polish and British English

Abstract: Taboo is a multifaceted cultural phenomenon. Socio-cognitive and cultural aspects of taboo are dimensions that require further analysis, especially since contact between various cultures is becoming increasingly frequent. This paper investigates linguistic taboos in Polish and British English societies with regard to the social context in which they are exploited and the socio-cultural factors which influence their employment in various contexts. Specifically, the paper identifies the categories of linguistic taboos in Polish and British English and investigates the strategies employed by native speakers to avoid using taboo expressions. A major means of avoidance involves the substitution of taboo words with more proper expressions. These include jargon terms, constructions, euphemisms, creative synonyms, metaphoric expressions and circumlocution. The paper also studies why definite words are taboo in a society and why certain taboo words are complemented by specific conventionally-fixed words. The taboo words in Polish and English societies are divided into general and context specific categories, each with their own subcategories. The outcome of this study should provide a useful basis for the study of differing sensitivity arising from the discussion of taboo topics in Polish-British English intercultural communication. The study began with the distribution of questionnaires 80 Polish and 80 British English speakers of varying educational background and age. The subjects were chosen on the basis of convenience random sampling and the data were analyzed employing SPSS 21.0. The results show that many respondents believed that taboo words should not be used publicly or openly where certain topics should not be discussed candidly. Nevertheless, the cultural norms and the notion of politeness play significant roles in restricting the open use of these taboo words. The British English respondents seemed to be more expressive in using taboo words in expressing their emotions than the Poles. It is also apparent that the acceptability of taboo words depends on the domains and contexts of use.

Keywords: socio-cognitive aspects of taboo, culture and taboo, socio-cultural aspects of taboo

https://doi.org/10.1515/9783110582758-010

1 Introduction

Language, or words of a language, cannot be inherently good or bad but may reflect individual or societal values (Farba 2015). Two or more words or expressions can have the same linguistic meaning, with one acceptable and the others not. This seems to agree with Holme's (2001) remark that people in some communities share principles for language use, such as rules of speaking, attitudes and values along with socio-cultural understanding regarding speech. Cognitively, however, people often rely on mental constructs that explain one's thought process about how something is perceived in the real world. They often offer their own intuitive perception about another's acts and their consequences. These are mental models (Idealized Cognitive Models) that can help shape behaviour and set an approach to solving problems and doing tasks. A mental model becomes a kind of internal symbol or representation of external reality, hypothesized to play a major role in cognition, reasoning and decision-making manifested in the use of language.

As a result, language is one device by which the moral conduct of a society is determined. Therefore, people generally try to be careful in their use of words in order not to break the linguistic rules of their community, since if this happens, it is perceived as violating a linguistic taboo.

A taboo tends to be a significant subject of the study of linguists and specialists in cross-cultural communication. It is topical due to the fact that the number of cultural contacts is constantly growing because of globalization. All cultures are different and every culture has its own values and taboos. While communicating with the individuals of other cultures it is crucial to know the themes which are prohibited to talk on. It is vital to remember that communication has a specific aim and is considered effective only if this aim has been reached. The knowledge of taboo and the capability to deal with them is the key to success in the process of communication. The objective of this paper is to analyze the significance of taboo for the cross-cultural communication and to observe the ways to deal with forbidden themes for discussing. The research question is as follows: Do perceptions of the Polish or British English speakers vary in terms of the use of linguistic taboo in their culture based on specific domains? The goal of this study is to analyze the specific character of taboos in the communicative processes of different levels, study the influence of taboos on the process communication and analyze taboos from the point of view of English and Polish culture.

2 Taboo

The concept of taboo is defined as "ny prohibitions which carry no penalties beyond the anxiety and embarrassment arising from a breach of strongly entrenched custom" (Steiner 2013: 143).

Linguistic taboos are recognized as words or expressions to be avoided because using them directly in public is perceived as violation of certain moral codes. That is, linguistic taboos have their usage controlled by certain circumstances or reasons such as religious or cultural norms. The obscenity or beauty of language ought to then be in the ear of the listener, or in the collective ear of the audience.

Crystal (1995) mentions that taboos are the issues individuals avoid in a polite society, either because they are felt to be hurtful, embarrassing or offensive. Taboo words also include blasphemies, obscenities and profanities (Hughes 2015). Forbidden performances or words frequently reflect the specific customs and views of the society.

Linguistic taboo takes place when individuals avoid talking about specific things. Some individuals choose not to mention the prohibited words at all, since they are certain that saying these words will welcome evil spirits or invite bad fortune. Conversely, others believe that these topics should not be discussed at all, and if they do talk about these things, it is only indirectly, with euphemisms. Fromkin and Rodman (1993) added that a euphemism is a word or phrase that substitutes a taboo word or helps to avoid frightening and unpleasant topics.

It also appears that linguistic taboo differs from one culture to another, even if the generic reason for the taboo is the same. Words that have religious connotations are considered profane if employed outside of formal or religious ceremonies. Among Poles, certain expressions such as *o boże* ('oh my God'), is believed to be profane and cultured people do not use these words. In England the word *bloody* is a taboo word (Joseph 2006), though the reason is obscure. Jamaliah (2000: 6) has observed that in each culture, one can find a polite system that exemplifies specific codes of verbal and non-verbal behaviour. In other words, speakers are usually open to those who show good manners in face-to-face interaction.

Hass (1964) confirms that specific language taboo appears to rise from bilingual situations, namely intercultural environments. Some Vietnamese names may create embarrassment in English, for example, the word *phuc,* which is pronounced [fʊk], like 'fuck' in some English dialects.

There are not many studies about taboo and it is worth investigating the possible trends that can be observed. This study investigates the perceptions of English and Polish speakers concerning linguistic taboos. Sometimes specific words can be taboo in one society but seen as suitable in others. Consequently, this study wants to observe whether individuals from different societies (Polish, English) perceive the taboo level of certain domains in a different way. It will be verified by the empirical study that will place special attention to the aspect of politeness. But before determining the inventory of taboo expressions in Polish and English, we must discuss politeness in language. It should be taken into consideration the concept of taboo, politeness and culture are closely related.

3 The concept of politeness in language

Examination of linguistic taboos requires consideration of the aspects of 'face' and 'Politeness Theory', as postulated by Brown and Levinson (1978, 1987). Brown and Levinson created a Model Person (MP), who is a fluent speaker of a language and who has two special qualities, namely rationality and face. By 'rationality', Brown and Levinson understand that the MP will exploit a specific mode of reasoning to select means that will satisfy his/her ends. By the concept 'face', Brown and Levinson (1987: 61) recognize the "public self-image that every member wants to claim for himself." Face contains two related aspects: a) negative face: "the want of every 'competent adult member' that [their] action be unimpeded by others" (p.62), and b) positive face: "the want of every member that [their] wants be desirable to at least some others" (p. 62) and "... [the] perennial desire that [their] wants (or the actions / acquisitions / values resulting from them) should be thought of as desirable" (p.101). Consistent with the needs of positive face, rational members of a given society frequently seek to present themselves in the best form possible. They attempt to keep face and present themselves as worthy of respect, as self-reliant, pure, and free from bad or filthy matters that may injure the integrity of their face. They need reinforcement in their concept of themselves as polite, considerate, respectful members of their society. From this perspective, such an image should be reflected both physically and linguistically. Douglas (1966) claims that by default individuals are polite, and euphemistic; and people censor their own language use to avoid taboo topics in pursuit of well-being for themselves and for others.

4 Methods and materials

4.1 Choice of subjects

This study is primarily qualitative in nature. Questionnaires were given to 80 Polish and 80 British English speakers. They were chosen randomly on the basis of convenience random sampling, disregarding the differences in age, educational background and occupation. The data were analyzed using SPSS 21.0.

4.2 Research question

RQ: Do perceptions of the Polish or British English speakers vary in terms of the use of linguistic taboo in their culture based on specific domains?

4.3 Instrumentation

A set of questionnaires was distributed to each respondent in order to identify the linguistic taboos in their own cultures. The questionnaires were divided into three parts. The first part gathered respondents' demographic information such as gender, age, and occupation or qualifications. In the second part, the respondents were asked to offer their general perception of linguistic taboos employing a 5-point Likert scale: from Strongly Disagree (1) to Strongly Agree (5). The third part was founded on four categories of linguistic taboo, namely *sex, body parts, bodily functions, death* and *dying*, again with a 5-point Likert scale. A frequency scale from Never (1) to Always (5) was included. This scale was employed because the investigators wanted to discover 'if' and 'when' taboo words were used in Polish and British cultures. The respondents were provided with brief instructions on the questionnaires. The examination of the results is focused mostly on the differences between Polish and English cognitive perceptions towards linguistic taboos.

The data obtained from the questionnaires was then examined by Statistical Package for Social Science (SPSS) version 21.00, with descriptive statistics frequency, distribution, mean and mode.

5 Results and discussion

5.1 Reliability analysis and the overall perception of linguistic taboo in Polish and English

A Kappa reliability test was carried out to confirm the validity of the technique employed. The outcome indicates that the Alpha value is satisfactory (0.9652). This shows that the method employed is valid, since the Alpha value is greater than 0.6000. The average mean for the general perception of Polish and English speakers about linguistic taboos is 3.23. This confirms that most interviewees agree on all the elements listed in the questionnaire.

Table 1 shows the frequency distribution of each element the general perception of Polish and English speakers on the use of linguistic taboos.

Table 1: General Perception of Linguistic Taboo

Statement	Strongly Disagree (%)		Disagree (%)		Undecided (%)		Agree (%)		Strongly Agree (%)	
	P	E	P	E	P	E	P	E	P	E
1. I am certain that taboo words are generally acceptable.	5.0	3.8	7.5	6.3	11.3	11.3	26.0	25.	1.3	2.5
2. I believe that taboo words help to transport meanings more clearly.	1.3	3.8	12.5	8.8	11.3	10.0	17.0	28.0	6.3	2.5
3. I do not believe taboo words are offensive or repulsive.	1.3	1.3	20.0	11.3	11.3	10.0	19.5	29.3	0.0	1.3
4. I do not believe taboo words are vulgar	1.3	0.0	15.0	8.8	18.8	16.3	17.0	23.0	1.3	3.8
5. I do not think taboo words are dirty.	2.5	0.0	15.0	8.8	6.3	15.0	25.0	11.3	1.3	2.5
6. I believe taboo words should not be used in public.	3.8	1.3	15.0	3.8	5.0	11.3	17.5	20.0	8.8	13.8
7. I am embarrassed to use taboo words with others.	3.8	1.3	16.3	6.3	15.0	18.8	8.8	13.8	6.3	11.3

Table 1 (continued)

Statement	Strongly Disagree(%)		Disagree (%)		Undecided (%)		Agree (%)		Strongly Agree (%)	
	P	E	P	E	P	E	P	E	P	E
8. I avoid using taboo words in my speech.	2.5	1.3	16.3	3.8	5.0	7.5	16.3	21.3	10.0	16.3
9. Taboo words should only be used with close friends.	2.5	3.8	13.8	7.5	5.0	8.8	27.5	26.3	1.3	3.8
10. I do not believe taboo words should be used even though one is in anger.	1.3	0.0	10.0	6.3	11.3	12.5	22.5	23.8	5.0	7.5
11. I detest those who use taboo words openly.	0.0	0.0	13.8	10.0	8.8	15.0	21.3	20.0	6.3	5.0
12. I believe that those who frequently use taboo words are from lower status background.	8.8	6.3	16.3	15.0	8.8	12.5	10.0	11.3	6.3	5.0
13. 1 believe those who use taboo words frequently are uneducated.	10.0	7.5	20.0	17.5	6.3	11.3	10.0	8.8	3.8	5.0

Note: P= Poles, E= English speakers

The results demonstrate that half of the respondents (51.3 %) agreed with the first statement, "I am certain that taboo words are generally acceptable" (26.0 % of Poles and 27.3 % of English speakers expressed that belief). The second statement "I believe that taboo words help to transport meanings more effectively" also shows both nationalities agree, although the percentage for the English speakers believing this statement to be true is higher (28 %) than the Polish (17 %). Therefore, it shows that most Polish and English speakers are certain that taboo words are mostly acceptable (see Statement 1). For the third statement, "I do not believe taboo words are offensive or repulsive", most Polish speakers (19.5 %) do not agree but 29.6 % of the English respondents showed their agreement to the statement. This appears to be interesting and may indicate that Poles, although they usually perceive taboo words to be acceptable, find these words to be offensive or repulsive, but the English speakers are mostly tolerant of such taboo words. 17 % of the Polish and 23 % of the English speakers agreed with the fourth statement, "I do not believe taboo words are vulgar." Among the Polish speakers, 18.8 % seemed to be unsure in comparison to 15 % who agreed.

This appears to suggest that Polish speakers, recognized for their refined and gentle ways, still hold strong to their culture that treats certain issues in a very sensitive way (Dyczewski 2002). 25 % of the Polish and 11.3 % of the English speakers agreed with the fifth statement, "I do not think taboo words can be considered dirty." However, among the English speakers, 15 % are unsure, as compared to the 13.3 % who approved of this statement. One can see that 17.5 % Poles and 20.0 % English speakers, accepted the statement that taboo words should not be used in public. Nevertheless, for the statement "I am embarrassed to use taboo words with others", 16.3 % of the Poles disagreed, versus 8.8 % who agreed, while more English speakers agreed (13.8 %) with the statement than disagreed (6.3 %). For the statement "I avoid using taboo words in my speech", an equal number of the Polish respondents agree and disagree (16.3 %), while more English respondents agree with the statement than disagree. Both the Polish and English respondents agree with the statements "Taboo words should only be used with close friends" and "I do not believe taboo words should be used even though one is in anger" (22.5 % Polish and 23.8 % English speakers). This is possibly because in the eyes of the Polish and English speakers, a person who exploits taboo words is insensitive to the dignity of others or perceived as impolite and offensive.

A total of 21.3 % of the Polish respondents and 20.0 % of the English respondents indicate that they agree with the statement "I detest those who frequently use taboo words openly." The greatest number of respondents disagree (16.3 % of the Polish and 15.0 % of the English speakers) with the statement "I believe that those who frequently use taboo words are from lower status background." Similarly, the greatest number (20.0 % of the Polish and 17.5 % of the English speakers) disagree with the statement that taboo words are used often by uneducated people. Consequently, the employment of these taboo words is not perceived to have anything to do with the characteristics mentioned above.

5.2 Categories of linguistic taboo used in accordance with domains

The descriptive statistics depicts the mean value for the statement "I use taboo words related to sex when I am..." The mean value provided is less than 2.0, except for the fifth statement with a mean value of 2.21. The mode value for the five statements is 1.

Table 2 shows the frequency distribution for the employment of taboo words connected with sex, consistent with specific domains[1].

Table 2: I use taboo words related to sex when I am:

Item	Never (%)		Seldom (%)		Occasionally (%)		Frequently (%)		Always (%)	
	P	E	P	E	P	E	P	E	P	E
a) Alone	26.5	29.5	19.8	13.7	8.8	5.0	3.8	5.0	1.3	0.5
b) At home	37.0	24.5	12.5	15.0	6.3	6.3	1.3	2.5	0.0	1.3
c) At the office	35.0	26.7	13.8	13.8	6.3	13.0	2.5	2.5	2.5	0.0
d) At school	23.0	22.4	12.5	11.0	6.3	13.8	5.0	3.8	1.3	1.3
e) At informal gatherings	16.3	18.8	15.0	11.3	12.3	18.0	6.3	3.8	2.9	1.6

The frequency distribution in Table 2 reveals that the majority of respondents from both cultures have chosen the option 'never' or 'seldom' to characterize their use of sex-related taboo words. For example: "In using sex related taboo words when being alone", 26.5 % Polish respondents, declare 'never' and 19.8 % said 'seldom'. The English speakers, however, declared 29.5 % for 'never' and 13.7 % for 'seldom'. For the next statement, employing sex-related taboo words among family at home, the Poles indicated 37.0 % 'never' versus 24.5 % for English speakers.

This is barely astonishing, as Poles come from cultures that pay much attention to family values with a puritanical approach to sex, particularly in the presence of children. However, the exploitation of sex associated taboo words displays a higher frequency during informal gatherings with the option 'occasionally' designated by the Polish (12.3 %) and the English speakers (18.0 %). Informal gatherings frequently encompass close friends and both Polish and English speakers appear to be comfortable speaking about sex in the company of friends rather than in the company of family members.

The informal context (e) gives a mode value of 3.0 as compared to the other contexts. This is consistent with the answer 'occasionally' for using sex-related taboo words among close friends.

---

[1] *Domain* is used to mean context of use.

Table 3 shows the frequency distribution of the use of taboo words connected with sex with specific individuals.

Table 3: I use sex-related taboo words with

Item	Never (%)		Seldom (%)		Occasionally (%)		Frequently (%)		Always (%)	
	P	E	P	E	P	E	P	E	P	E
a) Older close family members	29.6	37.0	8.8	10.0	10.0	2.5	2.5	1.3	0.0	1.3
b) Younger close family members	37.5	33.8	6.3	10.0	5.0	5.0	1.3	1.3	0.0	0.0
c) Older relatives	32.5	35.0	6.3	10.0	10.0	3.8	1.3	1.3	0.0	0.0
d) Younger relatives	37.6	31.3	6.3	12.5	3.8	3.8	1.3	2.5	0.0	0.0
e) Close friends	11.0	11.0	11.3	15.0	16.3	12.5	7.5	6.3	6.0	7.5
f) Friends	15.0	8.8	7.5	16.0	16.0	8.8	10.0	12.5	3.5	6.0
g) Colleagues	16.3	1.3	8.8	15.0	15.0	10.0	7.5	6.3	3.5	6.0
h) Peers	15.0	15.0	12.5	14.8	12.5	13.8	7.5	5.0	4.5	4.5
i) Acquaintances	22.5	25.0	8.8	15.0	13.8	10.0	3.8	0.0	2.3	0.5
j) The man in the street	33.7	34.3	15.0	8.8	1.3	5.0	0.0	0.0	1.7	0.6
k) People I do not like	27.5	25.0	10.0	8.8	6.3	8.3	3.4	5.0	2.3	2.2
l) Strangers	37.5	38.8	10.0	3.8	0.0	5.0	1.3	2.5	1.2	0.0

The employment of sex-related taboo words with "Older close family members", "Young close family members", "Older relatives" and "Younger relatives" seemed to be comparatively infrequent. The frequency distribution in Table 3 indicates that 29.6 % of Polish speakers and 37.0 % of English speakers did not employ sex-related taboo words when they communicated with "Older close family members". Conversely, for the use of sex-related taboo words among "close friends", "friends", "colleagues" as well as "peers" for both cultures, the selection is "occasionally". This could be a result of the intimacy feature, where the more intimate they are with the other party, the less shy or reserved they seem to be. However, when coping with "the man in the street", "People I do not like" and "strangers", most respondents declared "never" or "seldom" in exploiting sex-related taboo words.

The descriptive statistics for 'I use taboo words related to sex when' (Table 4) reveals that the mean value varies from 1.0 to 2.50 with the mode at 1.0. This indicates that most participants have a higher tendency to choose "never" or "seldom".

The employment of sex-related taboo words with the option when "I am angry" among both groups has a similar occurrence (18.7 % for 'never' and 16.3 % for 'seldom' among Poles and 17.5 % and 8.2 % respectively for English speakers). The majority declared 'never' to the use of sex-related taboo words for items (b) to (h), as seen in Table 4.

Table 4: I use taboo words related to sex when:

Item	Never (%)		Seldom (%)		Occasionally (%)		Frequently (%)		Always (%)	
	P	E	P	E	P	E	P	E	P	E
a) I am angry	18.7	17.5	16.3	8.2	13.8	12.5	3.8	3.8	1.3	7.5
b) I want to show affection	25.6	23.5	11.3	12.5	13.8	12.5	1.3	1.3	0.0	1.3
c) I want to be offensive	23.8	20.0	10.0	12.5	10.0	7.5	5.0	6.3	1.3	3.8
d) I want to shock	26.3	25.0	10.0	6.3	10.0	15.0	3.8	2.5	0.0	1.3
e) I am happy	38.8	27.5	3.7	6.2	6.3	13.8	1.3	2.5	0.0	0.0
f) I am excited	30.0	22.5	10.3	6.5	7.5	12.8	0.0	2.5	1.3	1.3
g) I want to emphasise	20.0	22.5	12.5	6.3	8.8	16.3	7.5	4.0	1.3	0.0
h) For no reason	36.5	33.5	8.5	7.5	3.7	8.4	0.0	1.3	0.0	0.0

The statement "I use taboo words related to body parts when I am" (Table 5) showed a mean value of less than 2.0 and a mode value of 1.0. This shows the tendency of the majority to opt for "never" and "seldom" as their selections to the statement.

The occurrence analysis in Table 5 indicates that the majority of responses from both cultural groups for the five items are frequently directed towards the option "never". For example: 30.5 % of the Polish respondents chose "never" in employing taboo words connected to body parts when alone, while 37.0 % of the English speakers do so. The situation seems to be similar when they are at school. Most of them chose "never" in using taboo words associated with body parts: 34.6 % (Polish) and 29.5 % (English speakers).

Table 5: I use taboo words related to body parts when I am:

Item	Never (%)		Seldom (%)		Occasionally (%)		Frequently (%)		Always (%)	
	P	E	P	E	P	E	P	E	P	E
a) Alone	30.5	37.0	12.5	8.8	2.5	1.3	2.5	2.5	1.5	2.5
b) At home	26.5	30.5	16.6	14.5	3.8	2.5	0.0	2.5	0.0	0.0
c) At the office	32.5	31.3	10.0	10.0	5.0	6.3	1.5	2.5	1.5	0.0
d) At school	34.6	29.5	6.5	7.5	6.3	8.8	2.5	5.0	1.3	1.3
e) At informal gatherings	26.5	29.0	11.3	6.3	8.5	8.5	1.5	3.5	2.6	1.4

The result was to be expected, as among the Polish and the English speakers, politeness appears to be a significant aspect of their everyday interaction, both within the group and outside of it. Politeness for both groups means indicating respect for others and conforming to social rules and etiquette. Furthermore, it is the cultural traits of both the Polish and English speakers not to cause offence to others. Consequently, the employment of taboo words associated with body parts is firmly prohibited (except for close friends).

Most mean values are between 1.27 to 2.30 for the statement "I use taboo words related to body parts" with items such as older and younger close family members, older and younger relatives, friends, colleagues and peers. The non-use of taboo body part names is strongly indicated in the two cultural groups, except when they are with close friends, as shown in Table 6.

Table 6: I use taboo words related to body parts with:

Item	Never (%)		Seldom %		Occasionally (%)		Frequently (%)		Always (%)	
	P	E	P	E	P	E	P	E	P	E
a) Older close family members	32.0	35.5	13.8	10.0	3.8	3.8	1.3	2.5	1.3	0.0
b) Younger close family members	42.0	45.0	8.8	3.8	1.3	6.3	0.0	0.0	0.0	0.0
c) Older relatives	36.3	40.0	8.8	5.0	3.8	2.5	1.3	2.5	0.0	0.0
d) Younger relatives	38.8	35.0	10.0	8.8	1.3	3.8	0.0	1.5	0.0	1.5

Table 6 (continued)

Item	Never (%)		Seldom %)		Occasionally (%)		Frequently (%)		Always (%)	
	P	E	P	E	P	E	P	E	P	E
e) Close friends	17.5	12.5	17.5	18.8	7.5	6.3	3.8	10.0	4.8	3.5
f) Friends	23.8	15.0	13.8	13.5	5.0	13.8	6.0	8.5	3.5	1.6
g) Colleagues	25.0	18.8	12.5	13.5	8.5	14.8	2.5	2.5	2.5	2.5
h) Peers	25.0	23.8	8.8	8.8	8.8	13.8	6.3	2.5	1.7	1.7
i) Acquaintances	30.0	28.8	12.5	10.0	5.0	10.0	2.5	0.0	0.0	1.3
j) The man in the street	42.5	37.5	7.5	7.5	1.3	5.0	0.0	1.3	0.0	0.0
k) People I do not like	32.5	28.8	10.0	8.8	3.5	6.3	3.8	5.0	1.5	1.5
l) Strangers	41.3	36.3	9.5	5.0	0.0	3.8	1.5	3.9	0.0	1.5

About 32.0 % of the Polish respondents and 35.5 % of the English speakers chose the option 'never' on the use of taboo words associated with body parts when communicating with older close family members. One can observe that when Polish and English speakers are communicating with younger family members, the predisposition is more towards 'never'. When they communicate with older and younger relatives, most of them chose 'never' or 'seldom'. This is possibly out of respect for the elders. Among the Polish speakers, the elders are respected and are treated accordingly. Yet, it seems that most of the respondents admit to using taboo words connected with body parts when they communicate with their close friends.

The participants also chose the option 'never' and 'seldom' for the use of body part taboo words when they talk with a 'man on the street' and 'strangers'. 42.5 % of the Polish respondents and 37.5 % of the English speakers specified the answer 'never', while 8.5 % chose 'seldom' in such a case. This indicates that 'the sense of familiarity or intimacy' is one of the features which could affect the use of taboo words during verbal interaction.

One can observe that a high mean value of 2.19 for the item "I use taboo words related to body parts when I am angry" is present, compared to the other choices with a mean value under 2.0 (cf. Table 7). This shows that most respondents regularly use taboo words concerning body parts when they are angry, possibly to release their anger or to express a strong degree of anger. This appears to be consistent with Tannen's (1979) observation that when individuals speak they do it in ways that contribute to the impression others derive about the speaker's intentions, personalities and styles. The study participants may have used taboo words deliberately. The majority of the participants chose the option 'never' or 'seldom' for the use of body part taboo words in many situations. Beside anger, Polish and English speakers most often chose the option 'occasionally' but with differences. For the entry 'I want to show affection', the English speakers (15.5 %) chose 'occasionally', Polish speakers 6.5 %.

The other two elements, 'I want to shock' and 'I am happy' also validate the higher inclination of the English speakers to use the related taboo words, compared to the Polish respondents, as indicated in Table 7. These findings specify that most English speakers are possibly more open and expressive in displaying various emotions.

Table 7: I use taboo words related to body parts when:

Item	Never (%)		Seldom %)		Occasionally (%)		Frequently (%)		Always (%)	
	P	E	P	E	P	E	P	E	P	E
a) I am angry	23.5	16.53	10.0	11.7	13.5	13.5	7.7	9.5	0.0	1.5
b) I want to show affection	24.0	26.5	17.5	7.5	6.5	15.5	1.5	2.5	0.0	0.0
c) Iwant to be offensive	29.8	21.5	10.0	11.3	7.5	7.5	3.8	6.5	0.0	2.5
d) I want to shock	34.5	27.5	8.5	8.5	6.3	8.8	1.3	3.8	1.8	4.5
e) I am happy	35.8	28.5	12.3	8.5	2.5	11.3	2.5	1.3	0.0	1.3
f) I am excited	37.5	27.5	7.5	7.5	2.5	12.5	2.5	1.3	0.0	1.3
g) I want to emphasise	27.5	27.6	11.5	7.5	6.3	7.5	2.5	5.0	1.5	1.5
h) For no reason	42.5	29.5	3.8	7.5	1.5	9.8	3.5	1.5	0.0	18

Let us now consider the response to the question "I use taboo words related to bodily functions when I am" in different contexts, namely alone, home, office, school and informal gatherings. The mean value is between 1.50 to 1.80 for the options 'never' and 'seldom'. Table 8 reports the outcome for the use of taboo words related to body functions in numerous situations. It is clear that most participants did not select 'frequently' or 'always' for the use of bodily function taboo words most recommended situations. For example: only 3.0 % of Polish and English speakers chose 'always' for most places with the exception of 'at informal gatherings' with 4.0 %.

Table 8: I use taboo words related to bodily functions when I am:

Item	Never (%)		Seldom (%)		Occasionally (%)		Frequently (%)		Always (%)	
	P	E	P	E	P	E	P	E	P	E
a) Alone	33.8	31.7	6.3	7.5	2.5	6.3	6.3	1.3	1.5	1.5
b) At home	30.0	30.0	13.5	10.0	2.5	8.8	3.8	0.0	1.5	15
c) At the office	32.5	34.0	13.5	3.6	1.3	7.5	2.5	3.9	0.0	0.0
d) At school	30.0	30.0	13.5	6.7	3.8	8.5	3.9	3.9	0.0	1.5
e) At informal gatherings	25.5	33.5	13.5	4.0	6.3	8.5	2.5	3.9	2.5	1.5

Acts of bodily functions are private and are not discussed openly. Consequently, words concerning bodily functions are recognized as impolite and people do not refer to them in polite situations, particularly during formal events.

These words are also not used in the company of elders or superiors and with acquaintances or strangers. This is consistent with the belief that Poles are expected to respect elders in their speech as well as behavior. The mode value for the bodily function taboo corresponds to the participants' communicating.

For the statement 'I use taboo words related to bodily functions', the following elements display high mean values: close friends, friends, and colleagues, with values of 2.0 or more. This reveals that the respondents frequently use such taboo words with their friends and colleagues than with their relatives. Correspondingly, in Table 9, a low occurrence distribution is indicated for the options 'frequently' and 'always'.

Table 9: I use taboo words related to bodily functions with:

Item	Never (%)		Seldom (%)		Occasionally (%)		Frequently (%)		Always (%)	
	P	E	P	E	P	E	P	E	P	E
a) Older close family members	26.8	35.8	12.8	2.7	4.5	8.3	4.8	1.5	0.0	0.0
b) Younger close family members	37.5	36.3	7.5	5.0	2.5	6.3	2.5	1.3	0.0	1.3
c) Older relatives	35.0	35.0	6.3	5.0	5.0	7.5	3.8	2.5	0.0	0.0
d) Younger relatives	36.3	31.3	8.9	11.3	2.5	5.0	2.5	1.3	0.0	1.5

Table 9 (continued)

Item	Never (%)		Seldom (%)		Occasionally (%)		Frequently (%)		Always (%)	
	P	E	P	E	P	E	P	E	P	E
e) Close friends	22.5	13.8	13.5	16.0	7.5	6.3	5.0	11.3	2.5	3.8
f) Friends	20.0	20.0	16.3	8.8	10.0	11.3	1.3	8.7	2.5	1.3
g) Colleagues	21.3	21.3	21.0	8.8	3.8	13.8	3.5	7.3	2.5	0.0
h) Peers	20.0	23.8	21.0	11.3	5.0	11.3	3.5	4.8	2.5	0.0
i) Acquaintances	27.5	30.0	13.8	11.3	6.4	7.5	3.5	1.3	0.0	0.0
j) The man in the street	35.5	38.3	10.0	8.8	2.5	2.5	0.0	1.3	0.0	1.3
k) People I do not like	31.0	26.5	12.5	7.5	2.5	6.3	5.0	7.5	0.0	2.5
l) Strangers	38.5	38.5	10.0	6.0	1.5	2.5	1.5	3.4	0.0	1.5

The items 'friends', 'colleagues' and 'peers' involve high percentages for the choice 'occasionally', compared to other groups, particularly among the English respondents. This suggests that they are more open when they are with their close friends than with their own family members. Perhaps they are attempting to set a good example in front of younger family members and demonstrate respect towards elders.

The mode and mean values for "I use taboo words related to bodily functions when" appear to be higher than any other elements when respondents are angry. The mean value at 2.24 and the mode value at 2.00 shows that respondents from both cultures 'occasionally' employ taboo words connected with bodily functions when they are angry. Table 10 indicates that 25.3 % of the Polish respondents and 15.5 % of the English speakers chose 'seldom' when replying to the statement "I use taboo words related to bodily functions when I am angry". Yet, 16.0 % of the English speakers also chose 'occasionally', versus 11.0 % for the Polish respondents. This indicates that English speakers employ taboo words related to bodily functions when they feel angry more regularly than the Polish respondents.

Table 10: I use taboo words related to bodily functions when:

Item	Never (%)		Seldom (%)		Occasionally (%)		Frequently (%)		Always (%)	
	P	E	P	E	P	E	P	E	P	E
a) I am angry	16.0	16.0	25.3	15.5	11.0	16.0	3.8	1.3	0.0	6.5
b) I want to show affection	26.5	22.5	15.0	11.3	7.5	10.0	0.0	5.0	0.0	1.5
c) I want to be offensive	24.8	20.0	17.5	13.8	5.0	10.0	3.8	3.8	0.0	2.5
d) I want to shock	37.3	29.5	8.8	7.5	5.0	11.3	5.0	2.5	0.0	1.5
e) I am happy	34.0	25.5	6.3	8.5	6.3	10.0	2.5	4.8	0.0	1.5
f) I am excited	36.8	27.3	7.5	6.3	7.5	12.5	1.5	4.8	0.0	1.5
g) I want to emphasise	28.3	24.0	16.3	8.5	5.0	7.5	2.5	7.5	0.0	1.5
h) For no reason	30.5	36.6	11.0	6.0	7.3	8.5	4.8	1.5	0.0	0.0

Conversely, the Polish respondents reply 'Never' in more cases than the English speakers. This might be because in the Polish community one should demonstrate proper refined behavior at all times (cf. Dyczewski 2002). The percentage of English speakers selecting 'Occasionally' is more than 10.0 % for most items.

With regards to "death and dying", the five elements analyzed showed a low mean value which was less than 2.00 with a mode at 1.00. Most participants chose 'Never' or 'Seldom' for the statement "I use taboo words related to death and dying when I am..." (Table 11). The greatest number of respondents chose 'Never' or 'Seldom' when using taboo words related to death and dying at all times in this experiment. For instance, 30.5 % of the Polish respondents and 34.0 % of the English speakers stated that they 'Never' exploited taboo words related to death and dying at informal gatherings. It can be seen that 16.5 % of the Polish and 8.5 % of English speakers chose 'Seldom' in response to the statement, as illustrated in Table 11.

Table 11: I use taboo words related to death and dying when I am:

Item	Never (%)		Seldom (%)		Occasionally (%)		Frequently (%)		Always (%)	
	P	E	P	E	P	E	P	E	P	E
a) Alone	34.5	31.5	12.3	14.3	3.5	2.3	3.5	4.8	1.5	2.5
b) At home	27.5	22.6	18.3	15.0	6.0	6.0	1.5	5.0	0.0	1.5
c) At the office	38.5	32.5	6.5	11.5	6.0	6.0	2.5	1.5	0.0	1.5
d) At school	31.5	26.5	11.0	12.3	7.5	8.8	1.5	1.5	0.0	2.5
e) At informal gatherings	30.5	34.0	16.5	8.5	4.8	8.5	5.0	2.8	0.0	2.9

No Polish respondents replied 'Always' in using taboo words related to death and dying when they are at home, office, school and at informal gatherings. Very few replied 'Always' when alone.

Now, we consider the use of death/dying taboo words with different groups of people (Table 12). The 'friends' and 'close friends' elements had a very high mean value. All elements had a mode value of 1.00. In sum, respondents normally chose "Seldom" or "Occasionally" when employing taboo words related to death and dying with their close friends.

Conversely, the elements for 'older and younger close family members' and 'younger and older relatives' showed a high percentage for 'Never' and 'Seldom' regarding the use of taboo words related to death and dying. The 'friends' element was the only element having a high percentage for the feedback 'Occasionally' among the English speakers. This suggests that having a close relationship with someone does not stop the use of taboo words related to death and dying.

Table 12: I use taboo words related to death and dying with:

Item	Never (%)		Seldom (%)		Occasionally (%)		Frequently (%)		Always (%)	
	P	E	P	E	P	E	P	E	P	E
a) Older close family members	28.8	35.0	17.5	7.5	15.6	10.3	2.5	5.0	1.3	2.5
b) Younger close family members	36.3	35.0	8.8	8.8	2.5	0.0	2.5	5.0	0.0	1.3
c) Older relatives	33.8	35.0	12.5	7.5	1.3	1.3	2.5	2.5	0.0	3.8

Table 12 (continued)

Item	Never (%)		Seldom (%)		Occasionally (%)		Frequently (%)		Always (%)	
	P	E	P	E	P	E	P	E	P	E
d) Younger relatives	38.8	35.0	7.5	10.0	1.3	2.5	2.5	1.3	0.0	1.3
e) Close friends	22.5	16.3	17.5	16.3	5.0	8.8	3.8	2.5	1.3	6.3
f) Friends	23.8	16.3	20.0	15.0	1.3	10.0	3.8	5.0	1.3	3.8
g) Colleagues	28.8	21.3	14.8	14.8	2.5	7.5	3.8	5.0	1.3	2.5
h) Peers	31.3	22.5	14.8	14.8	0.0	8.8	3.8	2.5	1.3	2.5
i) Acquaintances	35.0	28.8	10.0	12.5	2.5	6.3	2.5	1.3	0.0	1.3
j) The man in the street	38.8	37.5	5.0	6.3	3.8	3.8	2.5	2.5	0.0	0.0
k) People I do not like	35.0	27.5	10.0	7.5	1.3	8.8	2.5	5.0	1.3	1.3
l) Strangers	50.0	40.5	5.0	5.0	1.3	3.8	3.8	3.8	0.0	0.0

Yet when communicating with strangers, the greatest number of participants (50.0 % of the Polish speakers and 40.5 % of the English) chose 'Never' in reply to the statement.

The condition "I am angry" has a mean value of 2.20 for this statement, whereas other items have a mean value under 2.00. This result is somewhat clarified by responses in Table 13. Subjects select 'seldom' and 'occasionally' for use of taboo words related to death and dying when angry. A higher percentage of English speakers (12.5 %) choose 'Occasionally' in response to the entry "I am angry," as compared to the Polish respondents (9 %).

Table 13: I use taboo words related to death and dying when:

Item	Never (%)		Seldom (%)		Occasionally (%)		Frequently (%)		Always (%)	
	P	E	P	E	P	E	P	E	P	E
a) I am angry	21.0	15.8	17.5	15.0	9.0	12.5	2.5	5.0	1.3	5.0
b) I want to show affection	29.7	26.5	13.8	10.0	5.0	5.0	2.5	6.3	0.0	1.3
c) I want to be offensive	27.5	20.0	15.0	13.8	2.5	7.5	3.8	5.0	1.3	3.8
d) I want to shock	36.0	25.8	12.5	11.3	0.0	8.8	1.3	3.8	1.3	2.5

Table 13 (continued)

Item	Never (%)		Seldom (%)		Occasionally (%)		Frequently (%)		Always (%)	
	P	E	P	E	P	E	P	E	P	E
e) I am happy	37.5	33.8	6.3	6.3	5.0	3.8	1.3	3.8	0.0	3.5
f) I am excited	35.0	26.5	7.5	11.3	7.5	3.8	0.0	6.0	0.0	3.5
g) I want to emphasise	31.3	26.0	7.5	12.5	5.0	6.5	6.3	6.0	0.0	1.5
h) For no reason	36.0	36.0	8.5	9.5	6.0	6.0	0.0	1.5	1.5	1.5

No Polish respondents answer 'Always' for "I want to shock", "I am happy", "I am excited" and "I want to emphasize". This suggests that the Polish respondents are more careful in using taboo words connected with death and dying than the English speakers, again suggesting that the English speakers tend to be more responsive and honest in articulating their feelings.

6 Conclusions

This study seeks a better comprehension of how taboo words function in Polish and English cultures as a function of the types of taboo word and the context of their use. The two groups of respondents differ culturally and linguistically, yet perceptions of linguistic taboo appear to cross cultural barriers. Yet there are differences. The present study identifies some of these areas but does not correlate them with potential causation. The next step in this direction is to determine the different methods of avoidance, e.g. euphemism, circumlocution, scientific terms, and correlate them with the cultural and cognitive variables used here. As Holmes (2001:67) points out, "Choosing the appropriate linguistic forms for friends and foreigners involves the dimension of solidarity (or social distance) and social status (or power)." These dimensions affect the cognitive process of perception of linguistic phenomena like politeness. Therefore, it is expected this analysis might help disclose whether linguistic taboo plays a main role in the way individuals perceive and communicate with one another and how it can raise sensitivity and diminish embarrassment or offence when communicating.

References

Brown, P. and C.Levinson.1978. Universals in Language Usage: Politeness Phenomena. In Goody, E. (ed.) *Questions and politeness: Strategies in social Interaction*, 56–289. Cambridge: Cambridge University Press.

Brown, P. and C. Levinson 1987. *Politeness: Some Universals in Language Usage.* Cambridge: Cambridge University Press.

Crystal, D. 1995. *The Cambridge Encyclopedia of Language.* New York: Cambridge University Press.

Douglas, M. 1970. *Natural Symbols.* Middlesex, England: Penguin.

Douglas, M. 1966. *Purity and Danger: An Analysis of the Concepts of Pollution and Taboo.* London: Ark-Routledge and Kegan Paul.

Dyczewski L. 2002. *Values in the Polish Cultural Tradition.* Washington: The Council for Research in Values and Philosophy.

Farba P. 2015. *Word Play: What Happens When People Talk.* New York: Vintage.

Freud, S. 1950 [1913]. Totem and Taboo, trans. James Strachey. London: Routledge & Kegan Paul.

Hass, Mary R. 1964. Interlingual Word Taboos. In Dell Hymes (ed.), *Language in Culture and Society: a Reader in Linguistics and Anthropology,* 489–494. New York: Harper & Row.

Holmes, J. 1992. *An Introduction to Sociolinguistics.* London and New York: Longman.

Hongxu, H., & Guisen, T. 1990. A Sociolinguistic View of Linguistic Taboo in Chinese. *International Journal of Society and Language* 81. 63–85.

Hughes, G. 2015. *The Social History of Oaths, Profanity, Foul Language, and Ethnic Slurs in the English-speaking World.* London and New York: Routledge.

Jamaliah Mohd. Ali. 2000. *Verbal Communication: A Study of Malaysian Speakers.* Kuala Lumpur: University of Malaya Press.

Leech, E. 1964. Anthropological aspects of language: Animal categories and verbal abuse. In Eric H. Lennenberg (ed.), *New Directions in the Study of Language,* 23–36. Cambridge, MA.: M.I.T. Press.

Malinowsky, B. 1923. The problem of meaning in Primitive Languages. In Ogden C. K. & I. A. Richards (eds.), *The Meaning of Meaning* (suppl. 1). New York: Harcourt Brace.

Mead, M. 1937. Tabu. *Encyclopaedia of Social Sciences.* London: Macmillan, vol. 7: 502–505.

Steiner, F. 2013. *Taboo.* Harmondsworth, UK: Penguin Books.

Wardhaugh, R. 1994. *An Introduction to Sociolinguistics.* Second Edn. Cambridge: Blackwell Publishers.

Barbara De Cock and Ferran Suñer
10 The influence of conceptual differences on processing taboo metaphors in the foreign language

Abstract: In this paper, we analyze to what extent well developed multilingualism goes hand in hand with an adequate integration of conceptual differences between the different languages, with a focus on the comprehension of taboo metaphors in the second language (L2). Despite the growing body of theoretical approaches, empirical studies on the concrete functioning of mechanisms involving metaphor interpretation are not conclusive. In this study, we report on a pilot study among French-speaking students of L2 Spanish with a focus on the influence of the conceptual and sociocultural differences between the L1 and the L2, as well as the presence of context. The results show that the impact of context on the ability of students to infer the correct interpretation is less straightforward than suggested in the literature. In general, students perform as well at interpreting conceptually similar metaphors than conceptually different ones, suggesting that they rely on general embodied experiences. The triangulation with a questionnaire concerning their linguistic biography reveals that students who have spent a prolonged stay in a Spanish-speaking country are better at interpreting taboo metaphors, regardless of their overall language level.

Keywords: taboo, metaphor, metaphoric competence, L2 acquisition, Spanish

1 Introduction

Although research on the language-specific encoding of experiences has stressed the importance of the conceptual system and the socio-cultural embedding of languages for teaching purposes, teaching and learning foreign languages is often limited to the formal aspects of language (Roche 2014; Danesi 2008; Littlemore 2009). In line with Danesi (2008), we assume that well developed multilingualism goes hand in hand with an adequate integration of conceptual differences between the different languages. This includes the ability to use different conceptual contents and varied sources of knowledge (e.g. pragmatic, sociocultural knowledge) when interpreting expressions in the foreign language (cf. Trim 2012). Despite the growing body of theoretical approaches, empirical studies on the concrete functioning of these mechanisms are lacking. This is even more the case for the study of taboo expressions in the foreign language, related to the fact that some taboo topics are not dealt with in foreign language learning or are avoided when speaking with non-natives, and/or that some of these expressions are part of more informal registers, which are not always included in foreign language teaching. Furthermore, assuming that taboo expressions often draw upon metaphorization to avoid a direct reference of the target concept (Crespo Fernández 2011), the acquisition of a metaphoric competence in this domain becomes even more important. Therefore, the purpose of the present study is to shed light on the influence of conceptual and sociocultural differences as well as the linguistic context on processing taboo metaphors in a foreign language. This was tested by means of a comprehension test on metaphoric taboo expressions with learners of Spanish as a foreign language, which allowed to examine both single effects of the dimensions as well as their interplay.

First, we will describe the specific position of taboo in foreign language learning (section 2) before presenting a theoretical overview of research concerning the impact of sociocultural knowledge on metaphor interpretation by foreign language learners (section 3). We will then present our pilot study and discuss the main findings (section 4), before proceeding to discussing these findings and formulating conclusions as well as avenues for further research (section 5).

2 Taboo and foreign language learning

In this section, we will mainly focus on the input of taboo expressions that foreign language learners would be exposed to, taking into account the register-specificity of (sexual) taboo expressions (section 2.1) and students' contact with discourse concerning taboo topics (section 2.2). We will focus on speakers who received (also) formal instruction in a foreign language, not on speakers who acquired a foreign language through informal learning only.

2.1 Taboo and register use

The use of taboo expressions is known to be register-dependent in that the use of taboo words gradually diminishes when abandoning the more informal register and changing to the more formal one (López Morales 2005; Pizarro Pedraza this volume, Ruette this volume). A logical question is then to which extent are foreign language learners in contact with informal registers.

We will now discuss to which extent students may be familiar with this type of data. The Common European Framework of Reference for Languages (CFR), which is used as the basis for many teaching materials and official curricula throughout Europe, associates appreciating register shifts to the C1-level and considers that "in early learning (say up to level B1), a relatively neutral register is appropriate, unless there are compelling reasons otherwise. It is a register that native speakers are likely to use towards foreigners and strangers generally. Acquaintance with more formal or more familiar registers is likely to come over a period of time, perhaps through the reading of different text-types, particularly novels, at first as a receptive competence. Some caution should be exercised in using more formal or more familiar registers, since their inappropriate use may well lead to misinterpretation and ridicule" (CFR s.d.: 120). The CFR then bases its recommendation on the fact that natives are likely to use a neutral register when addressing non-natives. This may be due to the fact that natives may consider this register easier to understand for non-natives and/or they may consider that they have to set a good example to non-natives and avoid non-neutral registers. As we will see, the students involved in our study are situated at levels B2–C1 and are, as such, still acquiring register differences. In addition, students may have been confronted with more explicit information concerning register differences when analyzing artistic productions (literary texts, movies,...) in their literature classes and/or in linguistics classes.

2.2 Exposure to discourse on taboo topics

While foreign language teaching has focused during a long time on grammar and lexicon acquisition, more relatively recent approaches such as the communicative approach or task-based language learning aim more explicitly at preparing students for everyday interaction, involving also certain elements of intercultural and pragmatic competence. Moreover, "research of the past three decades has shown almost unanimously that the teaching of pragmatic skills to language learners is not only feasible (...) and desirable (...), but also more effective than mere exposure to the target language" (Glaser 2013: 151). The expression of taboo is situated mainly at the semantics-pragmatics interface and often also includes cultural knowledge (Pizarro Pedraza 2015: 62; Pizarro Pedraza and De Cock 2018). Thus, the changes in foreign language didactics imply a more prominent place for some competences that are useful for the comprehension of taboo expressions.

When looking more specifically into the teaching or acquisition of the comprehension of discourse on taboo topics, it is noticeable that the major taboo topics (death, illness, sex, bodily fluids, cf. Allan and Burridge 2006) are treated in a very unequal way in traditional language teaching. If we look into the CFR, it is clear that, at a theoretical level, taboo knowledge is considered part of the ability to learn declarative knowledge and intercultural knowledge (CFR s.d.: 12, 103). Torres Sánchez' study (1997) shows that students from different countries have different appreciations of which topics are taboo, to which extent they are so, and what is the appropriate way to deal with it. Yet, no concrete reference is made to learning to talk about or understand taboo topics in the actual description of the CFR framework. More concretely, we see that the only taboo topic explicitly mentioned is illness, mostly from a very practical perspective, namely in order to allow students to deal with emergencies. Indeed, in the global scale descriptions of the B1-level, for instance, we find "[the student] can deal with most situations likely to arise when travelling in an area where the language is spoken" (ibid. 24). While this leaves room for discussion concerning the (taboo) topics likely to arise when travelling (lexicon concerning contraception, for instance, is virtually absent from textbooks), in practice textbooks seem to include reference to illnesses only and, in general, typically to relatively frequent and "less taboo" afflictions, such as a cold, a flu or a fracture. These are likely to have a lower "revoltingness rating" (Allan and Burridge 1991). Menstruation, by contrast, was proven to have a high revoltingness rate (Allan and Burridge 1991), and the term itself does not appear in typical foreign language textbooks. Yet, one could argue that, for female students, menstruation is much more likely to arise when travelling than a flu or a fracture. A possible exception is the more general descriptions concerning belly aches, which may be linked both to bodily functions and/or sexual reproduction. Diseases which are considered to have a higher degree of tabooization, such as cancer (Grondelaers and Geeraerts 1998), remain generally absent in textbooks.

The ALTE (Association of Language Testers in Europe) framework, a standard for international language exams such as the Cambridge Certificates in English as a Foreign Language, has issued a set of descriptors for each level. Level 5 contains: "can advise on or talk about complex or sensitive issues" (Council of Europe: 251). ALTE Level 5 is associated with CFR level C2, viz. the highest level. Assuming that taboo expressions can be considered "sensitive" issues, this shows again that using taboo expressions is situated at the highest levels of proficiency.

As with register issues, taboo topics may come up in discussion of more specific productions. It is known that some taboo topics, such as death and sex, are likely to appear in literary works and/or cinematographic production. Depending on the genre, this may be produced in a much more formal register, though.

3 Metaphoric competence in the L2

As mentioned above, it is widely recognized that taboo expressions often draw upon metaphorization to avoid a direct reference of the target concept (Crespo Fernández 2011). That means that speakers need to perform some cognitive tasks which typically belong to the so called metaphoric competence in order to ensure their adequate comprehension and/or production. In order to have a clear understanding of which mechanisms underlie metaphor comprehension in the L2 and which factors influence this process, this section reports on previous research concerning (non-taboo related) metaphoric competence in the L2 on cognitive and sociocultural aspects (section 3.1) and on previous studies (section 3.2).

3.1 Cognitive and sociocultural aspects of metaphoric competence in the L2

Assuming that taboo expressions are highly relevant for everyday life communication in the foreign language, coping with them in the context of foreign language learning requires an advanced metaphoric competence. Indeed, learners do not only need to master the formal aspects of a language and the literal meaning of the words, but also to deal with metaphorical extension in a culturally sensitive way in order to adequately encode experiences in the L2 (cf. also Danesi 2008; Pavlenko 2009; Roche 2013; Roche and Roussy-Parent 2006; Charteris-Black 2002; Jessen and Suñer 2017, Kuzio in this volume). In fact, metaphoric taboo expressions are especially suitable to exemplify to what extent linguistic forms are conceptually motivated and embedded in a sociocultural context. For example, the Spanish expression *mojar el churro* 'to dip the churro' is used in colloquial contexts to refer to *having sex*. In this case, speakers need to use their sociocultural knowledge about the source domain *churro* (a long, slender fried pastry which can be dipped into hot chocolate) in order to activate the relevant features and map them through onto the target domain *sex*, e.g. by means of analogical reasoning and image formation. However, when creating such a figurative meaning in the foreign language, learners are likely to face major challenges, since the relevant sociocultural knowledge often differs from their own L1 sociocultural knowledge and cannot, therefore, be accessed for this purpose. In this sense, learning a foreign language implies that at least two different conceptual systems are in contact and can influence each other in different ways (cf. Danesi 2008). For example, conceptual interferences often lead learners to erroneously map conceptualization patterns from their L1 onto the foreign language and, thus, fail getting access to the relevant conceptual content of the source domains to structure more abstracts concepts (Jessen and Suñer 2017). In order to avoid such conceptual interferences and the associated communicative impairments, Danesi (2008) stresses the importance of teaching learners how to "express oneself in the target language (L2) while utilizing the conceptual system of the target language, rather than using the target language, but relying primarily on the conceptual system of the first language" (Danesi 2008: 243). In other words, learners should be able to identify language-specific conceptualization patterns, restructure their own conceptual categories and create links between languages which reflect the respective conceptual and sociocultural differences. The acquisition of such a competence is, in turn, an important condition for qualitatively developed multilingualism (cf. Roche 2013).

Whereas research on language acquisition points out the importance of metaphoric competence for vocabulary retention, grammatical, textual, illocutionary and sociolinguistic competence (Littlemore and Low 2006; Doiz and Elizari 2013; Azuma 2009; Cameron and Low 1999), textbooks and current curricula are slow in accepting such findings. Indeed, metaphors are often still presented as semantically opaque phrasal idioms or frozen metaphors which should be taught at upper levels. In contrast to this view, a recent study by Littlemore et al. (2014) found that the use of metaphors is relatively widespread among learners at all levels of L2 proficiency, although the overall density of metaphors increases from the lower levels (A2–B1) up to the upper levels of proficiency (B2–C2). Furthermore, the authors found some qualitative difference between the different groups of proficiency: whereas learners at upper levels made more often use of metaphoric expressions based on items from open-class items (e.g. verbs, nouns, etc.), learners at lower levels used metaphors which relied on closed-class items (e.g. prepositions). The authors conclude that metaphors are ubiquitous and serve different communicative functions at each level. As a consequence, Littlemore et al. (2014) formulate a set of descriptors at every level of the CFR involving metaphor use. For instance, they propose that learners at C1 level "should be able to make use of direct, indirect, and personification metaphors in clusters, with appropriate phraseology, for persuasive or rhetorical effect, to write emotively about topics that they feel strongly about" (p. 142).

3.2 Previous studies on the role of context and sociocultural knowledge for metaphor comprehension in the L2

In very broad terms, metaphor comprehension can be understood as the ability to comprehend one entity in terms of another entity (cf. Littlemore and Low 2006a; cf. also Littlemore et al. 2014). More concretely, learners need "to identify the source and target domain terms, use the target domain to single out those aspects of the source domain that seem relevant within the given context and decide between competing alternative solutions" (Littlemore and Low 2006b: 50). Especially in the context of foreign language, metaphoric expressions are likely to be novel to learners at the moment of processing (cf. Littlemore 2008), so that special processing strategies are needed to cope with potential comprehension difficulties, even if learners are familiar with the literal meaning of the single words contained in the metaphor. Indeed, there is some evidence suggesting that L2 literal meanings are often more salient than figurative meanings and are, thus, often first accessed when dealing with idiomatic expressions (cf. Liontas 2002; Cieslicka 2006). Some authors, however, claim that the way to access and use literal and figurative meanings when processing idiomatic expressions varies according to the L2 learner's proficiency in the target language. As a result, learners tend to adapt their comprehension strategies according to their needs and the situational cues available (cf. Littlemore and Low 2006b). Among others, they use mental imagery, analogical reasoning, context guessing, transfer from L1 and creation of figurative extensions from existing L2 vocabulary (cf. Azuma and Littlemore 2010, cf. also Azuma 2009). Especially at the upper levels of L2 proficiency, learners often rely on the transfer from L1 which helps when metaphors in the L2 are similar or identical to those in the L1, but can lead to misinterpretations when metaphors in the L2 are different from those in the L1 (cf. Boers 2000). In this vein, some scholars have pointed out that conceptual, sociocultural and linguistic differences between both languages can impair metaphor comprehension for several reasons: a) the existence of unfamiliar conceptual metaphors in the L2, b) the existence of different, or partially different, linguistic expressions (due to overlaps between both conceptual systems), c) the existence of conceptually equivalent metaphoric expressions with different linguistic realizations and d) the existence of (conceptually and linguistically) equivalent metaphoric expressions with different connotations or use in the two languages (cf. Charteris-Black 2002: 111; Roche 2012).

As pointed out by Suárez and Hijazo-Gascón (in press), research on the comprehension of metaphors by students of Spanish as a foreign language is very limited (but see Masid 2015). To the best of our knowledge, also in other languages only a small number of studies have addressed the question of to what extent the use of learners' L1 knowledge and culture may affect metaphoric processing in the L2 (cf. Hoang 2014). The study by Charteris-Black (2002) aimed to find out which type of figurative units in the L2 were more or less difficult for learners with the same L1. To this end, the figurative proficiency of a group of 36 Malay-speaking learners of English was tested by means of a set of production and comprehension tasks. The results showed that learners performed better when metaphorical expressions were conceptually and linguistically similar to those in their L1. However, metaphoric expressions with an equivalent linguistic form but a different conceptual basis as well as conceptually and linguistically different metaphoric expressions reflecting culture-specific contents were found to be the most difficult. The author points out that not only the conceptual and linguistic distance between both languages may affect the production and comprehension of metaphoric expressions, but also the frequency of exposure to L2 figurative language and the intra-lingual transfer. This goes hand in hand with the view sustained by Boers' (2003) who states that culture-specific metaphoric expressions often consist of complex metaphors drawing upon primary metaphors. Once learners understand that a couple of complex metaphors belong to a set sharing the same primary metaphors, they are going to be able to better understand complex metaphors via intra-lingual transfer. Further empirical evidence supporting the findings by Charteris-Black (2002) is provided by Chen and Lai (2013) who explored the role of conceptual and sociocultural distance between the L1 and the L2 in metaphor comprehension. Results from a translation task administered to 28 Taiwanese learners of English showed better performances for shared conceptual metaphors in both languages and worse performances for different conceptual metaphors. In addition, the authors point out that culturally universal concepts could help learners to create conceptual links between the L1 and the L2 and thus enhance comprehension, though learners sometimes fail to recognize the similarities and used context clues to infer more general interpretations of the expressions.

Finally, the study by Ferreira (2008) addressed the question of what sort of knowledge foreign language learners use when trying to understand novel metaphors in the L2. More concretely, the study investigated the differences when processing metaphoric expressions with and without a context. For this purpose, 221 Brazilian students were presented with a comprehension test consisting of a list with metaphoric expressions from online editions from English speaking newspapers, once with and once without a short context. The results show that learners rely more on general embodied experiences to interpret the metaphoric expressions, rather than on contextual clues. This, however, can be explained by the fact that the learners already knew the vocabulary which was part of the metaphors and, therefore, they did not need to make use of the context information. Interestingly, the metaphoric expressions for which the Brazilian learners of English achieved the higher scores were also judged as easier by a group of 16 native speakers. This suggests that speakers make use of a universal pattern based on embodied experiences to structure abstract concepts by which metaphoric comprehension can be enhanced both in the L1 and in the L2.

In sum, the studies presented in this section suggest, on the one hand, that linguistic, conceptual and sociocultural differences between metaphoric expressions in the L1 and the L2 influence their comprehension. On the other hand, context seems to play a limited role when facing novel metaphors in a foreign language. However, if learners do not know the vocabulary used in the metaphoric expression, they tend to rely on context to guess the metaphoric meaning. Furthermore, intra-lingual transfer and exposure frequency to figurative language may also affect metaphor comprehension. To date, all these dimensions have been investigated separately for their influence on metaphor comprehension. In what follows, we present a pilot study which aims to explore the interplay between the use of context and the conceptual and sociocultural distance between the L1 and the L2 when processing metaphoric taboo expressions in the L2.

4 The study: Comprehension of metaphoric taboo expressions in the L2

4.1 Research questions

The present study addresses the following research questions:
- RQ1: Are metaphoric taboo expressions with conceptually different L1 equivalents more difficult to comprehend than conceptually similar taboo expressions?
- RQ2: Are metaphoric taboo expressions which rely on different sociocultural knowledge more difficult to comprehend than those relying on shared sociocultural knowledge?
- RQ3: To what extent does contextual information facilitate the comprehension of metaphoric taboo expressions?

4.2 Participants

A comprehension test on taboo metaphors was presented to third year Belgian students and to master students of a degree in languages and literatures at the Université catholique de Louvain (Belgium). Their L1 is French and the age ranges from 21 to 27 (mainly 21- to 23-year olds). These students take a university degree comprising Spanish and another language, for which they study language, linguistics and literature. The third year students averaged at the time of the test a B1-level, with B2 for certain comprehension skills. However, we discarded their results for the present research since many of them left all items blank and seemed not to understand any of the taboo metaphors presented. The master students averaged B2 or C1-level. Thirty five students completed the test and the questionnaire. At a more analytical level, part of the students involved attended a linguistics class which dealt with register differences, albeit that no discourses specifically on taboo topics were studied. If we take into account that the students involved in this test also study literature, then we know that they may have been exposed to discourse on taboo topics in some of the literary works studied, yet this is likely to be a production of a more formal register. In all, taking into account the place held by informal registers and by discourse on taboo topics in official curricula, we may conclude that students have relatively limited contact to discourse concerning taboo topics in formal L2 instruction.

4.3 Instruments

For the experimental part of our research, we created a questionnaire containing eight conditions in four pairs. We distinguished taboo metaphors which have the same conceptual base vs. those with different conceptual bases, and taboo metaphors which require specific sociocultural knowledge vs. those who do not. For each of these, we presented one expression in an isolated way and one with linguistic context. Table 1 summarizes the design with the variables tested in the study:

Table 1. Summary of the variables tested in the study

		Presentation mode	
		With context	Without context
Conceptual distance	Similar	CSC	CSA
	Different	CNC	CNA
Sociocultural distance	Similar	SSC	SSA
	Different	SNC	SNA

All the examples were taken from the *MadSex* corpus (Pizarro Pedraza 2013). This is a sociolinguistic corpus of interviews with inhabitants of Madrid. The corpus is based on an opinion questionnaire in order to indirectly elicit discourse concerning taboo topics. As such, they represent samples of authentic spoken language from Madrid in a rather informal language register (Pizarro Pedraza 2013: 140–142). We asked the students to give the *signifié* (reference) of the underlined taboo metaphor and the equivalent expression in their L1. For every correct answer the students were credited with one point, so that they received at most two points for each item and 16 points for the whole test. Our test also included the following example in order to explain the task.

Que signifient les mots soulignés en français? Connaissez-vous des mots/ expressions équivalent(e)s en français ?

Par ex. : *como mucho dicen los niños tienen colita*
=> *Signifié : pénis ; autres expressions/mots : queue*

'What do the underlined words mean in French? Do you know equivalent words/expressions in French?

E.g. 'at the most they say boys have a little tail'
=> Signifié : penis ; other expressions/words : tail'

In parallel to this test, students were asked to fill out a questionnaire. In addition to standard sociolinguistic variables, this questionnaire contained questions concerning their linguistic biography, languages spoken and the self-assessed foreign language level for speaking, writing, listening and reading skills. Moreover, we explicitly asked whether students had spent an Erasmus stay or in any other way had spent prolonged periods in a Spanish-speaking country.

4.4 Procedure

Both the test and the questionnaire were administered to a class group. Students were asked to sign a form of consent. Given that the test deals with taboo subjects, we wanted to maximally guarantee the anonymity of the students, not only in the practice of our analysis, but also in their experience of the test. Therefore, they did not have to fill out their name but could use a pseudonym and they could drop the forms in the back of the classroom without having to hand them in in person. We preferred to proceed by means of paper forms filled out in class rather than a computer test at a distance in order to exclude the use of external sources.

4.5 Data analysis

With regard to the test on the comprehension of metaphoric taboo expressions, eight examples for metaphors were selected from the corpus and assigned to the different variables of the study design. An external rater was brought in to examine the accuracy of the assignments. In case of disagreement, discussions took place until consensus was reached. Before the study was conducted, alternative answers were formulated for each item and validated by two external raters, which were native speakers of French and highly proficient in Spanish. For most items, several answers were accepted as correct. For instance, when trying to define the literal meaning of the expression *los bebés vienen de París* 'the procreation of children', also answers that only partially referred to the target domain were counted as correct, e.g. *la naissance des enfants* 'the birth of children'. As for the equivalent expressions, the full range of colloquial expressions were counted as correct, e.g. for *los huevos* 'the eggs, the testicles' the following French equivalent expressions such as *couilles, boules, bourses, burnes* were accepted as correct.

4.6 Results

Table 2 represents the overall results obtained in the metaphor comprehension test, which will be discussed in this section.

Table 2: Descriptive statistics of participants' scores in the test per item

		Presentation mode		N
		With context	Without context	
Conceptual distance	Similar	M= 0.342 SD= 0.683	M=1.257 SD=0.918	35
	Different	M= 0.171 SD= 0.568	M=1.200 SD=0.994	35
Sociocultural distance	Similar	M=0.657 SD=0.905	M=0.457 SD=0.807	35
	Different	M=1.271 SD=0.825	M=0.057 SD=0.338	35

Note. M = Mean score for each item; SD = Standard deviation of mean scores

If we compare the mean scores of the items containing the taboo expressions with different and similar conceptual metaphors (RQ1), we can conclude that students' performance in those items was not strongly affected by the conceptual distance between the L1 and L2. In fact, the total mean score ($M_{total}=M_{CSA}+M_{CSC}:2$) for the items with conceptually similar expressions (CSA and CSC) is M=0.800

with SD=0.926 and for conceptually different expressions (CNA and CNC) M=0.686 with SD=0.956. In a next step, we conducted an inferential test in order to examine whether these differences were significant. Assuming that the sample data were not normally distributed given their large standard deviation scores, a non-parametric test was used for the analysis. The Wilcoxon signed rank test for dependent samples showed that the difference between the total mean scores for the items with conceptually similar and conceptually different expressions was not significant ($Z=-0.481$, $p=0.630$). With regard to the influence of sociocultural differences on metaphoric taboo expression (RQ2), the analysis of the total mean scores for the corresponding items shows that metaphoric taboo expressions which rely on different sociocultural knowledge (SNA and SNC) were slightly easier to comprehend than those relying on shared sociocultural knowledge (SSA and SSC). In fact, participants scored an average of 0.557 (SD=0.858) for both items with socioculturally similar expressions and 0.664 (SD=0.875) for both items with socioculturally different expressions. However, the Wilcoxon signed rank test for dependent samples showed that the difference between the total mean scores was not significant ($Z=0.613$, $p=0.540$).

We will now discuss these results in more detail. If we look at the influence of the context on the comprehension of conceptually similar and different taboo expressions (RQ3), the items with conceptually similar and conceptually different taboo expressions both without context (CSA and CNA) ranked first and second respectively (M=1.257, SD=0.918; M=1.200, SD=0.994), whereas the items containing the counterparts with context (CSC and CNC) were found to be more difficult to comprehend (conceptually similar M=0.342, SD=0.683; conceptually different M=0.171, SD=0.568). According to these results, the context does not necessarily seem to facilitate coping with conceptual aspects when processing taboo expressions, as participants' performances for the items with context were worse than for items with context independent of the conceptual distance between the L1 and the L2. The Wilcoxon signed rank test showed that the difference between the total mean scores for the items with context (CSC and CNC M=0.514, SD=0.818) and without context (CSA and CNA M=2.457, SD=1.509) was highly significant ($Z=-4.612$, $p=0.000$).

As to the effect of the context on the comprehension of taboo expressions with and without shared sociocultural knowledge (RQ3), comprehension of metaphorical taboo expressions was considerably impaired by sociocultural differences when the context was not available to the participants (SNC M=1.271, SD=0.825; SNA M=0.057, SD=0.338). Although to a lesser degree, the same picture was observed for the items with shared sociocultural knowledge: the mean score for the item with context (SSC) was better (M=0.657, SD=0.905) than for the counterpart without context (SSA M=0.457, SD=0.807). In sum, we can observe that participants systematically performed better when the context was available (with context M=1.928; without context M=0.514). The Wilcoxon signed rank test indicated that the differences between the total mean scores for the items with and without context were highly significant (Z=-3.717, p=0.000) independent of the sociocultural distance between the L1 and the L2. Given the small size of the sample and the extremely large variances observed between the different items, no further statistical tests (e.g. logistic regression) were conducted in order to analyze the interaction effects between the factors tested in the study.

To find out whether the comprehension of metaphoric taboo expressions was influenced by the exposure frequency to discourse on taboo topics, we compared the mean scores of participants with and without experience in a Spanish-speaking country. The analysis revealed that participants with experience in Spanish-speaking countries systematically performed better in almost all the items except for the item with a metaphoric taboo expression without shared sociocultural knowledge and context (SNC), where an extremely small difference of 0.1 was found due to extremely low performances of both groups. For the item with a conceptually similar metaphoric expression without context (CSA) both groups showed similar performances. In contrast, the greatest differences between both groups were found for the item with a conceptually different metaphor without context (CNA) and with a conceptually similar metaphor with context (CSC) with a difference of 1.16 and 0.56 respectively.

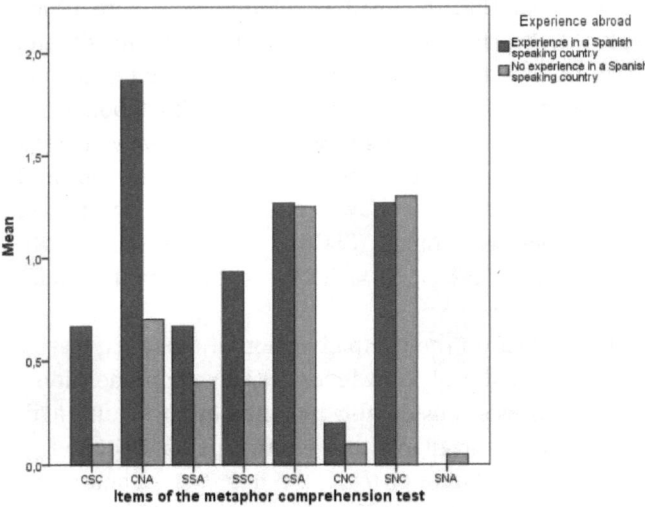

Figure 1: Mean scores for the different items in the test sorted by groups with and without an experience in a Spanish-speaking country

In order to determine whether the total mean scores between both groups were significantly different (experience abroad M=7.033; SD=2.709; no experience abroad M=4.200; SD=2.324), further inferential statistics were conducted. Assuming that the sample data were not normally distributed given the limited number of individuals in each group (experience abroad n=15, no experience abroad n=20) and the large standard deviation values, a non-parametric test was used for the analysis. The Mann-Whitney U Test for independent samples indicated that the differences were highly significant (U=64.000, p=0.003). Finally, we looked into the relationship between the level of proficiency and the mean scores. We assumed that more proficient participants were more likely to access the literal meaning of some of the single words contained in the presented taboo expressions and thus better interpret the figurative meaning than lesser proficient participants. No significant correlation coefficients (Spearman's rho) were obtained between the total mean scores in the test and the level of proficiency of the participants (r=0.034, p=0.808). Thus, in our study the level of proficiency of the participants did not affect the comprehension of the metaphoric taboo expressions contained in the test. These results are in line with Masid's (2015) results concerning an experimental study on metaphors based on body parts in Spanish as a foreign language, where she showed that there was no significant difference in the interpretation/production of body metaphors depending on the level of the CFR. The fact that the third-year students which we had to discard from our study overall had great difficulty to try to offer a possible interpretation, may be due to the fact that the lexemes in the taboo metaphors concerned in this study are more difficult than the more basic lexemes concerning body parts from Masid's study.

4.7 Discussion

On a methodological level, it became clear that not all students managed to distinguish at an analytical level between the reference ('signifié') and an equivalent, i.e. some students answered by means of an equivalent in their L1 to the question concerning reference, or answered both questions with the same form. The latter is especially the case when there is an equivalent metaphor in the L1, e.g. *cigüeñas – cigognes* 'storks'. Moreover, some students gave equivalents belonging to a more formal register. It is unclear whether this is due to their inability to assess the register of the original Spanish utterance and/or to their reluctance to answer with a colloquial term, which they often consider vulgar.[1] However, we retained the distinction between reference and equivalent, since it reflects different degrees of metaphor comprehension in terms of conceptual fluency.

As shown in the literature overview, foreign language students (and especially those of the levels we deal with) do not seem to receive a lot of input concerning taboo expressions, especially those from colloquial registers. This is due both to the limited input of the colloquial registers and to the limited presence of taboo expressions in curricula. In that sense, for the interpretation of taboo metaphors, students have to rely on other contact with the foreign language and/or on their competence to understand metaphorical meanings. We see that students who have had an Erasmus stay (or similar) in a Spanish-speaking country, are better at interpreting the metaphors included in the task (especially the conceptually different metaphor presented without contextual information). Contrary to our expectations, this difference was not limited to metaphors for which cultural knowledge is necessary, but also for metaphors that have the same conceptual basis in French. Different hypotheses may be formulated: it is possible that students who have the experience of a prolonged stay abroad are more familiar with the informal register used in the task, given that they have had a prolonged input of Spanish in non-classroom contexts. They may also (have learned to) rely more on their abilities to infer information from the context and, thus, to make more (and better) educated guesses. The fact that no correlation was found between language level and metaphor interpretation seems to suggest indeed that the overall language level (and possible benefits of a stay abroad in this respect) are not the questions at stake, but rather the familiarity with contexts and registers that are underrepresented in formal learning processes.

We also looked into the wrong answers given in order to gain a better insight in the interpretative processes (even when the interpretation is wrong) and to see in which cases students make an educated guess vs. those where they leave the answer blank. In general, we see that access to the source domain is crucial for attempting an interpretation. Thus, the students who made an attempt to interpret *huevos* 'balls' but interpreted it wrong, answered *ovules* 'ovules' or *ovaires* 'ovaries'. They know the word *huevo* (lit. 'egg') and seem to try to link it to a word they know in the domain of sexual taboos and which has a common etymology. These students (a minority, since most of them did interpret it correctly) then rely

---

1 It is interesting to point out that also some colleagues from the linguistics research group who volunteered to test our questionnaire (and whose results have not been included in this study) explicitly asked whether we really wanted them to answer by means of colloquial terms and/or apologized for the perceived 'vulgarity' of some of their answers.

more on the etymological link than on the metaphorical link based on the similar form of eggs and testicles. The importance of accessing to the source domain for attempting an interpretation becomes particularly apparent if we compare it with the fact that *la tiene morcillona* 'he has a softie' was left blank by all students, except for one of them, who did know the meaning. In this case, lexicon can be assumed to play a role, in that *morcilla* 'a type of blood sausage' is a highly specific term, both from a lexical and from a cultural perspective. It is highly likely that most students lacked knowledge of the term, which left them without any clue to even make an educated guess. At this point, it is worth mentioning that presenting conceptually different metaphoric taboo expressions with a context does not facilitate metaphor comprehension, but rather distracts learners from using their embodied experiences to properly interpret the metaphors (see also Ferreira 2008).

While we focused on the processing of metaphors in L2, it is important to point out that students may rely on other types of information to infer an interpretation. Thus, the expression *se te empalma* 'you get a hard one' was interpreted correctly by few students (3/35) but most students who attempted a wrong interpretation, answered 'to masturbate'. This may be due to the fact that interpreting the Spanish middle passive construction is quite challenging. Students may have interpreted *se* as a reflexive rather than a middle marker and thus opted for the interpretation as *se masturber* or the more colloquial equivalent *se branler*, which are reflexive in French. Thus, they relied more on constructional clues than on a metaphoric interpretation, possibly due to lack of access to the source domain. The fact that the grammatical structure served as a distractor may explain the surprising difference that conceptually different metaphors with context were less well interpreted than those without context.

Context turned out to be important especially with socioculturally different metaphors. This shows that the interpretation of taboo metaphor is easier when embedded in a larger interaction context, which is of course also the case in normal interaction. Moreover, it suggests that, when there is a higher sociocultural and conceptual similarity with the L1, students can rely on this similarity as much as on the context to correctly interpret taboo metaphors.

5 Conclusions

The present study provides further evidence of how different aspects such as conceptual and sociocultural distance between languages and the contextual information affect the comprehension of metaphoric taboo expressions in the foreign language. The findings show that the existence of conceptual differences does not directly affect metaphoric taboo expression comprehension, which suggests that learners were able to use general embodied experiences underlying the metaphoric taboo expressions in order to guess their figurative meaning. Such conclusion goes against Charteris-Black's (2002) findings that conceptual distance between languages accounts for differences in metaphor comprehension among L2 learners. The language pair he analyzed was however both linguistically and culturally at much greater distance than our language pair. In addition, a broader context, which is expected to help students, seems to have led to misinterpretations of the presented taboo expressions independent of the conceptual distance between both languages, which is consistent with the study by Ferreira (2008). In contrast, presenting metaphoric taboo expressions without shared sociocultural knowledge in a context turned out to support guessing their figurative meaning and, thus, helped learners accessing the relevant aspect of the source domain. In sum, the relative importance of the context for the comprehension of metaphoric taboo expressions is in line with studies showing that the presence of verbal information does not automatically lead learners to use the contextual clues (cf. Littlemore 2004). In fact, Littlemore (2004) suggests that the cognitive styles of the learners (e.g. verbalizers vs. imagers) can influence the way they deal with context. In addition, other authors have claimed that not every contextual information does affect metaphor comprehension in the same way and propose to differentiate between literal and figurative-biasing contexts (Cieslicka 2006). Thus, as a suggestion for further research, such differentiation could provide new insights for a deeper understanding of the role of context in metaphor comprehension. At this point, it is worth mentioning that, although such contextual dimensions were not easy to control due to the limited exemplars for each taboo expression in the corpus, the presented taboo expressions were embedded in usage events and, thus, reflected authentic communication. This aspect, in turn, has been lacking in most studies on metaphor comprehension conducted to date (cf. Boers 2013).

Furthermore, we found that participants with prolonged experience in Spanish-speaking countries systematically performed better in almost all the items, which suggests that exposure frequency to different registers and discourse types (possibly including discourse on taboo topics) can facilitate the comprehension of taboo expressions. At this point, it should be mentioned that frequency exposure to figurative language alone does not automatically guarantee a proper comprehension of the metaphoric taboo expressions as such. Rather, it seems that aspects such as the discursive function in a given context, the communicative relevance and the immersion in the culture can affect the comprehension of taboo expressions (Kecskes 2015: 34; Roche et al. 2012). In general, it remains to be seen whether the effects observed in the study can be systematically found to hold across many different groups with other L1, which would corroborate the relevance of the tested variables for the comprehension of metaphoric taboo expressions.

This study has also some limitations. First, due to the reduced number of items of the test (8) and the relatively small group of participants (n=35) no generalizations can be made about the effects observed in the study. Second, it should be mentioned that metaphor comprehension is likely to be influenced by other variables which were not tested in the study. For instance, the results from the item with the conceptually different taboo expression with context suggest that formal distance between the equivalents in both languages may affect deciding between competing alternative solutions which can, under certain conditions, lead learners to misinterpretations. Furthermore, assuming that accessing the relevant aspects of the source domain is essential to metaphor comprehension (cf. Littlemore and Low 2006), the vocabulary knowledge of the participants about the L2 words comprised in the taboo expressions needs to be assessed in order to better control this variable. This will allow for a fine-grained analysis of the difficulties learners face when processing metaphors in the foreign language. Third, it should also be noted that categorizing taboo expressions according to their conceptual or sociocultural distance is highly complex. In our study, we assumed that whereas some metaphors using embodied experiences can be interpreted on the basis of general cognitive processes such as analogical reasoning and/or image formation (even if they are different in both languages), other metaphors reflecting sociocultural practices require a deeper processing due to the use of culture-specific knowledge. In the present study, the different sources of knowledge used for interpreting figurative meaning were the determining criterion for assigning the metaphoric taboo expressions to the variables tested. As a suggestion for further research, a set of indicators should be formulated in order to better differentiate the conceptual and sociocultural dimensions of taboo expressions.

Despite these limitations, the present study provides first promising insights into the comprehension of metaphoric taboo expressions in the foreign language. With regard to the pedagogical implications to be derived from these findings, we argue that, to help learners increasing their metaphoric competence and their knowledge about taboo expressions, instruction cannot be limited to decontextualized form-focused exercises, such as mere descriptions, and that exposure to a variety of discourses is paramount. In this sense, the use of corpus-informed teaching approaches seems to be best suited to support teaching taboo expressions, since they reflect common patterns of usage, make the correspondent discursive functions transparent and provide rich contextual information.

6 References

Allan, Keith & Kate Burridge. 1991. *Euphemism and dysphemism*. New York: Oxford University Press.
Allan, Keith & Kate Burridge. 2006. *Forbidden words: Taboo and the censoring of language*. Cambridge: Cambridge University Press.
Azuma, Masumi. 2009. Positive and negative effects of mother-tongue knowledge on the interpretation of figurative expressions. *Papers in Linguistic Science* 15. 165–192.
Azuma, Masumi & Jeannette Littlemore. 2010. Promoting creativity in English language classrooms. *JACET Kansai Journal* 12. 8–19.
Boers, Frank. 2000. Metaphor awareness and vocabulary retention. *Applied Linguistics* 21(4). 553–571.
Boers, Frank. 2003. Applied linguistics perspectives on cross-cultural variation in conceptual metaphor. *Metaphor and Symbol* 18. 231–238.
Boers, Frank. 2013. Cognitive Linguistic approaches to teaching vocabulary: Assessment and integration. *Language Teaching* 46(2). 208–224.
Cameron, Lynn & Graham Low. 1999. Metaphor [Survey article]. *Language Teaching, the International Journal for Language Teachers, Educators and Researchers* 32. 77–96.
CFR = Council of Europe. S.d. *Common European Framework of Reference for Languages: learning, teaching, assessment*. https://www.coe.int/t/dg4/linguistic/Source/Framework_EN.pdf (last accessed 30/08/2016)
Charteris-Black, Jonathan. 2002. Second language figurative proficiency: A comparative study of Malay and English. *Applied Linguistics* 23(1). 104–133.
Chen, Yi-chen & Huei-ling Lai. 2013. The influence of cultural universality and specificity on EFL learners' comprehension of metaphor and metonymy. *International Journal of Applied Linguistics* 23. 312–336
Cieslicka, Anna. 2006. Literal salience in on-line processing of idiomatic expressions by second language learners. *Second Language Research* 22. 115–44.
Crespo Fernández, Eliécer. 2011. Conceptual metaphors in taboo-induced lexical variation. *Revista Alicantina de Estudios Ingleses* 24. 53–71.
Danesi, Marcel. 2008. Conceptual errors in second-language learning. In Sabine De Knop & Teun de Rycker (eds.), *Cognitive Approaches to Pedagogical Grammar*, 231–256. Berlin & New York: Mouton de Gruyter.
Doiz, Aintzane & Carmen Elizari. 2013. Metaphoric competence and the acquisition of figurative vocabulary in foreign language learning. *ELIA* 13. 47–82.
Ferreira, Luciane Correa. 2008. A psycholinguistic study on metaphor comprehension in a foreign language. *ReVEL* 6(11). 1–23.
Giora, Rachel. 1999. On the priority of salient meanings: studies of literal and figurative language. *Journal of Pragmatics* 31. 919–929.
Glaser, Karen. 2013. The Neglected Combination: A Case for Explicit-Inductive Instruction in Teaching *Pragmatics* in ESL. *TESL Canada Journal*, 30(7). 150–163.
Grondelaers, Stefan & Dirk Geeraerts. 1998. Vagueness as a euphemistic strategy. In Angeliki Athanasiadou and Elsbieta Tabakowska (eds.), *Speaking of emotions: Conceptualization and Expression* (Cognitive Linguistics Research 10), 357–374. Berlin & New York: Mouton de Gruyter.

Hoang, Ha. 2014. Metaphor and Second Language Learning: The State of the Field. *TESL-EJ* 18(2). http://www.tesl-ej.org/wordpress/issues/volume18/ej70/ej70a5/
Jessen, Moiken & Ferran Suñer. 2017. Language acquisition and teaching of conceptual competence in L2: the case of motion events. In Laura Torres-Zúñiga & Thomas Schmidt (eds.), *New Methodological Approaches to Foreign Language Teaching*, 7–30. Cambridge: Cambridge Scholars Publishing.
Kecskes, Istvan. 2015. Is the Idiom Principle Blocked in Bilingual L2 Production? In Roberto Heredia & Anna Cieslicka (eds.), *Bilingual Figurative Language Processing*, 28–53. Cambridge: Cambridge University Press.
Liontas, John I. 2002. Context and idiom understanding in second languages. *EUROSLA Yearbook* 2, 155–185
Littlemore, Jeannette & Graham Low. 2006a. Metaphoric competence and communicative language ability. *Applied Linguistics* 27(2). 268–294.
Littlemore, Jeannette & Graham Low. 2006b. *Figurative Thinking and Foreign Language Learning*. Basingstoke, UK/New York: Palgrave Macmillan.
Littlemore, Jeannette. 2008. The relationship between associative thinking, analogical reasoning, image formation and metaphoric extension strategies. In Mara Sophia Zanotto, Lynne Cameron & Marilda do Couto Cavalcanti (eds.), *Confronting metaphor in use: An applied linguistic approach*, 199–222. Amsterdam & Philadelphia: John Benjamins.
Littlemore, Jeannette. 2009. *Applying Cognitive Linguistics to Second Language Learning and Teaching*. Basingstoke & New York: Palgrave Macmillan.
Littlemore, Jeannette, Tina Krenmayr, James Turner & Sarah Turner. 2014. An investigation into metaphor use at different levels of second language writing. *Applied Linguistics* 32(4). 208–429.
López Morales, Humberto. 2005. *Sociolingüística del tabú*. Salamanca: Universidad de Salamanca.
MacArthur, Fiona. 2010. Metaphorical competence in EFL. *AILA Review* 23. 155–173.
Masid, Ocarina. 2015. *La metáfora lingüística en el desarrollo de la competencia léxica en ELE. Propuesta semántica y didáctica sobre el léxico somático desde un punto de vista cognitivo*. Unpublished PhD Thesis Universidad Complutense de Madrid.
Nation, I. S. Paul. 2001. *Learning vocabulary in another language*. Cambridge: Cambridge University Press.
Pavlenko, Aneta. 2009. Conceptual representation in the bilingual lexicon and second language vocabulary learning. In Aneta Pavlenko (ed.), *The Bilingual Mental Lexicon: Interdisciplinary Approaches*, 125–160. Clevedon, UK: Multilingual Matters.
Pizarro Pedraza, Andrea. 2013. *Tabú y eufemismo en la ciudad de Madrid: estudio sociolingüístico-cognitivo de los conceptos sexuales*. PhD Thesis. Universidad Complutense de Madrid.
Pizarro Pedraza, Andrea. 2015. Who said 'abortion'? Semantic variation and ideology in Spanish newspapers' online discussions. *Australian Journal of Linguistics* 35(1). 53–75. DOI: 10.1080/07268602.2015.976901
Pizarro Pedraza, Andrea. Submitted. *MadSex*: Collecting a spoken corpus of indirectly elicited sexual concepts.
Pizarro Pedraza, Andrea & Barbara De Cock. 2018. Taboo effects at the syntactic level: reducing agentivity as a euphemistic strategy. *Pragmatics* 28(1). 113–138.

Roche, Jörg. 2012. Zum überfälligen Paradigmenwechsel in der Fremdsprachendidaktik. In Andrea Birk & Claudia Buffagni (eds.), *Linguistik und Sprachdidaktik im universitären DaF-Unterricht*, 33–52. Münster: Waxmann.

Roche, Jörg. 2013. *Mehrsprachigkeitstheorie – Erwerb, Kognition, Transkulturation, Ökologie*. Tübingen: Gunter Narr Verlag.

Roche, Jörg. 2014. Language Acquisition and Pedagogy. In Jeanette Littlemore & John Taylor (eds.), *Companion to Cognitive Linguistics*, 325–351. London: Continuum.

Roche, Jörg and Mélody Roussy-Parent. 2006. Zur Rolle der kontrastiven Semantik in interkultureller Kommunikation. *Fremdsprachen Lehren und Lernen (FLuL)* 36. 228–250.

Roche, Jörg, Janin Reher & Mirjana Simic. 2012. *Focus on Handlung. Zum Konzept des handlungsorientierten Erwerbs sprachlicher, sozialer und demokratischer Kompetenzen im Rahmen einer Kinder-Akademie*. Münster: Lit Verlag.

Suárez-Campos, Laura & Alberto Hijazo-Gascón. In press. Metáfora conceptual y enseñanza de ELE. In Teresa Cadierno, Alejandro Castañeda, Irraide Ibarretxe-Antuñano (eds.), *Lingüística cognitiva y el español como lengua extranjera (ELE)*. Londres: Routledge.

Torres Sánchez, María Ángeles. 1997. Tabú y enseñanza de español como lengua extranjera. In Francisco Moreno, María Gil and Kira Alonso, *VIII Congreso Internacional de ASELE. La enseñanza del español como lengua extranjera : del pasado al futuro*, 811–822. Alcalá de Henares: Universidad de Alcalá.

Trim, Richard. 2012. The limits of comprehension in cross-cultural metaphor. Networking in drugs terminology. In Fiona MacArthur, José Luis Oncins-Martínez, Manuel Sánchez-García & Ana María Piquer-Píriz (eds.), *Metaphor in Use. Context, culture and communication*, 217–236. Amsterdam: John Benjamins.

Part III: Cognitive Sociolinguistics

Tom Ruette
11 Why do the Dutch swear with diseases?

Abstract: In this paper, we address the general problem of dealing with a complex and interwoven set of influential factors, potentially both linguistic and extra-linguistic factors, behind linguistic choices. We do so by investigating the rare phenomenon of swearing with diseases in Dutch, rather than with the more common Western taboo concepts of (among others) religion and sexuality. The standing hypothesis is that swearing with diseases is related to the Calvinistic cultural background of the Dutch. Methodologically speaking, we perform a corpus-based analysis of a large database of location-specific tweets from Flanders and The Netherlands in which we observe "bad language". Since the hypothesized influential factor of Calvinism shows an outspoken geographical pattern, we intuitively expect clear overlap of the area in which we observe a preference for disease-based swearing and the area in which Calvinism is the predominant religion. We do not find a straightforward overlap in the geography of Calvinism and disease-based swearing. Although the locations where disease-based swearing is conspicuously frequent are all within the Calvinistic area of The Netherlands, disease-based swearing is more likely in the highly-urbanized region around Amsterdam. Therefore, we can only conclude that urbanity, socio-economic factors, religious affiliation and nationality play intertwined roles in the choice for disease-based swearing versus swearing with words from other lexical domains. Consequently, we end up with a complex and interwoven set of extra-linguistic factors that influence the lexical choice for a taboo word from a specific domain for swearing.

Keywords: Taboo, swearing, Twitter, sociolinguistics, variational linguistics

1 Introduction

In this paper, we address the general problem of dealing with a complex and interwoven set of influential factors, potentially both linguistic and extralinguistic factors, behind linguistic choices. We do so by investigating the rare phenomenon of swearing with diseases in Dutch, rather than with the more common Western taboo concepts of (among others) religion and sexuality. As an example, we wonder why the Dutch consider an annoying alarm clock a 'teringwekker' *typhus alarm clock* whereas one could also refer to this as a 'godverdomde wekker' *goddamned alarm clock*. In addition to this clearly sociolinguistically inspired methodology of working with alternation variables, we adopt a Cognitive Linguistic take on swearing, enriched with insights from taboo research, to address the hypothesis that swearing with diseases is a Northern Dutch phenomenon that is motivated by a Calvinistic cultural background (in contrast to the southern region of the Dutch language area, consisting of Flanders and the South of the Netherlands, which has a historical Roman-Catholic cultural background).

Methodologically speaking, we perform a corpus-based analysis of a large database of location-specific tweets from Flanders and The Netherlands in which we observe "bad language" (Andersson and Trudgill 1990). As such, we can literally chart the geographical variability in the preference for a disease-word over other potential swearwords. In other words, for each location we can measure the ratio of tweets in which the swearwords draw from the domain of disease rather than from other taboo domains such as religion or sexuality. Since the hypothesized influential factor of Calvinism also shows an outspoken geographical pattern, we intuitively expect clear overlap of the area in which we observe a preference for disease-based swearing and the area in which Calvinism is the predominant religion.

However, foreshadowing the results of our empirical investigation, we do not find a straightforward overlap in the geography of Calvinism and disease-based swearing. Although the locations where disease-based swearing is conspicuously frequent are all within the Calvinistic area of The Netherlands, disease-based swearing is more likely in the highly-urbanized region around Amsterdam. Moreover, in the truly outspoken Calvinistic strongholds, disease-based swearing is not booming, despite far reaching efforts to balance the dataset across all locations.

In addition, census data shows a clear levelling of religious affiliation, i.e. no religious preference, across the entire language area, which complicates the contemporary relation between Calvinism and disease-based swearing even more. In total, from the data alone, we can only assume that urbanity, socio-economic factors, religious affiliation and nationality play intertwined roles in the choice for disease-based swearing versus swearing with words from other lexical domains. Consequently, we end up with a complex and interwoven set of extra-linguistic factors that influence the lexical choice for a taboo word from a specific domain for swearing.

In the remainder of this paper, we go into further details of this investigation. Section 2 offers some background on the relationship between taboo and swearing, and also digs deeper into the relationship between Calvinism and swearing with diseases. This section ends with embedding the research of this paper in the framework of Cognitive Sociolinguistics. Section 3 then elaborates on the methodological apparatus for the empirical part of the corpus-based analysis. Section 4 discusses the results of the corpus analysis, while Section 5 concludes by linking the results to findings in taboo research, Cognitive Linguistics and swearing research.

2 Background

2.1 Taboo and swearing

Taboo concepts are often used for swearing (Cruse 1986: 273). Commonly cited taboo concepts are religion, sexuality, genitals, feces, direct family relationships, etc. (Allan and Burridge 1991, 2006; Nübling and Vogel 2004; Ljung Magnus 2010; Drange, Hasund, and Stenström 2014) But why are these taboo concepts so likely to occur in bad language? The rationale for this is that using taboo language may achieve some speaker-internal cathartic effect (Jay 1992: 241), or it may even have the inter-speaker function of convergence (Dynel 2012: 29), i.e. by swearing a speaker may create a social connection or an atmosphere of solidarity, or it may achieve a speaker-external aggression (Wajnryb 2005: 30). All of this is facilitated by transgressing the social norm that is implicit in taboo, i.e. not to speak about something.

Therefore, it is valuable to look a bit more into what taboo is. An interesting approach is the notion of "tabooness" as developed in Jay (1992: 168): "tabooness is the degree to which a word is inhibited". Interestingly, Jay (1992: 13) already introduces a sociological component by relating tabooness to the speaker: "Tabooness focuses on the speaker's inhibitions and his or her decision about what can or cannot be said in a given setting". Jay then contrasts this with obscenity, which is in the ear of the beholder: "the notion of obscenity focuses on the listeners or recipient of the information". Consequently, inhibition and obscenity are two concepts that must be negotiated between speaker and hearer (Bartsch 1987; Harder 2012) to reach a maximum of effect in terms of catharsis, inter-speaker convergence and/or speaker-external aggression.

Building on this, we would like to put forward that the negotiation between speaker and hearer is specifically for taboo in the context of swearing of a most interesting nature. Could the effect of a swearword lie in finding a delicate, implicitly socially debated balance in acceptability? More specifically, one could hypothesize that if a swearword is not taboo enough, the cathartic effect of swearing will not be obtained; to obtain inter-speaker convergence, inhibition and obscenity must be carefully balanced; and to obtain speaker-external aggression, the speaker must be capable to transgress his/her own inhibition far enough to surpass a threshold of obscenity that triggers aggression in the hearer.

Nonetheless, a logical consequence of this clear socio-interactional perspective is that the gradual nature of "tabooness" must coincide with variability dimensions in both the choice for swearwords and also the extra-linguistic realm. Quite obviously, we know that taboo is culturally influenced, and many examples for this can be found in scientific (Aman 1996; Ljung Magnus 2010) and popular articles. However, due to the social nature of taboo, it is not unthinkable that variation exists below a holistic cultural level, i.e. communities of practice. As mentioned above, we touch upon this more sociological aspect by focusing on a geographical dimension.

2.2 Calvinism and swearing with diseases

Of course, several hypotheses about why Dutch use disease words for swearing have been put forward. The hypothesis we are pursuing (van Sterkenburg 2000, 2008) revolves around the notion that there is a taboo in Dutch society on being in poor health, which can be linked to Calvinism. Being unhealthy is supposedly considered a sign of damnation, from a religious conviction that God decides over one's wellbeing. Indeed, in the North of the language area (cf. Figure 1), the predominant religious confession is Calvinism, and some aspects of the Calvinistic tradition have been said to incentivize a healthier lifestyle than roman Catholics (Mackenbach 2007), the historically predominant religious confession in the South of the language are. This could be a historical-cultural foundation for the taboo, which in its turn may have inspired swearing. Notice that in the hypothesis of Van Sterkenburg, there is no mention of Flanders.

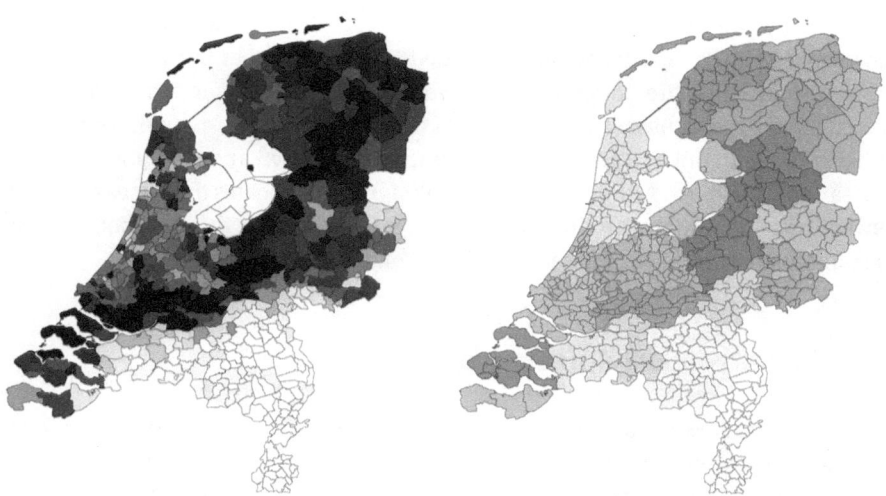

Figure 1: Calvinism in The Netherlands (1899 on the left, 2002 on the right). Black indicates 100 % Calvinistic population, white indicates 0 % Calvinistic population). Source: cbs.nl

Swearing with diseases is conspicuously a part of contemporary Dutch, but not exclusively. Currently, swearing with diseases outside of Dutch is indeed quite rare, and only some attestations in Yiddish and Polish (Nübling and Vogel 2004: 30–31) are regularly passed on from publication to publication. Moreover, Lötscher (1981) already observed disease-inspired swearing as early as the 14th/15th century in what is now known as the south of Germany, e.g. he found in R. Brandstetter's "Blasphemiae accusatae" the phrase *das dich das nun vallende übel an gienge* 'that you may get epilepsy' – basically a polite predecessor of the *krijg X* 'get X' template (see this section below for an excursion into the idea of templates). This is clearly well before the Calvinistic era. And also later on, in Shakespeare's Romeo and Juliet, Mercutio famously wishes "a plague on your houses" (plague is considered to be referring to the pox). So, from the onset, we can already point out that it is not Calvinism, and Calvinism alone, that is driving this contemporary Dutch peculiarity of swearing with diseases.

Nonetheless, it is valuable to investigate the relation between Calvinism and swearing with diseases. Indeed, even if Calvinism is not the instigator for the productive disease-based swearing we observe today, it may have been a power to conserve the existing forms of disease-based swearing from earlier times. Although our contemporary Twitter data is not the most suitable dataset to address this historical-diachronic question, it is not unlikely that a trace of that potential conservatism is still present today, in the form of a geographic distribution.

Finally, we have not found literature in which the disease-based forms of swearing in Yiddish or Polish are described as productive, in the sense that new forms of swearing are being produced. This could however happen, perhaps by referring to recent diseases such as ebola or AIDS. Curiously enough, we do find observations in our Twitter corpus of swearing with AIDS and also informally of swearing with ebola. Although this is a weak signal, it indicates that disease-based swearing is potentially productive; whether it is productive due to taboo-related mechanisms or purely for paradigmatic reasons, we cannot conclude.

2.3 Cognitive Sociolinguistics

Given this framework of lexical variability (in choosing a word from one taboo domain rather than a word from another taboo domain), where words function as expletives due to their special taboo status, which is in its turn heavily influenced by a range of cultural, historical and societal factors, it is straightforward to position this paper in the realm of Cognitive Sociolinguistics (Geeraerts, Kristiansen, and Peirsman 2010; Kristiansen and Dirven 2008). Especially when one considers the tangible definition put forward by Martin Putz: "Cognitive Sociolinguistics would [...] take the characteristics of meaning as a non-discrete yet structured category to account for the variation of and within dialects, sociolects, cultures, registers, styles, stereotypes, etc."(Pütz, Robinson, and Reif 2014: 9). Following this definition, taboo gets "raised" to a part of the meaning of a word, which is, we think, in line with what Cognitive Semantics would allow for.

Apart from looking at taboo from a Cognitive Sociolinguistic perspective, this study also contributes methodologically to the field by presenting a unique and freely available database of geo-specific swearing utterances. Moreover, it also sheds light on the possibility of investigating rare phenomena with corpus material, because it is relatively straightforward to collect unprecedented amounts of words from social media. This is also showcased by the work of Jack Grieve et al. (Forthcoming), who has also compiled a very large corpus of geo-annotated tweets and investigates the rise of neologisms.

In this section, we would also like to point out that we will not go into the details of the purely linguistic side of swearing. In the current study, we have quite broadly defined the variation space to be words in utterances that can be bad language, with the alternation taking place between lexical fields, i.e. we observe that a bad word from one lexical field is used, rather than from some other lexical fields. However, it is not unthinkable that the use of a specific swearing word is not so interchangeable as we present it due to purely linguistic reasons. As an example, alliteration between the swearword and the object that is being cursed may be a reason to select one swearword, rather than another. Ignoring these potential linguistic constraints, we can try to see swearwords as fillers for slots in templates. And indeed, a number of interesting linguistic structures could be observed. One of them is the *krijg de X* 'get the X' template, with X being a disease: Sanders and Tempelaars (1998) position the first attestations of that popular template in the 16th century (Nübling and Vogel 2004: 22), which is indeed the era in which Calvinism is emerging widely (since more or less 1530). Moreover, the template is still productive, with attestations in our Twitter corpus (cf. Section 3 below) of *krijg aids* 'get AIDS', and an informally observed rise in the use of *krijg ebola* 'get ebola' during the ebola crisis of 2015. Clearly, such linguistic structures or (extra)linguistic constraints need to be investigated in more detail.

3 Data and methodology

In this section, we go into some details regarding the collected data and the methodology that we follow to perform a qualitative and quantitative analysis.

3.1 Twitter corpus

Investigations into swearing have either based themselves on anecdotal evidence (Montagu 1967; Aman 1996), textbook or undocumented examples (Nübling and Vogel 2004), questionnaire data (van Sterkenburg 2000) or psycholinguistic research (Jay 1992; Jay 1999). In recent years, one can also see a more corpus-oriented approach (McEnery 2004; Beers Fägersten 2012; Han and Wang 2014; Drange, Hasund, and Stenström 2014). The current paper subscribes to that corpus linguistic approach by investigating swearing by means of a geo-specific corpus of Twitter messages. Twitter is an application with which individuals can broadcast a short and usually public 140-character message. This message is brought to the attention of other Twitter users that follow the sender. They have the ability to re-broadcast that message to their followers, called "retweeting", which may have a recursive and quadratic effect on audience size. The messages are, in most cases, accessible to everybody, and not just the followers. From 2014 onwards, Twitter has become more of a branding tool, also used by companies, marketing agencies and professionals. This change in function of the medium has potentially had an impact on both the audience and the kind of language that can be observed. Nonetheless, even in today's format, personal messages and conversations remain on Twitter, albeit it to a lesser extent due to the rise of media such as Snapchat or Whatsapp that restrict public access to these conversations.

The messages in our corpus were collected in 2012 and 2013. The messages were selected from users that identify in their user profile a location; in many cases this aligns with where they are based (by crossing the GPS location of the tweet with the reported location). We did not look at the actual GPS location from where the tweet is sent, but considered the location in the user profile to be a better indication of the region with which the Twitter user identifies. To obtain a more or less balanced corpus, with respect to the (reported) locations, we tried to find about 200 Twitter users per location (by recursively collecting the followers of a number of seed users). Then for each Twitter user per location, we downloaded the 200 most recent messages. By doing so, we collected on average about 2.000 words per user and 350.000 words per location. In total, we look at about 75 million words from 6 million tweets by 46.000 Twitter users in 213 locations.

This corpus is available for download[1].

3.2 Search words

From this corpus, of course, we needed to derive a dataset of tweets that contains swearwords. We start from a list of taboo source domains with taboo lexical items that we could easily get from Sanders and Tempelaars (1998), a dictionary of swearwords, ordered by source domain. We extracted from that dictionary lexical items and their spelling variants for which we could search in the corpus. At some places, we added a few English and French swearwords that are known to be borrowed, e.g. *shit* and *putain* 'prostitute'. These lexical items are summarized in Table 1.

---

[1] http://perswww.kuleuven.be/tom_ruette/data/twitter, last access September 3, 2016.

Table 1: Source domains and lexical items for swearing

Source domain	Lexical items
GENITALS	*Kut* vagina, *vagina* vagina, *spleet* vagina, *reet* vagina, *muts* vagina, *eikel* penis, *lul* penis, *piemel* penis, *penis* penis, *pik* penis, *dick* penis, *kloot* balls, *klote* balls, *aars* ass, *kont* ass
FECES	*Kak* 'shit', *shit* 'shit', *crap* 'shit', *schijt* 'shit', *stront* 'shit', *keutel* 'shit', *pipi* 'piss', *merde* 'shit', *scheisse* 'shit', *diarree* 'diarrhea', *poep* 'shit', *pis* 'piss', *zeik* 'piss'
SEXUALITY	*Fuck* 'fuck', *hoer* 'prostitute', *slet* 'slut', *putain* 'prostitute', *neuk* 'copulate', *pijp* 'blow', *lek* 'lick', *kus* 'kiss'
RELIGION	*God* 'god', *dju* 'god', *dieu* 'god', *gatver* 'god damn', *jezus* 'jesus', *christus* 'christ', *duivel* 'devil', *hemel* 'heaven', *hel* 'hell', *heilig* 'holy'
DISEASES	*weitig* 'disease', *syfilis* 'syphilis', *stuipen* 'stroke', *beroerte* 'stroke', *mazelen* 'measels', *Lazarus* 'lazarus', *kramp* 'cramp', *krets* 'infection', *koorts* 'fever', *tering* 'tuberculosis', *tyfus* 'typhus', *bult* 'tumor', *influenza* 'influenza', *griep* 'influenza', *kanker* 'cancer', *pleuris* 'pleurisy', *jicht* 'gout', *pest* 'plague', *pokke* 'pox', *takke* 'attack', *cholera* 'cholera', *kolere* 'cholera', *lepra* 'lepra', *aids* 'AIDS', *ebola* 'ebola', *hoest* 'cough', *ziekte* 'disease', *kiezen* 'molar', *longen* 'lungs', *koliek* 'colic', *polio* 'polio'

A simple Python script filtered the 6 million tweets in the corpus down to a set of about 70.000 tweets that contain at least one of the lexical items from Table 1. However, not all of these tweets use the lexical items that we identified as a swearword, e.g. when the lexical item is actually used to refer to the disease, rather than using the word figuratively. Therefore, we had to manually go through all these tweets, yielding 20.000 tweets that we consider to be instances of swearing. The details of this annotation step are described in the following section.

3.3 Annotation

We have annotated each tweet, first, for whether or not it contains a swearing incident, and second, with the conceptual domain from which it draws for the swearing. For each tweet, we know from Twitter what the location is to which the Twitter user affiliates from his Twitter profile. The dataset has a format as in Table 2, with a typical KWIC layout, a column to indicate whether or not the observation is to be considered as swearing, an annotation of the conceptual domain from which the swearing draws, and the location. The raw dataset, as well as the R code that was used for the quantitative analysis can be downloaded[2] for further analysis.

The annotation of whether or not a tweet contains a lexical item that is used as a swearword is not trivial, mostly because it is impossible to classically define a linguistic category such as "swearing" with necessary and sufficient conditions. We followed a guideline that can be summarized as follows: under swearwords we understand expressive figurative language that draws from a domain that is typically considered to be taboo; the use of swearwords must have the function of emphasizing positive or negative emotions; furthermore, even if a lexical item from a potentially taboo domain is used in the above described fashion, it is not considered to be a swearword if that lexical item is not considered to be offensive, clearly crosses an inhibition or may be perceived as obscene.

Table 2: Excerpt from the raw dataset[3]

left	kw	acc?	right	domain	norm_loc
HaHa	!@ FUCKI-PEDIA		gets a compliment, thinks he's GOD, take the wrong path, doesn't know exactly who RT him & blocked me!Who's the faggot?	sexual	Heerlen, Netherlands, Heerlen, Netherlands
Wet renault afschaffen en da uit nen bek van socialist,het word tijd dat de politiekers gansters hunne kop is uit hunne	aars	t	trekken	genitals	Mortsel, Belgium, Mortsel, Belgium
Delen	!Fuck		! ♪ Epic Soundtracks http://t.co/a1ZJbTga #Spotify	sexual	Bilzen, Belgium, Bilzen, Belgium

---

2 http://perswww.kuleuven.be/tom_ruette/data/twitter_invectives/, last access September 3, 2016.

3 Column "left" shows the context words on the left of the keyword, column "kw" shows the keyword that was found in the corpus, column "acc?" indicates whether the observation was considered to be an actual observation of swearing, column "right" shows the context words on the right of the keyword, column "domain" shows the taboo domain from which the swearword draws, and column "norm_loc" shows the cleaned location names of the user profiles.

Table 2 (continued)

left	kw	acc?	right	domain	norm_loc
Nog voor de #kerst 2 nieuwe modellen #GedenkkastjeART op gedenkkastje.nl! Icoon Maria	& Jezus		en Engelen van Brigita Silovic	religion	Nijmegen, Netherlands, Nijmegen, Netherlands
@MiekeInc naar de ondemand stream, niet naar de ‚ik wil het luisteren als ik tijd heb' stream ;-) of kijk ik met mijn #	aars	t	?	genitals	Amsterdam, Netherlands, Amsterdam, Netherlands
(Schijn	)heilig		boontje op fiets gemhuis in in #Losser. Alter-ego bgm #Sijbom. En nu weer naar buiten: optocht start! http://t.co/5CNsPt9m	religion	Netherlands, Netherlands
*Tousse	*Bullshit		*Tousse* http://t.co/X8wYf2KbCe	faeces	Namur, Belgium, Namur, Belgium
Spitaels	‚"Dieu		„is overleden.Allez, ik zal maar beginnen bleiten zeker?	religion	Kortrijk, Belgium, Kortrijk, Belgium
"Landgenoten	‚Fuck	t	this shit, I'm outta here! Latertjes, woord aan je moeder." #aftreden	sexual	Gouda, Netherlands, Gouda, Netherlands

3.4 Quantitative analysis

Given our research focus on the geographical pattern of swearing with diseases, and the potential relation with the geographical spread of Calvinism, we have to fall back to a geospatial analytical instrument. We identified Spatial Autocorrelation as the most appropriate statistical method to detect geographical patterns in data.

Spatial Autocorrelation comes in two flavors. Global Spatial Autocorrelation indicates whether the data contains a geographical pattern. Local Spatial Autocorrelation indicates for each observed location whether it belongs to an area in which the phenomenon under investigation reaches high values or low values. This method has already found an application in linguistics (and is described in detail by Grieve 2014; Grieve 2012; Grieve 2013; Grieve, Speelman, and Geeraerts 2013; Grieve, Speelman, and Geeraerts 2011). For details on the statistical method, we refer to the aforementioned publications; here, we restrict ourselves to introducing the intuition behind the method.

3.4.1 Global spatial autocorrelation

The first flavour of spatial autocorrelation is Global Spatial Autocorrelation and indicates whether the phenomenon at hand exhibits a geographical pattern. The strength of the geographical pattern is expressed with Moran's I (Moran 1948; Odland 1988), which can be compared to an effect size in a more common inferential statistical analysis. Moran's I lies between −1 and 1, with 0 indicating a random geographical pattern. A value of Moran's I close to −1 indicates that nearby locations have different values; a value of Moran's I close to 1 indicates that nearby locations have similar values. In the case of our swearing patterns, we are expecting that nearby locations will have similar values, so that we can discern areas, i.e. groups of locations, with a specific swearing pattern. As with any effect size, it is insightful to also return a p value that indicates the statistical significance of that effect size. A Moran's I value close to 1 might be indicative of a strong geographical pattern, but if the p value suggests that this pattern is just a chance finding, one needs to attenuate the conclusions. Vice versa, a statistically significant pattern ($p < 0.05$) may very well be random, i.e. with Moran's $I = 0$.

3.4.2 Local spatial autocorrelation

Whereas Global Spatial Autocorrelation indicates whether the phenomenon under investigation exhibits a geographical pattern in the full territory, Local Spatial Autocorrelation zooms in on the individual locations. For each location, Local Spatial Autocorrelation calculates a value that indicates "the degree to which that particular location is part of a high- or low-value cluster" (Grieve 2011: 13). So, rather than returning the one value of Moran's I for the full territory as in Global Spatial Autocorrelation, Local Spatial Autocorrelation returns one value for each location. The returned value is referred to as Gi^* (Ord and Getis 1995) and it is at heart a z-score "indicating the degree to which a location is surrounded by locations with similar values" (Grieve 2011: 13).

We visualize these z-scores per location with color-coded dots on a map. Each location in the dataset is represented by a dot, and the color ranges from blue over white to red. A white dot indicates that the location is in an area with transitional values, somewhere between the highest and lowest values that are observed. A blue dot indicates that the location is in an area with very low values, and a red dot indicates that the location is in an area with very high values. Note that these dots are thus indicative of the area in which the location resides, and not about the location itself. As an example, a location with a very low observed value that is amidst a group of locations with very high observed values will nonetheless receive a reddish color. Because of this, it is also possible to think of local spatial autocorrelation as a geographical smoothing function that smothers out local aberrations.

3.4.3 Spatial weighting function

Both Global and Local Spatial Autocorrelation depend heavily on a so-called Spatial Weighting Function. For Global Spatial Autocorrelation, the Spatial Weighting Function defines what 'nearby' means in the calculation of Moran's *I*. For Local Spatial Autocorrelation, the function defines the scope of the area to which a location is compared to come up with a z-score.

The most straightforward approach for this Spatial Weighting Function is to work with a threshold: locations within a range of X kilometers are considered nearby. Of course, this rather crude function does not take into account that some locations may be isolated, so that no other locations fall within this threshold and no reference values can be calculated.

Rather than a threshold based approach, we decided to apply a continuous weighting function. The inverse of the distance is used as the Spatial Weighting Function. In other words, the farther away a reference location is to the location that is currently being tested, the less impact this reference location will have. Although we used a linear function, the idea of continuous weighing is in line with a fundamental finding of dialectology, i.e. that geographical distance is non-linearly and inversely correlated with linguistic similarity (Séguy 1971). This weighting function is also called a reciprocal Spatial Weighting Function, and is explained in more detail in Grieve, Speelman, and Geeraerts (2013).

3.4.4 Values per location

The spatial autocorrelation method assumes that we have been able to quantify the phenomenon at hand, i.e. swearing with words from taboo domains, into a value for each location. From the dataset we gathered, this is not difficult, as it boils down to constructing a commonly used pivot table. In Table 3, an excerpt of the frequency counts of the different types of swearing in a couple of locations is presented.

Table 3: Quantitative representation of swearing with lexical items from taboo domains per location

Locations	Diseases	Religion	Feces	Sexuality	Genitals
Antwerpen	8	72	133	68	88
Gent	15	172	234	156	193
Amsterdam	12	63	213	79	193
Groningen	18	34	68	34	110

From the absolute values in Table 1, we have to calculate relative frequencies, to be able to say something about how people swear across the territory. However, relative frequencies can be calculated in several ways. First, one could calculate the frequency of tweets containing swearwords relative to the total number of tweets per location. As an example, consider Figure 2, in which the number of tweets containing swearing in a certain location is made relative to the total number of tweets in that location.

Note that, as explained above, the maps that are shown in this section have been treated with a Local Spatial Autocorrelation analysis to bring forward geographical patterns. That is why we see the values per location as red-white-blue dots. In addition, we also provide the summary statistic from the Global Spatial Autocorrelation. In Figure 2, we see that Flanders is an area in which we observe more swearing per location than in the Netherlands. This pattern is (globally speaking) significant, with the indication from Moran's I that this is only a modestly strong pattern.

4 Results and discussion

So, we will investigate the geographical pattern of disease-based swearing, as it occurs in contrast to the other domains for swearing that we incorporated, i.e. RELIGION, GENITALS, FECES, and SEXUAL. The pattern that we observe is presented in Figure 3. On the left-hand side, we show the raw proportions that we observed, with darker dots indicating a higher proportion of disease-based swearing tweets. On the right-hand side, we show the map after treating it with spatial autocorrelation. The pattern we observe has a modest effect size, with Moran's I at 0.1374, and a very small p value.

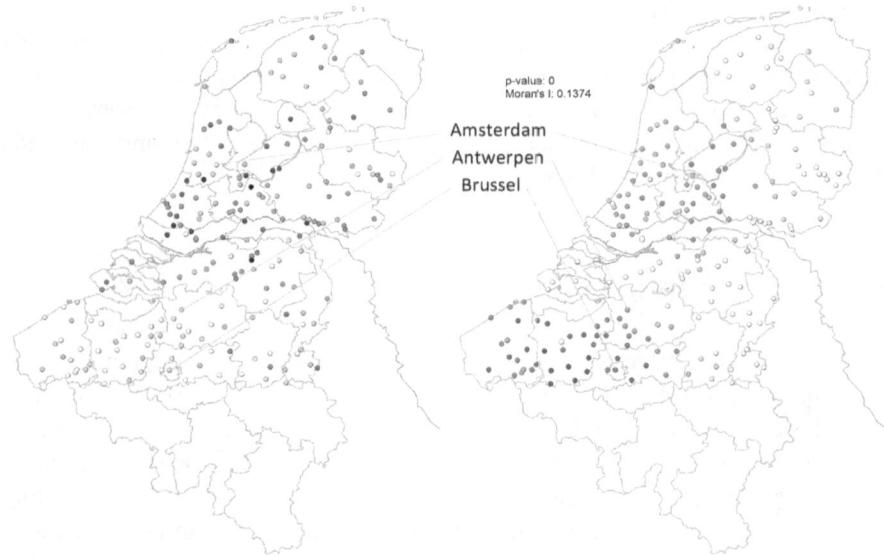

Figure 2: Disease-based swearing in contrast to swearing based on other domains.

We observe that disease-based swearing occurs with elevated probability in the Rim city area (South of the lake). In fact, almost all red dots are located north of the river Maas and Waal, which is historically speaking the border between the Calvinistic North and the Catholic South. Some red dots do occur below these rivers, especially in the neighborhood of 's-Hertogenbosch. 's-Hertogenbosch is the capital of North Brabant, and an important economic center, home to the brewery Heineken (among other international industries), so it may attract people from a wide area. The red dots are mostly absent in the North of the Netherlands, and along the border with Germany.

In Flanders, we observe mostly blue dots, indicating that swearing with diseases is very uncommon. Here and there we do see some white dots, which indicate a region of transition. Rather than attributing too much importance to and trying to interpret these white dots, we can safely say that the coloring of the dots may be here an artifact of the quantitative method and may be potentially due to some data scarceness. As a matter of fact, due to the use of a reciprocal Spatial Weighting Function, there will always be a range of white dots between the blue and the red dots, so one should not over-interpret this.

We observe that there is clearly an overlap between the area where we observe disease-based swearing and the historical area in which Calvinism was the strongest religion (cf. map in Figure 1). The overlap is not complete, though. In the Calvinistic North-East of the territory, and also in the Calvinistic area of Zeeland (in the South) we do not observe many disease-based swearing tweets. Moreover, in the Catholic province of North Brabant, we do observe disease-based swearing in the vicinity of 's-Hertogenbosch. The highest concentration of disease-based swearing is to be found in the socio-economic center of the Netherlands, around Amsterdam in the so-called Rim City.

5 Discussion and conclusion

In this study, we started from the observation that within the contiguous Dutch language area (North of Belgium and The Netherlands), some Dutch speakers draw swearwords from the DISEASE domain, whereas others don't. One of the standing hypotheses is that this can be related to Calvinism – whereby Calvinism puts diseases under a spell of taboo, and thus making them accessible for swearing. Empirical support for this hypothesis was found, but only to the extent that disease-based swearing seems to occur practically exclusively in the traditionally Calvinistic region of The Netherlands, and not in the traditionally roman Catholic South. However, disease-based swearing could not be observed in the entire Calvinistic region, but predominantly in the Rim City area in and around Amsterdam. This latter observation indicates that also sociological factors, e.g. urban/non-urban, influence the way people swear or, perhaps more basal, what they perceive as taboo.

The question one may ask now is related to untangling the phenomena of swearing, tabooness and cultural background. We know that there are ties between swearing and taboo, and it is also trivial that taboo relates to cultural background. But these relationships are not impervious to confounding influences. As a consequence, we are left with wondering: does the urban/non-urban cline influence the tabooness of diseases, and thus indirectly the geographical swearing pattern we observe? Or is the urban/non-urban distinction directly operating on the level of the linguistic practice of swearing, without the go-between of taboo? In other words, do people in urban regions swear with diseases because this is how their peers swear and how people commonly swear in their community of practice? Or do people in urban regions experience the taboo on diseases differently than the people in non-urban regions?

The latter possibility seems to be supported by research that was performed by the Dutch "Bond tegen vloeken" (Union again swearing) in 2015[4]. This research showed that *kanker* 'cancer' and *tering* 'tuberculosis' are both in the top 5 of the most hurting swearwords (in The Netherlands). And some years earlier, a campaign was launched to keep people from swearing with *kanker* 'cancer'[5]. These are two examples that indicate that diseases still have a high symbolic – certainly taboo? – value in the culture of the Dutch.

So, why do the Dutch swear with diseases? At the end of this paper, we are still in doubt whether it is because they have a taboo on diseases, or if it is due to their Calvinistic background, or maybe it has to do with a unique urban fad that is currently hip in Amsterdam? The swearing pattern that we observe indicates at least that the choice for a disease as a swearword is a complex interaction of sociological influences on both language use and the tabooness of concepts.

6 References

Allan, Keith and Burridge, Kate. 1991. Euphemism and dysphemism: language used as shield and weapon. Oxford: Oxford University Press.
Allan, Keith and Burridge, Kate. 2006. *Forbidden words: taboo and the censoring of language*. New York: Cambridge University Press.
Aman, Reinhold. 1996. *Opus Maledictorum: A Book of Bad Words*. New York: Marlowe & Company.
Anderson, Lars-Gunnar and Trudgil, Peter. 1990. *Bad language*. Oxford: Basil Blackwell.
Bartsch, Renate. 1987. *Norms of Language: Theoretical and Practical Aspects*. London & New York: Addison-Wesley Longman Limited.
Beers-Fägersten, Kristy. 2012. *Who's Swearing Now?: The Social Aspects of Conversational Swearing*. Newcastle: Cambridge Scholars Publishing
Cruse, D. Alan. 1986. *Lexical Semantics*. Cambridge: Cambridge University Press.

---

4 http://www.bondtegenvloeken.nl/files/Bond%20tegen%20vloeken/onderzoeken/adviesrapport-bond-tegen-vloeken-2015---samenvatting.pdf, last access September 3, 2016.
5 http://www.stopscheldenmetkanker.nl/, last access September 3, 2016.

Drange, Eli-Marie Danbolt, Ingrid Kristine Hasund, and Anna-Brita Stenström. 2014. 'Your Mum! 'Teenagers' Swearing by Mother in English, Spanish and Norwegian. *International Journal of Corpus Linguistics* 19 (1). 29–59.

Dynel, Marta. 2012. Swearing Methodologically: The (im) Politeness of Expletives in Anonymous Commentaries on Youtube. *Journal of English Studies*, no. 10. 25–50.

Geeraerts, Dirk, Gitte Kristiansen, and Yves Peirsman. 2010. *Advances in Cognitive Sociolinguistics*. Berlin, Boston: De Gruyter Mouton. https://www.degruyter.com/view/product/177073.

Grieve, Jack. 2011. A Regional Analysis of Contraction Rate in Written Standard American English. *International Journal of Corpus Linguistics* 16 (4). 514–46.

Grieve, Jack . 2012. A Statistical Analysis of Regional Variation in Adverb Position in a Corpus of Written Standard American English. *Corpus Linguistics and Linguistic Theory* 8 (1). 39–72.

Grieve, Jack. 2013. A Statistical Comparison of Regional Phonetic and Lexical Variation in American English. *Literary and Linguistic Computing* 28 (1). 82–107.

Grieve, Jack. 2014. A Comparison of Statistical Methods for the Aggregation of Regional Linguistic Variation. In Szmrecsanyi, Benedikt & Bernhard Wälchli (eds.), *Aggregating Dialectology, Typology, and Register Analysis: Linguistic Variation in Text and Speech*, 53–88. Berlin & New York: Walter De Gruyter.

Grieve, Jack, Dirk Speelman, and Dirk Geeraerts. 2011. A Statistical Method for the Identification and Aggregation of Regional Linguistic Variation. *Language Variation and Change* 23 (02). 193–221.

Grieve, Jack . 2013. A Multivariate Spatial Analysis of Vowel Formants in American English. *Journal of Linguistic Geography* 1 (01). 31–51.

Grieve, Jack, Andrea Nini and Diansheng Guo. Forthcoming. Analyzing lexical emergence in American English online. *English Language and Linguistics*.

Han, Chong, and Kenny Wang. 2014. Subtitling Swearwords in Reality TV Series from English into Chinese: A Corpus-Based Study of The Family. *Translation & Interpreting* 6 (2). 1–17.

Harder, Peter. 2012. Variation, Structure and Norms. *Review of Cognitive Linguistics* 10 (2). 294–314.

Jay, Timothy. 1992. *Cursing in America: A Psycholinguistic Study of Dirty Language in the Courts, in the Movies, in the Schoolyards, and on the Streets*. Amsterdam/Philadelphia: John Benjamins Publishing.

Jay, Timothy. 1999. *Why We Curse: A Neuro-Psycho-Social Theory of Speech*. Amsterdam/Philadelphia: John Benjamins Publishing.

Kristiansen, Gitte, and René Dirven. 2008. *Cognitive Sociolinguistics, Language Variation, Cultural Models, Social Systems*. Berlin/Boston: De Gruyter Mouton. https://www.degruyter.com/view/product/40053.

Ljung Magnus. 2010. *Swearing: A Cross-Cultural Linguistic Study*. New York: Palgrave Macmillan.

Lötscher, Andreas. 1981. Zur Sprachgeschichte Des Fluchens Und Beschimpfens Im Schweizerdeutschen. *Zeitschrift Für Dialektologie Und Linguistik* 48. 145–60.

Mackenbach, Johan. 2007. Jean Calvin, Calvinism, and Population Health: Impressions from Switzerland. *The European Journal of Public Health* 17 (1). 1.

McEnery, A. 2004. Swearing in Modern British English: The Case of Fuck in the BNC. *Language and Literature* 13 (3). 235–68.

Montagu, Ashley. 1967. *The Anatomy of Swearing*. Philadelphia: University of Pennsylvania press.

Moran, P. A. P. 1948. The Interpretation of Statistical Maps. *Journal of the Royal Statistical Society. Series B (Methodological)* 10 (2). 243–51.
Nübling, Damaris, and Marianne Vogel. 2004. Fluchen Und Schimpfen Kontrastiv. *Germanistische Mitteilungen* 59. 19–33.
Odland, John. 1988. *Spatial Autocorrelation.* London: Sage Pub.
Ord, J. Keith, and Arthur Getis. 1995. Local Spatial Autocorrelation Statistics: Distributional Issues and an Application. *Geographical Analysis* 27 (4). 286–306.
Pütz, Martin, Justyna A. Robinson, and Monika Reif, eds. 2014. *Cognitive Sociolinguistics: Social and Cultural Variation in Cognition and Language Use.* Vol. 59. Benjamins Current Topics. Amsterdam: John Benjamins Publishing Company. http://www.jbe-platform.com/content/books/9789027270276.
Sanders, Ewoud, and Rob Tempelaars. 1998. *Krijg de Vinkentering!* Amsterdam/Antwerp: Contact.
Séguy, Jean. 1971. La relation entre la distance spatiale et la distance lexicale. *Revue de Linguistique Romane* 35. 335–357.
van Sterkenburg, Piet. 2000. *Vloeken: Een Cultuurbepaalde Reactie Op Woede, Irritatie En Frustratie.* Den Haag: Sdu Uitgeverij.
van Sterkenburg, Piet. 2008. Vloeken Is Niet Meer Wat Het Geweest Is. *Taalschrift.org*.
Wajnryb, Ruth. 2005. *Expletive Deleted: A Good Look at Bad Language.* New York: Simon and Schuster.

Andrea Pizarro Pedraza
12 Calling things by their name: Exploring the social meanings in the preference for sexual (in)direct construals

Abstract: This chapter is a cognitive sociolinguistic approach to the preferences for direct versus indirect construals and their social meanings. The study is based on the analysis of 906 expressions of sexual concepts (body parts and physiological processes) from the corpus *MadSex* (Pizarro Pedraza, 2013). These are divided in direct (based on sexual concepts, *vulva*) and indirect expressions (based on domains other than sexuality, *little cupcake*) and included in a logistic regression model with internal (sex of the concept, topic of the interview question) and external factors (gender, age, education level, prudishness of the speaker) as independent variables. The results show that direct construals are used more by speakers with higher studies and in questions about more formal topics, where they can be interpreted as orthophemistic or straight talking (Allan and Burridge 2006). Indirect construals are more heterogeneous and therefore their use can be explained by different motivations: as a marker of a semi-conversational style in questions about informal topics, as an affective resource for male speakers talking about aspects of their own sexuality, and as euphemistic strategy for older speakers and prudish speakers, with a true intention of concealing the taboo meanings.

Keywords: sexual concepts; construal; orthophemism; euphemism; cognitive sociolinguistics

1 Introduction

Talking about sexuality is considered taboo in many societies and as such it is forbidden or subject to communicative restrictions (Allan and Burridge 1991, 2006). These restrictions are motivated by more or less implicit linguistic ideologies of particular social groups (Andersson & Trudgill 1992: 35) about when, how, why or who can express sexual concepts. The way these ideologies actually affect lin-

---

The research reported in this chapter has been carried out with the support of a MOVE-In Louvain Postdoctoral fellowship. I would like to thank the reviewers for the very useful comments on the first versions of this chapter.

https://doi.org/10.1515/9783110582758-013

guistic behaviour can be observed in the preference of certain social groups for particular expressions: for instance, the often mentioned feminine preference for avoidance strategies (euphemism), versus a preference for offensive strategies (dysphemism) in the case of men (Allan & Burridge 2006: 89). The literature on linguistic taboo has mostly focused on these extremes of the x-phemistic continuum (euphemism-dysphemism), but much less is known about the middle point, orthophemism, which refers to the pragmatic intention of "straight-talking" (p. 32). Euphemism and dyphemism are semantically often based on indirect construals (through metaphor, metonymy, vague expressions...), while orthophemism relies on the use of a literal or direct expression of the concept. Orthophemistic expressions are also subject to linguistic ideologies, such as "calling things by their name", as explained by the speaker in (1):

(1) *las cosas hay que llamarlas por su nombre / [...] eh... porque luego te encuentras casos / que por ejemplo / al pene / le llama- le llaman de 1500 formas / que tú no eres capaz de descifrar / y a la vulva le llaman "magdalenita" /* (MR13[1])
'you have to call things by their name / [...] hm... because then you encounter situations / where for instance / the penis / they call- they call it by 1500 ways / that you are not able decipher / and they call the vulva "little cupcake" /'

Speaker MR13 (a young woman with university studies) advocates for straight-talking: she prefers the direct expressions *pene* and *vulva* ('penis' and 'vulva') to indirect expressions evoked by '1500 ways' and 'little cupcake'. This chapter aims at observing *whether there is a significant link between aspects of social identity and the choice for a direct* (like 'vulva') *or an indirect construal* ('little cupcake'). To do so, it explores the conceptual onomasiological variation (Geeraerts, Grondelaers & Bakema 1994) of sexual concepts as possibly related to the social characteristics of a group of Spanish speakers, through a usage-based cognitive sociolinguistic approach (Kristiansen and Dirven 2008, Geeraerts, Kristiansen & Peirsman 2010, Geeraerts & Kristiansen 2014, Pütz, Robinson & Reif 2014) to *MadSex*, a sociolinguistic corpus of sexuality in Spanish (Pizarro Pedraza 2013, submitted) (cf. 3.1). The study includes traditional macro-social information (gender, age, education level) but we also operationalize as a micro-social variable the speakers' stance towards sex talk, in order to analyse the possible relation of conceptual variation with that stance. Our global hypothesis is that we will find patterns of variation

---

[1] All the examples are followed by the code of the speaker in the corpus *MadSex* (cf. 3.1).

related to social and conceptual features and their interactions, for instance, women will use expressions that conceal sexual content (indirect expressions) more than men. Due to the limited amount of data and the complexity of the phenomenon itself, we would like to stress that this chapter is a first exploration of an understudied phenomenon within linguistic taboo.

The paper addresses first the link between linguistic taboo and cognitive sociolinguistics (section 2), then, the analytical apparatus of the study will be explained (section 3), followed by the presentation of the results (section 4), which will be interpreted subsequently (section 5). The paper will end with some conclusions (section 6.)

2 Linguistic taboo and Cognitive Sociolinguistics

Linguistic taboo is the term used to refer to two types of phenomena: referential taboo (dealt with in this chapter), that is, the expression of concepts belonging to "forbidden" or problematic semantic fields, such as sexuality (e.g. sexual activities, identities or body parts) and non-referential taboo, the expression of swearwords and insults (e.g. *fuck* or *cunt*). The phenomenon of linguistic taboo can be primarily situated at the semantic level (Uría Varela 1997: 18, Casas Gómez 2012, this volume) in the sense that the prohibition falls on meanings, or conceptualizations (Pizarro Pedraza & De Cock 2018), rather than on particular words, and it is highly dependent on the pragmatics of the situation (Allan & Burridge 1991, 2006). Each reference (variant) to a forbidden meaning (variable) in discourse is the speaker's particular solution to the taboo problem. In that sense, the study of the different expressions of a target taboo concept is a matter of onomasiological variation (or "cross-varietal synonymy" Allan & Burridge 2006:29) which is subject to conceptual, contextual and social constraints and motivations (p.48–49).

The categorization of a concept as taboo has its roots in the extralinguistic context, since the prohibition originates in ideologies which are socioculturally motivated (Andersson & Trudgill 1992). In their experiential and encyclopaedic nature (Geeraerts 2006), taboos are not different from other concepts, but they are particularly meaningful because prohibitions are key pillars of the regimes of thought of particular societies (Irvine 2011). Not all taboo realities are equally problematic or subject to the same level of prohibition (Allan & Burridge 2006: 163), which is reflected in a different degree of tabooization between different domains (sex, death, aging, ...), and also between different concepts within each domain, which shows prototypicality effects (Jay 2009: 154). Crucially, these conceptual differences vary as well through time and social groups, whose particular experience of reality may affect what is a taboo and how taboo it is.

Until now, not many empirical approaches have given quantitative proof of the sociolinguistic variation of taboo concepts in use, partly due to the problems of Sociolinguistics in the study of variation implying semantic differences (Labov 1972), such as lexical-semantic variation, which have been tackled by Cognitive Sociolinguistics (Kristiansen & Dirven 2008, Geeraerts & Kristiansen 2014). The combination of cognitive semantics and sociolinguistics allows to analyse semantic variation against the speakers' social background, in order to determine empirically the social meanings of particular semantic preferences.

A cognitive sociolinguistic approach to linguistic taboo can have at least two possible outcomes; first, to observe the effects of taboo at the semasiological level, for instance, in changes in the salience of particular meanings in the semantic structure of a concept (Geeraerts, Grondelaers & Bakema 1994: 89) due to taboo contamination[2] (Allan and Burridge 2006: 43), and second, to analyse taboo effects at the onomasiological level, for example, in the use of different expressions to refer to a particular taboo concept (Grondelaers & Geeraerts 1998). This is especially relevant at the conceptual onomasiological level, since taboo variants often present conceptual differences. Moreover, a cognitive sociolinguistic analysis of these phenomena would allow establishing what the links are between semantic preferences and conceptual, contextual and social features, through statistical analysis. This chapter wants to contribute to this rather unexplored area. In the following, we will explain the design of a cognitive sociolinguistic study applied to sexual concepts at the conceptual onomasiological level in relation with a number of external variables.

---

[2] Linguistic taboo studies have observed that euphemistic expressions are quite fast "contaminated" by the negative load of the taboo they are replacing, therefore losing the ability to conceal the taboo. This motivates the permanent need for new euphemistic expressions, a process which is known as the "domino theory of euphemism" (Bolinger, 1980: 74, in Crespo-Fernández 2007: 86).

3 Analysis of the variation of sexual concepts

3.1 Description of corpus and data extraction

Our analysis is based on data from *MadSex* (Pizarro Pedraza 2013, submitted), a self-collected sociolinguistic corpus of 54 face-to-face interviews in Madrid (Spain), designed for the indirect elicitation of sexual concepts in Spanish. The sample was pre-stratified by age, gender and education level. The interviews were collected in two districts with very different social and ideological profiles: Chamberí (wealthier, more conservative) and Villa de Vallecas (working class, more liberal). The interviewees answered 35 open-ended questions about their opinions and experiences related to a variety of sexual aspects in Spain. Questions were divided in five modules: sexuality in the media, social changes related to sexuality, sexuality in everyday life, sexual education and sexual laws. This last module was introduced to elicit argumentative sequences and a more formal style. The corpus has approximately one million words and contains very varied sexual concepts and social information about the speakers.

For this study, we focused on a subcorpus of questions dealing with body parts and physiological processes (present in 53 of the interviews). We used Rodríguez González's (2011) dictionary of sexual and erotic language in Spanish to create a basic list of 21 target concepts related to body parts and physiology at different levels of granularity, e.g. MALE SEXUAL ORGAN, PENIS, SCROTUM. Then, every expression referring to those concepts was extracted manually from each interview. We excluded extremely vague cases with irretrievable reference, anaphors and immediate repetitions due to emphasis or reformulation, which would increase the presence of a variant for pragmatic or syntactic reasons, rather than conceptual motivations. The rest of the expressions for the target concepts were considered valid (N=906) (cf. Table 1). They were coded with semantic, contextual and social variables of the speaker (cf. 3.2 and 3.3.).

Table 1: Distribution of tokens for the selected target concepts (body parts and physiological processes) in *MadSex* in raw numbers (n=906).

Feminine		Masculine	
Body parts			
FEMALE SEXUAL ORGANS	77	PENIS	100
BREASTS	46	MALE SEXUAL ORGANS	60
VAGINA	22	TESTICLES	7
CLITORIS	13	SCROTUM	2
FALLOPIAN TUBES	2	GLANS	2
HIMEN	1	FRENULUM	1
Physiological processes			
PREGNANCY/GET PREGNANT	281	EJACULATION	16
MENSTRUATE	122	ERECTION	15
MENSTRUATION	69	SEMEN	5
UNWANTED PREGNANCY	50		
GET SOMEONE PREGNANT	14		
MENOPAUSE	1		

There are in general more feminine than masculine concepts, and more physiological processes than body parts, which are related, since most of the former refer to female physiology, like PREGNANCY and MENSTRUATION. The relatively higher presence of these concepts with respect to those of male sexuality might be partially related to the questionnaire design (the questions about sexual education and the abortion law elicited more of such concepts).

3.2 The construal of sexual concepts

The sexual concepts expressed by the informants take the form of varied linguistic expressions, however they all share one semantic feature that we can call DIRECTNESS OF CONSTRUAL. When expressing sexual concepts, speakers may opt for a sexual source concept (direct construal) and others for a source concept that is not specifically sexual (indirect construal), with different communicative intentions. The variants of each particular concept do not only differ in their form (which would be a question of formal onomasiological variation), but they also imply differences in meaning, which situates this analysis at the level of conceptual onomasiological variation (Geeraerts, Grondelaers & Bakema 1994).

Semantically, direct construals convey a sexual target concept directly through a sexual source concept, that is, through the option that could be considered literal (as in the dictionary), such as in examples (2a-2c).

(2) a. CLITORIS: *en el caso de los hombres / pues... les- les harán una vagina / o... un **clítoris** /* (CC01)
'in the case of men / so... they- they'll make them a vagina / or... a **clitoris**'
b. TO MENSTRUATE: *cuando **tuve la menstruación** [...] / me dijo / "ponte... esta compresa y tal / y esto te pasará todos los meses" /* (IA13)
'when I **got my menstruation** [...] / she said / "put... this sanitary towel and so / and this will happen to you every month"'
c. ERECTION: *pero no sé... científicamente decir pues cómo puede llegar a tener **una erección** / o... no lo sé /* (GP02)
'but I cannot... scientifically explain how they can have **an erection** / or... I don't know'

Indirect construals do not rely on the domain of sexuality to express a sexual target concept, but on different domains, either through metonymy (3a), metaphor (3b) taxonomical shifts or generic expressions, such as in (3c):

(3) a. CLITORIS: *o sea si es un chico... que quiere ser chica por ejemplo / pues eh... le cortan el... el... el pene y con... eh... pues... eh... ciertas partes que son más sensibles del hombre ((lo que)) le hacen ponerle **las partes más sensibles de la mujer** /* (GP02)
'so if it's a boy... who wants to be a girl for instance / so uh... they cut his... his... his penis and with... uh... so... uh... certain men's parts that are more sensitive ((what)) they do is to put him **women's most sensitive parts**'
b. ERECTION: *le desnudó / y le echaba un espray para que se... **empitonase** / [risas] /* (CC06)
'she undressed him / and she put him a spray so that he would... **get the shape of a bull's horns** [metaphorically, "to have an erection"]'
c. MALE SEXUAL ORGAN: *sí / en... pues aparte de hormonarse / ¿no? / en... ponerle **cosas de hombre** a... una mujer /* (CR10)
'yes / in... so apart from taking hormones / right? / in... putting **men's stuff** to... a woman'

We have relied on dictionary information (Real Academia Española 2014) to code for directness of construal: if the token appears in the dictionary first with a sexual meaning, it is coded as 'direct construal', otherwise, it is considered 'indirect construal'. In our data, there are 448 direct and 458 indirect construals. The choice for a direct construal, can be considered the neutral, orthophemistic option in some situations (Allan & Burridge 2006) when opting for a straightforward mention of the sexual concept seems more adequate, for instance in medical consultations (López Morales 2001). On the other hand, indirect construals are an alternative different than orthophemism, chosen by the speaker even if there is a certain degree of conventionalization of the sexual meaning. DIRECTNESS OF CONSTRUAL is the dependent variable in this study. We will present now the independent factors that may affect the use of direct or indirect construals.

3.3 Independent variables

3.3.1 Internal factors

SEX OF THE CONCEPT: Since our data is composed of concepts that refer to body parts and physiological processes of one sex or the other, we can classify our concepts as feminine or masculine. Feminine sexuality is loaded with a stronger taboo (Allan & Burridge 2006), so we would expect that feminine body parts and physiology will trigger more indirect construals to conceal the direct reference (see also Gatambuki et al., this volume). Nonetheless, this prediction will possibly be the opposite for women speakers, their own embodied experience of these concepts will probably reduce or eliminate the taboo.

TOPIC: The interview answers analysed for the creation of the corpus are taken from two modules: everyday life and sexual laws. The former revolve around sexuality in day-to-day aspects. It usually elicited more narrative answers. On the other hand, the questions about sexual laws (abortion, homosexual marriage, transsexuality or prostitution) triggered more formal argumentative answers. Previous results from written questionnaires or lexical availability studies have related formal situations with a higher tendency for orthophemistic variants (López Morales 2001, Samper Padilla 2006). Therefore, we expect a higher presence of direct construals when talking about sexual laws than when talking about everyday life.

3.3.2 Social factors

GENDER: This variable has two variants: men and women. The gender of the speaker is often responsible for sociolinguistic variation (see Klann-Delius 2004, for a brief overview) and it is especially relevant in linguistic taboo studies. It is usually stated that women use less dysphemistic expressions than men (López Morales 2001: 13) and that their use of taboo words is judged as inappropriate (Christie 2013: 162), patterns that have been explained by social imposition or by a higher sensitivity to linguistic politeness (García Mouton 2003). The hypothesis in this study is that women will use less direct construals.

AGE GROUP: We divide the speakers in three age groups (G1: 20–34, G2: 35–54, G3: 55 and more years old), following Spanish sociolinguistic studies (PRESEEA 2003, Cestero Mancera, this volume). It has been proved that younger speakers use more taboo words and dysphemistic expressions (López Morales 2001: 6). The recent history of Spain (specifically, the forty-year conservative dictatorship followed by forty years of democratic system) has had a strong impact on sexuality (Iglesias de Ussel 1981), which has undergone a recent process of destigmatization (Ayuso Sánchez & García Faroldi 2014). We expect that the younger speakers (G1) will use more direct expressions for sexual concepts than the other two groups. If the sociological change is reflected sociolinguistically, we could also find a decreasing pattern in the use of direct expressions with age.

EDUCATION LEVEL: We divide our speakers according to the education received in three levels: primary, secondary and university studies, since it has been proved that educational achievements have an impact on language use (Blas Arroyo 2005: 228). There is evidence that speakers with a higher educational level tend to use more technical terms (López Morales 2001: 11), which are direct construals. On the other hand, taboo words have covert prestige among men with lower education level (Trudgill 1972, Stapleton 2010). The hypothesis is that speakers with higher studies (university degrees) will tend to use more direct construals. Possibly, lower education in interaction with gender might bring patterns of covert prestige to the surface.[3]

PRUDISHNESS: In addition to the macro-social variables, we also include a micro-social variable: the stance of the speakers in our corpus towards talking about sexuality. Mostly, the answers to question 18 contained relevant information about the speakers' stances, since it asked about who they thought spoke more about sex, men or women, which triggered metadiscursive sequences about

---

[3] Although DISTRICT (Chamberí, Villa de Vallecas) didn't have an impact on variation in our previous studies, we controlled for it.

sex talk. The analytical procedure included a qualitative analysis of the answers with the purpose of finding potential common stances across speakers that could be operationalized for the quantitative analysis. We found that we could classify speakers basically in two groups according to their stances: those speakers who admitted some embarrassment when talking about sexual experience (4a), and those who expressed feeling comfortable talking about it (4b). We decided to name the variable as PRUDISHNESS with the levels 'yes' and 'no' so as to portray the local cultural relevance of the key concept of *tener pudor* ("being prudish"), present in our interviews. Our hypothesis is that prudish speakers will use less direct construals in order to avoid sexual meanings.

(4) a. *¿en una conversación de mujeres? / bueno / pues depende de con quien la tengas / puedes estar hablando a lo mejor con alguna amiga tuya... muy amiga / y contarle algo... que te haya surgido... pero eso- pero si no yo creo que las mujeres de sexo no hablan /* (PB14)
'in a women's conversation? / well / it depends on who you're talking to / you may be talking with a friend of yours... close friend / and tell her something... that has happened to you... but that- but otherwise I think women don't talk about sex'
b. *sí / los hombres nos cortamos menos / también es verdad / o sea yo creo... sí / qué coño / para nosotros estamos hablando de sexo todo el rato /* (CC06)
'yes / we men are less shy / that's also true / I mean I think... yes / what the fuck / for us we are talking about sex all the time /'

Once the data were coded according to the previous variables, we proceeded to the quantitative analysis.

3.4 Mixed effects logistic regression model

The aim of this study is to measure the relative effect of a number of factors on the preference for a direct or an indirect construal, therefore, we opt for building a binary logistic regression model with the variable DIRECTNESS OF CONSTRUAL as response. This method allows to predict the probability of direct versus indirect construals in our data taking into account the effect of the independent variables included in the model. In this case, we include as predictors all the variables listed above, since we want to explore whether the variation is due to internal or social factors, or interactions of both. No major collinearities were found between the independent variables. Table 2 shows a summary of the variables.

Table 2: List of variables and variants included in the study.

Response Variable	Variants
DIRECTNESS OF CONSTRUAL	Direct / indirect
Factors	**Levels**
SEX OF THE CONCEPT	Masc, Fem
TOPIC	Life, Legal
GENDER	Women, Men
AGE GROUP	1, 2, 3
EDUCATION LEVEL	Primary, Secondary, University
PRUDISH	Yes, No

Apart from these fixed effects, we also included two random variables that we suspected could have an influence in the variation of our data. In total there are 53 speakers who, despite having some common social features, might potentially show a degree of individual variation that cannot be generalized with the results of social categories. This is especially true for linguistic taboo, which is related to a variety of aspects of personality which are not included in our model, and which might affect how a particular speaker behaves linguistically (Jay 2000 ch. 13). Similarly, out of the 21 target concepts in our data (cf. Table 1), some might be subject to a greater taboo than others and trigger more indirect expressions, or viceversa (Jay 2000, López Morales 2001). In order to account for these two sources of variation, we include PARTICIPANT (53 speakers) and TARGET CONCEPT (21 concepts) as random variables, in order to adjust the effect of the fixed effects to each participant and each target concept.

Building a logistic regression model with mixed effects means searching the model that explains the data better, a goal that requires a numbers of tasks. First, we built a model with all the fixed effects and the interactions and we applied a stepwise automatic model selection (using AIC as a comparative criterion). With the resulting model, we checked the measures of its explanatory power to confirm that it was possible to include random effects: R2 indicates how much of the variation is explained by the model (0.207) and C-value indicates whether the model is able to predict variation (0.727). Then we included our random variables and proceeded to manually eliminate non-significant predictors one by one (starting from the least important, according to our ANOVA test), while checking for a reduction in AIC. All fixed effects were kept in the model. Two interactions were also retained: AGE GROUP: SEX OF THE CONCEPT and AGE GROUP:STANCE.

The model with the random variables improves considerably, as shown by the decrease in AIC (1090.7) and the increase in C that reaches almost 0.8. We also took into consideration a pseudo-R2, whose value is 0.255 for this model. Furthermore, the model didn't have problems of fit and the blups have a normal distribution. The results will be described in 4 and interpreted in 5.

4 Results

Table 3 shows the significant factors in order of importance according to the ANOVA test for the fixed effects model. One level of each factor contributes to the intercept (first line of table 3) and the other levels are listed individually. In the first column, we see the estimate, that is, the effect of each predictor on the response variable: positive numbers indicate that the predictor favours significantly more the use of sexual source concepts for referring to the target (direct construal), and negative numbers show that the predictor favours source concepts that are not sexual (indirect construal). In the last column, significance is marked with stars for an easier visualization. The last two rows show the adjustment imposed by each random variable: PARTICIPANT has a lower standard deviation than TARGET CONCEPT, which means that there is less variability among speakers than among concepts[4].

Table 3: Output of the mixed effets logistic regression model (performed with R).

Predictor	Estimate	Std. Error	z value	Pr(>|z|)
(Intercept)	−0.12256	0.41286	−0.297	0.766570
Topic Everyday Life	−0.67785	0.17381	−3.900	9.62e−05 ***
Age Group 2	−0.05899	0.27928	−0.211	0.832705
Age Group 3	−0.59452	0.27380	−2.171	0.029906 *
Age Group 2 : Prudish Yes	1.50814	0.57794	2.610	0.009067 **
Age Group 3 : Prudish Yes	1.86317	0.56023	3.326	0.000882 ***
Prudish Yes	−1.19270	0.46437	−2.568	0.010216 *

---

[4] For instance, the concepts MENSTRUATE and VAGINA favour mostly indirect construal, while UNWANTED PREGNANCY and GET PREGNANT are mostly expressed through direct construal.

Table 3 (continued)

Predictor	Estimate	Std. Error	z value	Pr(>|z|)
Education level: secondary	0.75099	0.26140	2.873	0.004066 **
Education level: university	0.84335	0.26053	3.237	0.001208 **
Age Group 2 : Sex Concept masculine	−1.10389	0.43659	−2.528	0.011458 *
Age Group 3 : Sex Concept masculine	−0.05762	0.45367	−0.127	0.898935
Random variables	**Variance**	**Std. Dev**		
Participant	0.08098	0.2846		
Target concept	0.64888	0.8055		

At the top of the table, two main effects reach significance on their own: the TOPIC of the question acts as predicted, the questions related with everyday life don't favour the use of sexual source concepts for the target, but rather indirect construals.

The variable AGE GROUP reaches significance for the older speakers (age group 3), who use significantly less direct construals, a result that is also coherent with our initial hypothesis. Although the estimate for the second age group is not significant, it shows that this group also uses less direct construals than the younger group but more than the third. The age results seems to point to a pattern where direct construals are less and less used as age advances.

When interactions between factors have significant effects, the global effects need to be nuanced by the more fine-grained picture given by the interaction. Independently AGE and PRUDISHNESS are related to less use of direct construals but the result of their interaction seems counterintuitive: prudish people from the second and the third age groups tend to use more direct construals than younger prudish speakers. In order to inspect the data according to the two variables in interaction, we visualize it through a mosaic plot (Fig. 1).

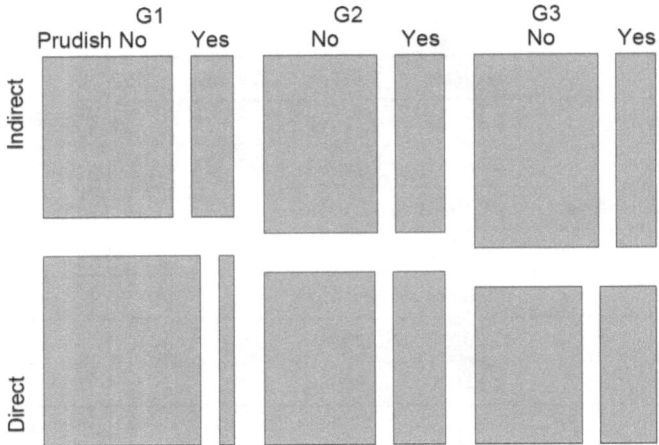

Figure 1: Mosaic plot of the effect of the interaction of AGE GROUP and PRUDISHNESS on DIRECTNESS OF CONSTRUAL.

The first age group uses in general more direct construals than the second and the third groups, but this tendency is reversed for those younger speakers who consider themselves prudish. Their very low use of direct construals contrasts with the prudish speakers of the other two age groups, which results in a significant positive value in our model. Indeed, younger people are the only ones that show a pattern coherent with our hypothesis, in the sense that the young prudish speakers use less direct construals, and the non-prudish use more. For the second age group the fact of being prudish doesn't affect the use of more or less direct construals. On the other hand, the third age group has an overall preference for indirect construals, which is significantly reversed in the case of prudish people of this group, who show a preference for direct construals. Although this might seem illogical, it is not so much if we look at the kind of concepts they use (table 4): 26 out of 46 direct construals are related to PREGNANCY/GET PREGNANT, which has a low degree of tabooization, and therefore, is less problematic to be construed directly (cf. foot note 4).

Table 4: Distribution of tokens per target concept used by prudish speakers of age group 3 according to directness of construal (raw numbers).

Target concept	Indirect	Direct	Total
FEMININE SEXUAL ORGAN	1	5	6
MASCULINE SEXUAL ORGAN	2	1	3
TO GET SOMEONE PREGNANT	1	1	2
PREGNANCY/GET PREGNANT	6	26	32
UNWANTED PREGNANCY	1	2	3
MENOPAUSE	–	1	1
MENSTRUATION	10	1	11
BREASTS	4	–	4
PENIS	4	6	10
TO MENSTRUATE	9	2	11
TESTICLES	1	–	1
FALLOPIAN TUBES	–	1	1
VAGINA	1	–	1
Total	**40**	**46**	**86**

In short, when it comes to the effect of PRUDISHNESS on conceptual onomasiological variation, it seems that it affects directness of construal mostly when speakers are young.

The next factor, EDUCATION LEVEL, also acts as predicted: the higher the education level of the speakers, the more they use sexual source concepts for the target. This can be related to the preference for orthophemism present in speakers with longer studies, a result that has also been found in other sociolinguistic studies and interpreted as an intention of straightforwardness and precision, through technical denominations (López Morales 2001).

Finally, the last significant effect of the table is again related to the age group of the speaker, which is also in interaction with the conceptual variable SEX OF THE CONCEPT. The result indicates that the speakers from the second age group (35–54) tend to express concepts of male sexuality more through indirect construals than the rest of the groups (Fig. 2).

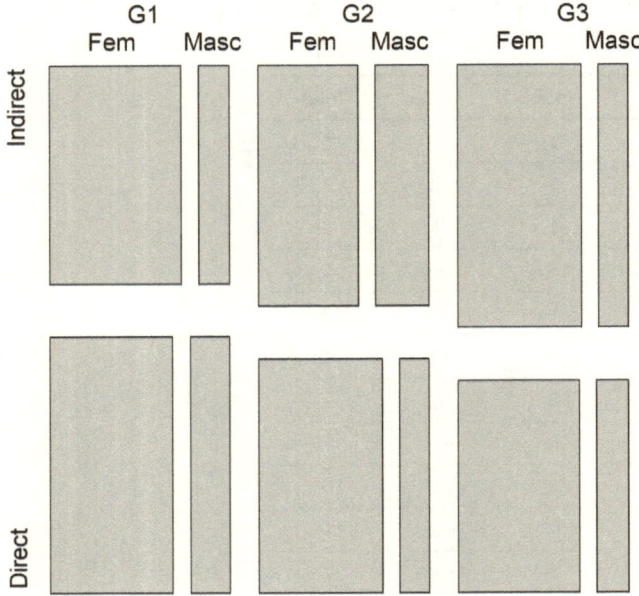

Fig. 2: Mosaic plot of the effect of the interaction of AGE GROUP and SEX OF THE CONCEPT on DIRECTNESS OF CONSTRUAL.

As shown in the plot, male sexuality is in general far less represented in the data for all age groups. In this distribution, it stands out that the proportion of masculine concepts that are construed indirectly in the second age group constitutes almost a third of the tokens for that group. In order to further explore this interaction, we observe how these data (the indirect construals of masculine concepts (n=52)) are distributed according to the social variables, for the second age group. Table 5 shows that most of these construals are uttered by men (n=40/52), especially those who consider themselves non-prudish, with secondary or university studies (n=17+14/52). This combination is particularly interesting because it seems to go against all our initial hypotheses about direct construals: men, non-prudish speakers, speakers with higher education levels, and masculine concepts would favour them, but combined, their effect is the opposite.

Table 5: Distribution of indirect construals of masculine sexual concepts within the second age group, according to SEX, EDUCATION LEVEL and PRUDISHNESS (raw numbers).

	Non prudish	Prudish	Total
Men	36	4	40
Primary education	5	4	9
Secondary education	17	–	17
University	14	–	14
Women	9	3	12
Primary education	8	3	11
Secondary education	1	–	1
Total	45	7	52

Table 6: Indirect construals of concepts of masculine sexuality used by men of the second age group (raw numbers).

Target concept	Total
MASCULINE SEXUAL ORGAN	4
ERECTION	8
EJACULATION	4
FRENULUM	1
GLANS	1
PENIS	20
SEMEN	1
TESTICLES	1

A further look into the specific examples used by men (n=40) sheds some light into this apparent contradiction: most of the concepts of masculine sexuality are represented (except SCROTUM), but the most frequent is PENIS (see table 6). Most of these indirect construals rely on highly conventionalized indirect expressions, based on metaphors (*nabo* 'turnip', *cola* 'tail', *pito* 'whistle') or on the accusative pronoun (*la* 'it') without explicit reference. ERECTION also relies repeatedly on a few source concepts, both metaphorical (*empalmarse* 'to splice oneself together', *empitonarse* 'getting the shape of a bull's horns') and metonymical (*dura* 'hard').

Since these source concepts can be found on the discourses of different speakers with similar social characteristics (men, second age group, non-prudish...), we can assume that it shows a pattern of indirect onomasiological preferences for men of that generation when referring to their own sexuality, whose connotations are socially meaningful for this group (for other axiological values of sexual concepts, see also Crespo-Fernández, this volume).

Interestingly, the SEX of the speaker doesn't reach significance in our model. Therefore, although we may find interesting distributions (as previously mentioned), overall onomasiological preferences for men and women cannot be detected in our data.

5 Interpretation

In this section, we will give an interpretation of our results so as to answer our research question; *Is there a significant link between aspects of social identity and the choice for a (in)direct construal?* In the following, we will argue that our results prove that the answer to our question is positive: the speakers' attitudes towards what they consider forbidden can be found not only in their explicit metadiscursive stances about taboo, but is also performed through their conceptual onomasiological variants. In the particular choices with regard to DIRECTNESS OF CONSTRUAL, social and conceptual features interact.

By now, there is enough proof that taboos are not equally distributed across individuals and social groups (Jay 2000, Allan & Burridge 2006, Cestero Mancera 2015, this volume, Crespo-Fernández 2015, this volume, Finkelstein, this volume, Ruette, this volume), since the degree of tabooization of particular concepts varies, as well as the very fact of being taboo. In our analysis, the considerable differences across concepts illustrate that idea, which is reflected by the different construal preferences associated to each of the 21 target concepts included in our data: as expected, highly tabooed concepts of feminine sexuality show a higher preference for indirect construals, such as 'vagina' and 'to menstruate', while 'to get pregnant' or 'unwanted pregnancy' are associated with direct construal (cf. footnote 4).

Directness of construal implies using an expression with less connotative load, and can consequently be attributed to an intention of being neutral or orthophemistic. Little is known about this pragmatic function (it is actually not always present in accounts about linguistic taboo), apart from its semantic definition as the literal expression of taboo, and its general consideration as a straight-talking strategy (Allan & Burridge 2006: 33). In our data, this is only partially the case. The increasing preference for a direct construal related to higher education levels points indeed in that direction: the expression of taboo concepts through neutral and sometimes technical expressions indicates a positive consideration of orthophemism as a strategy. The explanations for this could be found in the exposure to academic discourse, where technical jargon is often used. It indicates, moreover, that speakers with higher education levels evaluate the interview as a rather formal environment.

If the tendency to direct construals happened across all sorts of concepts, even the most tabooed, it would be safe to say that directness means straightforwardness and clarity, as an index of lack of taboo. That, in our view, would be a prototypical example of orthophemism: a choice for direct construal when other naming strategies would have been more delicate. But when directness only happens with rather unproblematic concepts, the tendency cannot be safely related to an intention of straightforwardness, because a mitigated expression is not pragmatically needed. This is the case of our prudish older speakers, whose proportionally high number of direct tokens is not related to lack of taboo, but rather to their almost exclusive use of less problematic concepts, such as PREGNANCY. Although it is impossible to measure it with our study, it is logical to consider that the strongest taboo is not the concept that the speaker conceals, but the concept that s/he doesn't even include in their discourses, that which is not talked about.

It is important to bear in mind that the group of direct construals is more homogeneous than that of indirect construals, in the sense that the semantic link between source and target is comparable across concepts. On the other hand, indirectness is a broad category whose internal heterogeneity can provoke that some components are more salient than others in the significant correlations with independent factors. In our view, indirect construals rely on two basic semantic effects: meaning reduction (specializations and generic expression) – potentially more euphemistic (see Chamizo Domínguez, this volume)– and categorical shifts (metaphor, metonymy) –which may be imbued with affective and axiological connotations (Allan 2007, Casas Gómez 2012, Crespo-Fernández, this volume, Gatambuki et al., this volume, Moritz, this volume). The different ways of construing meaning of the four resources can be at the origin of differences in social and contextual distribution of the 'indirect' category as a whole, which would need further investigation.

Sociolinguistic interviews are usually considered a semi-formal environment (Albelda Marco 2004, Moreno Fernández 2016), where dysphemistic expressions or any form of verbal aggression would be highly unexpected. Within our interviews, formality was experimented with through changes in the topics of the questions: the last long section was dedicated to discussing sexual laws with the aim of eliciting argumentative answers, while the rest of the interview focused on different aspects of the speakers' everyday lives related to sexuality (cf. 3.1). The purpose was precisely to test the effect of the topic (as a trigger of formality) on onomasiological variation. Interestingly enough, the change in topic is the factor that explains the most variation in our data. When talking about everyday life, there is a higher tendency to use indirect construals, as opposed to legal subjects, where the precision imposed by the topic requires unambiguous direct expressions. This preference for indirectness can lead to two interpretations. On the one hand, lack of semantic precision is typical of conversational styles, in the form of vague language (Jucker, Smith & Lüdge 2003). In our data, it would indicate that speakers behave as if they were having a conversation, performing a more informal style through the semantic indirectness of their sexual concepts, especially with those who are based on meaning reduction.

Nonetheless, a different interpretation could also hold, at least for the indirect construals that rely on categorical shifts. A preference for these expressions, which carry varied connotations, would possibly be related to an intention of conveying axiological and affective meanings. Since connotative meanings are experientially-based, they vary among groups and individuals (Allan 2007: 1049). In sexual concepts, source domains are related, for instance, to ideologies about gender roles, in the sense that conceptualizing sexual intercourse as violence is typical of heteronormative discourses of male speakers (Crespo-Fernández 2015). In our data, a similar reasoning is behind the preference of the speakers of the second age group for indirect construals of masculine concepts: it is not so much a tendency to conceal sexual reference as a preference for construing concepts of their own sexuality through categories (food, objects and animal concepts) that are meaningful for their users, which are mostly non-prudish men (Fig. 2). Since their interviewers were also men, it is likely that these onomasiological variants contribute to an in-group communicative style.

Besides the conversational style and the affective style, a purely euphemistic function is in all likelihood behind the preferences related to older speakers and prudish speakers. It is proved that older generations are more euphemistic, but the reasons for that age pattern are very often under-problematized and attributed to life stage – older speakers being more conservative regarding taboo (López Morales 2001), when it is most probably also due to generation. Indeed, when studying linguistic taboo, we need to consider historical contexts. The concept of "pudor" in Spain was related to the catholic ideology during Franco's dictatorship (cf. 3.3.2), when sexual "decency" was promoted through a number of official and unofficial means, from school to church, and from cinema to family education (Regueillet 2004, Osborne 2012). The effect on individuals who lived during those years was sometimes determinant for their sexual lives and the difference with younger generations is apparent for them (5).

(5)   *a lo mejor / no sé / nosotros / con nuestra edad / tenemos un sentido del pudor que a lo mejor la gente joven no lo tiene /* (RT01)
'maybe / I don't know / us / at our age / we have a sense of being prudish that young people might not have /'

It is clear both from the metadiscursive stances and from the semantic variation that what it means to talk about sexual experience varies for speakers of different age groups. While younger speakers manifest their prudishness by using more indirect construals, the older prudish speakers restrict themselves to concepts of low tabooization, making indirectness unnecessary. Although an age grading pattern cannot be completely discarded, our data seem to indicate rather an evolution in the taboo of sexuality related to a sociohistorical change. Together with the weakening of the moral discourse, what it means to be prudish about sexuality has changed, which shows through the onomasiological variation of different age groups who lived fully, partially and not at all under Franco's regime.

6 Conclusion

The goal of this study was to explore the links between social identity and directness of construal in sexual concepts. The analysis shows that the preference for (in)direct construals is influenced by internal (sex of the concept, topic of the question) and social factors (age group, education level and stance towards taboo) and their interactions.

The function of direct construals can be related to orthophemism, especially in its significant correlation to higher education levels and questions that trigger more formal, argumentative answers. Especially in the expression of more tabooed concepts, direct construal indicates an intention of straightforwardness. Indirect construals have more varied functions (and certainly require further investigation): as a marker of semi-conversational style, when talking about everyday life; as a source of affective meanings, for the speakers of the second age group for masculine concepts, and as euphemistic function for older speakers and prudish speakers. Moreover, the interaction of age and stance seems to point to an evolution of patterns regarding taboo, rooted in a socio-historical change in the destigmatization of sexuality. Against the initial expectations, the factor 'gender' is ruled out by the model.

With our analysis, we have tried to prove that a cognitive sociolinguistic approach can provide new insights into the relative importance of social factors for the variation of taboo expressions, and consequently contribute to determine what is behind each speaker's solution to the problem posed by taboo concepts in discourse.

References

Albelda Marco, Marta 2004. Cortesía en diferentes situaciones comunicativas. La conversación coloquial y la entrevista sociológica semiformal. In Diana Bravo & Antonio Briz Gómez (eds.), *Pragmática sociocultural : estudios sobre el discurso de cortesía en español*, 109–136. Barcelona: Ariel.

Allan, Keith. 2007. The pragmatics of connotation. *Journal of pragmatics* 39(6). 1047–1057.

Allan, Keith & Kate Burridge. 1991. *Euphemism and Dysphemism. Language Used as Shield and Weapon*. New York & Oxford: Oxford University Press.

Allan, Keith & Kate Burridge. 2006. *Forbidden words*. New York: Cambridge University Press.

Andersson, Lars-Gunnar & Peter Trudgill. 1992. *Bad Language*. London: Penguin Books.

Ayuso Sánchez, Luis & M. Livia García Faroldi. 2014. *Los españoles y la sexualidad en el siglo XXI*. Madrid: Centro de Investigaciones Sociológicas.

Blas Arroyo, José Luis. 2005. *Sociolingüística del español. Desarrollos y perspectivas en el estudio de la lengua española en contexto social*. Madrid: Cátedra.

Bolinger, Dwight. 1980. *Language. The loaded weapon.The Use and Abuse of Language Today*. London: Longman.

Casas Gómez, Miguel. 2012. De una visión léxica y pragmático-discursiva a una dimensión cognitiva en la caracterización extralingüística y lingüística del eufemismo. In Marc Bonhomme, Mariela de la Torre & André Horak (eds.), *Études pragmático-discursives sur l'euphémisme*, 53–72. Frankfurt am Main: Peter Lang.

Casas Gómez, Miguel. 2012. El realce expresivo como función eufemística: a propósito de la corrección política de ciertos usos lingüísticos. In Ursula Reutner & Elmar Schafroth (eds.), *Political Correctness*, 61–77. Frankfurt am Main: Peter Lang.

Cestero Mancera, Ana María. 2015. La expresión del tabú: estudio sociolingüístico. *Boletín de Filología* 50(1). 71–105.

Christie, Christine. 2013. The relevance of taboo language: An analysis of the indexical values of swearwords. *Journal of Pragmatics* 58. 152–169.

Crespo-Fernández, Eliecer. 2015. *Sex in Language. Euphemistic and Dysphemistic Metaphors in Internet Forums*. London: Bloomsbury.

García Mouton, Pilar. 2003. *Así hablan las mujeres*. Madrid: La esfera de los libros.

Geeraerts, Dirk. 2006. Introduction. In Dirk Geeraerts, (ed.), *Cognitive Linguistics: Basic Readings*. Berlin: Mouton De Gruyter.

Geeraerts, Dirk, Stefan Grondelaers & Peter Bakema. 1994. *The structure of lexical variation*. Berlin: Mouton De Gruyter.

Geeraerts, Dirk & Gitte Kristiansen. 2014. Cognitive Linguistics and Language Variation. In Jeanette Littlemore & John Taylor (eds.), *Bloomsbury Companion to Cognitive Linguistics*. London: Bloomsbury.

Geeraerts, Dirk, Gitte Kristiansen & Yves Peirsman (eds.). 2010. *Advances in Cognitive Sociolinguistics*. Berlin: De Gruyter Mouton.
Grondelaers, Stefan & Dirk Geeraerts. 1998. Vagueness as a euphemistic strategy. In Angeliki Athanasiadou & Elzbieta Tabakowska (eds.), *Speaking of emotions: conceptualisation and expression*, 357–374. Berlin: Mouton de Gruyter.
Iglesias de Ussel, Julio. 1981. La sociología de la sexualidad en España: notas introductorias. *REIS: Revista española de investigaciones sociológicas* 21. 103–134.
Irvine, Judith T. 2011. Leaky Registers and Eight-Hundred-Pound Gorillas. *Anthropological Quarterly* 84(1). 15–39.
Jay, Timothy. 2000. *Why we curse*. Philadelphia/Amsterdam: John Benjamins.
Jucker, Andreas H., Sara W Smith & Tanja Lüdge. 2003. Interactive aspects of vagueness in conversation. *Journal of pragmatics* 35 (12). 1737–1769.
Klann-Delius, Gisela. 2004. Gender and language. In Ulrich Ammon, Norbert Dittmar, Klaus J. Mattheier & Peter Trudgill (eds.), *Sociolinguistics. Soziolinguistik. An International Handbook of the Science of Language and Society. Ein internationales Handbuch zur Wissenschaft von Sprache und Gesellschaft vol. 2*, 1564–1581. Berlin: Walter De Guyter.
Kristiansen, Gitte & René Dirven (eds.). 2008. *Cognitive sociolinguistics. Language Variation, Cultural models, Social systems*. Berlin: De Gruyter Mouton.
Labov, William. 1972. *Sociolinguistic Patterns*. Philadelphia: University of Pennsylvania Press.
López Morales, Humberto. 2001. Estratificación social del tabú lingüístico: el caso de Puerto Rico. *Actas del I Congreso de la Asociación de Lingüística y Filología de América Latina (ALFAL) Región Noroeste de Europa. Estudios de Lingüística del Español* 13. http://www.raco.cat/index.php/Elies/article/view/195450 (accessed 5 December 2017).
Moreno Fernández, Francisco. 2016. *A Framework for Cognitive Sociolinguistics*. New York: Routledge.
Osborne, Raquel (ed.). 2012. *Mujeres bajo sospecha: memoria y sexualidad (1930–1980)*. Madrid: Editorial Fundamentos.
Pizarro Pedraza, Andrea. 2013. *Tabú y eufemismo en la ciudad de Madrid. Estudio sociolingüístico-cognitivo de los conceptos sexuales*. Madrid: Universidad Complutense de Madrid. PhD thesis.
Pizarro Pedraza, Andrea. Submitted. *MadSex:* Collecting a spoken corpus of indirectly elicited sexual concepts.
Pizarro Pedraza, Andrea & Barbara De Cock. 2018. Taboo effects at the syntactic level: reducing agentivity as a euphemistic strategy. *Pragmatics: quarterly publication of the International Pragmatics Association* 28(1). 113–138.
PRESEEA. 2003. Metodología del Proyecto para el estudio sociolingüístico del español de España y de América, http://www.linguas.net/portalpreseea/Metodolog%C3%ADa/tabid/474/language/es-ES/Default.aspx. (accessed 22 August 2017)
Pütz, Martin, Justyna A. Robinson & Monika Reif, (eds.). 2014. *Cognitive sociolinguistics: social and cultural variation in cognition and language use*. Amsterdam/Philadelphia: John Benjamins.
Real Academia Española. 2014. *Diccionario de la lengua española*, 23rd edn. http://www.rae.es/rae.html (accessed 5 June 2017).
Regueillet, Anne-Gaelle. 2004. Norma sexual y comportamientos cotidianos en los diez primeros años del franquismo: noviazgo y sexualidad. *Hispania* 64(218). 1027–1042.
Rodríguez González, Félix. 2011. *Diccionario del sexo y el erotismo*. Madrid: Alianza Editorial.

Samper Padilla, José Antonio. 2006. Disponibilidad léxica y sociolingüística. In José Luis Blas Arroyo, Manuela Casanova y Mónica Velando (eds.), *Discurso y sociedad: contribuciones al estudio de la lengua en contexto social*, 99–121. Castellón de la Plana: Servicio de Publicaciones de la Universidad Jaume I.

Stapleton, Karyn. 2010. Swearing. In Sage Graham & Miriam A. Locher (eds.), *Interpersonal Pragmatics*, 289–306. Berlin: Mouton de Gruyter.

Trudgill, Peter. 1972. Sex, Covert Prestige and Linguistic Change in the Urban British English of Norwich. *Language in Society* 1(2), 179–195.

Uría Varela, Javier. 1997. *Tabú y eufemismo en latín*. Amsterdam: A. M. Hakkert.

Ana M. Cestero Mancera
13 The perception of the expression of taboos: a sociolinguistic study

Abstract: The study of linguistic taboos has experienced considerable, although still limited, development in recent decades. These studies have especially approached the topic from disciplines that deal with speech, such as sociolinguistics or pragmatics, which has led to an expansion of the subject of these studies and also to the use of interdisciplinary approaches. However, one of the least studied aspects regarding the linguistic expression of taboo concepts, behaviours and realities is variation conditioned by social factors. With the aim of broadening knowledge of the discursive functions and the influence of certain social factors (sex, age, education level and social class), we are performing a study on linguistic taboos in the speech from Madrid. This study will focus on two different angles: on the one hand, what occurs in oral discourse, in a semi-formal register; and on the other, the perception that speakers have of the use of taboo expressions. In earlier works, we have shared the results from the first part of our research and the conclusions we have reached regarding sociolinguistic patterns in expressing taboos (Cestero 2015a, 2015b); this time our main focus is the analysis of results obtained from administering a questionnaire, which was designed for the study and follows the model used in earlier sociolinguistic studies (López 1990, 2001, 2005; Martínez 1995; Drange 1997; Calvo 2008). This questionnaire has been distributed in Madrid, with the aim of advancing our knowledge based on the analysis of the perception of speakers from different genders, age groups or socio-cultural statuses, of how they act with respect to the use of taboo expressions in formal, semi-formal and informal registers.

Key words: Cognitive Sociolinguistics, taboo, linguistic interdiction, dysphemism

1 Introduction

In the 21st century, after the spectacular technological and social advances of the last fifty years which appear to have greatly flexibilized and liberalized human behaviour, we still interact according to long-established sociocultural conventions. The ancestral sociocultural values of fear, decency, embarrassment or respect directly motivate *taboo*, which, since the beginning of the 20th century, is understood as a communicative prohibition, a form of social behaviour reflected directly in speech acts. This causes certain areas to be forbidden, as well as rendering the resulting lexical and semantic units unmentionable or unusable.

Linguistic taboo has been dealt with at length in the bibliography of the 20th and early 21st centuries. The evolution of the concept has gone hand in hand with the disciplinary perspectives from which it has been studied (Martínez 1998; Calvo 2011), which have produced varied and interesting results, allowing us to link and combine the resulting discoveries in order to establish all the factors to which this phenomenon is related, so that any study carried out may be more inclusive and lead to a deeper knowledge of the subject. However, there is a clear lack of consensus regarding the implied plane of the phenomenon, although nowadays linguists consider that it is behaviour and realities, conceptualized through language, that have been tabooed in society, and, consequently, the lexical elements used to express them.

The classifications of linguistic taboo that have been made in the course of different studies start from the psychological reasons that motivate it – ancestral taboo, caused by fear, and social taboo, motivated by decency, embarrassment and respect (Casas 1986; Crespo 2007)-; these four causes enable us to group concepts and realities into four areas (Montero 1981): magical-religious, sexual, scatological and social. This typology forms a reference base on which to arrange the forbidden realities and linguistic elements to be examined here, although, as Uría (1997) points out and Pizarro (2013: 74) reminds us, it must not be forgotten that the causes of taboo are exclusively contextual and do not organize fixed and immovable categories of elements. Therefore, the use of taboo elements or their substitutes is finally determined by the communicative situation. This directly links up with the study of linguistic taboo from a pragmatic perspective, which focuses on the function of certain elements of communication.

The existence of taboo concepts does not prevent us from referring to them, but it does mean that we make a choice of expression, which enables us to distance ourselves to a greater or lesser extent from the forbidden meaning, depending on the linguistic element chosen (Pizarro 2013: 81). On this basis, linguistic taboo has traditionally been linked to two concepts, euphemism and dysphemism, and to their linguistic resources, with the addition of the direct, neutral expression or orthophemism[1]. The choice of particular linguistic elements, having a referential or non-referential function, to fulfil certain communicative aims, means that the phenomenon with which we are dealing is variable. The chosen option may concern pragmatic functions, in which case it is a pragmatic-discursive strat-

---

1 There is a wide and varied bibliography on euphemism, dysphemism and orthophemism which is dealt with in other chapters of this book and for which reason we will not repeat it here.

egy. Alternatively, its use may be determined by the social characteristics of the interlocutors and the context, meaning that we are faced with different sociolinguistic patterns. Finally, as Pizarro points out (2013: 80), it may respond to cognitive conditioners[2] or conditioners of the discursive construction of certain identities[3]. This could be an example of different behaviour patterns requiring an interdisciplinary approach: pragmatic, sociolinguistic and cognitive, this being the approach adopted in this research.

2 The sociopragmatic study of taboo: theoretical framework and research methodology

With the aim of going more deeply into the linguistic expression of taboo and the influence of certain social factors (gender, age and level of education) in its use, we have carried out a study on linguistic taboo in the speech of Madrid. This study approaches its object from two different angles: on the one hand, what actually occurs in semiformal speech, and, on the other, our perception as speakers of our use of forbidden expressions. In previous papers we have published the results of the first part of the study and the conclusions reached on sociolinguistic patterns in the expression of taboo (Cestero 2015a, 2015b). We will now deal with the results obtained in a purpose-designed questionnaire, following the model used in previous sociolinguistic studies (López Morales 1990, 2001, 2005; Martínez 1995; Drange 1997; Calvo 2008), which has been used with the aim of increasing our knowledge through the analysis of the perception of speakers of different genders, age groups and sociocultural levels of how they behave in relation to the use of forbidden expressions, in formal, neutral and informal registers[4]. We embrace Contreras' comments (2008) regarding the fact that the answers given

---

2 The most recent works by Casas (2012a and b) present a typology of the functions of euphemism and dysphemism on a pragmatic-discursive and cognitive basis. He very rightly establishes three basic functions: to cover, to attenuate and to enhance or emphasize. This, in my opinion, should be the functional framework which is the starting point for current and future research.
3 The results obtained by Pizarro (2013) in her study on sexual taboo are a clear example of this.
4 It must be remembered that questionnaires of the type used here inform us of the informants' perception of the use of direct linguistic expressions to refer to taboo elements or concepts, rather than confirming results or data. The perception documented here therefore enables us to discover the sociolinguistic awareness of speakers, as well as their vision of the functioning of communicative activity, which is more a consequence of their concept of correct or proper linguistic use than of their life experiences.

by the subjects have to do, albeit indirectly, with the psychological and social models of their sociolectal and geolectal groups, and, as such, show what these groups consider to be proper and correct, or inform about marks of identity and strategic linguistic resources.

2.1 The sociolinguistic and cognitive study of taboo

There is no doubt that linguistic taboo has a social origin and that it operates in society. It consists of the limitation of the use of linguistic elements under the assumption that these are a direct reflection of the reality to which they refer, which is tabooed (Pizarro 2013: 69). Given that social configurations are cultural, taboo is a cultural phenomenon and, as such, is socially and culturally variable. Thus we are faced with a subject of study that can be prioritized from a sociolinguistic standpoint. In this sense, research has been carried out over the last decades, starting from works by López Morales (1990, 1997, 2001, 2005), with complementary and enriching responses by Martínez (1995) Drange (1997) and Calvo (2008, 2013), aiming to discover the effect on the frequency of use of certain forbidden terms, largely related to the area of sex, of social factors such as gender, age, level of education and social class.

In the above-mentioned works, the fact that variability may affect the level of stigmatization of concepts and elements is taken into account, which as Pizarro says (2013: 76), links directly with prototypical effects, and, consequently, with cognitive sociolinguistics[5], in which research line this study is included. This explains the decisive effects of contextual and social factors in the expression of taboo and adds to these the influence of some personality components, individual characteristics and identities. This study is, of necessity, interdisciplinary and Pizarro's theory and methodology (2013) are used as the base for wider and more profound research on linguistic taboo, leading to the description and explanation of its real use.

Sociolinguistic and cognitive sociolinguistic studies of taboo have clearly shown, as López Morales already suggested in his early works, that linguistic taboo is conditioned by age, gender, level of education or social class and by the context in which it is used. The findings presented by sociolinguists have

---

[5] Regarding cognitive sociolinguistics from a multidisciplinary standpoint, see Moreno Fernández (2012).

informed us, in general lines[6], that more direct or dysphemistic expressions are used in an informal register, by the middle and upper classes, by middle age groups and by men, in contrast to lower social classes and women, who prefer indirect or euphemistic expressions.

Without losing sight of all the contributions which, with different aims and from different linguistic levels and disciplines, have brought us to our present position, in this cognitive sociopragmatic paper, we intend to offer new data on the use and functioning of linguistic elements and expressions which specifically refer, or have referred, to taboo realities in the speech of Madrid, and the incidence of certain social factors [7], dealing with the people's perception of their own expression of taboos.

2.2 Research methodology

In order to offer quantitative data on the frequency and functional performance of linguistic expressions of taboo concepts and realities, as well as their sociolinguistic and cognitive conditioning, it is necessary to start from oral production data and the speakers' own information on their perception of the frequency of use.

From a sociolinguistic viewpoint, using data obtained with questionnaires concerning the use in oral interaction of *ad hoc* or non-specific corpora, it is possible to study the expression of taboo from two different perspectives: one informs on the expressions of tabooed realities used, with greater or lesser frequency, in spoken language and the social factors implied in their variability. The other explains the functions with which linguistic expressions of taboo realities or concepts are used, in their different areas. These are studies on formal variation which, as we have mentioned, were initiated by López Morales and were carried out using specific questionnaires and oral interviews, in order to discover which expressions of certain sexual taboos show interdictions or limitations in correlation with variations in situational and social variables. Recently, Pizarro (2013) has carried out an extensive study on conceptual variation, also centred

---

[6] See works by López Morales (1990, 1997, 2001, 2005), in San Juan de Puerto Rico; Martínez (1995), in Las Palmas de Gran Canaria; Drange (1997), in Viña del Mar; Calvo (2008, 2013), in San José de Costa Rica; Pizarro (2013), in Madrid, y Fernández de Molina (2014), in Mérida (Badajoz).
[7] This paper is included on the research project "Estudio complementario de los patrones sociolingüísticos y procesos de integración sociolingüística en Madrid", funded by the Ministry of Economy and Competitivity (Ref. FFI2015-68171-C5-4-P).

on sexual taboo, using a specially created corpus, which contributes to the completion of previous studies, advances in the creation of an adequate theoretical and methodological base and confirms the incidence of social, situational and cognitive factors in the expression of taboos.

Our current research is included in the international macroproject known as 'Project for the Sociolinguistic Study of Spanish from Spain and America (*PRESEEA*)', and its general aim is to discover sociopragmatic and cognitive patterns through speakers' oral production, and in this particular case, through the speakers' perception of their behaviour in this respect. The focus is on discovering which linguistic expressions refer to taboo realities – both past and present – in different areas traditionally considered to be forbidden, used in oral discourse, in a semiformal register, what their communicative function is and the proportion in which they appear, and if there are sociolinguistic or sociopragmatic conditioners which could enable us to talk of patterns and confirm or complete the findings of previous research. We have started by analysing a sub corpus of the oral corpus of PRESEEA-MADRID (Salamanca and Vallecas districts[8]), in order to discover what occurs naturally in oral interaction, in a neutral register (Cestero 2015a, 2015b). We have then gone on to study the results obtained from a questionnaire, similar to the one used in preceding sociolinguistic studies, in the same districts, using a specially created digital application, with which we have been able to learn more, studying what the speakers do or their perception of what they do, in formal, neutral and informal registers.

Our objectives were the following:
1) To discover the frequency of use of certain words or expressions that refer directly, non-neutrally, to taboo concepts and realities, as well as their level of tabooization.
2) To identify expressions that refer directly or indirectly to certain taboo concepts or realities, according to the perception of the speakers, and the frequency of their use.
3) To establish the influence of the communicative situation – and with this the language register – in the use of direct and indirect expressions which, according to the speakers' perception, are used habitually, and which refer,

---

8 Due to the size of Madrid, we have chosen two districts which quantitatively and qualitatively represent two major socioeconomic areas: the Salamanca district, located in the city centre, whose population can be defined as upper middle class and long-established in the area, and the neighbourhood of Vallecas, situated in the south-east, a working class area that accommodates national, and, more recently, foreign migrants.

or have referred at some point, to taboo concepts and realities, which, again, informs us of their level of tabooization and of sociolectal patterns.

Previous sociolinguistic studies have dealt almost exclusively with forms belonging to the sexual sphere. We have lengthened the list and, although we have asked about ten forms related to sexual interdiction (*cojones [balls], polla [dick], coño [cunt], tetas [tits], follar [to fuck], cabrón [cuckold], puta [whore], estar salido/a, [to be horny] maricón [faggot] and marimacho [butch]*), we have also tried to discover the use of expressions from the magical-religious sphere *(¡hostia! [the host!], muerto [dead], ¡Virgen! [the Virgin])* and the scatological sphere *(mear [to piss], cagar [to shit], culo [ass], pedo [fart])*. In order to know the informants' perception of the frequency with which they use these direct expressions, we have used a scale of answers, asking the subjects if they used the expressions 'never', 'seldom', 'sometimes', 'often' or 'always'.

Following López Morales' suggestions, to discover the diaphasic variation, in the design of the questionnaire we have taken into account the use of linguistic elements in formal, semiformal and informal situations, established according to the context and the interlocutors[9].

In this study we have used a sample of 72 informants, 36 from each district, with two men and two women from each age group (20–34, 35–54 and over 55) and level of education (low, intermediate and high).

The answers given were encoded and tabulated using a template created in Excel©, which has served as the base for qualitative and quantitative analyses of the data[10]. Here follow our most significant findings.

---

9 The informal contexts suggested are: use of expressions with a friend, with a boyfriend/girlfriend or spouse or close relative; the semiformal contexts are: with an acquaintance, with a work colleague, with a distant relative; finally, the formal contexts mentioned in the questionnaire are: with a stranger, in a job interview, talking to a teacher or a superior and at the doctor's surgery. In each contextual block informants are asked to write down expressions or words that they would use with these interlocutors.
10 Analysis has been carried out based on descriptive statistics, complemented, when necessary, by some statistical tests using the SPSS program (version 15.0).

3 The perception of the expression of taboo

In previous papers, we have explained the use and frequency of linguistic expressions that refer to forbidden concepts or realities pertaining to the taboo domains habitually established in the bibliography in oral discourse, in a semiformal register, together with the use and frequency of marked or unmarked direct expressions, or indirect ones, to refer to taboo concepts and realities and related factors of production and linguistic context, as well as sociopragmatic patterns (Cestero 2015b). The data show that the passing of time has considerably diminished the weight and effect of taboo, but there are still vestiges of interdiction. This can be seen in oral discourse in the low frequency of linguistic elements referring to scatological, religious and sexual areas, as well as in the way that they are produced. The interdiction regarding these types of expressions was also clear in the fact that, in speech, most of the lexical units chosen to refer to taboo items were direct and neutral rather than marked: only 11.3 % of the expressions documented were direct and marked (dyphemistic or used dysphemistically), showing the infrequent use of forbidden elements in a semiformal register, as well as confirming a high level of tabooization of the realities and concepts to which they refer (express or displaced reference), and consequently, of the related linguistic units. For this reason we have chosen, as the specific subject of our study, direct, non-neutral, expressions of magical-religious, sexual and scatological spheres.

The general results obtained from the analyses of the oral corpus do not contradict those that come directly from the speakers' beliefs regarding the frequency of use of the linguistic units with which we are dealing. However, regarding the average use of these expressions, it is interesting to note that the lexis pertaining to the sexual sphere are reported by the subjects to be used least (an average of 1.89, which means the average frequency is 'seldom'[11]), followed by those of the religious sphere (an average of 2.2, between 'seldom' and 'sometimes') and, finally, those related to scatology (an average of 2.37, which also falls between 'seldom' and 'sometimes').

---

11 For our quantitative analysis, the reported frequencies of use were given the following values: 'never' = 1, 'seldom' = 2, 'sometimes' = 3, 'often' = 4 or 'always' = 5.

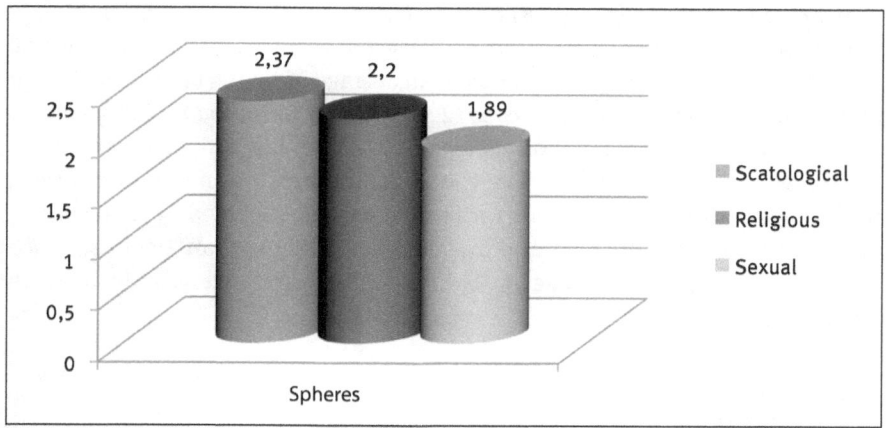

Graphic 1: Perception of the expression of taboos: spheres

As can be observed, the most tabooed sphere is the sexual one, followed by the magical-religious and, finally, the scatological sphere. This is an inversion of order with regard to what occurs in the oral production of the inhabitants of Madrid in our corpus and shows the sociocultural stigmatization that exists regarding taboo concepts and realities and the forbidden terms used to refer to them. The lexical items used to make direct, non-neutral, reference to natural body functions and the related body parts (*cagar, mear, pedo* and *culo*) can be used 'sometimes', which is justified, in spite of their lack of embarrassment, by the fact that they are natural. The dysphemistic use of expressions of the magical-religious sphere, forbidden by the taboo of fear, are perceived to have 'a certain use' due to their expressivity, which means that this is either a displaced reference (*¡hostia!* and *¡Virgen!* are presented as exclamatives), or a natural phenomenon (*muerto*). Finally, there appears to be no justification for the use of sexual dysphemisms, which infringe upon decency. Thus, most of our informants consider that they use them, on average, 'seldom' (*cojones, polla, cabrón* and *maricón*; *coño, tetas, puta* and *marimacho*; *follar* and *estar salido/a*).

As could be expected, the communicative situation determines the use of the expressions that concern us and the subjects' perception of it, according to established sociocultural conventions. A close relationship with the interlocutor (like those proposed above as informal situations) relaxes, to a certain extent, prohibitions due to embarrassment, fear or decency. Therefore, the participants in our corpus consider that, on average, in these situations, they use expressions such as the following between 'sometimes' and 'often': *culo* (an average of 3.60), *mear*

(3.41), *muerto* (3.36), *cabrón* (3.18) or *pedo* (3.17)[12]. Semiformal situations conditioned the consideration of an 'occasional' use (on average between 'seldom' and 'sometimes') of expressions such as *culo* (an average of 2.99), *muerto* (2.96), *mear* (2.70), *cabrón* (2.53), *pedo* (2.53), *coño* (2.33), *¡hostia!* (2.26), *tetas* (2.20), *cojones* (2.14), *puta* (2.13), *cagar* (2.13) or *maricón* (2.04)[13]. Finally, formal situations are generally considered to inhibit direct, non-neutral expression of a taboo; thus, the average use of the expressions with which we are concerned, with the exception of *muerto*, the most neutral of them, is never higher than 2 points, which means that the frequency of use by Madrid speakers is considered to be between 'never' and 'seldom'.

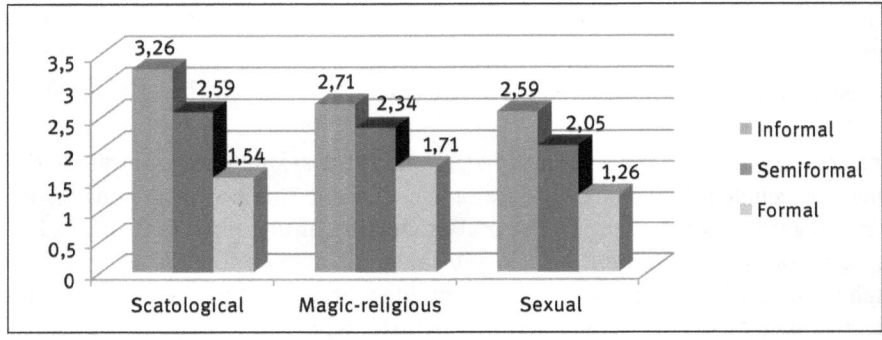

Graphic 2: Perception of expression: situations/registers

We find some of the data obtained in research particularly interesting, pointing directly to our informants' perception of levels of tabooization of realities and concepts, which, in turn, is related to the cognitive categorization of these realities and concepts.

The expressions belonging to the scatological sphere are decreasingly used depending on whether they refer to body parts or significantly, to defecation or urination. Therefore, '*culo*' is a lexical item apparently considered to be of frequent use since it is considered neutral; as alternatives, however, the participants propose direct, non-neutral, expressions that can be considered humorous (*pandero, ojete, posadera*) [*bum, little eye, situpon*] and more neutral and indirect expressions in which softening strategies are used (*glúteos [glutes], nalgas [buttocks], ano [anus], trasero [backside], cachas [cheeks], parte más baja de la*

---
12 The rest of the linguistic units included in our study had an average that was lower than 3.
13 The rest of the linguistic units included in our study had an average that was lower than 2.

espalda [tail], culete [bottom], culito [botty] o *pompis [derrière]*), always conditioned by the communicative situation. The three remaining expressions appear in order according to the type of excretion, from lesser to greater, which has a direct influence on the level of tabooization for reasons of embarrassment. Again, the subjects mentioned humorous dysphemistic expressions as alternatives, or more neutral euphemistic ones, always related to the level of formality of the communicative situation: for *mear, orinar [urinate], hacer necesidades [relieve oneself], cambiar el agua [pass water], hacer un alto técnico [take a leak], ir al baño [go to the bathroom], ir al servicio [go to the lavatory], ir al tigre [go to the loo], hacer pis [have a pee]* and *hacer pipí [do a wee]*; for *pedo, cuesco [bomber], ventolera [hot wind], escape nuclear [nuclear escape], bufado [parp], fuyo [poot], gas [gas], aire [wind], flatulencia [flatulence], caerse algo [let off]* and *pedete [stink bomb]*; and for *cagar, jiñar [crap], poner un huevo [drop a brick], descargar [drop a load], plantar un pino [pitch a log], liberar a Nelson Mandela [free Nelson Mandela], ir al baño [go to the bathroom], ir al excusado [go to the restroom], ir al tigre [go to the loo], defecar [defecate], evacuar [evacuate], hacer de vientre [have a bowel movement], hacer necesidades [relieve oneself], aguas mayores [number twos], hacer caca [do a poo], hacer popi [poop], hacer popó [poo]* and *dejar un regalo [leave a deposit]*.

Of the expressions in the magical-religious sphere included in our study, essentially tabooed for reasons of fear of the unknown or of higher beings, *¡hostia!* and *¡Virgen!* are used as interjections with a displaced reference and are considered by the speakers to be of very infrequent use *(¡Virgen!* is the least common, according to the informants, of all the expressions with which we have worked, which means it seems to have fallen into disuse, as well as having a high level of tabooization). For this reason, subjects consider it to be of some use only and suggest alternative interjections with similar values or functions, in the different situations proposed. These are either more widely used – and belong essentially to the sexual sphere – or euphemistic – the more formal the situation, the more indirect the expressions are – such as *¡¡joder! [fuck!]* or *¡¡jopé! [feck!]* or *¡¡joé! [freak!] ¡coño! [cunt!]* or *¡coña!, ¡contra!*[14], *¡ostras! [oysters!], ¡me cago en...! [I shit on/in...!], ¡una mierda! [shit!], ¡leche! [milk!], ¡Dios! [God!], ¡hombre! [man!], ¡macho! [man!], ¡vaya! [damn!], ¡bueno! [well/good!] , ¡anda! [wow!], ¡ahí va! [there it goes!] ¡bien! [well/good!], ¡buff! [Huh!]* or *¡ups! [oops!]*. The other expression included in this area, *muerto*, has a medium level of tabooization and, consequently, shows the considerable repercussion of the prohibition for reasons of

---

14 The preceding expressions are minced oaths substituting *cunt*. No English equivalent is available.

ancestral fear, since, although it is one of the terms that the informants consider to be most common, the average is no more than 3.5 points, and, more importantly, the use of the lexical item is usually orthophemistic or neutral. The people of Madrid who took part in the survey, suggest as alternatives some direct, non-neutral and notably humorous expressions – always in informal situations –, such as *tieso [stiff], irse al huerto [to be pushing up the daisies], palmar [snuff it]* and *"ha caducamigoado" [has passed his/her sell-by date]*[15], but, fundamentally, expressions considered to be more neutral and indirect, such as *fallecido [passed away], difunto [defunct], cadáver [corpse], fenecido [departed], finado [deceased]*[16].

Finally, regarding the words from the sexual sphere with which we have worked, we should emphasize that, referring to the informants' perceptions of use, the cognitive categorization of the realities alluded to is directly related to the level of sociocultural tabooization of these concepts or realities, and, as before, to the communicative situation. Generally, there is a perception of a lesser use, and therefore a higher level of tabooization for reasons of decency, of expressions alluding to women's sexual organs/attributes than those of men, and expressions referring to the sexual act or sexual desire are highly tabooed. However, this information must be put into context. The two dysphemistic expressions that appear to be most tabooed, according to the frequency of use in the study, are *marimacho [butch]* and *polla [dick]*. The first is used to refer to a woman's sexual condition, rather than an option, which, for its scant use in all situations, shows a clear sociocultural stigmatization, regarding both the condition and the linguistic interdiction. The informants suggest few alternatives, all of which are either dysphemistic or neutral: *machorra [dyke], bollera [butch], tortillera [lezzie] hombruna [masculine] camionera [lorry driver], chicazo [tomboy], parecer un hombre [look like a man], masculina [masculine], travelo [transvestite], lesbiana [lesbian], gay* and *homosexual*. It is interesting that the masculine equivalent, *maricón*, does not have the same level of stigmatization and, therefore, of tabooization, possibly due to a greater acceptance of the condition nowadays, to a different consideration towards this sexual orientation, or to its frequent use as an appellative, often indicating familiarity, among men. The more frequent perceived use means that the alternatives suggested are varied, going from the most direct and non-neutral to the most indirect: *amariconado [fairy], trucha [ponce], homosexual, gay, afemi-*

---

15 This expression was given by one informant but we have seen no other occurrence of it.
16 Some subjects showed an express dislike for this term.

nado [effeminate], *mariquita* [pansy], *mariposa* [poof], *sarasa* [faggot], *tener un poco de pluma* [to be a bit camp], or *panelista* [panellist][17].

Polla is the expression considered by the informants to be the least used in the sexual sphere. This is a dysphemistic reference to the male member and so it is not used in semi-formal or formal situations, and thus the speakers' perception of the frequency of its use is reduced. In this case, some direct, non-neutral, expressions are proposed: *pollón* [cock], *pito* [willy], *cacharro* [thing], *nabo* [dick], *cimbel* [prick] *pene* [penis], *órgano sexual* [sexual organ], *partes* [private parts] and *colita* [weenie]. Related to this expression we also find *cojones*, perceived to be used more often, especially in informal situations, but also rather stigmatized when not an exclamation; the subjects in our sample suggested the following alternatives: *huevos* [balls], *testículos* [testicles], *cuyons* [from the Catalan *collons*, bollocks] and *cataplines* [nuts]. The suggested lexical items for female sexual organs are a little less stigmatized and tabooed, judging by our informants' perception of greater frequency of use. As direct non-neutral, neutral and indirect alternatives, the corpus includes *fafarique* [fanny], *chocho* [twat], *chumino* [pussy], *seta* [muff], *vagina*, *vulva*, *partes* [private parts] and *chumi* [puss]. And, as alternatives to *tetas*, the most widely used expression, Madrid speakers propose: *ubres* [udders], *almendras* [almonds], *domingas* [boobs], *senos* [bosoms], *pechos* [breasts], and *pecho* [chest].

The expressions *follar* and *estar salido* are accompanied by a strong sense of stigmatization, indicating "primitive" and "animal" sexual acts and states which, therefore, debase the human condition. As alternatives to *follar*, subjects mentioned the following direct, non-neutral, neutral and indirect expressions *joder* [fuck], *chingar* [shag], *mojar* [get laid], *chiqui chiqui* [happy happy], *triki triki* [slap and tickle], *echar un polvo* [get laid], *pillar* [catch], *pinchar* [screw], *tirarse a...* [do...], *fornicar* [fornicate], *copular* [copulate], *hacer el amor* [make love], *relación sexual* [sexual relations], *acto sexual* [sex act], *tener sexo* [have sex], *tener relaciones* [have relations], *acostarse con...* [go to bed with ...], *hacer las paces* [make peace], *darle* [give... one] and *ir a Ávila* [go to Ávila, go all the way]. And, instead of *estar salido/a*, the subjects say they use the following dysphemistic, neutral and indirect expressions in informal situations: *estar más salido que otra cosa* [to be horny as hell], *estar más salido que la tapa de un piano* [to be hot to trot], *estar como el pico de una mesa* [to be up for it], *estar bruto* [to be ruttish], *estar salidorro* [to be turned on], *estar cachondo* [to be randy], *estar caliente* [to be hot], *estar*

---

[17] On the communicative, i.e. euphemistic and dysphemistic, functions that metaphors used to refer to homosexuals and homosexual-related issues perform in discourse, see Crespo (this volume).

excitado [to be excited], estar muy necesitado [to be in need], estar desesperado [to be desperate], estar alegre [to be happy], picar [to bang] and *mostrar demasiado interés [to show too much interest]*.

Finally, it would appear that *puta* is much more stigmatized than *cabrón*, which is directly related to the level of tabooization of expressions used to refer to undesirable sexual behavior, both in men and women, or to insult, expressively, based on a negative consideration which is an offence against decency. The perception of frequency of the lexical items reveals sociocultural values, as do the alternatives mentioned by our informants; for *puta*, direct, non-neutral expressions, essentially *golfa [slag], guarras [slut], zorra [vixen]* and *zorreta [little vixen], ramera [whore], bruja [witch], hija de puta [daughter of a bitch], putón [harlot], prostituta [prostitute], mujer de mala vida [loose woman], fresca [easy], prosti [pro], putilla [tramp], chica de la calle [street walker]* and *señorita de compañía [escort]*; and for *cabrón*, only other types of informal insults: *hijo puta [son of a bitch], maricón [faggot], capullo [prick], gilipollas [asshole], malo [evil], bicho [animal], malnacido [bastard], mala persona [wicked person], imbécil [imbecile], mendrugo [dimwit], cretino [cretin]* and *cabroncete [little sod]*.

Let us now examine the influence of the social characteristics of the speakers in their perception of their use of the expressions included in our study.

4 The perception of taboo: sociolinguistic conditioners

As could be foreseen, in accordance with the results of previous studies, women admit using direct expressions referring to taboo concepts or realities in a smaller proportion than men (an average of 1.88, compared with 2.24, meaning that women consider they never or seldom use these terms, and men, seldom or sometimes). These data are very significant, and show the existence, not only of the taboo, but also the social role assigned and self-assigned to women, even in the 21st century, which is consequently an identifying value. And, as was also expected, the frequency of use of forbidden terms is strongly conditioned by the register, included here through the characterization of the communicative situation. Thus, without exception, the direct, non-neutral, expressions dealt with here are used in informal situations, much less in semiformal situations and hardly ever in formal registers, according to the speakers' perception, which is a product of their sociolinguistic awareness.

The most strongly tabooed sphere, for both men and women – but always more so for women (an average of 1.72, as opposed to 2.07 for men) – is the sexual one, followed by the religious one (an average of 2.06 for women and 2.33 according to men) and finally the area of scatology (an average of 2.16 for women and 2.58 for men). This fact appears to be related to the fact that actions and items from the scatological domain are considered natural, as opposed to those of the sexual sphere, and to the exclamative use of the elements belonging to the religious sphere.

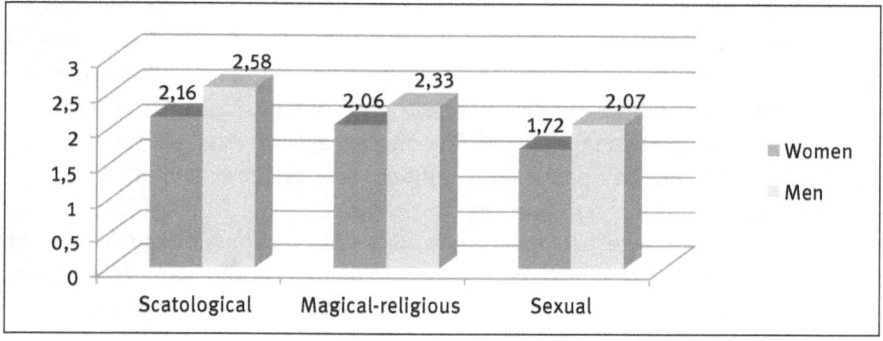

Graphic 3: Perception of the expression of taboo: gender and spheres

In spite of their being natural, actions and parts of the body belonging to the scatological sphere are tabooed by embarrassment, and women are more sensitive to this than men. The direct, non-neutral, expression for 'defecate' (*cagar*) is the most forbidden word, and presents a considerable difference in the average perceived use by men and women (an average of 1.78, as opposed to 2.86), although the greatest difference is found in the use of the expression for 'urinate', *mear* (2.02 *versus* 2.86), which indicates a high level of interdiction of scatological acts as far as women are concerned. However, the infrequent perceived use, both by women and men, of direct expressions like *muerto* is caused by fear. Furthermore a significantly smaller proportion of women use the interjection *¡hostia!* (1.66 as opposed to 2.48), although it is interesting to note that it is women who make a greater use of *¡Virgen!* (an average of 1.75, and 1.62 for men), which associates the religious sphere with the female condition.

The differences in frequency of perceived use by men and women of expressions belonging to the sexual sphere in our study are very interesting. Women consider that behaviour and body parts associated with men are more strongly tabooed, whereas the opposite is true for men, with the exception of the word *tetas*. In both cases female homosexuality is strongly tabooed, much more than masculine homosexuality, especially in men's perception. This is clearly reflected in the scant use of the direct expression *marimacho* (an average of 1.5 for women and 1.78 for men), which suggests a different conceptualization of this fact, strongly conditioned by social and cultural factors. The sexual act and sexual desire, according to our subjects, present a high level of tabooization, more so in women than men. Women consider that they make less frequent use of direct, non-neutral, expressions to refer to these facts (1.56, as opposed to 1.94, in the case of *follar*, and 1.73 against 1.79, in the case of *estar salido/a*).

Age is, once more, a conditioning factor in the perceived frequency of use of the expressions with which we are dealing. The level of tabooization of realities and concepts increases with age – or else it has decreased with the passing of time, that is, it is now lower than in the past. Moreover, as has already been established, it depends on the formality of the situation, which, in this case, leads to a strong interdiction in formal contexts. The only exception is in the level of tabooization on expressions belonging to the religious sphere, meaning that, according to the perception of our subjects, young people are more in fear of death and seem to have a greater respect for religious terms, as is shown by the differences in the use of *muerto*, (2.88 in young people, 2.77 in mature adults and 2.93 in older people) and of *¡Virgen!* (1.54 in young people, 1.67 in mature adults and 1.84 in older people).

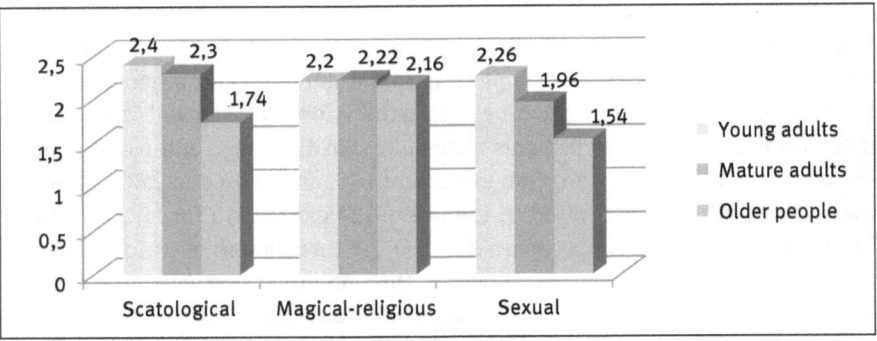

Graphic 4: Perception of the expression of taboo: age and spheres

The general behaviour patterns are those registered with regard to the use of direct, non-neutral, expressions belonging to the scatological sphere. The young people's perception reveals a lower level of tabooization, especially compared to that of older people, who give more importance to decency (an average of 2.40 in young people, as opposed to 2.30 in mature adults and 1.74 in older people). The most tabooed act is, again, defecation, especially for older people (an average of 1.64 for older people, 1.90 for mature adults, and 2.52 for young people). It is striking that, regarding the use of expressions in this sphere, young people consider that they make frequent use of *culo*, even in a formal register (an average of 2.34), which appears to suggest that this concept is nowadays associated with human anatomy rather than scatology.

Although we have also documented general patterns of perception with regard to expressions of the sexual sphere, and again among young people there seems to be a lower level of tabooization than with mature adults, and especially, than the older age group (an average of 2.26, compared with 1.96 for mature adults and 1.54 for older people), the results of the research are interesting and significant. The use of expressions referring to the sexual act or sexual desire are perceived as strictly forbidden by the older people and mature adults in our study, and less so by the youngest group; these data suggest that there is still tabooization for the sake of decency or modesty, even today and among young people, although it is more evident for the two older age groups, especially in informal and formal registers (see Pizarro Pedraza, this volume). Furthermore, young people consider female body parts to carry a stronger interdiction than male ones (*coño* and *tetas* are less used than *cojones* and *polla*) as opposed to the older groups for whom the reverse is true. In all three age groups, the direct allusion to undesirable feminine behaviour (*puta*) is considered to be more strongly forbidden than its male counterpart (*cabrón*), which shows a differing sociocultural concept of these behaviours, still existing even today. Finally, references to homosexuality (*maricón* and *marimacho*), especially the female variety, are strongly tabooed, although to a lesser extent for young people, which indicates a lower level of tabooization for reasons of modesty nowadays.

The informants' level of education also turned out to be a conditioning social factor in the perception of the use of direct non-neutral expressions and, consequently, in the level of tabooization of the realities and concepts to which they refer. Contrary to what could be expected, the averages suggest that those with an intermediate level of education consider that they make the greatest use of the forbidden expressions and lexical items included in our research (an average of 2.18, compared with 2.01 for subjects with a low level, and 2.00 for those with a high level), always with increasing tabooization at higher levels of formality in the communicative situation. This is true for the sexual and scatological spheres, but not for the religious one, as, in this case, the subjects with the lowest level of studies have a slightly higher average frequency of use, although this occurs with their use of the exclamations *¡hostia!* and *¡Virgen!* but not with the term *muerto*, which leads us to consider that interjective expressions have a pragmatic purpose rather than being an expression of taboos, and that the subjects with a lower level of education are more conditioned in their linguistic expression by fear, which decreases as education levels rise.

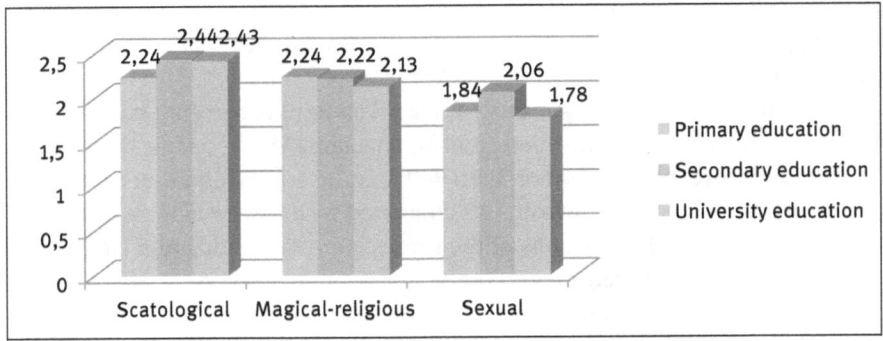

Graphic 5: Perception of the expression of taboo: education and spheres

As regards the scatological sphere, it is interesting to discover that, once more, defecation is the most tabooed action, and in our subjects' perception, the level of tabooization rises in proportion to the level of education (an average of 2.10 for those with primary education, 2.05 for those with secondary studies, and 1.90 for subjects with university studies). In other spheres, the opposite is true, and so the level of tabooization is reduced in proportion to the level of studies. Of these expressions, *pedo* seems to be subject to the strongest interdiction, followed by *mear*, and, finally, *culo*, which indicates a gradual categorization situating the part of the anatomy related to scatology on the periphery.

According to our informants, the sexual sphere is the most strongly tabooed. The general pattern of behaviour with regard to the direct expressions related to this area is more marked, and so, in all cases, the informants with secondary studies have the highest perceived use of these expressions, and thus appear to be rather less sensitive to the sociocultural conditioning imposed by decency. For those with the lowest level of education, the strongest interdiction applies to *estar salido/a* (an average of 1.55), followed by *marimacho* (1.60), *follar* (1.64) and *polla* (1.67). Therefore, they consider the sex act, female homosexuality, sexual desire and the male sex organ to be strongly tabooed; moreover, in this case, direct expressions regarding male genitalia are considered to be more strictly forbidden than those referring to female ones, and inappropriate sexual conduct in a woman (*puta*) is considered more taboo than that of a man (*cabrón*); likewise female homosexuality is more taboo than male homosexuality. These results are repeated for subjects with secondary studies, although, in this case, the most taboo expressions, in descending order, are as follows: *polla* (1.72), *marimacho* (1.82), *follar* (1.92) and *estar salido/a* (2.01). Finally, the informants with higher studies, who admit to the lowest level of use of direct non-neutral expressions, follow the same behaviour pattern, considering the term *polla* (1.42) to be the most strictly forbidden, followed by *marimacho* (1.50), *maricón* (1.63) *follar* (1.70) and *estar salido/a*, which means there is also a high level of tabooization regarding male homosexuality.

The data offered here show a level of tabooization of sexual, scatological and religious realities and concepts that is always high, above all in the sexual sphere, but which is variable according to the subjects' level of education. However, the last factor to be considered, the home district or residence of the informants, related to social class, has not proved to be so influential as the others. The subjects from Vallecas have a higher perceived use of the expressions included in our study, which reflects a lower perceived level of interdiction and, therefore, that the concepts and realities referred to are less taboo. However, the differences with regard to the informants of the Salamanca district are negligible.

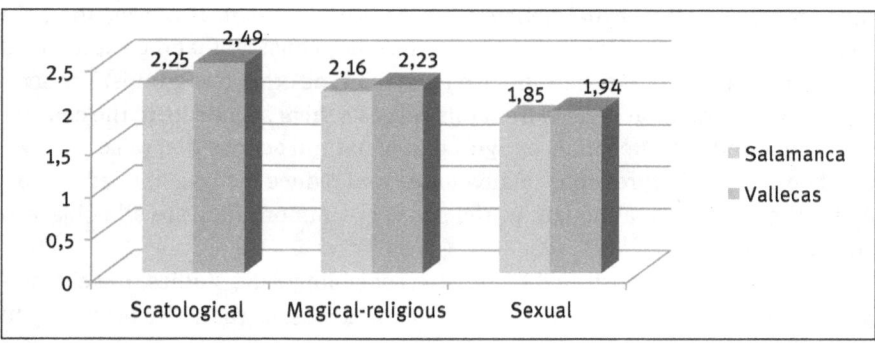

Graphic 6: Perception of the expression of taboo: Madrid district and spheres

It is interesting to note the cases in which the informants from Vallecas indicate a lesser use of certain expressions than those from the Salamanca district. Thus, it is noteworthy that the former seem more susceptible to fear and use the term *muerto* less than their counterparts from the Salamanca district, which could indicate a certain relationship between ancestral taboo and social class. Besides, for the Vallecas informants, the allusion to concepts and realities related to male sexuality are more tabooed than those related to female sexuality, whereas for those from the Salamanca district the reverse is true.

5 Conclusions

The results obtained in our research show that linguistic taboo still exists in the 21st century, albeit at different levels in the various spheres and conceptual areas, as well as in communicative situations, related to the pragmatic aim and the social factors that normally condition its use.

The study of the incidence of the social characteristics of the informants, more specifically gender, age and level of education has produced data of great interest highlighting the existence of sociopragmatic and sociocognitive patterns in their perception and the existence of expressions that refer to, or have referred to taboo realities and concepts. In this regard, it would seem significant that, in speech, in a semiformal register, the most strongly tabooed expressions are those belonging to the scatological sphere, followed by the religious one, and finally those relative to the sexual sphere (Cestero 2015a, 2015b). However, the subjects' perception of this is very different, since they consider that the expressions belonging to the sexual sphere are used less than the other two groups. The sociocognitive information derived from this suggests great sensitivity to the concept of decency and the categorial configuration of natural actions that raise the level of tabooization of expressions related to sex and reduce the level related to scatological expressions, although, in the subjects' opinion, they are all subject to strong interdiction.

As has been demonstrated by previous sociolinguistic studies, the communicative situation conditions the expression of taboos, so that, also according to the informants' perception, it is indeed possible to refer to concepts and realities related to sex, religion and death or scatological matters in informal contexts, but not in semiformal or formal ones, which shows the subjects' sociolinguistic awareness, as well as the level of tabooization of the concepts and realities and of their direct, non-neutral linguistic expression.

Finally, as has also been shown previously, according to the speakers' own perception, in general, men, young people and those with an intermediate level of education use more direct, non-neutral, expressions of taboo realities, although the sociopragmatic patterns that appear in the study are directly related to the informants' motivation for the interdiction (decency, embarrassment, fear or respect) and to the sociocultural and cognitive configuration of taboo realities and concepts.

References

Calvo Shadid, Annette. 2008. *Análisis sociolingüístico sobre el tabú sexual en el español de Costa Rica*. Bergen: Bergen University PhD thesis.
Calvo Shadid, Annette. 2011. Sobre el tabú, el tabú lingüístico y su estado de la cuestión. *Kañina* XXXV (2). 121–145. http://revistas.ucr.ac.cr/index.php/kanina/article/viewFile/558/617 (accessed May 2016).
Calvo Shadid, Annette. 2013. El tabú sexual en el español de Costa Rica: análisis sociolingüístico. *Kañina* XXXVII (1). 177–201. http://163.178.114.46/latindex/index.php/kanina/article/view/10582 (accessed May 2016).
Casas Gómez, Miguel. 1986. *La interdicción lingüística. Mecanismos del eufemismo y disfemismo*. Cádiz: Publications services of the University of Cádiz.
Casas Gómez, Miguel. 2012a. De una visión léxica y pragmático-discursiva a una dimensión cognitiva en la caracterización extralingüística y lingüística del eufemismo. In Marc Bonhomme, Mariela de la Torre & André Horak (eds.), *Études pragmático-discursives sur l'euphémisme*, 53–72. Frankfurt am Main: Peter Lang.
Casas Gómez, Miguel. 2012b. El realce expresivo como función eufemística: a propósito de la corrección política de ciertos usos lingüísticos. In Ursula Reutner & Elmar Schafroth (eds.). *Political Correctness*, 61–77. Frankfurt am Main: Peter Lang.
Cestero Mancera, Ana M. 2015a. Estudio sociolingüístico del tabú en el habla de Madrid: propuesta metodológica y primeros resultados. In Ana M. Cestero Mancera, Isabel Molina Martos & Florentino Paredes García (eds.). *Patrones sociolingüísticos de Madrid*, 287–348. Frankfurt am Main: Peter Lang
Cestero Mancera, Ana M. 2015b. "La expresión del tabú: estudio sociolingüístico", *Boletín de Filología* L (1). 71–105.
Crespo Fernández, Eliecer. 2007. *El eufemismo y el disfemismo. Procesos de manipulación del tabú en el lenguaje literario inglés*. Alicante: University of Alicante publications.
Contreras Fernández, Josefa. 2008. Test de hábitos sociales en un análisis contrastivo sobre el uso y la interpretación de la cortesía lingüística. In A. Briz Gómez et al. (eds.), *Cortesía y conversación: de lo escrito a lo oral. Actas del III Coloquio Internacional del Programa EDICE*. 642–656. Valencia: Universitat de València & Universitat Politècnica de València.
Drange, Eli-Marie Danbolt. 1997. *La mujer y el tabú. Un análisis sociolingüístico del tabú en el lenguaje femenino de Viña del Mar*. Bergen: Bergen University MA thesis.
Fernández de Molina Ortés, Elena. 2014. La presencia de eufemismos y disfemismos en el campo semántico del cuerpo humano. Estudio sociolingüístico. *Pragmalingüística* 22. 8–30.
López Morales, Humberto. 1990. *Sociolingüística del tabú. El caso de Puerto Rico*. Madrid: MS.
López Morales, Humberto. 1997. Papel del nivel sociocultural y del estilo lingüístico en el uso del eufemismo. In Francisco Moreno Fernández (ed.). *Trabajos de sociolingüística hispánica*, 27–33. Alcalá de Henares: Publications services of UAH.
López Morales, Humberto. 2001. Estratificación social del tabú lingüístico: el caso de Puerto Rico. *Estudios de lingüística del español* 13. http://elies.rediris.es/elies13/index.htm#indice / http://elies.rediris.es/elies13/lopez.htm (accessed May 2016).
López Morales, Humberto. 2005. Sociolingüística del tabú. *Interlingüística* 16 (1). 7–20. http://dialnet.unirioja.es/servlet/articulo?codigo=2514205 (accessed May 2016).

Martínez Valdueza, María del Pilar. 1995. *El tabú lingüístico: estudio sociolingüístico de Las Palmas de Gran Canaria*. Las Palmas de Gran Canaria: Las Palmas de Gran Canaria University PhD thesis.

Martínez Valdueza, María del Pilar. 1998. Status quaestionis: el tabú lingüístico. *Lingüística* 10. 115–139.

Montero Cartelle, Emilio. 1981. *El eufemismo en Galicia (Su comparación con otras áreas romances)*. Verba. Anuario Galego de Filología (Anexo 17). Santiago de Compostela.

Moreno Fernández, Francisco. 2012. *Sociolingüística cognitiva. Proposiciones, escolios y debates*. Madrid/Frankfurt: Iberoamericana/Vervuert.

Pizarro Pedraza, Andrea. 2013. *Tabú y eufemismo en la ciudad de Madrid. Estudio sociolingüístico-cognitivo de los conceptos sexuales*. Madrid: Universidad Complutense de Madrid PhD thesis. http://eprints.ucm.es/24937/1/T35255.pdf (accessed May 2016).

Uría Varela, Javier. 1997. *Tabú y eufemismo en latín*. Ámsterdam: A. M. Hakkert.

Part IV: **Interdisciplinary Approaches**

Habibollah Ghassemzadeh

14 Scrupulosity, sexual ruminations and cleaning in Obsessive – Compulsive Disorder

Abstract: A major goal of this chapter is an exploration of the nature of taboo and the concept of scrupulosity as appear in obsessive-compulsive disorder (OCD). There are many religious unacceptable thoughts and taboos, which show themselves in the forms of doubts, blasphemies, and moral transgressions with sexual nature. Sexual obsessions and ruminations with different forms and contents are one of the main sources of distress in OCD patients. In many cultures washing and cleaning has been advised to get rid of such distresses. One important aspect of washing in OCD is the fact that cleaning does not necessarily take place because of physical contaminations, as most often the individual is aware that his/her acts are excessive and senseless. As a conclusion, it has been emphasized that many aspects of obsessive-compulsive pattern of behavior have been shaped in the evolutionary history of mankind. Although these aspects might be considered as "pathological" today, they have probably had an adaptive function in the past.

Keywords: OCD, Scrupulosity, Sexual ruminations, Taboo, Washing

1 Introduction

My main purpose in this chapter is to explain some aspects of taboo as appear in obsessive-compulsive disorder (OCD). The word taboo, as Freud (1913/1919) has mentioned in his *Totem and Taboo,* is a Polynesian word, which diverges in two contrary directions. It stands for "sacred" and "consecrated" on the one hand, and for "forbidden" and "uncanny", on the other (p.30). In the continuation of the definition, Freud tries to challenge the idea proposed by Wundt (1912/2013) that "the division between sacred and unclean does not yet exist in the first primitive stages of taboo" (pp.41–42). According to Freud taboo as a prohibition is imposed from "without" (culture) and directed against the strongest desire of man and at the same time the desire to violate it continues in the unconscious. Therefore, individuals who are controlled by taboo have "an ambivalent feeling toward what is affected by the taboo" (p.54), and this ambivalence exists in all of the stages of primitive thinking.

Taboos are usually characterized by prohibitory norms. Incest and cannibalism are two important taboos that are considered to be universal. Touching or being in contact with human corpse is another example that often is considered unclean in some religions and requires a cleaning ritual by the person who touches the dead body. In some cases the violation of a taboo may attract a death penalty, while in others the violation can be rectified by performance of the appropriate purification ritual (such as praying or washing oneself).

A thesis proposed in this chapter is a possible connection between OCD and the concept of scrupulosity arising from the guilt feeling and rectified by performing some rituals such as praying, washing and some other acts. Freud may be the first psychologist to pay attention to a link between obsessions and scrupulosity as shows itself in OCD. To discuss the matter in detail, I start with a short description about OCD and then switch to the concept of scrupulosity. The last section will be devoted to washing ritual in OCD and religious traditions.

2 Obsessive-compulsive disorder

Obsessive-compulsive disorder (OCD) is characterized by recurrent, intrusive and unwanted thoughts or images that evoke an extreme distress in the sufferer (*obsessions*) and/or repetitive behavioral or mental rituals that are usually performed to reduce the evoked distress in the patient (*compulsions*).

Clinical features of OCD are manifested in the form of many symptoms or clusters of symptoms. Obsessions regarding contamination are combined with excessive washing and cleaning and obsessions regarding responsibility for harming others are combined with reassurance seeking and certainty which shows itself in the form of checking. Obsessional ruminations with aggressive, violent or sexual and blasphemous themes are usually combined with compulsions, either covert (mental neutralizing) or overt (repeating behaviors in a ritualistic manner). One of the main characteristics of OCD patients is that they often realize that their different obsessional concerns and neutralizing rituals are excessive, unnecessary and "senseless" but they feel forced to perform such intrusive and unwanted acts (Abramowitz 2006).

Assuming anxiety as the core element of OCD, it used to be classified in the category of anxiety-based or anxiety-related disorders in the past. But since DSM-5 (The *Diagnostic and Statistical Manual of Mental Disorders*, the reference manual by mental health professionals to diagnose mental disorders, starting from DSM-1) it has been removed from this category and has been included in a new classification of obsessive-compulsive disorder spectrum (OCDS) (APA 2013).

One of the themes of obsessions that will be discussed here is scrupulosity or as sometimes called "I am going to hell" condition.

2.1 Scrupulosity

The word scrupulosity is derived from the Latin *scrīpulum* (variant *scriptulum*) meaning a small, sharp stone or pebble which may cause discomfort if someone walk with such a thing in his/her shoes. Later, it was used metaphorically evaluating an action, a thought or feeling as sin where it should not be evaluated in such a way. Today, it means an uneasy feeling arising from conscience or principle that tends to hinder action, or moral and ethical consideration or standard that acts as a restraining force or inhibits certain actions (Ciarrocchi 1998). But we are dealing with the concept of scrupulosity as it happens in OCD.

The history of OCD as a psychological disorder starts with religious concerns. In the seventeenth century, obsessions and compulsions were explained as symptoms of religious melancholy. In *Anatomy of Melancholy*, Robert Burton reports a case which is very close to today's description of "pure obsession": "If he be in a silent auditory, as at a sermon, he is afraid he shall speak aloud and unaware, something indecent, unfit to be said" (1621, cited in Parmar and Shah 2014: 13). Later, in 1660, Jeremy Taylor explained something very similar to obsessional doubts and called them as "scruples". He defines scruples as a trouble when the trouble is over, a doubt when doubts are resolved (cited in Collins 1961). In 1691, John Moore, a Bishop, refers to some "Naughty, and sometimes blasphemous thoughts which start in the individuals minds, while they are exercised in the worship of God [despite] all their endeavors to stifle and suppress them... the more they struggle with them, the more they increase" (cited in Parmar and Shah 2014:13; Collins 1961).

Three of the greatest figures in Christian history suffered from what would now be called obsessive-compulsive disorder. The young Martin Luther had severe obsessional fears of loss of salvation and compulsions of repeated confessions and prayers. John Bunyan (http://www.ocdhistory.net/firsthand/bunyan.html), author of one of the most influential Puritan classics, *The Pilgrim's Progress*, suffered a serious struggle with OCD that at times became paralyzing. In this book he is describing his blasphemous thoughts that came to his mind posing questions against the very being of God. Saint Therese of Lisieux, the most influential and popular Catholic saint of modern times, developed OCD at age 11 and spent many years with such a disabling problem. She also had extreme doubts about God's existence and at the same time was trying to propose suffering as a prerequisite for salvation. Apparently, all three, after receiving some advice from church authorities, found a way to deal with their problem through developing what could be called "Christian therapy for OCD": trusting absolutely in God's power and mercy. In psychological terms, they allowed God to take responsibility for their obsessional fears (Collins 1961; Rachman and Hodgson 1980). Today we may refer to this type of therapy as a version of "spiritual therapy".

Although the whole picture of OCD has changed since seventeenth century, the concept of scrupulosity has remained more or less the same. Today, when we talk about OCD, one of the main categories of obsessive thoughts and urges is still scrupulosity, which literally means "fearing sin where there is none" (Abramowitz and Jacoby 2014). Part of this feeling has been rooted in the assumptions of some religious beliefs that human being is sinful by nature, and therefore, every individual is doomed to do something to "wash out" that sin.

There is variety of religious unacceptable thoughts and taboos, which show themselves in the forms of doubts, blasphemies, denial of God and moral transgressions. Some examples are: "Do I have sufficient faith in God?" "What if God does not help me to get rid of the problems?" "What if I kill my beloved person?" and "I will not be forgiven by God". The core themes of these thoughts are three mechanisms that make them extraordinarily difficult to tolerate. The first one is *fear of danger,* expecting that bad things will happen in the future (e.g. losing the loved ones). The second one is "the fusion of thought and action". For OCD patients, thinking has the same power, as well as the same value, of action. Therefore, thinking about something is more or less the same as doing that thing. The third mechanism is *perfectionism*, which reflects itself in excessive praying, repeating the rituals, and most importantly seeking unnecessary reassurance from religious figures or family members and friends. Individuals with such a burden try to avoid situations and stimuli that activate such patterns of behavior. In some cases, even good believers prefer to avoid praying and going to the places of worships. Avoidance, however, makes the situation worse. In fact, the opposite of avoidance, exposure, has been proved to be effective to resolve this problem (e.g. Clark 2004). In the framework of cognitive-behavior therapy (CBT) cognitive strategies may be used to challenge erroneous or irrational beliefs to "detoxify" the obsessions (Salkovskis 1999). For example, the patient is encouraged to accept the notion that scruples are just ruminations or temptations and not sins while allowing him/her to adhere to one's faith and spiritual practices. In the next step, the therapist asks the patient to list all blasphemous thoughts and record them on an audiotape and repeatedly listen to these thoughts. It is believed that a process called habituation or extinction happens in this way which leads to alleviation to anxiety (Ghassemzade, Rothbart and Posner, 2017; Purdon 2004).

Scrupulosity manifests itself in various ways such as general ego-dystonic intrusive thoughts about sex, violence and immoral acts; ego-dystonic thoughts specific to religion, such as using profane expression, about God or holy figures; obsessional thoughts about faithfulness and observing the religious rules correctly (Abramowitz and Jacoby 2014). Although it is difficult sometimes to distinguish scrupulosity from normal religious acts, one of the major characteristics of scrupulosity is its excessive, rigid, and ironic "selective" nature. Such an individual may concern with some aspects of faith and forget some other important aspects of it (e.g. the patient may experience extreme fear of being punished for having intrusive "impure" thoughts when she enters some religious places for worship. But this may force her to avoid such places altogether). Another difference is the degree of distress associated with scrupulosity, which is more severe than a usual violation of adherence as measured by some scales such as the Penn Inventory of Scrupulosity (Abramowitz et al. 2002).

Scrupulosity has been indicated as a common presentation of OCD. In Foa and Kozak's (1995) study, religious concern was the fifth most common theme among 425 OCD patients with 5.9 % of patients endorsing it as a primary obsessional symptom. But in our studies with 135 OCD patients in each study (Ghassemzadeh et al. 2002, 2005) we found blasphemous thoughts in 30 % and 34 % of our two samples in Iran. The rates were significantly higher in the men. However, as Olatunji et al. (2007) have mentioned, scrupulosity appears to be influenced by many factors such as the method used to measure it plus the individual's religious affiliation and level of devoutness. Although some scales have been developed, there are many unexplored areas in this regard (Abramowitz et al. 2004; Abramowitz et al. 2002; Olatunji et al. 2007).

2.2 Sexual obsessions

Individuals with OCD often feel ashamed about their obsessions and compulsions, and this shame can go even deeper when their obsessions are sexual, violent, or blasphemous. These taboo topics are difficult to talk about, and OCD sufferers sometimes wait to get help.

Sexual obsessions have been categorized as one of the main sources of distress in OCD (Ball, Baer, and Otto 1996; Gordon 2002). Although all forms of OCD can be paralyzing, sexual obsessions can be especially difficult to handle for sufferers because they constitute and shape one's fundamental identity as a social being. This symptom cluster may take many different forms with different contents. OCD patients report sexual obsessions as their primary symptoms (Foa et al. 1995). Current and lifetime prevalence of sexual obsessions among OCD individuals is 16.8 % and 26.3 %, respectively (Williams and Farris 2011). One particular form of sexual obsessions is sexual-orientation fears, which may include a fear of experiencing an unwanted change in sexual orientation, fear that others may perceive that one is homosexual, or fear that one has latent homosexual desires. Lifetime rates for homosexual obsessions have been reported at 9.9 % and 11.9 % among research and treatment-seeking populations, respectively (Pinto et al. 2008; Williams and Farris 2011).

In addition to anxiety, which is the most salient characteristic of most obsessions, individuals with sexual obsessions experience a high degree of guilt, shame, hopelessness, and depression, and often, mistakenly, consider themselves deviant, disgusting, or evil.

There is a basic difference between sexual fantasies that some of non-OCD people experience and the sexual obsessions in OCD, which are unpleasant and provoke guilt, rather than being enjoyable. As a result, the thoughts cause distress, which may be connected to unwanted emotions, such as lust, disgust, anger, and frequently guilt. This distress is directly related to the frequency of the sexual obsessions, and may lead to depression, difficulties in concentrating, and anxiety (Gordon 2002; Grant et al. 2006).

Sexual obsessions include various forbidden thoughts which are mostly ego-dystonic, intrusive, recurrent and persistent thoughts, images or concerns about sexual matters that do not usually prompt sexual behavior (Dell'Osso et al. 2012: 1). Intrusive thoughts, including sexual concerns occur in many non-clinical people, as well (Salkovskis and Harrison 1984). But normal individuals try to dismiss them or find a way to cope with the situation. In a study, Rachman and De Silva (1978) found some results suggesting that experience of obsessive thoughts is not an exclusive feature of OCD. However, as Rassin and Muris (2006:1068) have declared there are some clinical obsessions that can be identified as being abnormal and there are significant differences in content between clinical obsessions and their non-clinical counterparts. It seems the most important difference between two groups lies in the fact that obsessive ruminators try to evaluate their thoughts and images and for that reason they feel greater distress about their unacceptable thoughts.

Sexual obsessions can take many forms such as fears of being attracted to children, fears of engaging in a forbidden sexual activity, and bizarre sexual images. But the most distressful urges that come to the minds of OCD patients are sexual approach toward children, animals, and incest. They might experience intrusive images of sexual organs, imagining themselves performing unwanted and unacceptable sexual acts, or have persistent doubts about their own sexual or gender identity. Some of the experienced thoughts, images and urges may take a form of doubtful questions like: "What if I have an affair with that person?" "What if I expose my genitals to that person or to the public?" or "What if I lose control and act out sexually?" Most often, it is difficult for them to explain the situation verbally and they concern about the judgments that other people or even the therapist may make on their thoughts and urges (Abramowitz 2009; Hyman and Pedrick 2010). All of these thoughts are forbidden according to many religions and cultures and it is unlikely to happen in many cases but cause very serious distress leading to seek help at least in 10 % of patients (Foa et al. 1995). In our studies (Ghassemzadeh et al. 2002, 2005) we found sexual ruminations happening in 41 % and 39 % of our two OCD samples and the rate of these ruminations was almost equal in men and women. As mentioned before some sexual ruminations may happen in the normal subjects as well. But they are not usually evaluated and interpreted as something happening in an evil or sinful mind. It seems this happens when something is wrong with the normal psycho-sexual development.

Freud (1913) was the first to pay attention to the role of sex – in a very broad sense – in human "normal" and "abnormal" development. For Freud, unless an individual can accomplish the transition in his/her sexual life from the infantile auto-erotic interests characteristic of the oral, anal, and genital stages to a post-pubertal stage of sexual maturity at which he/she is able to relate his/her erotic desires to other human sentiments and attitudes of an altruistic or other – regarding nature, he/she cannot be said to have attained a condition of "normal sexual life" (Carr 1987).

2.3 Linguistic aspects of sexual taboos

One of the main manifestations of taboos happens in language. Language as the most important tool and/or mechanism of relationship and communication is very sensitive to any "violation" or "anomalies" considered as taboos. This sensitivity is notably salient in the case of sex and sex related words, particularly when they are supposed to be communicated by women. Even sometimes the word "woman" is considered equivalent to "sex". In some Middle-Eastern societies if a man wants to speak about his wife, he uses words such as "home", " mother of kids", "s/he – without indicating the gender", instead of her name.

The genital organs are always subject to some sort of taboo. The organs related to women are usually more tabooed and inhibited than those of men, and women are supposed to observe this kind of taboos more strongly than men. Linguistic taboos have their usage controlled by certain social, cultural and religious factors which implement their control through creating and monitoring some "rules", "norms", and "expectations". Therefore, most part of linguistic taboos takes the forms of euphemism: proverbs, idioms, metaphors, and paraphrases. In American culture, it was not very usual for ladies of the nineteenth century to use "breast" or "leg", not even of chicken. The words "white meat" and "dark meat" were used instead. It was not elegant to speak of "going to bed"; the word "to retire" was considered to be polite (Gao 2013). Although the situation has changed a lot after the sexual revolution of the 1960s, there are still many taboo words such as words related to bodily excretions, "four letter words" and swear words which are considered more or less as taboo words. Moreover, sexist language and racist language are still used in some books, journals and communications.

There are many expressions, which have been generated and used in Persian as well as Azeri languages that substitute sex and sex-related words. "Going to one (shared) bed", " sleeping together", " being in privacy", even in some contexts "being together" are examples of "dressed-up" terms which are used for having sex. These terms may be called as euphemisms as they are used to reduce the harshness of taboo words. But sometimes in some cases or situations other equivalent words or expressions are used which are not very elegant or polite, but still they are substitutions. The term "penetration" meaning to do something with some degree of force and pressure is just an example of this category of words.

In general, there is a mental set representing a cluster of attitudes toward sex in the "normal" population. One of the ways to have access to this cluster is using association tests. In an unpublished preliminary study (Ghassemzadeh et al. 2016) the investigators gave 67 female and 36 male students the word "sex" and asked them to write down the words that came to their minds. These words were considered as associated to the word "sex". Some of the frequent associated words in women were *pleasure* (27%), *love* (24%), *sexual relation* (17%), *peace of mind* (15%), *marriage* (9%), *friendship* (9%), *sleeping room* (7.5%), *feelings* (7.50%), and *needs* (7.5%), and in men were *pleasure* (36%), *peace of mind* (22%), *love* (11%), *sexual relation* (11%), *genital organ* (11%), *porn films* (11%), *breast* (8%), *lust* (8%), and *friendship* (8%). Some of the words that were absent (zero frequency) from the women associations were: *breast, genital organ, masturbation, fetish, bosom, porn films, sincerity, power, instinct, vaginal sex, anal sex, lip, fiancé, extramarital affair, aggression, anxiety, feet, dominance, elegance, sex position* and *sucking*, which occurred at least one time in the list of men. Although it is not possible to generalize the findings, it shows a kind of inhibitory mechanism in the women, which can be interpreted as the effect of taboos in their mind and as a representation of a more conservative attitude toward sex.

Violation of the taboos including sex taboos usually demands a process of purification that most often takes the form of washing in a ritualistic way. Washing may take place with two purposes: physical cleaning on the one hand and "spiritual" or psychological cleaning on the other.

2.4 Psychological aspects of washing

Physical cleansing has been advised in many life and religious situations. However, in many societies it has a specific cultural meaning, which goes beyond the concept of "cleanliness" in the usual sense. Baptism is a water purification ritual, which is practiced by Christians, Mandaeanists, and Sikhs. Christians follow the admonition, "Arise and be baptized, and wash away your sins". It is believed that with symbolic cleansing of their bodies they might also achieve a cleansing of conscience. In Islam, "wudu" ("ablution") or washing parts of the body is a necessary requirement to get ready for worship. Also, in Hinduism washing the body is very important. In general, washing the body in many religious traditions take place with the purpose of purifying the soul (Zhong and Liljenquist 2006: 1451).

Washing is also one of the major symptom clusters in OCD and often manifests itself as a compulsive pattern of behavior. OCD compulsions are repetitive behaviors that an individual feels driven to perform. These repetitive behaviors are performed to prevent or reduce anxiety related to obsessive urges or to prevent something dangerous to happen. Compulsions include the themes such as washing and cleaning, checking, counting, reassurance seeking, hoarding and orderliness. One of the most common types of compulsions is washing and cleaning compulsion in which individuals repeatedly wash themselves (Jenike, Baer and Minichiello 1990).

Compulsive hand washing or hand sanitizer use is so prevalent in OCD that "washers" has become a widely accepted category of OCD patients. The urge commonly stems from a fear of germs (the most common obsession seen in OCD), but it also can be rooted in fears of making others sick or of being impure or immoral. This pattern of behavior can become excessive, at times resulting in raw and broken skin. In some cases washing in the bathroom may take several hours, during which the individual washes the different parts of his/her body according to rigid ritual rules. Excessive washing may show itself as excessive showering, bathing, tooth brushing, grooming, toilet routines, and cleaning household items.

One important aspect of washing in OCD is the fact that cleaning does not take place because of physical contaminations, as most often the individual is aware that his/her acts are excessive and senseless. As a matter of fact, an OCD patient washes himself/herself to get rid of the anxiety and distresses which arise because of some touching of or thinking about something which has been labeled as dirty and has been inhibited in the society (Krapp and König 2015; Zhong and Liljenquist 2006). As our studies on the prevalence of obsessions and compulsions in two samples of Iranian OCD patients show (Ghassemzadeh et al. 2002,

2005) washing was the most prevalent compulsive symptom, which happens in 72% and 73% of the total groups (study 1 and study 2, respectively). Most of the washers were women (82% in the first study and 84% in the second one). Both of them were significantly higher than the number of washers in the men (45% in the first group and 49% in the second). Our reports were consistent with reports from other Middle-Eastern settings (Mahgoub and Abdel-Hafiz 1991; Okasha, et al. 1998) but different from some Western settings where compulsive checking (repeated and ritualistic checking to make sure that things have been done in a correct way) was more common than compulsive washing (Antony, Downie and Swinson 1998; Foa et al.1998).

To get rid of contamination takes many forms: avoiding dirt, germs, poison (fear that food is poisoned), doorknobs, electric switchers, newspapers, and pollution from more specific contaminants like urine, feces, seminal fluid, animal fur, dust, sweat, and blood. Cleaning rituals may take the form of repetitive washing of hands, feet, whole body, doorknobs, chairs, and walls for several hours, and/or washing and cleaning according to a rigid manner: for example washing the arms five times carefully while asking someone else to keep the track of the number of times and more importantly, to reassure the individual that he/she is now clean.

Washing and cleaning behavior, in general, has a sense of restitution or putting things right. In Iranian culture, washing behavior has an additional connotation of restoring "spiritual purity". A practice of religious faith requires a symbolic cleaning and washing ritual in preparation for daily prayers. This washing ritual is not identical with bodily cleaning as such; rather, it symbolizes spiritual purification. Washing compulsions also sometimes carry this symbolic meaning.

2.5 Semantic implications

One factor that contributes to the linguistic aspects of OCD in general and washing compulsion in particular, is the psycho-semantic aspect of the term in Persian language. The word for obsessive-compulsive in Persian is *waswas* (originally from the Arabic root *waswaseh*-whisper, temptation). In the context of the religious ritual, *waswas* often refers to excessive doubts about the proper and orderly completion of the cleaning ritual in preparation for prayer or the prayer itself. The individual may find it hard to terminate the cleaning ritual or doubt whether the right words have been recited the right number of times. Occasional doubts are not rare and there are some religious instructions to resolve them. But when the doubts become excessive and/or interfere with the other activities of daily life, they are considered to be abnormal and as manifestations of *waswaseh*. Excessive doubting is often attributed to the devil's temptation and religious teachings instruct to "seek refuge from these temptations in God" and ignoring the doubts completely. In a more secular sense, however, the term *waswas* in Persian daily language has a positive implication, referring to such attributes as carefulness, conscientiousness and orderliness to the point of perfectionism. A mild cleanness and washing *waswas* in a housewife or a mild orderliness *waswas* in a student might be treated as a positive character. In such cases, the boundaries of normal and pathological are not always clear.

In many Middle-Eastern cultures being clean semantically means two different and yet related things. They are different because the origins of distress are basically different. They are similar because in both cases washing and cleaning are the necessary response to get rid of it. Washing may mean: 1) to get rid of germs, dirt, and any other contaminations, which may cause disease or harm (type-I); and 2) to get the feeling of being clean enough to carry out the prayer in an acceptable manner (type-II). It is the latter type, called *Tahareh* which may cause more distress, as it relates to the internal feeling of purification and piety.

Tahareh is not identical with body cleanliness as such; it has a spiritual component attached to it. A number of different events may interfere with *Taharah* including contact with dirty and contaminated objects, sexual contact or even touching a member of opposite sex (Ghassemzadeh et al. 2002, 2005).

Some of OCD patients refer to the clergy to make sure that their prayer is acceptable. In these cases, getting contaminated means to be guilty or "bad" and some type of "symbolic" processing of cleanliness is going on in the mind of the patient. While the patients of type-I try to avoid sources of contamination like public restrooms and doorknobs, type-II patients try to avoid themselves and some of them think that their own body is the dirtiest thing in the world. In one of our studies 67 % had fear of impurity (mostly women), 58 % had fear of contamination (also mostly women), 57 % had the feeling of self-devaluation, and 30 % had the feeling of self-impurity (again mostly women) (Ghassemzadeh et al. 2005).

In some cultures the use of ceremonies may be explained as means of placating anxiety and fears provoked by the presence of natural phenomena that are unexplainable to man. A ceremony or a ritual pattern is a careful elaborated attention to form and detail. Ceremonies are performed to emphasize rules of hygiene, to celebrate past events in a social context, or to worship God. Ceremonies are seen in the hand washing performed during the Catholic mass, a form of purification, or in the hand washing of the Romans to excuse themselves from responsibilities (e.g. Pontius Pilate), and also in the hand washing of a patient who has just touched a contaminated object (Taryura-Tobias and Neziroglu 1983:

1). The main point is that one of the important factors in the continuation of the rituals is the assurance and feeling of certainty which are produced as a result of purification which, in turn, acts as a reinforcement of the rituals.

3 "Macbeth effect"

The psychological and moral aspects of washing have also been studied in normal individuals. Many studies, which have been done in the framework of embodiment theory (the idea that cognitive activities in the human beings happen in relation to the sensory-perceptual processes), have shown this effect. In one of their studies, Zhong and Liljenquist (2006) asked the participants to recall an ethical or unethical deed from their past and explain any feelings that they could relate to them. Then they participated in a word completion task, which could be completed as words related or unrelated to cleansing. They found that participants who recalled unethical deed responded more with cleansing words than the other group. It seems that recalling bad memories lead the subject to try to wash out the negative emotion related to it. In the second study the participants were asked to hand-copy a short story written in the first person in which an ethical good deed (such as helping someone) or an unethical deed (such as sabotaging a co-worker) should be described. Then the participants were asked to rate the desirability of some products including cleansing products such as Dove soap or other categories such as Energizer batteries, from 1 to 7 – (low to high). Writing the unethical story increased the desirability of cleansing products as compared to writing down the ethical story. In the third study, the procedures of the first and the second study were combined. The participants were asked to engage in the recall task and were offered a gift either an antiseptic wipe or a pencil. Again, those who recalled an unethical act mostly took the antiseptic wipe.

Based on these studies we may hypothesize that a need for physical cleansing in many cases is dependent on an exposure to our feeling about moral threats. In the fourth study, the participants described an unethical act and after that either cleansed their hands with an antiseptic wipe or not. Then they were asked if they were interested in a good volunteer activity. It was found that physical cleansing significantly reduced volunteerism.

What can be learned from these four studies? It seems there is an association between physical and psychological cleanness and this association possesses a compensatory nature, at least with the direction from morality toward physicality. In other words, threats to moral cleanness activate a need to physical cleansing. Zhong and Liljenquist (2006) refer to this mechanism as "Macbeth effect", as Lady Macbeth – in Shakespeare's famous play – was looking for a little bit of water to wash away her bloodied conscience. She was crying: "Out, damned spot! Out, I say!"(p.1451). There is a parallel between the emotion we experience in dealing with physical contaminations on the one hand, and moral transgressions on the other. This kind of association finds its manifestation in facial expression (such as oral-nasal rejection in disgusting situations), activation of overlapping neural networks, subjective feeling, and language use. For example we have expressions such as "dirty hands", "dirty language words", "pure heart", "pure life" and "pure conscience". Just as we want to clean our body part when we are in touch with a physical contaminant, we want to clean the body part involved in a moral transgression (Lee and Schwarz 2011:308). It has also been suggested that cleaning may wash all our past memories. Then, the metaphoric concept of "washing away one's sins" seems to reflect a generalized notion of "wiping the slate clean" (Lee and Schwarz 2010).

There have been some explanations about such an association. Anderson (2010) has proposed the terminology of "neural reuse" emphasizing on the evolutionary role of disgust responses, which kept the animal away from health-threatening contaminants. In the framework of conceptual metaphor and embodiment theory the abstract moral purity is grounded on a physical ground of experience (Lakoff and Johnson 1980/2003, 1999; Landau, Meier and Keefer 2010). In any case, once a concept such as " dirty", "clean" or "pure" is generated it does not remain in its limited area of language usage rather it goes beyond and explain many things on the basis of similarity, relevance, category, extension of meaning and structural mapping (Gentner and Markman 1997; Ghassemzadeh 1999; Glucksberg 2010).

4 General conclusions

Unacceptable thoughts tend to be ego-dystonic with a repugnant nature. These are thoughts that have been shaped and evolved in the history of mankind. Dealing with such forbidden themes has always been dependent on the level of our understanding of mental life of individuals on the one hand and on the social life of the people on the other. The concept of scrupulosity that had once been considered as a sin, today is a symptom of OCD and the therapists are trying to help the patients to view these ruminations and urges not as sin or guilt, but as something that may happen in the minds of many including OCD as well as non-OCD individuals. Therefore, it is subject to an intervention and change.

However, there is an issue here which should be emphasized and that is the concept of "normality". It is very difficult to propose a comprehensive and categorical definition of normality as it has varied over time and across different societies. So many behaviors that were forbidden a few decades or even a few years ago have been adopted in the value system of today's communities. Tolerance has become one of the most important concepts in the real life of people today. One of the best expressions of tolerance is actualized in language. Words as Vygotsky (1962) has explicitly stated are not just something happening at the linguistic level. They have evolved in the thinking process along with powerful emotional and motivational processes happening in the human brain. Taboos in the languages are the product of many cognitive, emotional and motivational mechanisms that play an important role in the daily activities. To change these taboos so many underlying mechanisms, including the concept of "abnormality" should change.

Regardless of the status of human being in the ladder of evolution, science and technology, each person lives in a concrete situation with specific demands and constraints. The representation of the world in the mind of individuals is based on sensory-motor experiences. Even for the most abstract ideas there are experiential bases, which can be found in the life history of the people (Lakoff and Johnson 1999). In the real world, we are dealing with real environment, real relationships, and real people.

Many aspects of obsessive-compulsive pattern of behavior have arisen as an adaptive response in the evolutionary history of mankind and might have had an important function in the survival of human being. Although many ideas of Freud have been a subject of criticism today, his idea about the nature of mental "pathology" is interesting. He believes that the difference between "normal" repression and the kind of repression which results in neurotic illness is one of degree, not of kind. Many aspects of obsessive-compulsive pattern of behavior exist in our daily life, in different religious activities, as they were salient in the primitive societies. As Rapoport and Fiske (1998) have properly stated, " People conduct culturally meaningful rituals when they need to create, affirm, and coordinate the meaning of an ambigous or stressful situation..."(p.171). This is exactly what happens in OCD cases, although it may not be "adaptive" anymore!

References

Abramowitz, Jonathan S. 2006. The psychological treatment of obsessive-compulsive disorder. *Canadian Journal of Psychiatry* 7. 407–716.

Abramowitz, Jonathan S. 2009. *Getting over OCD*. New York: Guilford Press.

Abramowitz, Jonathan S., Brett J. Deacon, Carol M. Woods, David F. Tolin. 2004. Association between protestant religiosity and obsessive-compulsive symptoms and cognitions. *Depression and Anxiety* 20. 70–76.

Abramowitz, Jonathan S., Jonathan D. Huppert, Adam B. Cohen, David F. Tolin & Shawn P. Cahill. 2002. Religious obsessions and compulsions in a non-clinical sample: The Penn Inventory of Scrupulosity (PIOS). *Behaviour Research and Therapy* 40. 825–838.

Abramowitz, Jonathan S. and Jacoby, Ryan J. 2014. Scrupulosity: A cognitive-behavioral analysis and implications for treatment. *Journal of Obsessive-Compulsive and Related Disorder* 3. 140–149.

Al-Issa, I. and Oudji, S. 1998. Culture and anxiety disorders. In S.S. Kazarian and D.R. Ivans (Eds.), *Cultural clinical psychology – Theory, research and practice*. New York: Oxford University Press. 127–141.

American Psychiatric Association. 2013. *Diagnostic and Statistical Manual of Mental Disorders*. 5 ed., Washington, DC: American Psychiatric Publishing.

Anderson, Michael L. 2010. Neural re-use: A fundamental organizational principle of the brain. *Behavioral and Brain Sciences* 33. 1–69.

Antony, Martin M., Fiona Downie & Richard P. Swinson. 1998. Diagnostic issues and epidemiology in obsessive-compulsive disorder. In R.P. Swinson, S. Rachman, and M.A. Richter (Eds), *Obsessive-compulsive disorder: Theory, research and treatment*. New York: Guilford Press. 3–32.

Ball, Susan G., Lee Baer, Michael W. Otto. 1996. Symptom subtypes of obsessive-compulsive disorder in behavioral treatment studies: A quantitative review. *Behaviour Research and Therapy* 34. 47–51.

Carr, David. 1987. Freud and sexual ethics. *Philosophy*, 62, 361–373.

Ciarrocchi, Joseph W. 1998. Religion, scrupulosity, and obsessive-compulsive disorder. In M.A. Jenike, L. Baer and W.E. Minichiello (Eds.). *Obsessive-compulsive disorders- Practical management* (3 ed), 555–569. St. Louis: Mosby.

Clark, David A. 2004. *Cognitive-behavioral therapy for OCD*. New York: Guilford Press.

Collins, Eduardo F. 1961. *The Treatment of scrupulosity in the Summa Moralis of St. Antoninus: A historical-theological study*. Rome: Pontificia Universitas Gregoriana dissertation.

Dell'Osso, Liliana, Giulia Casu, Marina Carlini, Ciro Conversano, Paola Gremigni & Claudia Carmassi 2012. Sexual obsessions and suicidal behaviors in patients with mood disorders, panic disorders and schizophrenia. *Annals of General Psychiatry* 11. 1–9.

Foa, Edna B., & Michael J. Kozak.1985. Treatment of anxiety disorders: Implications for psychopathology. In A. H. Tuma and J. D. Maser (Eds.), *Anxiety and the anxiety disorders*. Hillsdale, NJ: Erlbaum. 421–452.

Foa, Edna, Michael J. Kozak, Wayne K. Goodman, Eric Hollander, Michael A. Jenike & S.A. Rasmussen. 1995. DSM-IV field trial: Obsessive-compulsive disorder. *American Journal of Psychiatry* 152. 90–96.

Foa, Edna B., Michael J. Kozak, Paul M. Salkovskis, Meredith Coles and N. Amir. 1998. The validation of a new obsessive–compulsive disorder scale: The obsessive–compulsive inventory. *Psychological Assessment* 10. 206–214.

Freud, Sigmund. 1913/1919. *Totem and taboo*. New York: Moffat Yard and Company.

Gao, Chunming. 2013. A Sociolinguistic study of English taboo language. *Theory and Practice in Language Studies* 3. 2310–2314.

Gentner, Dedre & Arthur B. Markman. 1997. Structure mapping in analogy and similarity. *American Psychologist* 62. 45–56.

Ghassemzadeh, Habibollah. 1999. Some reflections on metaphor and metaphoric processing: A move toward meta-sign formulation. *New Ideas in Psychology* 17. 41–54.

Ghassemzadeh, Habibollah, Akram Khamseh & Nargess Ebrahimkhani. 2005. Demographic variables and clinical features of obsessive-compulsive disorder in Iran: A second report. In B.E. Ling (Ed.), *Obsessive-compulsive disorder research*, 243–271. New York: Nova Science Publishers.

Ghassemzadeh, Habibollah, Ramin Mojtabai, Akram Khamseh, Nargess Ebrahimkhani & Zahra Saif-Nobakht. 2002. Symptoms of obsessive-compulsive disorder in a sample of Iranian patients. *International Journal of Social Psychiatry* 48. 20–28.

Ghassemzadeh, H., Raisi, F., Firoozikhojatefar, R. and Karamghadiri, N., Yahyavi, S. T. 2016. A preliminary study on the words related to the concept of "Sex". Unpublished manuscript. Roozbeh hospital, Tehran University of Medical Sciences. Tehran.

Ghassemzadeh, Habibollah. Rothbart, M.K. and Posner, Michael. I. 2017. Mechanisms of response prevention and the use of exposure as therapy for obsessive-compulsive disorder. *Int J Psychiatry* 2, 1–8.

Glucksberg, Sam. 2001. *Understanding figurative language- From metaphors to idioms*. Oxford: Oxford University Press.

Gordon, William M. 2002. Sexual obsessions and OCD. *Sexual and Relationship Therapy* 17.343–354.

Jon E. Grant, Anthony Pinto, Matthew Gunnip, Maria C. Mancebo, Jane L. Eisen, Steven A. Rasmussen. 2006. Sexual obsessions and clinical correlates in adults with obsessive-compulsive disorder. *Comprehensive Psychiatry* 47. 325–329.

Hyman, Bruce M. and Cherry Pedrick. 2010. *The OCD workbook*. Oakland, CA.: New Harbinger Publications, Inc.

Jenike, Michael A., Lee Baer, and William E. Minichiello. 1990. *Obsessive-compulsive disorders: Theory and management*. Chicago: Year Book Medica Publishers.

Krapp, Kai, Vanessa Krapp & Peter König. 2015. Hand washing induces a clean slate effect in moral judgments: A pupillometry and eye-tracking study. *Scientific Reports*, 5:10471 | DOI: 10.1038/srep10471, 1–10.

Lakoff, George & Mark Johnson. 1980/2003. *Metaphors we live by*. Chicago: University of Chicago Press.

Lakoff, George and Mark Johnson.1999. *Philosophy in the flesh: The embodied mind and its challenge to Western thought*. New York: Basic Books.

Landau, Mark J., Brian P. Meier & Lucas A. Keefer. 2010. A metaphor-enriched social cognition. *Psychological Bulletin*. 136. 1045–1067.

Lee, Spike W.S. & Norbert Schwarz. 2010. Washing away post-decisional dissonance. *Science* 328. 709.

Lee, Spike W.S. & Norbert Schwarz. 2011. Wiping the slate clean: Psychological consequences of physical cleaning. *Current Directions in Psychological Science* 20. 307–311.

Mahgoub, Osama M. & Hassan B. Abdel-Hafiz.1991. Patterns of obsessive-compulsive disorder in Easter Saudi Arabia. *British Journal of Psychiatry* 158. 840–842.

Okasha, A., Khalil, A.H., El Dawla, A.S., Folstein, M, F. and McHugh, P.R. (994. Phenomenology of obsessive-compulsive disorder. *Acta Psychiatrica Scandinavica* 89. 191–197.

Olatunji, Bunmi O. , Jonathan S. Abramowitz, Nathan L. Williams, Kevin M. Connolly & Jeffrey M. Lohr. 2007. Scrupulosity and obsessive-compulsive symptoms: Confirmatory factor analysis and validity of the Penn Inventory of Scrupulosity. *Journal of Anxiety Disorders* 2. 771–787.

Parmar, M. and Shah, N. 2014. Phenomenology of obsessive compulsive disorder. *International Journal of Pharmaceutical and Medical Research* 2. 13–23.

Pinto, Anthony, Benjamin D. Greenberg, Marco A. Grados, O. Joseph Bienvenu, 3rd, Jack F. Samuels, Dennis L. Murphy et al. 2008. Further development of YBOCS dimensions in the OCD collaborative genetics study: Symptoms vs. categories. *Psychiatry Research* 160. 83–93.

Purdon, Christine. 2004. Cognitive-behavioral treatment of repugnant obsessions. *Journal of Clinical Psychology* 60. 1169–1180.

Rachman, Stanley J. and Ray J. Hodgson. 1980. *Obsessions and compulsions*. Englewood Cliffs, NJ: Prentice Hall.

Rachman, Stanley J. and Padmal De Silva. 1978. Abnormal and normal obsessions. *Behaviour Research and Therapy* 16. 233–248.

Rapoport, Judith L. & Alan Fiske. 1998. The new biology of obsessive-compulsive disorder: Implications for evolutionary psychology. *Perspectives in Biology and Medicine* 41. 159–175.

Rassin, Eric and Peter Muris. 2006. Abnormal and normal obsession: A reconsideration. *Behaviour Research and Therapy* 45. 1065–1070.

Salkovskis, Paul M. 1999. Understanding and treating obsessive-compulsive disorder. *Behavior Research and Therapy Supplement, 37*, S29-S52

Salkovskis, Paul M. and Jimm Harrison. 1984. Abnormal and normal obsessions: A replication. *Behaviour Research and Therapy* 22. 549–552.

Vygotsky, Lev S. 1962. *Thought and language*. Cambridge. Mass: MIT Press.

Williams, Monica T. and Samantha G. Farris. 2011. Sexual Orientation Obsessions in Obsessive-Compulsive Disorder: Prevalence and Correlates, *Psychiatry Research* 187. 156–159.

Wundt, Wilhelm. 1912/2007. *Elements of folk psychology – Outline of a psychological history of the development of mankind*. London: George Allen and Unwin LTD.

Yaryura,-Tobias, Jose A. and Fugen A. Neziruglu. 1983. *Obsessive-compulsive disorders- Pathogenesis, diagnosis, and treatment*. New York: Marcel Dekker.

Zhong, Chen-Bo and Katie Liljenquist. 2006. Washing away your sins: Threatened morality and physical cleansing. *Science* 313. 1451–1452.

Shlomit Ritz Finkelstein
15 Swearing as emotion acts
Lessons from Tourette syndrome

Abstract: This chapter explores swearing as *emotion acts*, speech acts that express and evoke emotions. The chapter focuses on a special kind of such acts – the involuntary verbal and gestural swearing of the neuropsychiatric disorder Tourette syndrome (TS).

Examined within the framework of pragmatics, behavioral data suggest that, by adhering to the Gricean rules while simultaneously violating the sociocultural norms of the society, TS-related involuntary swearing becomes an effective speech act. In violating norms, the automatic behavior of swearing demonstrates great sensitivity to them and to their relevance to the specific situation in which the swearing occurs.

The consequences of swearing, as the data show, can be very harmful. Automaticity contributes to the effects of the swearing on both speaker and hearer. Not only is the speaker's behavior mostly involuntary; the hearer's negative reaction to the speaker is often involuntary too. When the hearer responds non-automatically and considers the challenges of the speaker, the communication can change and reduce the harm done by the swearing to both speaker and hearer.

Keywords: Swearing, speech acts, pragmatics , coprolalia, emotion acts, Tourette syndrome (TS)

The 19th century British neurologist John Hughlings Jackson (1958) observes, "We scarcely say anything when we swear, although we utter words in relation." Indeed, swearing differs from other forms and usage of language. While words often denote objects and actions, describe events and share ideas, swearing does not. Swearing uses language to express and evoke emotions; often the emotions are negative, but sometimes they are positive as in in-group swearing that can express affection. Words that name emotions rarely evoke them: *Fear, disgust,* and *sexual desire* denote emotions but typically do not elicit them. Swearing does.

This chapter shares some data and ideas with Finkelstein et al. (2016).

https://doi.org/10.1515/9783110582758-016

1 Emotion Acts

Here we explore swearing as *emotion acts*, a sub-category of speech acts, which like other speech acts, act! They are special, as we will see later, in that their acts are that of expressing and evoking emotions. We focus on a special kind of swearing – *coprolalia*, the involuntary swearing of Tourette syndrome (TS), and *copropraxia*, the gestural swearing of TS, collectively referred to as *coprophenomena*.

Like all speech acts, swearing affects both the speaker and the hearer[1]. To be effective, coprophenomena simultaneously obey the pragmatic Gricean cooperative principle and challenge the cultural values by violating social norms. We examine the effect of coprophenomena on their speaker and hearers and the automaticities involved in performing these emotion acts and responding to them.

We start with introducing TS.

1.1 Tourette syndrome

Tourette syndrome (TS) is a neuropsychiatric disorder (APA 2013). According to its current definition its onset is before the age of 18 years, and more males are afflicted than females, with a ratio of about 3–4:1 (Tanner 2005). The understanding of TS has changed since it was described in the 19th century by the French neurologist Gilles de la Tourette. Until the 1960s TS was understood as psychogenic. In the second half of the 20th century the psychogenic paradigm was replaced by a biological paradigm (Kushner 1999). But despite advancements in understanding the neurobiology of TS it does not have yet any definite biological markers (Fernandez and State 2013) and its etiology – the cause of the disorder – is not known.

Therefore, TS is diagnosed by the patient's phenotype, by its signs and symptoms[2]. The most obvious signs of TS are the tics, which are sudden, rapid, recurrent nonrhythmic movements, or vocalizations. Both the motor and the vocal, some of which are a subset of the motor, can be simple tics that last only milliseconds, or can be complex tics that last seconds and be quite elaborate. The motor tics include and are not limited to eye blinking, shoulder shrugging, squinting, and hopping. The vocal tics include and are not limited to throat clearing, sniffing, and barking (Leckman et al., 1999).

---

[1] *Speaker* and *hearer* are used generically without regards to the modality used.
[2] Signs are objective observables like temperature or rash, or a certain behavior. Symptoms are subjective and can be known only through the report of the patient, like pain or nightmares.

1.1.1 Coprolalia

The most complex vocal tics of TS are *coprolalia*, which afflict less than 20 % of the TS population (Freeman 2007). The word *coprolalia* was coined by Gilles de la Tourette after the Greek *kopros* – 'excrement', and *lalia* – 'speech'. While he considered coprolalia as "always obscene" (cited in Meige and Feindel 1907/1990: 224), today it is widely accepted that "essentially it is a symptom that expresses something that is socially unacceptable... [C]oprolalia can be racial slurs, religious improprieties, political innuendoes, derogatory remarks, use of another person's name, or any other method of expressing something socially unacceptable or forbidden" (Shapiro et al. 1988: 151).

Coprolalia, then, is not limited to a specific semantic space. Instead, it mirrors the culture whose values it challenges by violating behavioral norms. And it does so in every possible way – by relying on semantics, prosody, hearer's social status, or any other aspect of discourse that is culturally defined. For example, Japanese speakers afflicted with TS and coprolalia often swear only with prosody as in Japanese culture, prosody can be socially inappropriate and very insulting even when the vocabulary is "clean." (Baron-Cohen and Robertson 1998).

Cultural values, of course, are not abstracts in a vacuum. They define situations, apply to them, and over time are informed and modified by them. We will see that the cultural sensitivity of the coprolaliac is demonstrated situationally. For example, racial slurs are typically uttered in racially mixed company and seldom otherwise (Chiten et al. 1994). Later we will examine specific data to further establish that coprolalia, despite being involuntary, is sensitive to the culture that it violates and to the specific situation within which the socially inappropriate utterances are relevant.

1.1.2 Copropraxia

Communicative behavior is not limited to the vocal modality. Gestures are considered by most linguists as integrated into language (McNeill 1996). In a study of adults with TS (Finkelstein 2009), Ted[3] raised his middle finger at the interviewer; the gentle and polite Dylan did the same; when Stuart was asked about his gestural coprolalia – copropraxia – the very question evoked the raising of his middle finger; Donna reported of many occasions of copropraxia; and Claire squeezed her breasts often and with great force.

---

[3] All the names are fictitious to protect the identity of the interviewees.

Compared to coprolalia, copropraxia is rare. In a 2008 study of close to 600 TS patients (Freeman et al. 2008), copropraxia was observed 3 times less than coprolalia. In a much smaller study, interviewing 16 adults with TS (Finkelstein 2009), all who suffered from copropraxia suffered also from coprolalia, but not vice versa. Therefore, there is much less data about copropraxia, and most of this chapter will discuss coprolalia. Towards the end we will reflect on the difference of the rate of occurrence between the two modalities and suggest a cultural-pragmatic explanation for it.

2 The pragmatics of coprolalia

Individuals with TS respond to social situations and the TS's signs are exacerbated by social stress (Leckman et al. 2013). Of all the tics associated with TS, coprolalia is the most socio-cultural phenomenon. Later we present data suggesting that the connection with culture is so deep and automatic that even though it embarrasses its utterers greatly and is experienced by many as involuntary, it is often very effective in providing release to the speaker and insult to the hearer. Its effect depends on deeply rooted knowledge of the speaker's culture, and on the speaker's sensitivity to the specific situation that provides the opportunity to violate the culture.

2.1 Coprolalia in situations

Most of the situations that trigger coprolalia include other people (Finkelstein 2009): Ted says, "people stimulate me," and indeed in many social situations he violates norms, always in a manner relevant to the specific situation: Black people evoke "nigger;" fat women evoke "you are so fucking fat;" a gay friend evokes "want to suck your dick;" and a woman with large breasts evokes "you got big tits." Dylan too demonstrates great sensitivity to the social situation and to the strong cultural prohibition on racist remarks and sexual harassment. "Spick" is reserved for his Hispanic physician; "nigger" for his black friends or a black passersby; and "I want to have sex with you" to the woman who exercises on the treadmill next to him. Neil is a psychiatrist:

> The worst was when I was a new... practitioner, [and the hospital] have me speaking about something... I [started] the lecture... with a joke... I was telling the audience [nuns and other nurses], that one reason I like [to speak about] movement disorders is because I have my own movement disorder.

> I have Tourette syndrome. I used to hate it but one day I asked my wife, 'honey... how can you stand living with me?' And she says, 'honey it's ok as long as you don't start saying fuck you bitch fuck you bitch.' As soon as... I got into the bitch part I said, 'I can't believe I just did that' and half the audience was in hysterics; the other half was staring at me like 'I cannot believe this man is up there. How dare you?'

Reflecting on this episode, Neil observed the situatedness of the event: "I probably blurt out things that are mostly true, in *settings* that they shouldn't be said."

Daniel's family is Christian fundamentalist, and for many years he was homeschooled. His coprolalia then was limited to his family's strict domestic culture. The worst words and phrases he knew were the family-forbidden "shut up" and "dudu" and these two made up his entire coprolalia. As he grew up and started to meet other children, his coprolaliac vocabulary expanded. With his exposure to a culture beyond his domestic one, Daniel learned more words, including culturally inappropriate ones. As he expanded his swearing vocabulary, he also internalized their tabooness and they were added to the pool of utterances that made up his coprolalia (Finkelstein 2009).

When the target of coprolalia is God, the rules of communication change even though there is still an interlocutor who is assumed to be present, to listen, and to understand. The culture is still present too, but the situations are different and therefore the pragmatics might change. David was raised Catholic and attended a Catholic school, but in high school he became atheist: "I had 'internal' coprolalia. I used to curse God all the time. It was scary because I believed God heard my internal coprolalia against Him. When I became atheist it stopped." When turning atheist, the situation between David and God did not exist anymore. As a Catholic, he could often violate his culture. As an atheist, no God-David situations and no God-cursing prohibitions existed. His God-directed coprolalia ended.

As a boy, David violated the most sacred values of his culture. Daniel, Dylan, and Neil insulted their human audience effectively. They represent the many more who are afflicted with coprolalia.

2.2 Social consequences of coprolalia

Violating the values of the culture with proscribed utterances can be intensely embarrassing. The 18th century French neurologist Jean Marc Gaspar Itard describes his patient the Marquise de Dampierre in the first documented case of coprolalia:

> In the midst of a conversation that interests her extremely, all of a sudden, without being able to prevent it, she interrupts what she is saying or what she is listening to with bizarre shouts and with words that are even more extraordinary and which make a deplorable contrast with her intellect and her distinguished manners. These words are for the most part gross swear words and obscene epithets and, something that is no less embarrassing for her than for the listeners (cited in and translated by Kushner 1999: 10).

The consequences can go beyond embarrassment: Donna cannot get a job and was threatened with eviction from her apartment. Ted lost his job of fifteen years after calling a customer "nigger." And to avoid such consequences, the coprolaliac often avoids public places like movies, cafes, libraries, or shopping malls. (Finkelstein 2009).

The coprolaliac is often stigmatized (Finkelstein, 2009). Social stigma greatly exacerbates stress; therefore, the signs and symptoms of all the tics, including coprolalia, get more frequent and intense; and the stigma deepens to produce greater stress – a vicious circle.

In his book *Stigma*, the sociologist Erving Goffman recognizes three kinds of people. Those who are stigmatized, those who stigmatize, and those who see the other not through the lens of a stigma. The latter he calls *wise*: "Wise persons are the marginal men before whom the individual with a fault need feel no shame nor exert self-control, knowing that in spite of his failing he will be seen as an ordinary other." (Goffman 1963). Later, we will discuss with some detail two examples of such wise friends in their dyadic interactions with the afflicted.

In a 2012 empirical study Rachel A. Smith tested the Goffman's categorization in relation to stigma (Small 2016; Smith 2012). Based on her findings she refined the category of the *wise* into *educating stigmatizers* and *challenging stigmatization*. The Tourette syndrome Association (TSA) has been *educating the stigmatizers* for decades by making the disorder better known to the general public and better understood. In some American schools, afflicted children or their parents are invited to introduce TS to their classmates with some successes, in which the stigma has diminished and made room for acceptance and empathy (Conners 2009).

Brad Cohen[4], himself with severe TS, has *challenged the stigmatizers* with great success. In *Front of the Class* he describes how his applications to teach in elementary school were repeatedly rejected. He persisted and continued to apply for a teaching position even though each rejection became more hurtful, presented a greater challenge to his self, and decreased his hope to succeed. When

---

4 Real name.

finally a school in Georgia accepted him he ended up an award-winning teacher and a teachers' teacher. (Cohen and Wyscocky 2005).

Most members of society are stigmatizers. Goffman recognizes it and therefore calls them *normals*. The wise, as he taught us above, are marginal. The normality of stigmatization is most likely due to its automaticity, what Goffman (Goffman 1963) refers to as *reflexive and embodied* like much of our social behavior.[5]

2.3 Is coprolalia automatic?

The emotion acts of coprolalia are often automatic in that they precede the feeling – the consciousness of the emotion; but not always.[6]

When Stuart was 19, a black man murdered his brother. "[This murder] engrained some racial negative stereotypes towards black people" and therefore black people often trigger swearing. By contrast, Dylan insists that he could not have any racial stereotypes since many of his friends are black. His father, though, is not so sure: "Some of his friends are black," says the father, "but the last 30 years living in the South may have developed some attitude along the way to start thinking in [racial] direction." Some of Dylan's insults seem to be intended in defining his social territory: "Somebody that I don't know... I'll tic more towards them..." And if there are several new people, the one that Dylan likes the least gets the most swears. Claire who often screams "nigger!" says, "I have a lot of black friend[s]." And when she is asked whether it matters if she likes the person or not, she first screams and then answers, "O gosh! No it don't matter. It don't matter." Steven refers to his coprolalia as "coprolalia contradiction... because it contradicts everything I want to say. Because I, if I look at someone and insult him, which had happened before, it's the opposite of what I think of that person." The intention, Steven says, is not there. Stuart thinks that his coprolalia is "not *completely* involuntary... [The tic] can be suppressed to some degree." And then he demonstrates a singing of "I'm a little faggot, yes I am, I eat shit as fast as I

---

[5] The study of stigma is theoretically and empirically rich and closely related to studies of prejudice and stereotyping. But despite their often negative social implications, they can be shown to have some evolutionary advantages. The scope of this chapter does not allow a further discussion of this topic.

[6] The neurologist Antonio Damasio distinguishes between emotions and feelings. Emotions are neurological processes that only when they interact with the neurological processes defining the self, rise to the level of consciousness and become feelings (Damasio 2000). As the distinction is sometimes difficult and as whenever there are feelings there are preceding emotions, I use mostly *emotions*.

can" to the tune of "I'm a little teapot." He laughs and adds, "With my father I sing this song. I can see that it aggravates him [because he hates my homosexuality]." (Finkelstein 2009).

Automaticity, intentionality, volition, and awareness are an active topic of research. In current research on TS, the main experimental paradigm for studying such complex relations combines different types of brain imaging capturing the temporal and spatial properties of neural activity. A review of this literature is beyond the scope of this paper. We confine our discussion within a behavioral-psychological-sociolinguistic framework.

Whether intended or not, some who cannot suppress their coprolalia try to disguise it. Henry covers his swearing under stuttering that otherwise he does not have. When he speaks about the "4-letter word" he stutters and deforms the word, almost to non-recognition. When Lionel started to swear at the age of 8, he tried "muttering the things under my breath." Kyle's "fuck, fuck" is so soft and melodic that it takes a while to recognize it for what it is. In addition, while "I will say [the] 4-letter word, and G-D, and bitch, and M-F," he says, he does not utter racial slurs. "I live in a black neighborhood. I don't think that will be good." (Finkelstein 2009).

Others who can suppress some of their swearing for a while try to minimize the public impact and leave the worst for a more private environment. Elaine Shimberg, a mother of a child with TS, reports, "coprolalia often is worse at home, when the individual feels safer" (Shimberg 1995: :31). Lionel, after disguising or suppressing his coprolalia in public, screams it out when he comes home or goes out to the woods. But even after the worst is reserved for home, what remains is embarrassing, and socially isolating.

Ted who cannot suppress his swearing tries substitution. He often replaces *nigger* with *Nick*, and *bitch* with *witch*. Sometimes he succeeds, but sometimes he fails, as when he lost his job, calling a client *nigger*. Dylan disguises his copropraxia: After raising his middle finger at his interviewer, he continues the middle-finger gesture as though to brush his hair from his forehead. Steven has achieved complete substitution replacing his *fuck, shit, nigger,* and *fucking slut* with a grunt: "I got rid of it by turning it all into grunts, all of it." However he does not know how long this solution will last (Finkelstein 2009).

A common disguise for coprolalia is humor. In the height of his pain and embarrassment after uncontrollably writing *shit* on the blackboard and causing his classmates to laugh at him, Cory Friedman got the idea that

> it will be better if I make it look like I'm doing everything on purpose, as a joke. The kids will think that I am funny and not just weird. So I make a few more silly faces, including a dopey grin. This makes the kids laugh again. I laugh along with them... I am feeling so

bad... But I also realize for the first time that I can get kids to laugh *with* me instead of *at* me when I do something inappropriate. I can become the class clown (Patterson and Friedman 2008: :40).

With a similar approach, Chuck started his "raspy-froggy" voices at a summer camp before his fourth grade. This earned him the title of the "froggy man," which he enjoyed. But not for long. After a while it got on everybody's nerves (Finkelstein 2009).

Some comedians and humorists with TS seem to have used similar strategies. Dan Ackroyd, who rose to stardom on *Saturday Night Live*, spoke with NPR's Terry Gross about his TS. He told her how he approached many of his problems by covering them up "with humor." (Gross 2004). In *Naked*, the American comedian David Sedaris describes his childhood with TS and obsessive-compulsive disorder (OCD)[7] (Sedaris 1997). Humor might reduce some of the social embarrassment but still leaves the experience of loneliness and isolation. And even though humor often serves as a protective shield, it can become involuntary and out of the control of the self: "If I can change myself," says Neil the psychiatrist, "that's a thing [, being funny, that] I would change." The shielding behavior, be it motor or verbal, sometimes turns into a new form of involuntary and uncontrolled behavior, into a new tic.

3 Coprolalia is an effective speech act

There are various levels of automaticity to coprolalia, as we saw, and accordingly, the success of suppressing or disguising it varies. Whether automatic or voluntary, partially suppressed or not, coprolalia hurts its audience. In return, the embarrassment and other possible penalties to the speaker are great and match the intensity of the insult to the hearers.

Coprolalia is an effective speech act whose power depends on the combination of obeying the Gricean cooperative principle and being sensitive to the cultural values and social norms so they can be violated. The pragmatic sensitivities of speaker and hearer and the adherence of the speaker to the Gricean cooperative principle establish cooperation between speaker and hearers in the sense that the

---

[7] OCD is often comorbid with TS. However, its signs typically differ from the "stand alone" OCD in that the contamination fear, which is common in OCD, is rarely present in the OCD that is comorbid with TS.

utterance is well understood, semantically and culturally. Therefore, when the utterance challenges the cultural values by violating social norms, the violation is obvious and the utterance hurts.

We will examine now the perspectives of both the speaker and the hearer and how their interaction contributes to the effectiveness of coprolalia as a speech act.

3.1 The speaker

The power of coprolalia as emotion act depends on four characteristics: First, coprolalia meticulously adheres to the four cooperative maxims of Grice: quality, quantity, relevance, and manner (Grice 1989). *Quality* – The utterance is true. "Fat woman" points to a fat woman. "Nigger" points to a black person. "I want to suck your dick" is directed by a man to a gay man. The other three maxims are clearly followed too: *Quantity* – The information provided is minimal and sufficient; just the right amount. *Relation* – The coprolalia is always relevant to the situation. And finally *Manner* – The speaker is perspicuous. There is no ambiguity, no obscurity.

Second, as we saw, while this communication follows the principle of cooperation, it simultaneously constitutes the most inappropriate messages that challenge cultural values by violating social norms.

Third, coprolalia, along with other forms of swearing, is a speech act that gets very close to the physical action of hitting. In that I follow Hughlings Jackson who said, "he who was the first to abuse his fellow-man [with swearing] instead of knocking out his brains without a word, laid thereby the basis of civilization." (Jackson 1958: :179). To the best of my knowledge, no studies have examined the possibility of following the four Gricean maxims in analyzing the rules of effective violence, but we can notice the similarity between applying the Gricean maxims in speech and in violent actions: The *Quality* is true in the sense that the action of hitting a target really happens. The *Quantity* is minimal. Often a person hits and typically does not stay involved in the physical encounter beyond this. The *Relation*, the relevance to the situation, is present as the very act of violence defines the situation. And the *Manner* is unambiguous; hitting is neither a hug nor a kiss. On its face, at least, it seems the four maxims that often define a speech act also often define a violent act.

Finally, in addition to the unlikely marriage between following the Gricean maxims and violating the social norms, coprolalia violates another pragmatic rule – that of turn taking (for example see Sacks et al. 1974). This is characteristic to all tics; they erupt and interrupt. Because motor tics, like excessive blinking or hopping, with the exception of copropraxia, have no social meaning, they might annoy some but they do not insult. By contrast, the combination of breaking the rule of turn-taking and effectively applying the Gricean principles to challenge social norms is not welcomed by the hearers. How inappropriate this threesome can be is demonstrated by the following event: Ted is Jewish, and one year, when the entire congregation gathered in the synagogue for the Jewish High Holidays, Ted interrupted the most sacred prayer with "I love Jesus." How concise in its meaning, how challenging to the values of this congregation, and how most disruptive in this particular time (Finkelstein 2009).

3.2 The hearer

There are two ways for a hearer to understand an utterance – by its semantics and by the intention of its speaker (Noveck and Reboul 2008). Often the two agree, but not always. The power of swearing and its ability to harm depend on how the hearer interprets the intention of the speaker (Allan 2016).

We observed the role of automaticity in the coprolalia of the speaker. But this is not the only automaticity in the delivery of swearing. The interpretation of the utterance by the hearer plays a role too. Along with acquiring one's native language and becoming enculturated, young children develop the indispensable skill of joint attention with their interlocutor and the ability to assign intentions to others (Tomasello 1999). As the child develops and grows, these abilities become automatic – quick and effortless. They are crucial to our interactions with others but their automaticity can become an obstacle when the semantics of an utterance and the intention of the speaker are in conflict; as Steven says, "coprolalia contradiction."

As with every undoing of automatic behavior, assigning a benign intention to a coprolaliac who swears is cognitively effortful. The hearer is required to perform a Stroop-like task[8] – to separate a strong and automatic association between the

---

[8] When the psychologist John Ridley Stroop asked college students to read the words PURPLE BROWN RED BLUE GREEN presented in ink colors different from their names (E.g., PURPLE was written in red), it took the students longer to read the words than when they were in black ink, and longer than it took to name colors that were presented just as painted squares. Stroop concluded that the (automatic) association formed through life exposure between a word and its meaning is stronger than the association formed between perceiving a color and identifying it. Therefore, dissociating the word – a color name – from its meaning – the perception of a color – was effortful and required more time than when such a dissociation of the established automaticity was not called for.

meaning of a word and the intention of its utterer. This is the distinction called for by Noveck and Reboul (2008) and when semantics and intention are incompatible, this is an effortful task. Often, as we saw, the intention of the coprolaliac is harmless.

Stroop training[9] teaches us that we can counter the automatic interpretation by automating the suppression of this interpretation (Stroop 1935). Some family members, friends, health professionals, and empathic individuals make the effort and accomplish such suppression. When Dylan, Caucasian, calls his best friend, who is black, "nigger," his friend responds with, "I am a nigger and you are a nigger." They laugh and hug and it brings an end to the emotional impact of the "nigger," which is not uttered again until the next meeting (Finkelstein 2009). Their friendship is long enough that Dylan's friend has had the opportunity to train himself to create a new cognitive process in which he suppresses the automatic association <'nigger' is an insult> with a new association:

> [The utterer of 'nigger' is Dylan + Dylan cannot control it; he has TS + Dylan is my friend; he does not intend to hurt me] → <This 'nigger' is not an insult>.

This process is effortful and Dylan is lucky to have a friend who values their friendship enough to be willing to invest such cognitive effort.

Kyle's friend Monica was his roommate. She stopped hearing his swearing. It seems she has trained herself to suppress the automatic association between certain strings of syllables and their meaning when uttered by Kyle. Instead she associated them with non-words. Kyle is not always this fortunate. His stepfather has never attempted to go through the cognitive self-training that would allow him to interpret Kyle's behavior as benign. He "thought that [Kyle] was just doing it to get on his nerves." (Finkelstein 2009).

In a typical speaker-hearer dyad, the speaker's utterances and intention are aligned and in agreement. Much of the utterance, including the choice of words, is voluntary. The hearer's interpretation of the speaker's intention is automatic (Sperber and Wilson 2002). To alleviate the suffering and embarrassment of those who involuntarily utter coprolalia, the hearer is invited to take on the burden of this dyadic interaction. The non-automatic part of the interaction should shift from speaker to hearer, as the speaker cannot carry this burden. Since now the

---

[9] In a consecutive experiment, Stroop trained the participants to perform the task of naming the ink color. The time performance shortened with training. Stroop interpreted the results as forming a *new automatic process*, suppressing the association of reading a word in favor of performing a new automatic association of identifying the ink color. Training made the color-name association more automatic and therefore less effortful and requiring less time.

speaker acts automatically, it is the hearer who needs to interpret the utterance non-automatically in order to cancel, or at least reduce, the harmful power of the coprolaliac speech act.

As long as both the speaker and the hearer act automatically, coprolalia is effective.

4 Copropraxia

Before concluding, we should revisit copropraxia. Gestures are part of language (McNeill 1996; Kendon 2000; Goldin-Meadow 2008). Like words, they can be used for communication and are culturally constructed and shared. Like with words, different cultures use different gestures to convey the same meaning. For example, the palm-back V sign, neutral or even positive in the US, has an obscene meaning and is inappropriate in Great Britain and Australia. Its American equivalent is a raised middle finger. The British who suffer from copropraxia gesture palm-back V sign. The Americans do not; instead they raise their middle finger (Morris et al. 2000).

Cognitively, gestures are more primitive than words. Some of them are beat gestures, many other are iconic and require only a simple mapping of resemblance (McNeill 1996). Often they do not require the full intricate and supportive network of linguistic symbols. Gestures also seem to be more automatic than speech as is suggested by the familiar scene in which a person speaking on the phone gestures enthusiastically or angrily to someone who cannot see her (de Rutter 1995).

It is therefore counterintuitive that the speech-form coprolalia is more common than the gesture-form copropraxia (Freeman et al. 2008; Shapiro et al. 1988). But what seems at first a paradox supports the centrality of culture in coprophenomena.

4.1 Coprolalia or copropraxia?

We saw many examples of how sensitive to the culture and the specific situation coprophenomena are. This sensitivity is demonstrated also in minimizing the *praxia* in favor of *lalia* – in swearing less with gestures than with words. There is almost always social penalty for coprophenomena, but the penalty for gestures might be harsher than for utterances since gestures are physical and might present greater threat to their target than words, and therefore might lead to a harsher response. Despite the automaticity involved in coprophenomena, it seems the coprolaliac often succeeds in preferring words over gestures. While control over coprophenomena is often lacking, we have seen that sometimes some control exists, even if only in part. We remember the example of Kyle who lives in a black neighborhood and succeeds in limiting himself only to sexual profanities. He avoids racial slurs, "I don't think that [racial slurs] will be good." (Finkelstein 2009). It is possible that a similar partial control is also activated to prefer the less damaging coprolalia over copropraxia.

Some consider speech as preventing physical violence. We remember Hughlings Jackson's words that swearing *replaces* violence and decreases harm. This can be observed in our close cousins. In *Our Inner Ape*, the primatologist Frans de Waal describes how a group of female chimpanzees barked at an alpha male to prevent him from attacking another male. The female violent vocalization *replaced* physical violence. "Had he [the alpha male] failed to stop, there would *undoubtedly* have been concerted *action* to end the disturbance." (de Waal 2005: 76, our italics).

Gestures, being physical, might trigger a violent response. Coprolalia – a special case of harming a fellow human by swearing – might point to a step in the evolution of human civilization in which physical acts have been replaced with speech acts. In this special form of swearing, possible violent acts are replaced by emotion acts. As painful as speech acts can be to the hearer and in turn to the speaker, they do not kill. Knowing the relations between acts and speech acts is part of being enculturated, and the coprolaliac, we have seen, is highly attuned to his culture. Thus, copropraxia occurs seldom, much less than coprolalia.

5 Discussion

Automaticity, as we saw, plays a central role in coprophenomena. Pragmatically, two built-in automatic conflicting processes contribute to these phenomena: On one hand the speaker adheres to the four maxims of the Gricean principle of cooperation and on the other hand s/he violates the cultural values and the norms of the society. For a full effect, though, coprolalia also relies on an automatic interpretation of the coprolaliac utterance by the hearer. Only when the hearer associates the utterance with the intention of its speaker, does the utterance hurt the hearer and in turn embarrasses the speaker. Because the coprolaliac, even when applying some strategies to disguise the tics or even postpone them, is a prisoner of his automaticity, it is left to the hearer, who is not afflicted with TS, to break out of her automatic interpretation of the coprolaliac utterance in order to minimize its effect as a hurtful speech act.

5.1 Coprophenomena are not random

The simultaneous adherence to pragmatic rules and violation of values that we discussed above is puzzling. Indeed, despite much data and millions of dollars invested in research (for instance, see https://www.tourette.org/), coprolalia is still a mystery. In an attempt to understand the phenomenon of coprolalia, Marc Nuwer suggests that it is just another tic as "certain obscenities are a concatenation of high-probability sequences of letters or phonemes." (Nuwer 1982: 366). In other words, Nuwer attempts to explain coprolalia not based on the socio-linguistic principles of pragmatics but as a vocal tic – a special motor tic – that takes a form which is highly present in the language. Van Lancker and Cummings tested Nuwer's claim. Their analysis concludes that the distribution of phonemes in English "is unable to account for coprolaliac utterances." (1999: 92). The data in the Finkelstein's (Finkelstein 2009) study support the relevance, rather than mere randomness, of coprolalia to culture and situations. Coprolaliac utterances are highly specific and socio-culturally contextualized.

Further support for the non-randomness of coprolalia might be provided by a rare case of coprolalia in a deaf man. Morris and colleagues describe a 29-year-old man who was found to be profoundly deaf at the age of 10 months. He learned sign language at the age of 7, and "when he mixed with children with normal hearing, he learned the obscene palm-back V sign and this was incorporated into his repertoire of tics." (Morris et al. 2000: 319). The young man's coprolalia was demonstrated in a non-verbal modality[10] and could not be considered as due to a high frequency sequence "of letters or phonemes."

Coprolalia is not random. As we have seen, it occurs within the context of specific cultural prohibitions and social situations. It demonstrates a degree of automaticity in the sense that speakers are compelled to produce these utterances and often hearers are compelled to understand them in certain ways. One major question for future study is how involuntary it is. What is the nature of the spectrum between Steven's "coprolalia contradiction" and Stuart's "With my father I sing this song. I can see that it aggravates him."

---

10 In sign communication there is a continuum between signing and gesturing that includes considerations of the space used in front of the signer and the linguistic structure of the signer "utterance." Therefore, to distinguish coprolalia from copropraxia the specific "utterance" has to be described. Because such a description is not provided in the cited paper we follow the authors' identification of the palm-back V sign as coprolalia. The possibility that this is a case of copropraxia rather than of coprolalia remains open.

5.2 Coprophenomena are emotion acts

Whether voluntary or not, whether very severe or mild, coprolalia is primitive in the sense that it has a mechanical quality; it lacks the richness of language. As we saw, the four maxims that make up the cooperative principle – quality, quantity, relations, and manner – are always obeyed in coprolalia. Jeremy Campbell, in his critique of the Gricean principle, points to its mechanical, formulaic, nature. His critique takes the form of rhetorical questions, "Would we want to have dinner with such a person [who only follows the four maxims]? And is that the purpose of language?" (2012: , Kindle location 3994). Maybe in the dawn of language, when language just emerged from gestures and basic vocalizations, the cooperative principle alone sufficed. But not anymore; not as we understand language today. Still, the four pragmatic maxims can be effective and useful .when performing an act.

Central to our discussion here is that coprolalia, like other forms of swearing, is a special kind of speech act that uses words but draws its performative power from the knowledge of the socio-cultural norms and the pragmatic rules of communication. As we learn from Hughlings Jackson, coprolalia, like all swearing, has the power to express emotions and to evoke them, not with semantics but by special use of the socio-cultural attunement of the coprolaliac. *Nigger* is not an *emotion word* in that it does not denote an emotion, but "nigger" is an *emotion act* because of the cultural context attached to it. Coprolalia, a special case of swearing, is not used to exchange ideas or information but to express and evoke emotions. It is an emotion act.

Along with the more general phenomenon of swearing, the automatic, sometimes reflexive, coprolalia might relate to a rung in the evolutionary ladder leading from animal violence, to animal vocalization, to automatic human vocalization, to coprolalia. And finally, from such automatic human swearing to non-automatic language, including voluntary swearing. But this is a question for further research.

Acknowledgement: I thank the anonymous reviewers for their careful reading and thoughtful comments. Lynne Nygaard and Aria Ritz Finkelstein offered helpful remarks and suggestions.

References

Allan, Keith. 2016. The pragmeme of insult and some allopracts. In K Allan, A Capone, I Kesckes, et al. (eds.) *Pragmemes and Theories of Language Use*. Cham, Switzerland: Springer.
APA. 2013. *Diagnostic and Statistical Manual of Mental Disorders, 5th Edition: DSM-5*. American Psychiatric Publishing.
Baron-Cohen, Simon and M. Robertson. 1998. *Tourette Syndrome: The Facts*. New York: Oxford University Press.
Campbell, Jeremy. 2012. *The Liar's Tale: A social history of Falsehood*. Ward & Balkin Agency, Inc.: Kindle Edition.
Chiten, Laurel, Paul Medley and Burl Russel. 1994. Twitch and shout. USA: PBS/POV
Cohen, Brad and Lisa Wyscocky. 2005. *Front of the Class: How Tourette Syndrome Made Me the Teacher I Never Had*. Acton, MA: VanderWyk & Burnham.
Conners, Susan. 2009. A teacher looks at Tourette syndrome. *Diagnosing and treating Tourette syndrome*. Bayside, NY: Tourette Syndrome Association.
de Rutter, J. P. 1995. Why do people gesture at the telephone? In M Biemans and M Woutersen (eds.) *Proceedings of the center for language studies opening academic year '95 96*. Nijmegen: Center for Language Studies.
de Waal, Frans. 2005. *Our Inner Ape*. New York: Rivehead Books.
Fernandez, Thomas V. and Matthew W. State. 2013. Genetic Susceptibility in Tourette Syndrome. In D Martino and J Leckman (eds.) *Tourette Syndrome* Oxford, UK: Oxford University Press.
Finkelstein, Shlomit Ritz. 2009. Adults with Tourette Syndrome. http://pid.emory.edu/ark:/25593/1cjcz. Atlanta, GA. https://etd.library.emory.edu/view/record/pid/emory:1cjcz: Emory University.
Finkelstein, Shlomit Ritz, Rob Poh and Jorge Luis Juncos. 2016. Swearing: Language for Feeling. Lessons from Tourette Syndrome. *Cognitive Semantics* 2: 237–261.
Freeman, Roger D, Samuel H Zinner, Kirsten r Muller-Vahl, et al. 2008. Coprophenomena in Tourette syndrome. *Developmental Medicine & Child Neurology* 51: 218–227.
Freeman, Roger D. 2007. Tic disorders and ADHD: answers from a world-wide clinical dataset on Tourette syndrome. *Eur Child Adolesc Psychiatry [Suppl 1]*.
Goffman, Erving. 1963. *Stigma: Notes on the Management of Spoiled Identity* Touchstone. Kindle Edition.
Goldin-Meadow, Susan. 2008. Gesture, speech, and language. In ADM Smith, K Smith and RFi Cancho (eds.) *The Evolution of Language*.
Grice, Paul. 1989. *Studies in the Way of Words*. Cambridge, MA: Harvard University Press.
Gross, Terry. 2004. Fresh Air with Dan Ackroyd.
Jackson, John Hughlings. 1958. *Selected Writings of John Hughlings Jackson. Vol. I*. New York: Basic Books, Inc.
Kendon, Adam. 2000. Language and gesture: unity or duality? In D McNeill (ed.) *Language and Gesture*. Cambridge, UK: Cambridge University Press.
Kushner, Howard, I. 1999. *A Cursing Brain? The Histories of Tourette Syndrome*. Cambridge, MA: Harvard University Press.
Leckman, James F, Robert A. King and Donald J. Cohen. 1999. Tics and tic disorders. In JF Leckman and DJ Cohen (eds.) *Tourette's Syndrome – Tics, Obsessions, Compulsions*. New York: John Wiley & Sons, Inc.

Leckman, James F., Micahel H. Bloch, Denis G. Sukhodolsky, et al. 2013. Phenomenology of tics and sensory urges: The self under siege. In D Martino and J Leckman (eds.) *Tourette Syndrome*. Oxford, UK: Oxford University Press.

McNeill, David. 1996. *Hand and Mind: What Gestures Reveal about Thought*. Chicago: University of Chicago Press.

Meige, Henry and E. Feindel. 1907/1990. *Tics and Their Treatment*. London: Sidney Appleton.

Morris, Huw R., Alice J. Thacker, Peter K. Newman, et al. 2000. Sign language tics in a prelingually deaf man. *Movement Disorders* 15: 318–320.

Noveck, Ira A. and Anne Reboul. 2008. Experimental Pragmatics: a Gricean turn in the study of language. *Trends in Cognitive Sciences* 12: 425–431.

Nuwer, Marc R. 1982. Coprolalia as an organic symptom. In AJ Friedhoff and TN Chase (eds.) *Gilles de la Tourette Syndrome*. New York: Raven Press.

Patterson, James and Hal Friedman. 2008. *Against medical advice: A true story*. New York: Little, Brown, and Company.

Sacks, Harvey, Emanuel A. Schegloff and Gail Jefferson. 1974. A Simplest Systematics for the Organization of Turn-Taking for Conversation. *Language* 50: 696–735.

Sedaris, David. 1997. *Naked*. New York: Back Bay Books.

Shapiro, Arthur K., Elaine S. Shapiro, Ruth D. Bruun, et al. 1988. *Gilles de la Tourette Syndrome. Second Edition*. New York: Raven Press.

Shimberg, Elaine. 1995. *Living With Tourette Syndrome*. New York, NY: Fireside.

Small, Steven L. 2016. Cover 2: Editorial Board. *Brain and Language* 163: IFC.

Smith, Rachel A. 2012. Segmenting an Audience into the Own, the Wise, and Normals: A Latent Class Analysis of Stigma-Related Categories. *Communication Research Reports* 29: 257–265.

Sperber, Dan and Deirdre Wilson. 2002. Pragmatics, Modularity and Mind-reading. *Mind and Language*, 17: 3–33.

Stroop, J. R. 1935. Studies of interference in serial verbal reactions. *Journal of Experimental Psychology* 18: 643–662.

Tanner, Caroline M. 2005. Epidemiology of Tourette's syndrome. In R Kurlan (ed.) *Handbook of Tourette's Syndrome and Related Tic and Behavioral Disorders*. New York: Marcel Dekker.

Tomasello, Michael. 1999. *The Cultural Origins of Human Cognition*. Cambridge, MA: Harvard University Press.

Van Lancker, D. and J. L. Cummings. 1999. Expletives: neurolinguistic and neurobehavioral perspectives on swearing. *Brain Research Reviews* 31: 83–104.

Index

A
âberu 143–145, 147, 149–150, 155–157
ablution 301
abnormal 299
adaptive 306
adjuration 127
age 246, 249, 253, 255–257, 259–262, 264–265
alternation variables 226
ambiguity 80, 83–84, 89- 91, 93–94
ambivalent 293
Anatomy of Melancholy 295
Arabic dialects 126
attenuated communication 23
– attenuated expression 25
automaticity 317, 319, 321–325
axiology 36–39, 41, 48, 50, 53

B
Baptism 301
blasphemy 119, 134, 137
body part terms 130

C
Calvinism 226, 229, 240
cannibalism 294
censorship 36, 43, 84
– self-censorship 84
circumlocution 198
cognate accusative 120
cognition 26, 39
compulsions 294
conceptualize 19, 26
construal 246, 250–265
cooperative principle 319, 324, 326
– cooperative maxims 320
– Maxim of Quantity 121
coprophenomena 312, 323–324
– coprolalia 311–326
– copropraxia 312- 314, 318, 321, 323–324
culture 39, 313, 315, 323, 325
– cultural aspects of taboo 179
– cultural schemas 107, 114
– cultural values 324
– Egyptian culture 126

– English and Polish culture 180
– Middle-Eastern cultures 299, 303
curse 121, 129, 131, 134, 136
– curse intensifiers 128

D
death 38, 124, 135
derogatory 38, 50, 82–83
desemanticisation 119, 135
diaphasic variation 275
discourse 21, 24, 26, 36–41, 43, 50, 53, 281
DSM-5 294
dysphemism 15–22, 24–27, 36–38, 40–43, 47–50, 52–53, 82, 246, 253, 263, 270–271, 277, 281
– euphemistic dysphemism 38
– dysphemistic substitute 15, 24

E
education level 246, 249, 253, 257, 260–261, 263, 265
effat 143, 145, 148, 154, 156
ego-dystonic 296
emotion act 311–312, 317, 320, 324, 326
eulogy 83
euphemism 14–28, 36–38, 40–43, 45, 46, 50, 52, 55–75, 80, 82–83, 85, 90, 93, 101–104, 112, 114, 135, 181, 198, 246, 248, 263–265, 270–271, 281
– dysphemistic euphemism 38

F
face 37–38, 45, 182
family 117, 123, 127–129, 134–137
fear of danger 296
forbidden concept 26
– forbidden content 23–24
– forbidden reality 14–15, 19–20, 23, 26
– forbidden term 19, 23–25
– forbidden word 14, 16
foreign language learning 202, 205
four letter words 300
fusion of thought and action 296

G

gender 246, 249, 253, 255
geographical variability 226
gestures 313, 323–324
gheirat 143, 147–148, 150–151
grammaticalization 119, 126, 135–137

H

hayâ 142–148, 150–157
healthy ageing 107, 114
heteronormative 41, 47–48, 50
homosexuality 35–37, 39–50, 52–53, 281
– homosexual discourse 42
– homosexual obsessions 298
– homosexuality metaphor 37, 40, 42, 50
human corpse 294
humor 318–319

I

Idealized Cognitive Models 180
implicature 82, 90, 94
impure 297
incest 294
insult 117, 129, 134, 136
– metonymic insult 128
intensifier 117, 119–120, 122–124, 129–131, 135–138
– insult intensifiers 127, 137
intention 39–40, 321–322, 324
interdiction 13, 18, 35
– conceptual interdiction 14, 18–20, 26–27
– linguistic interdiction 280
involuntary 318, 326

J

joint attention 321

K

Kappa 184

L

lexical substitution 14, 19, 23–26, 40
– lexicalized substitutes 15
lexical syncretism 15
lexical variability 230
lexicon 23, 25

M

Macbeth effect 304
Marquise de Dampierre 316
menstruation 161, 163, 165, 167, 169–171, 173–176
mental constructs 180
mental neutralizing 294
metaphor 36–50, 53, 79, 83, 101–102, 113–114, 125, 128–129, 141, 143, 145, 151–156, 158, 162–165, 168, 174, 202, 205–212, 214–219, 246, 251, 261, 263, 281
– animal 41–43, 48–50
– closet 43–44, 50, 53
– container 42–43, 50
– contemporary theory of metaphor 38
– cruises 46
– cruising 45–46, 50
– discourse metaphor 38–39, 53
– flower 39, 47–48, 53
– journey 42–43, 45–46, 50
– Metaphor Identification Procedure 41
– women 42–43, 47–48, 50, 53
metonymy 55, 57–58, 61–75, 107, 111, 125, 246, 251, 263
Model Person 182
modulation 19, 23

N

neural reuse 305
neutralization 15, 24
normality 299, 306

O

obsessions 294
obsessive-compulsive disorder (OCD) 293–294, 319
– Christian therapy for OCD 296
onomasiological variation 246–247, 251, 259, 264–265
orthophemism 14, 16–17, 20, 38, 80, 86, 270

P

perception (cognitive process of) 198
perfectionism 296
periphrasis 83, 88, 93
Persian 302

physical cleansing 301
physical contaminations 301
politeness theory 92–93, 121, 182, 190
– positive politeness 124–125, 127
political correctness 81, 84–87, 90–94
– politically correct language 26–27
– euphemisms political correctness 80
political incorrectness 81, 83–84, 87, 89–90, 93
pragmatic 311–312, 314–315, 319–320, 324–326
prohibition 52, 84–85, 87–89, 91–94
prudishness 253–265

Q
quasi-dysphemism 14, 17
quasi-euphemism 14, 17, 38, 43–46, 49–50

R
reconceptualization 104–105, 113
referent 17, 27
referential meaning 80, 90
register 202–203
religion 117, 123, 127, 130, 134–135, 137
repetition 121, 127
ruminations 294, 296

S
scrupulosity 294–295
semantic change 21–22
semantic structuralism 14
Semasiology 21–22
sexuality 117, 123–124, 127, 135, 245–247, 249–253, 259–262, 264–266
– sex associated taboo words 187
– sex taboos 300
– sexual concepts 245–246, 248–250, 253, 261, 264–265
– sexual maturity 299
– sexual obsessions 297–298
– sexual organs 298
shame 141–143, 145–148, 152–153, 155–157
situation 313–315, 320, 325
social embarrassment 319
social norms 320–321, 324
social stigma 35, 316–317
Sociolinguistics 273

Spanish 202, 205, 207, 209, 211–212, 214–218
Spatial Autocorrelation 235
speech act 84, 87, 89, 94, 311–312, 319–320, 323–326
spiritual purity 302
spiritual therapy 296
substitution 14–16, 19–20, 23–25, 28, 40
successful ageing 105–107, 112, 114
swearing 227, 229, 240, 311–312, 315, 317–318, 320–324, 326
synonymy 36, 80, 84–86, 90, 93

T
taboo 13–14, 17–28, 36–38, 43, 49–50, 52, 123, 125–127, 130–132, 137, 141, 143, 146, 148, 150–151, 153–154, 158, 227, 230, 232, 240, 293
– linguistic taboo 13, 18, 21, 27, 52, 179, 181, 183, 270–272, 288
– taboo concept 14, 17–19, 25–26
– taboo for the cross-cultural communication 180
– taboo word 14, 18–19, 26–27, 37, 198
– tabooed realities 17–18, 25
– tabooness 124–125
Tahareh 303
teaching 203–204, 206, 219
The Pilgrim's Progress 295
tic 312–313, 317–319, 321, 324–325
Totem and Taboo 293
Tourette syndrome 311–316, 318–319, 324
Twitter 231

V
vagueness 46, 80, 83–85, 90, 93
– vague expressions 246

W
washing 301
waswas 302
waswaseh 302
wudu 301

X
X-phemism 14, 16–17, 37–38, 40–42, 45, 50, 53
– x-phemistic continuum 17, 20, 246

www.ingramcontent.com/pod-product-compliance
Lightning Source LLC
Chambersburg PA
CBHW030605230426
43661CB00053B/1853